POWER AND PRAGMATISM

The memoirs of
Malcolm Rifkind

Biteback Publishing

First published in Great Britain in 2016 by
Biteback Publishing Ltd
Westminster Tower
3 Albert Embankment
London SE1 7SP
Copyright © Malcolm Rifkind 2016

ISBN 978-1-78590-003-7

10 9 8 7 6 5 4 3 2 1

A CIP catalogue record for this book is available from the British Library.

Set in Garamond by Adrian McLaughlin

Printed and bound in Great Britain by
CPI Group (UK) Ltd, Croydon CR0 4YY

MIX
Paper from
responsible sources
FSC® C020471

CONTENTS

To Edith, Caroline and Hugo

'Don't walk behind me; I may not lead.
Don't walk in front of me; I may not follow.
Walk by my side and be my friend.'

– ALBERT CAMUS

Introduction

'If I could flatter myself that this Essay has any merit, it is in steering betwixt the extremes of doctrines seemingly opposite.'

– ALEXANDER POPE, 'An Essay on Man'

I HAD BEEN THINKING of calling these memoirs *My Early Life: The First Seventy Years* but that might have been tempting Providence. I have called them, instead, *Power and Pragmatism*.

I admit that is a title that may not, immediately, excite the reader. Nor, as I discovered when I offered myself as party leader in 2005, did my promise to be pragmatic enthuse the party faithful.

However, I have chosen it for a reason every one of my fellow politicians will understand. All of us who tread the political path are either conviction politicians or pragmatists. I am one of the latter and have been so throughout my public life.

This book, the reader will be relieved to know, is not just about pragmatism and politics. It records my Scottish childhood, my school-days and my university years in Edinburgh, during which I was on

University Challenge and took part in an overland expedition to India where we got caught up in a war between India and Pakistan. I also, then, worked for a year and a half in rebellious Southern Rhodesia, where, amongst other adventures, I met Edith, my wife for the last forty-six years. After Rhodesia, there followed four years practising at the Scottish Bar in wig and gown, as well as being Edinburgh's youngest City Father, serving with Robin Cook on the Town Council.

I examine, in this book, what made me, with that background, a politician when there were other careers that could have attracted me.

The book covers, as well, my role in government. To my astonishment, and my family's growing concern, I was a minister for the full eighteen years that Margaret Thatcher and John Major occupied 10 Downing Street. I, Ken Clarke and only three other colleagues completed the longest uninterrupted ministerial service since Lord Palmerston in the early nineteenth century.

When we were informed by John Wakeham, the Chief Whip, in 1996, that we had broken the previous record held by Lloyd George, we were so surprised that the five of us had a splendid dinner to celebrate, so splendid that I cannot remember where it was held.

For almost nine of those years I dealt with foreign affairs in both the Foreign Office and the Ministry of Defence. For seven years I was in the Scottish Office, dealing, as a minister or as Secretary of State, not only with Scottish issues but with Scotland's relationship with the rest of the United Kingdom.

My ministerial life was, therefore, dominated by these two existential challenges with which the United Kingdom has grappled and not yet fully resolved over the last half-century.

What is the future of these islands as a united kingdom and will they remain united for generations to come? What should be Britain's relationship with the rest of Europe and the wider world?

So this book deals with these issues and with my own contribution in trying, with my colleagues, to resolve them.

When I describe myself as a pragmatist, I accept that to suggest that there is a stark choice between conviction and pragmatism is, of course, an oversimplification. Pragmatists have convictions and conviction politicians can be surprisingly pragmatic when it suits them.

The political world is not monochrome. It is dominated by a lot of people with strong personalities, colourful temperaments and considerable egos. While every political animal is different and unique, the species can, however, be divided into two sub-species: the conviction politician and the pragmatist.

The conviction politician is one who is guided by a clear doctrine, ideology or set of beliefs. When a new challenge appears, he looks to this doctrine or ideology to determine his response. He tends to be as much concerned with the consistency of his actions and policies as with the consequences that flow from them.

To his credit, the conviction politician is more likely to be concerned with strategy than with tactics. He will profess himself to be unconcerned by whether his policy is popular or unpopular; only whether it is right. He will say (and he may believe) that his concern is the verdict of history and not just that of his contemporaries.

The pragmatic politician approaches these issues in a quite different way. Of course, he has his beliefs and values, which are held with deep conviction, but one of these beliefs is that you must always consider the likely consequences of your actions and if you conclude that a proposed policy would do more harm than good, there is nothing sinful or improper in casting that policy overboard.

The conviction politician might reach the same conclusion but would be consumed by worry and guilt if he had to veer away from the true path. The pragmatist would be pretty relaxed and see it as living in the real world.

The problem for pragmatists such as myself is that we can be accused of not having any coherent strategy. It is suggested that we do not have a guiding principle or vision in our approach to the solution of problems. It is alleged that, unlike Margaret Thatcher, we are for turning when the going gets rough.

Conviction politicians believe that pragmatists are woolly-minded and unreliable. Margaret Thatcher, the supreme conviction politician, was contemptuous of pragmatism and any search for consensus. Once, when asked whether she believed in consensus, she replied that she did and then added, 'There should be a consensus behind my convictions.'

Mrs Thatcher disliked compromise either with her domestic opponents or in international negotiations. Sometimes, as I record in this book, she was right. That was so when she clashed with her Foreign Secretary, Francis Pym, during the Falklands War and refused to contemplate any compromise with General Galtieri that might have left the Argentinians on the Falklands or compromised British sovereignty.

But in most international negotiations, whether in the European Union or even with Iran over its nuclear programme, some compromise is both principled and unavoidable if there is to be a breakthrough.

Whenever I was negotiating with my EU colleagues, I took into account that they, too, had national parliaments and domestic critics to satisfy and that if I could accept some compromise without sacrificing any crucial British interest, that was preferable to a negotiating strategy of no surrender.

Again and again, John Major and I experienced hardline Tory Eurosceptics who saw any compromise with Brussels as a betrayal of British interests. That is not the real world, especially when you are negotiating with friends not enemies.

Many of my differences with Mrs Thatcher, when I was Secretary of State for Scotland, which I record in this book, were not because I disagreed with, for example, the educational reforms that she wanted to implement. They arose because I insisted that the timing of these reforms and some of their substance had to be amended to take account of very different Scottish circumstances. This, she, and those closest to her, found hard to accept. She suspected weakness and lack of principle.

In reality, pragmatists can be as hard and robust as any conviction politician when the circumstances justify it. Thus, during the Second World War, Winston Churchill, whose whole political career, including not one but two changes of party, was a supreme example of high-minded opportunism, never wavered or dithered in his determination to defeat Nazi Germany.

Justifying his alliance with his arch-enemy Stalin in order to defeat Hitler, he declared that 'if Hitler invaded Hell I would at least make a favourable reference to the Devil'. This was not conviction politics but realpolitik applied with fervour.

The chapters that follow are not just about different kinds of politician. Reader, be warned. They are also about me.

I very much agree with Arthur Balfour, who once remarked, 'I am more or less happy when being praised, and not very uncomfortable when being abused, but I have moments of uneasiness when I am being explained.' The only way one can try to avoid this is by explaining oneself. I have enjoyed doing so more than I expected.

Memoirs tickle the vanity of the writer. This book will, I presume, be read by my friends and family. Having had the good fortune to serve in the Cabinet, it may also be of interest to the wider world.

But that interest would not be there if this book was merely to recount a list of events I have taken part in, world figures I have met or amusing anecdotes.

The reader, I hope, will find a narrative that seeks to explain me, warts and all, and to put my personal contribution to national or international events into a wider historical context.

Writing a novel must be much easier than presenting one's own life. With a novel the author can roam far and wide. He can invent people and events to illustrate his argument or entertain the reader.

When you write your autobiography, you have no such freedom. I have been able to select what to leave in and what to leave out, but all that I have included must have actually happened. Perhaps not the beginning but the middle and the end of the book are already in the public domain.

As much as any conviction politician, I have strong principles and deep beliefs which have been central to my political life. These principles and beliefs are not that unusual. Some are Tory beliefs, others are shared by all parliamentarians. They include a fundamental commitment to democratic values, the rule of law, free enterprise, a property-owning democracy and personal responsibility towards one's family and the wider community.

Being a pragmatic rather than a conviction politician is not because of my DNA. It is, to a considerable degree, because I am a product of the twentieth century, a period of history which, in many respects, it was good to put behind us. It was the century when the most extreme exponents of conviction politics were able to gain power over a considerable portion of mankind, with terrible consequences.

Hitler, Stalin, Mao Tse-tung and Pol Pot were not mere brutal despots like Genghis Khan. Their barbarism was rooted in Marxist-Leninist, Fascist and Nazi philosophies which purported to provide total answers to society's needs. Once they, and millions of their followers, were convinced that the end justified the means, tolerance and moderation were thrown aside and every mode of behaviour was seen as legitimate. The 'Islamic State' extremists of today fall into a similar category.

The horrors of the twentieth century have led many politicians, and many members of the public, to be sceptical about those politicians and political writers, most of whom are as democratic as the rest of us, who claim to have ideological solutions or total answers to the needs of our society. Most of us, instead, prefer to get off such a train before it crashes into the buffers.

The choice that I and all politicians have to make between conviction and pragmatism is not confined to domestic politics. Foreign policy, too, is an arena where I found that the same challenges apply.

Tony Blair liked to present himself as a conviction politician when it came to foreign policy, and the wars in Iraq and Kosovo are his legacy. But the original conviction politician was Mr Gladstone, also concerned with the Balkans, who considered that he had a special relationship with the Almighty rather than with the United States.

While I have no doubt that there should always be an ethical dimension in the foreign policy of civilised states, to try to construct a foreign policy mainly on these considerations is foolish and dangerous.

Why must the implementation of foreign policy always be pragmatic? Why can it not rest on alliances only with those who share our values and beliefs? We all know the answer. If we declined, today, to work with undemocratic governments in the Middle East or Russia, sharing intelligence and taking joint military action to defeat Islamic extremist terrorism, we would make the struggle immeasurably harder and the outcome less certain.

I have been banned from Russia by President Putin because of my strong advocacy of financial and banking sanctions against Moscow for its aggression against Ukraine. But I have, simultaneously, been prominent in calling for a resumption of dialogue between NATO and Russia as well as cooperation on counterterrorism and nuclear non-proliferation.

This does not, as some suggest, demonstrate inconsistency or lack of resolve. It is plain common sense.

No one is suggesting that democratic governments should not be pressing for human rights improvements, nor that they should not be cautious in getting too close to dictators. My point, and it is an important one, is that these questions must be decided on the basis of the likely consequences of the policy one chooses and not simply on perceived ethical or moral considerations.

Tony Blair, when as Prime Minister he spoke to the Labour conference, referred to Rwanda and the Congo, where, he said, we had a moral duty to act. Why was there no reference to the Chechens, the Tibetans or the Kurds? That, of course, had everything to do with Mr Blair's warm relations with Mr Putin and his desire not to offend the Chinese and Turkish governments. Despite the rhetoric it was more of a pragmatic than a principled foreign policy.

Whether in domestic or in foreign policy, pragmatism should prevail; a pragmatism that is aware of the ethical dimension and sensitive to it but which will always give most attention to the likely consequences of any proposed course of action. If these criteria had been applied before the United States and Britain went to war in Iraq, much of the agony that country has experienced ever since would have been avoided.

The best advice for aspirant statesmen was given by Disraeli in Edinburgh in 1867 when he said:

> In a progressive country change is constant; and the great question is not whether you should resist change which is inevitable, but whether that change should be carried out in deference to the manners, the customs, the laws and the traditions of a people, or whether it should be carried out in deference to abstract principles, and arbitrary and general doctrines. The one is a national system; the other, to give it an epithet, a noble epithet – which it may perhaps deserve – is a philosophic system.

I am conscious that Disraeli was one of those who might, occasionally, be accused of opportunism. But then, none of us is perfect.

Throughout my political and ministerial career I have been fortunate in being the subject of many complimentary profiles. But it has also been my fate, as this book records, to be portrayed by political commentators, journalists and some politicians, not least Margaret Thatcher, as being difficult to categorise. It has been suggested that my politics are 'ill defined', that it has been 'difficult to know' what I stand for, that I have been a regular 'weathervane' and other such observations.

It will not surprise the reader that I disagree. I know what I stand for and I have always defined my views and opinions. But I do acknowledge that I may be difficult to categorise.

This is because I am a self-confessed pragmatist, which, by definition, means other people cannot assume they know my opinions on one subject by knowing what they are on others. I dislike labels like right-wing or left-wing Conservative. I am uncomfortable with being typecast as either a Europhile or a Eurosceptic, or a wet or a dry Tory.

This is not because I am constantly changing my mind. I have done so, on occasion, as has any other normal person, but on the vast majority of political subjects my views are much the same today as they were forty years ago. Sometimes the glass which I have presented has been half full; sometimes it has been half empty. But it has remained the same glass.

Forty years ago, as now, I was uncomfortable with the style and some of the substance of Thatcherism but was impressed by Thatcher as a potential Prime Minister. That was why I never regretted voting for her in 1975 in preference to Willie Whitelaw and Geoffrey Howe.

Then, as now, I was a deep and unqualified believer in the Union of England and Scotland, while also sympathetic to the need for some kind of devolution to reflect Scotland's distinct national, legal and cultural identity.

Then, as now, I believed in the desirability of a European Union and Britain's membership of it, while being sceptical and opposed to a single currency and unnecessary integration.

In having these nuanced views, I was not unique. Indeed, I probably reflected the opinions of a majority of the British people. But a lot of the commentariat expect their politicians to be predictable in their opinions and for many politicians that creates no difficulties. Ken Clarke is happy to be described as a Euro-enthusiast; John Redwood likewise sees himself as a Eurosceptic. I ended up, according to *Le Monde*, as a 'moderate Eurosceptic'.

My eclecticism did me no political favours and would probably have ruled me out of leading the Conservative Party even if I had held my seat in 1997. There have been Thatcherites and Blairites as well as Portillistas and Cameroons, but I was never aware of many Rifkindites.

I have no regrets about that. 'To thine own self be true and then thou canst not be false to any man' has been my guiding light over the years and has not done me any harm.

So I see myself as the kind of Tory who, through pragmatism and the rejection of sterile ideology, has enabled the Conservatives to remain Britain's natural governing party for almost 300 years.

This book is the record of a pragmatic politician. I am not certain that pragmatism needs a defender, but if it does, I am happy to be one of its champions.

CHAPTER I

EARLY DAYS

I CAN HARDLY CRITICISE my parents for the date of my birth, but it was the source of my first disillusionment with the wider world.

I was born on 21 June 1946. As a small child, I was informed by my parents that my birthday was the 'longest day of the year'. Not unreasonably, I assumed that that meant I had a longer birthday than any of my friends. When I was disabused of this assumption by my mother I felt that I had been misled; the first myth of my life had been shattered.

I was born in the Carnegie Nursing Home in Morningside, a southern district of Edinburgh.

Morningside had, until recently, an unfair reputation for being the epicentre of Scottish middle-class gentility. Its residents were all believed to speak like Miss Jean Brodie when she was in her prime. It was declared that in Morningside 'there were no *rates*, only mice', and that '*sex* was what the potatoes come in'.

Of course, just as one does not have to be a horse to be born in a stable, one did not have to be genteel to be born in Morningside.

It might have been recorded in my birth certificate as my birthplace. I was, actually, a child of Marchmont, a nearby solidly respectable locality but one with no social pretensions.

I grew up with my parents and my older brother, Arnold, in a flat at 34 Warrender Park Terrace. The flat was part of a rather imposing Victorian terraced edifice overlooking The Meadows, which, then as now, were open grassland, with only a short walk required to get to Tollcross, the Old Town and the city centre.

Our street has been well described by Alexander McCall Smith in his novel *The Sunday Philosophy Club*. As in another of his novels he uses me as one of his characters without my permission, I feel free to quote him on the same basis.

Warrender Park Terrace, he writes:

> was a handsome construction … a high tenement in the Victorian manner … in six storeys of dressed stone … Some of the roofs were bordered with turrets, like the slated turrets of French chateaux … the edge of the roofs had stone crenellations, carved thistles, the occasional gargoyle, all of which would have given the original occupants the sense that they were living in some style, and that all that distinguished their dwellings from those of the gentry was mere size. But in spite of these conceits, they were good flats, solidly built … originally intended for petit-bourgeois occupation.

I was struck when I read this description because I recalled, as a child coming home from school, in the winter months, getting off the bus in the lit streets of Tollcross and having to cross the unlit, undulating Meadows in order to get home.

For me this was an adventure as I made my way in the dark through *terra incognita* towards the crenellated roofs of Warrender Park Terrace, which, with its street lighting, seemed like some friendly castle or fortress where I could find sanctuary.

We lived in a modest, first floor flat. There was a living room, a lounge and two bedrooms, one of which I shared with my brother. There was also a large box room which had once been used to store coal. In it were all sorts of interesting objects, including my father's wartime tin helmet and gas mask. This was my home during my school and university days until I went to southern Africa at the age of twenty-one.

We were a typical Edinburgh family. I have often been told that I do not have a Scottish accent. There is some truth in that. My mother was English from Manchester and since the age of twenty-seven I have worked and lived mostly in London while keeping, until recently, my home in Scotland.

But Scots know better. They know that my accent is Edinburgh, middle-class professional. This is not surprising as my initial chosen career was as a member of the Scottish Bar, the Faculty of Advocates.

Growing up in Edinburgh was one of the most fortunate experiences of my youth, though I did not realise it at the time. It is one of the world's most imposing cities.

Where else, as from the city centre, at the top of the Mound, can one see a medieval castle, the open sea and an extinct volcano, such as Arthur's Seat? Which other city has a New Town which, far from being of concrete and glass, has streets, squares and crescents of residential eighteenth- and early nineteenth-century Georgian homes?

Where else in Britain, other than in Holyrood Park and Arthur's Seat, can you disappear into a valley at the very heart of a great city and see only hillside, boulders and lochs that, for a moment, make you feel you are in the Highlands of Scotland?

Edinburgh is not perfect. It has been remarked that other places have climate, Edinburgh has weather. Robert Louis Stevenson, writing about Scotland's capital in the nineteenth century, said that Edinburgh had the vilest climate known to man. He added that the weak died young and that the healthy often envied them their fate.

Edinburgh knows that it is special, however. Regardless of whether

Scotland is independent or not, Edinburgh has always been a capital city. Much of England talks about going up to London. People in Edinburgh go down.

When the good citizens of Edinburgh need to go to Glasgow, they invariably say they are going to the 'West', as if it was California rather than forty-three miles away.

The rivalry between these two cities is not new. It is said (in Edinburgh) that in Edinburgh breeding is good form while in Glasgow breeding is good fun.

As a youngster, I assumed that all cities were much like Edinburgh. They are not. Many have an industrial origin. They are vibrant, lively and impressive. They have some splendid individual buildings, excellent art galleries, busy concert halls. But most cities are not visually inspiring.

It is difficult to walk in Edinburgh's medieval Royal Mile, to descend down the Mound to the Georgian New Town, to walk along the Radical Road of the Salisbury Crags in Holyrood Park and see the historic skyline of the city in front of you, without feeling better at the end of your walk than you did at the beginning.

That is Edinburgh today, not that different from the Edinburgh of my childhood. It is what I miss most about living now in London.

I said we were a typical Edinburgh family. That is true but in one respect we were rather different. As well as being Scottish and British, we were Jewish.

Edinburgh's Jewish community was not very large. There were several hundred families in the 1950s and 1960s, though there are far fewer now. There was (and is) only one synagogue, which was Orthodox, but many of the members were non-observant and attended only on the High Holy days of the Jewish New Year and the Day of Atonement (Yom Kippur).

My own extended family, including my parents, were observant. While they were moderate in their views and secular in their lifestyle, my father (though not my mother) attended synagogue each

Saturday morning and until my middle teens I was expected to be with him.

My brother and I attended the Jewish equivalent of Sunday school until after we had each had our Bar mitzvah, which was the equivalent of Confirmation and which happened when one was thirteen. We kept kosher at home, which meant we did not mix milk and meat and did not eat bacon or shellfish as well as various other customs.

All religions have their rites and rituals, which can seem strange to others. I love the story of the rabbi and the Catholic priest travelling together on the train. The priest asks the rabbi whether he has ever eaten bacon and the rabbi confesses that he once did. He then asks the Catholic priest whether he had ever had sex. The priest confesses that he once did. 'It's better than bacon, isn't it?' says the rabbi.

Unlike many Orthodox families, my parents were never rigid. We could watch television or listen to the radio on the Sabbath, we used electric lights and when they were elderly my father did not object to using a car to help him get to the synagogue.

Most important for me, there was no objection to my attending my school debating society's meetings, although they always occurred on the Friday evening when the Sabbath had already begun. Having non-Jewish girlfriends was another matter, as marrying outside the faith was the ultimate sin at that time.

Until I was a teenager I did not object to the constraints imposed on my diet and on my Saturday mornings by my Jewishness. But nor did I consider that my social life and my interests should be solely within the parameters of the local Jewish community. Not only was it too small but, increasingly, I found myself stimulated by all that Edinburgh, my schoolfellows and, in due course, my fellow students had to offer.

Nowadays, in Britain, most of us are very used to the concept of dual or multiple identities. When asked, we all find ourselves referring to ourselves as British and Scottish, English and Muslim, West Indian and British rather than having to adopt one part of our identity at the expense of the other parts.

That was not so self-evident in the 1950s and 1960s. Professor David Daiches, a prominent Scottish literary historian, published, in 1956, his memoirs of his Edinburgh Jewish childhood. His father was the Edinburgh rabbi at that time. While proud of his father, and not rejecting his religious background, Daiches's own career was secular and not constrained by his Jewishness. He entitled his memoir *Two Worlds*.

Like other migrant communities in British history, subsequent generations were becoming fully integrated in the wider community of which they were part. Some, like Daiches and, later, myself, welcomed it. Others, quite reasonably, worried as to whether integration would lead to assimilation and be at the expense of religious observance.

Today's Jewish community in Britain can be said to be fully integrated, with shared values and equal opportunities. But there has been a polarisation. Many, such as our daughter, Caroline, and our son, Hugo, have intermarried with spouses of other faiths or none. Many other younger British Jews have become more religious in their observance while pursuing secular professional or business careers.

It is often said that anti-Semitism has increased in recent years in Britain. While that is statistically correct, most of it appears to be associated with the Israeli–Palestinian controversies and has little connection with the anti-Semitism of the 1930s or previous eras.

I have experienced virtually no anti-Semitism in my personal and public life. I can recall only one remark in my childhood, which was from a fellow pupil at school whom I sat next to and whom I must have annoyed.

Scotland has a well-deserved reputation for finding anti-Semitism abhorrent, which may have something to do with Presbyterianism and its special interest in the Old Testament and the 'People of the Book'.

Several years ago I had an unexpected phone call from a stranger who informed me that when he was a child he had known my grandfather, Charles Rifkind. As he had died in 1947, I had never known my grandfather and was interested to hear what he had to recall.

My caller told me that my grandfather had visited his parents in Fife, as they were customers of his business. As he was leaving their house a neighbour, who was the worse for drink, came up and hit him. When my grandfather remonstrated and asked him why he had done this, the man apparently replied saying that it was because he was a Jew and the Jews had killed Jesus Christ. When my grandfather pointed out that was 2,000 years ago, the man replied, through a haze of alcohol: 'Maybe, but I only heard about it yesterday.'

Scotland has, however, not been free of religious prejudice. Protestant–Catholic dislike and discrimination was rife for many years. Indeed, anti-Catholic prejudice could be more virulent than anti-Jewish sentiment.

When Michael Ancram and I both applied for the Conservative candidature in the Scottish Borders in the early 1970s, I got through to the final two before losing, while Michael, whose home was near Jedburgh, never got to the shortlist. Some thought that his family's position as prominent Scottish Catholics might have been held against him. To be fair, the fact that he was the heir to a marquisate might also have been relevant.

On that occasion, my being Jewish was mentioned only once, by a lady at a sherry reception for all the aspirant candidates. She remarked to me, 'I don't think there are many synagogues in the Borders.' It didn't seem to worry her.

Much of the sectarian rivalry in Scotland was witnessed on the football terraces between Rangers and Celtic. I am one of the few that can claim to have helped bring the rival football supporters together. When I was a junior minister at the Scottish Office in the early 1980s, I managed to get 60,000 of them booing me simultaneously.

The government had just introduced legislation banning alcohol at football matches at the request of the Scottish football authorities. I was invited by the police superintendent to walk round the pitch before the match began. Foolishly, I agreed. Although the Rangers and Celtic fans were strictly segregated in the stadium, there developed what can be best described as a Mexican wave of booing as the police officer and I did the full round. Fortunately, the alcohol ban meant that the fans had no cans or bottles to add to their booing.

Our family was not small. My father was one of ten children. My mother was one of four. One of the consequences was that I had nineteen first cousins. At our wedding, as the guests arrived, Edith occasionally asked if they were my relatives. Unless they were at least a first cousin, I often did not know.

A fair proportion of my uncles, aunts and cousins did not live in Edinburgh, but some did and they formed the core of my parents' social life. Uncle David and Auntie Ena, as well as Uncle Jack and Auntie Rose, lived round the corner. Auntie Bessie and Uncle Joe lived across the Meadows.

The reader will be relieved to know that I do not intend to give an exhaustive account of all my relatives or of previous generations of the Rifkind family or my mother's family. I have often found that to be the part of an autobiography I am inclined to skip. As was said once about an MP's overlong speech, it can 'exhaust time and encroach upon eternity'.

However, we were a close family. I was fond of my cousins and still am. We keep in touch with each other and some I see quite often.

I will, however, say a little about my parents and grandparents. Our family first arrived in Edinburgh in 1896 when my grandfather's brother settled there, having travelled from his home in Russia. There was substantial emigration of Russian Jews to Western Europe and the United States in those years. We do not know why he made the fortunate choice of Edinburgh as his destination. I suspect it was because of the close links between the Baltic and Scotland, which went back many centuries.

Three years later, in 1899, my grandfather joined him in Edinburgh. My grandmother and their first child, aged one, followed him the following year. They were what would now be called economic migrants. Eight years after arriving in Scotland they had four more children, including my father, born in 1907. Five more were still to come.

When, as a child, I had asked my father as to the family's origins, he said that he had been told by his father that they came from Mshad, a small town in a part of Lithuania called Kovno Governo. That was all he knew. It appeared that neither he nor his parents, once settled in Scotland, had much continuing interest in their past.

Although I never knew my grandfather, my grandmother lived until 1964, when I was eighteen. I saw her often but, with the foolishness of youth, I never thought to ask her about her childhood until it was too late.

In 2003, I and three of my cousins, Marion and Gabrielle Rifkind and David Kaplan, decided to visit the now independent Lithuania and see for ourselves the town that had been home to our family in the nineteenth century.

The first problem was that we had no idea where Mshad was, as no such place appeared on any map or atlas that we consulted. Browsing on the internet, I discovered that a book entitled *The History of the Jews of Lithuania* had been recently published and I acquired a copy.

At the back of the book there was a list of the main towns of the country where there had been a sizeable Jewish community. This was a breakthrough, as the book listed those towns both in Lithuanian and in Yiddish. One such town was Mshad, whose modern equivalent is Mosėdis.

That was real progress, but we still had a problem. My father had been told that Mshad was in Kovno Governo, which translates as the governorship or province of Kovno, now known as Kaunas. But Mosėdis was nowhere near Kaunas. The same book, however, revealed that when the Russians acquired Lithuania after the Napoleonic wars they insisted on calling the whole country the Province of Kaunas, rather than Lithuania, to discourage Lithuanian nationalism and transform the population into loyal Russians.

We were able, by paying a small fee, to get access to the Lithuanian archives of births, marriages and deaths. Although the historical archives were incomplete, we were able to confirm that there had been Rifkinds in Mosėdis and were able to trace family links two generations earlier than my grandfather.

The earliest ancestor we could trace was my great-great-grandfather, who was known as Bere of Salant, a small town near Mosėdis. He is likely to have been born around 1810. He was a grain merchant and he married a lady called Esther from Mosėdis (Mshad), where they settled.

Mosėdis, in the 1897 Census, had a population of around 800, of which 40 per cent were Jewish.

There is a fascinating family story about the history and origins of our surname for which I also, unexpectedly, found corroboration.

I had been told by my father, who had been told by his, that the name went back to the early part of the nineteenth century. When the Tsar wanted conscripts for his armies, he would send soldiers into the towns and villages around Russia and draft as many young men as he needed. Being conscripted was no short-term inconvenience. Often, you were required to serve for up to twenty-five years and only then allowed to return home.

If the army was about to conscript a young man, the only consideration that would deter them would be if the youngster was the only son of a widow and, therefore, her sole means of support. Birth records were unreliable in those days and so if you had more than one son, you looked for a widow who would claim the young man to be her own when the army arrived, so he would not be press-ganged.

Our family story is consistent with this historical record. It is that an early nineteenth-century ancestor was a young man 'adopted' by a widow called Rebecca, or Rivka, and was known thereafter in the town as 'Rivka's *kind*', *kind* being the German or Yiddish for 'child'. When, after 1845, surnames were required in Russia, Rifkind was the one chosen.

Bere's son, Joseph, also a grain merchant, was the youngest of five children and married a Sarah Kangiser. The youngest of their eight children was my grandfather, Charles, born in 1877.

Occasionally people I have met in England, knowing my Scottish background, have asked if my surname is Gaelic or Scandinavian. From time to time it is misspelt. On one splendid occasion, while Edith was lecturing at Napier College in Edinburgh, she saw a colleague who had written to her but had spelt our surname with two Fs.

My wife, without realising how it sounded to other people who could hear her, said, 'No, you're quite wrong. There's only one *f* in Rifkind.' To those who heard her it must have sounded like 'There's only one effin' Rifkind', which they probably thought was one too many.

When we visited Mosėdis, we were taken by surprise. We had expected a drab, industrial town and found a national heritage site with houses with thatched roofs clustered around a baroque church.

I had once asked my father what had happened to his grandparents. He had told me that they had remained in Mosėdis but that his grandfather had died in a fire around 1909. I had never thought of this remark for many years.

When in Mosėdis, I asked an elderly resident if the Jewish community a hundred years ago had lived in any particular part of the town. He pointed to the thatched roof houses, near the church, and said that that was where most had lived. I asked whether these were the actual houses that would have been there at that time. He replied that they were not because there had been a major fire near the beginning of the twentieth century and most had been destroyed.

I had a strange feeling when I suddenly remembered what my father had told me years ago. It is curious how chance remarks can provide essential corroboration of family history.

We were told that the traditional Jewish graveyard had been on an island near the town centre but that it was now desolate and there was no way of visiting it. We drove to the shore opposite the island to visit a memorial that had been constructed by the Lithuanian government to the Jews of the town who had been murdered during the Second World War.

As we were about to leave, we saw a man rowing his boat between us and the island. He had been fishing. My cousin, Marion, who had studied Russian at university, asked him whether he could take us to the island, which he did.

When we got there we found two dozen gravestones, many from the early twentieth century but some could have been much older. Some had Russian lettering; others were in Hebrew. It was strange to feel that some of our nineteenth-century ancestors were likely to have been buried there. We said a prayer in their memory.

My grandfather was very pious and might have become a rabbi, but my grandmother, when she became engaged to him, made it clear that was unacceptable. In those days that would have meant that they would have been dependent on the contributions of a small congregation for their income, which she did not want.

He became a self-employed credit draper with regular customers in the mining villages of Fife. But his real love was the study of the Torah, which he did all his life. He often led prayers in the synagogue on High Holy days, was a member of the Synagogue Council and held the position of Warden. He died in 1947, having suffered from Parkinson's. A stained glass window dedicated to his memory is situated in the vestibule of the synagogue. Three of his grandsons are named after him.

My paternal grandmother, known as Nechama or Emma, can best be described as a matriarch. Small of stature, she had a strong will and was ambitious for her family. Her daughter Etta described her as clever, full of life, with charm, humour and intellect.

For many years she lived at 19 Bernard Terrace, a flat in the Newington district of Edinburgh. It was a large flat but furnished in what was to me an old-fashioned style. In the corridor to the hall, as you entered, there were two large prints on the wall. On the left was a large, coloured print of the royal family. I think the monarch was King Edward VII but I am not entirely certain. On the right was a large print of the 'Worthies of Edinburgh'. Who they were I cannot recall.

There was a formal dining room with a large table and dresser and also a polished wooden bookcase. Inside were some religious volumes but also various sets of encyclopaedia which must have been published and then sold, perhaps by subscription, volume by volume.

My grandmother used that room only on special occasions and an even more formal drawing room was never used in her later years. There was a living room which combined with a kitchen. Until her last years she did not have a fridge but used a traditional wooden box with lattice wire sides which was positioned outside the window and kept her milk, eggs and other foodstuffs fresh.

That print of the royal family on the wall said something about the commitment that my grandparents had made to their new country. They naturalised as British citizens in the 1920s.

The Jewish community in Britain has never been equivocal about its civic duties and its embrace of British values. Over a hundred years ago it was decided that the Sabbath service in all synagogues throughout the United Kingdom would always include a prayer for the royal family and for the government.

That continues to this day. It is an example that could be followed to remind children, regardless of their religion or ethnic or cultural background, that they have a shared obligation to uphold British values and our way of life.

In my late teens, I used to be sent by my parents to see my grandmother once a week to see if she needed any shopping done. Occasionally I had lunch with her. Although having lived in Edinburgh for over sixty years, she never lost her strong foreign accent.

She had great likes and dislikes. I was told that she approved of me but I was never told why. Her sons and daughters, even when they were adult, respected her authority and were dutiful to her. Every

Saturday after synagogue, her three sons, who lived in Edinburgh, walked with their children to her flat, where we stayed for twenty minutes, shared with her a glass of Sabbath wine and then went home for our lunch.

When she died in 1964, I asked if I could keep a memento of her. I have to this day a charming Russian silver sugar bowl, made in Moscow in 1874, which I think that she and my grandfather may have brought from Lithuania in 1899, as it has hallmarks with Cyrillic letters.

My mother's parents, Barnet and Rachel Cohen, were of a similar background. I did not know my maternal grandmother well, as they lived in Manchester when I was a child and she died while I was still quite young. My grandfather, however, lived his last years with my uncle and aunt round the corner from us and I saw him often. He had been born in Lithuania in 1882 and had come to Britain in the early 1900s and married his wife, Rachel Lichtenstein, in 1910 in Glasgow.

He moved to Manchester, where he started a hosiery business called the Prima Donna Hosiery Company in Turner Street. It was a wholesale warehouse and my mother, before she married, worked as the manageress, with three other staff.

My maternal grandfather was dapper, well-dressed and more anglicised than my father's parents. I remember him as a fairly gentle person sitting in our home wearing what I think was a stiff white collar and smoking his pipe. His wife Rachel died in 1958, aged sixty-nine. He died while on holiday in Southport from a heart attack in 1964, aged eighty-three.

My father was born in 1907 in Edinburgh and my mother in 1912 in Stockport.

My father went through life with one unfortunate possession and that was his name. Unlike his brothers and sisters, who were, simply, David, Jack, Etta, Annie and the like, my grandparents chose to give him the exotic Old Testament name of Elijah.

It was a name I never heard him use or be addressed by. He was known universally as Elky and on his card he was simply E. Rifkind. My mother, on the other hand, enjoyed the fine Anglo-Saxon, though rather Edwardian, name of Ethel, which, unlike some others of that period, has not yet come back into fashion.

Being one of ten children in a modest-income family could not have permitted my father many luxuries during his childhood. He attended Sciennes Primary School and then Boroughmuir, an excellent secondary school run by the Edinburgh Town Council.

Like most of his brothers and sisters, he left school at sixteen. I imagine that by that age they were expected to start bringing money into the home rather than just spending it.

My father informed me that he had been given the opportunity, by his parents, of further education but, at that time, it did not appeal to him. Only his youngest brother, Joe, born in 1920, had higher education. He graduated in Medicine from Edinburgh University and served as an officer and a doctor in the Army in India during the war.

When my father left school in 1923 he was offered a job in a chemist's shop but his parents objected, as the wages were small and he would have had to work on the Sabbath.

His mother had a drapery shop near the Royal Mile in St Mary's Street and my father worked there for around twenty years until after the war.

When the war began in 1939, my father was already thirty-two and was not conscripted into the armed forces. Instead, he became an air raid warden in the Air Raid Precautions (ARP).

He was the first to acknowledge that his contribution towards winning the war was not very substantial. There were very few air raids in Edinburgh as most of the German interest was in the Clyde shipyards and in industrial targets elsewhere in central Scotland.

On one of the few occasions that the air raid sirens went on during the night, my father instantly woke, put on his helmet, grabbed his gas mask and left their flat to ensure that all his neighbours got to the air shelters.

As he rushed down the stairs he found everyone else climbing up them. It turned out that he and my mother had slept through the original siren and had been woken by the all clear.

My father was a self-employed small businessman in the years after the war. His business was of a type that no longer exists, having been overtaken by the modern world.

He described himself on his card as a general warehouseman. During his early working years, he built up a substantial number of regular customers in working-class communities in several small towns near Edinburgh. Port Seton and Penicuik in the Lothians and Burntisland in Fife were amongst them.

In those days, low-income families in small towns had little choice of shops when it came to buying clothes, carpets or furniture. In any event, hire-purchase was not yet common and credit not always available. My father and others like him were in effect middle men and suppliers of credit. His customers indicated, in general terms, what kind of carpet or furniture they needed and what they could afford. They trusted my father to make the specific choice. He took orders, provided credit and arranged for wholesalers or manufacturers to deliver the goods. The sums outstanding were paid over weeks or months.

Once during the school holidays I spent a day with him in Burntisland. He visited his regular customers, was often invited in for a cup of tea, caught up with the family and local gossip and then moved on. It was a relaxing way of earning a living.

My father had had a car for a short time while unmarried in the 1930s. Despite his daily travelling throughout his working life, he never owned another one but was happy to use public transport.

My father shared with my paternal grandfather certain qualities. Both were content with what life offered. But although my father was content, he was not always tranquil.

He had a healthy enjoyment of a good argument and liked nothing better than informing his younger son of the weaknesses of government policy. He expressed his views about people in a forceful, colourful and often critical way but there was no malice in him and he did not bear grudges. He lost his temper easily but regained it quickly. He was sentimental and a tear could come easily to his eye, a tendency that can be found throughout the Rifkind family.

Throughout his life he was unimpressed by wealth and more interested in achievement. He was stubborn both when he was in the right and when he was, occasionally, in the wrong.

To me, he seemed a happy man, taking the seasons as they came. For those of us who have a more restless temperament, that attitude to life can sometimes be difficult to understand but never difficult to envy.

My mother was brought up in Manchester with her two sisters and one younger brother. She was a distant cousin of my father's. They married in Manchester and honeymooned in Llandudno.

Their marriage was successful and it seems to have been a love match. I have a photograph of her dated August 1939 which must have been sent by her to him at the time of their engagement. She is on the balcony of her home in Brooklands Road in Manchester. On the back she has written in blue-green ink 'Where is Romeo?' I never thought of my father as a Romeo. Perhaps all Rifkinds are suppressed Romeos.

Her life was not a mountain range; rather, it was a plain. There were no great summits in her life and, until she was seventy-five, there were no great valleys either.

Sadly, during her last years, after my father died in 1987, she developed Alzheimer's, which destroyed her personality. In 1990, I visited her with my son Hugo, who was then thirteen. My mother's memory was beginning to go and she could not remember a cousin's party she had been to only a day before.

I was a bit depressed but Hugo cheered me up, remarking, 'Don't worry, Dad. The best parties are those you can't remember the following day.' I couldn't help wondering how my thirteen-year-old son was already aware of this.

Although we were not well off, we had a comfortable standard of living during my childhood. My parents owned the flat we lived in. We had regular two-week summer holidays at a seaside resort and my brother and I attended fee-paying schools.

I have always found it sad that part of the human condition is that one never knows one's parents while they are young. My father was thirty-nine when I was born; my mother thirty-four.

Parents also seemed older and more formal in those days. I rarely saw my father without a tie except on holiday. Although not demonstrative, my parents' life was their family, and my brother and I enjoyed both emotional and financial security. It was not an exciting childhood but it was a happy one, for which I can only be grateful.

There is not a much better start that you can be given in life.

CHAPTER 2

AN EDINBURGH CHILDHOOD

WE ALL HAVE a fascination with earliest memories. Mine goes back to when I was around two years old.

I was having my tonsils out in the Sick Children's Hospital in Sciennes in Edinburgh.

Sciennes (pronounced Sheens) is not as Scottish as one might think. It is named after a convent of the Ladies of Sienna that was on this site before the Reformation.

I distinctly remember being in a cot while the other children in the ward were obviously older and were in normal beds. I was thinking that one day I would be old enough to be promoted to a bed as well.

I also think I remember being outraged when I discovered that the ice cream that my parents had brought for me had to be shared with the other children. I suspect that this is not a true recollection but something my mother told me about later. The cot recollection could only be mine.

Memory is a strange phenomenon. Pretty well everything we have experienced is locked away somewhere in our brains but it needs the right code to extract it. Margaret Thatcher once, in my presence, referred to 'the filing cabinet of the mind'. In this respect if in little other she had something in common with Marcel Proust and his madeleines.

I recall being on holiday with my parents and Arnold, my brother, in Whitley Bay in Northumberland when I must have been three or four. There is a lighthouse off the shore which one was able to walk to when the tide was out.

It was around this time that my short life almost came to a premature end. I was playing with my toys on the carpet in the living room at the base of a large kitchen cabinet where was kept crockery, glassware and the like.

Arnold, who was (and remains) more than three years older than me had climbed onto a chair to get something from the top of the cabinet. He lost his balance while doing so and managed to bring the cabinet crashing down. Although I was underneath, the angle of the fall left me entirely unscathed.

My other trauma, which in a modern age would have had me recommended for counselling, was when I and my brother were leaving the Woolworths store in Lothian Road.

As the glass door swung shut, I did not remove my hand soon enough and the forefinger of my left hand was trapped. Although I made a full recovery, I was left with a permanent slight disfigurement of the tip of that finger. If they ever need to identify my remains they need not bother with my DNA. All they need to do is look at the tip of my left forefinger. Like Tamerlane's limp, it is all there.

My brother, Arnold, and I shared a bedroom until he was eighteen and went off to Newcastle to study optometry. We have always been close, though we are very different. He is easygoing and is, perhaps, closer to my parents in temperament than I am.

He practised as an optician. A local child, when asked why

Malcolm Rifkind was famous, replied that it was because his brother was the optician in Morningside.

I sometimes felt that Arnold knew more of my constituents than I did. Once, when canvassing, I introduced myself to an elderly man on the doorstep. 'I know your brother,' he replied. 'He gave me these teeth.' He paused. 'Oh, no, he didn't. It was these glasses.'

Arnold has been married to Hilary since 1968. For many years she taught mathematics at my old school, George Watson's. She is my favourite sister-in-law and not just because she is my only one. They have two sons, Richard and Michael, my only nephews.

My first educational experience was in Miss Rankine's kindergarten (as child nurseries were known in middle-class Edinburgh at that time) near Tollcross. From there, I went to James Gillespie's Primary School at the age of five.

James Gillespie's was, at that time, a prominent girls' secondary school, situated just up the road from where we lived. Muriel Spark had been a pupil and she made it the model for Marcia Blaine School where Miss Jean Brodie taught in the 1930s during her infatuation with Mussolini.

In Marchmont Road, nearby, there was the boys' primary school with the same name, which was a bit confusing when you indicated which school you attended. I was there for two years but recollect little of that period other than that at the end of each day, at the tender age of five or six, my parents saw no reason not to let me make my own way home, a walk that took around fifteen minutes. Not all parents would be so relaxed nowadays.

I remember the Coronation in 1953, when I was six, for two reasons. Like tens of thousands of other families, we acquired our first television at that time in order to watch the new Queen being crowned.

When the TV arrived and was installed, I sat watching my first ever TV programme. I am pretty certain it was *The Lone Ranger* (and

Tonto, his faithful Indian), a highly popular Western with theme music from the William Tell Overture.

The Coronation was both exciting and, for me, boring. Our living room was full of friends and neighbours who did not yet have their own TVs. It was extraordinary to know that we were watching this historic event as it actually happened.

But it went on hour after hour, which was interminable for a six-year-old child. When I have seen the Coronation replayed recently, I have been reminded, also, how dreadful the picture was by modern standards. It was black and white, on a small screen, and with a very fuzzy image.

Being bored after a couple of hours, I wanted to go outside and play with some friends, but even that was frustrated. As it looked like rain, my mother insisted on my putting on my navy blue school gabardine raincoat, which I disliked. I refused and, for my pains, found myself confined to quarters.

There was one matter that puzzled me at the time but has since become clearer. As a small boy I had got into the habit of muttering 'Fudge' whenever something happened that annoyed me.

When my mother heard me using this word she insisted that I must never use it again, without providing any explanation as to why it was unsuitable. Some years later I realised, one day, its similarity to an expletive that is not always deleted. My mother was more streetwise than I had realised.

My brother had been enrolled at George Watson's College and at the age of seven I was given the opportunity to join him. But as there was no guarantee that I would be offered a place, I also sat the exam for George Heriot's School. To my satisfaction and my parents' surprise, I was offered a place by both schools. I recall distinctly that my parents left it to me to choose which to accept. I chose Watson's mainly because Arnold was already there. It was quite remarkable that my parents left it to me, aged seven, to decide, as if I had opted for Heriot's it would have been a considerable nuisance to have two sons at different schools in different parts of town.

George Watson's College is a Merchant Company school founded in the eighteenth century and offering education right through from five to eighteen years of age. Today it is co-educational, but in my day there was a separate ladies' college in George Square, near the university.

When I was a pupil there, I was a day boy but there were a significant number of boarders who were accommodated in nearby houses, each under the supervision of one of the masters. The boarders were, therefore, known throughout the school as bug hut boys.

Years later, when I was the local MP, I was invited to do the official opening of a smart new bug hut that was located in the school grounds and a plaque was unveiled which commemorated this event.

When my daughter, Caroline, became a pupil a little later, she was taken, with her fellow new pupils, on a tour of the school by a senior prefect. When they reached the new bug hut, the prefect pointed to the plaque and asked if anyone knew who Malcolm Rifkind was. 'He's my daddy,' piped up my daughter, triumphantly. This story went round the school and came back to me a few days later via the headmaster.

Edinburgh is unique for its large number of independent schools, mostly serving the local community. They range from the grand public schools like Fettes, Loretto and Merchiston to impressive day schools such as Edinburgh Academy, George Watson's, Daniel Stewart's and Melville, and George Heriot's, as well as St George's, a school exclusively for girls.

Altogether over 15 per cent of Edinburgh children attend fee-paying schools, compared to a UK average of around 7 per cent. Many were established by philanthropic merchants in the eighteenth century who, by lending their names to their schools, immortalised themselves in the process.

Being Edinburgh, there is not only a social divide between the independent and local authority schools. Even the independent schools have their own pecking order, with Fettes, Tony Blair's old school, being the most prestigious.

There is a delightful tale of two Edinburgh ladies having tea, some years ago, in Jenners, which used to be to Edinburgh what Harrods is to London.

Not knowing each other well and trying to establish her new friend's social position, one asks the other which school her children attend. 'Oh, we have no children,' says the other. Undeterred, the first replies, 'Ah, but if you did have any children, which school would they attend?'

Given my future career, it is worth pointing out that George Watson's, although in no way grand, had been the alma mater over the years of an impressive number of future Cabinet ministers.

During part of the First World War, two of the Cabinet were Watsonians, as was Sir John Anderson, the Home Secretary during the Second World War. In the 1950s, Watson's provided a Speaker of the House of Commons in W. S. (Shakes) Morrison.

David Maxwell Fyfe, the chief prosecutor at the war crimes tribunal at Nuremberg, who became Lord Chancellor in Harold Macmillan's government as Viscount Kilmuir, was also a Watsonian, as was David Steel, the former Leader of the Liberal Party.

Maxwell Fyfe recorded in his own autobiography that as a child he was sent to George Watson's, which 'was the best school in Edinburgh, and in Scotland, and therefore in the world'.

I began at Watson's in 1953. Although it was an exceptionally good school, the fees were around £30 a term, partly because, in those days, such schools received government grants. Now the fees run into thousands, which makes it unaffordable for so many. For a number of years I have been the honorary president of the George Watson's Family Foundation, which raises large sums of money to help pay the fees for children who would otherwise find the school unaffordable. George Watson would be impressed, as this is just what he had in mind 300 years ago.

I progressed through the primary school, a contented but unremark-able pupil. In those days we had school masters and mistresses rather than teachers. They were powerful people, as they could administer the belt, a leather strap, to the palm of the hand of a disobedient or difficult boy. We took such punishments for granted, not having been made aware of the provisions of the European Convention of Human Rights.

In my first year, aged seven, I had the pleasant Miss Anderson, then the diminutive Miss Dalgleish, followed by a Mrs Fraser. Thereafter, it was masters not mistresses until the end of my school days.

One of my form masters was Jim Smith, whose daughter Liz is now an impressive Member of the Scottish Parliament and a close friend and colleague.

In the secondary school we had different masters for each subject. How they acquired their nicknames I will never know but once chosen they stuck like limpets.

The senior music master was Norman Hyde, universally known as Pongo. He was a fine teacher and had published a book under the title *Music Doth Charm*, known within the school as *Music Doth Harm*.

On one occasion he invited to our class Joseph Cooper, a pianist and member of the TV panel game *Face the Music*. We expected to be bored but he won our hearts when, after his first piece, he said, 'Now that I've finished my little songo, it would be wrongo if I did not say thank you to Pongo.'

My maths master was Tiger Jamieson, who had cultivated a fierce, surly manner and was a regular user of the belt.

If one had an urgent need to leave the room during his period, he would point to a cocoa tin on his desk and invite the boy to use that. We subsequently found that the tin was stuffed with his fag ends.

On one occasion I got six of the best with his belt on my hands for what I considered to be a minor misdemeanour. I cannot even remember what it was. I felt considerable resentment but it never crossed my mind to complain either to him or to anyone else.

But one master's practices did lead to parental complaints. Our school uniform was a maroon blazer, striped tie, long grey trousers and plain socks. The school was usually relaxed about dress but occasionally there would be spasms of enthusiasm about getting us back into correct uniform.

This particular master had sent me home on one occasion to change my socks because they had a stripe in them and should have been plain.

He was responsible for a more disturbing practice. There was a fashion in drainpipe trousers. If he judged that a boy's trousers were too narrow he would call him into his room and require him to take off his trousers with his shoes still on. If he was unable to, he was punished.

This continued until parents objected to the headmaster and he was encouraged to find another way of ensuring observance of the rules. I have no reason to believe that there was any deliberate impropriety intended, but in today's climate, as opposed to the more relaxed attitudes of the 1960s, he could have got himself into serious trouble.

I recall two of my Latin masters, Geoff Suggett and Pip Paulin. Mr Suggett was an excellent teacher but he had a dreadful stutter. I admired the sheer guts of the man, with that disability, to choose school teaching as his career, working daily with curious and insensitive juveniles.

Pip Paulin was a rather Pickwickian figure with a deep love of the Classics and an inability to understand those who did not share it.

We studied Livy and Virgil's *Aeneid* with him and each boy was expected to translate a paragraph of the Latin prose as we worked our way through his beloved texts.

He was well aware that I and my close friend Mark Sischy, who sat next to me, were indolent and unlikely to be able to meet his expectations.

Without any formal negotiation, we had reached an understanding with him that as long as we were silent and reading something suitable, which in my case was an English translation of Plato's *Republic*, he would not bother us with demands to translate Virgil. This worked perfectly well and I have always thought of it as a civilised way of resolving a difficult problem.

My favourite master, and the one who influenced me most, was Robin Morgan, who taught history. He went on to be headmaster of Campbell College in Northern Ireland and then returned to Edinburgh as headmaster of Daniel Stewart's and Melville College.

He sounded and looked like a retired army officer and had a deep interest in military history, although, so far as I am aware, he had never been a soldier.

He had a striking personality, an infectious enthusiasm and curiosity. Most relevant to my future life, he was as interested in contemporary politics as in history.

Often, at the beginning of a period when we were supposed to be examining Europe in the nineteenth century, he would begin by referring to something in that day's newspapers that was happening in Britain or in the world, and invite us to comment on it.

Few of his pupils would immediately respond but I was one who usually did. My involvement in the school debating society had already created an interest in current affairs and the wider world, and served me well.

I spoke on two occasions, in later years, at Daniel Stewart's when Robin Morgan was headmaster, and stayed with him at his home in Yorkshire in 1995 after he had retired. He had tempted me to come and speak to his local Conservative association with the offer of a day's pheasant shooting.

The only real spat we had was when, as a pupil, I was the deputy editor of *The Phoenix*, the literary club magazine. We had a tradition of associating uncomplimentary remarks with individual masters. As he taught history, we had attributed to him the quote, 'Get your facts right first, then you can distort them as much as you like.'

He asked me to stay behind at the end of a period and then challenged me as to why I was making out that he was some sort of fascist who distorted history. I said, rather lamely, that it was intended to be a joke, but I don't think he was impressed.

My school days were inauspicious as regards both academic achievement and sporting prowess. Watson's is a school with an excellent and deserved reputation, but I was not stimulated by most of the lessons and I did not discover real enjoyment in studying until I was at university.

There was streaming within the school and I was content to find myself near the top of the second stream. This was sufficiently respectable to stop my parents rebuking me for my performance. I must confess I was also relieved not to be at the top of the second stream, as such pupils were transferred to the top stream for the following school session and I wanted to avoid the extra pressure and expectations that that might create.

My performance on the playing fields was no better. I was skinny as a child, which did not help when playing rugby, and I had no particular co-ordination skills when kicking a football.

I was occasionally the hooker in the rugger scrum. I can remember one occasion when I was passed the ball and realised there was no one in front of me who could prevent me from scoring a try. Unfortunately, I had forgotten those behind who could run faster than me. I was brought down by a tackle just before I reached the hallowed line.

Years later, when I was in my late thirties, I took up game shooting, which I greatly enjoyed. I was hugely amused when this recreation led to me being profiled, while Foreign Secretary, in *The Field* under the caption 'A Sporting Life'.

Only in two respects, while at school, did I achieve any significant plaudits and both were relevant to my future life. One was amateur dramatics; the other was public speaking.

I performed on the stage in several school plays. The first was a class play and was not very auspicious, as I had to act as the wife of one of the other performers and had to dress accordingly, which has put me off cross-dressing ever since.

The second was in Shakespeare's *Julius Caesar*, where I was the soothsayer. My lines were restricted to 'Beware the Ides of March', said twice. I remembered them perfectly and thereby began my career as one who has been recognised, over the years, as being able to speak without notes in even more challenging circumstances.

My moment of mini-glory was in the school production of Robert Bolt's *A Man for All Seasons*, where I played Cardinal Wolsey. It was not a major part but I could not resist the scarlet robes and the cardinal's biretta. Given Wolsey's status as Henry VIII's chief advisor, I suppose it is the nearest I have ever got to becoming Prime Minister.

I still have a splendid photograph that appeared in the *Edinburgh Evening News* showing me, in my robes, with my fellow actors, several of whom had rather distinguished futures.

They included Peter Farago, who remains one of my closest friends, who played Sir Thomas More and went on to become a very successful theatre director; Gavin Hewitt, who performed as Thomas Cromwell and ended his diplomatic career as the British ambassador to Belgium; and Mark Sischy, a future sheriff on the Scottish bench.

It was my interest in acting that, I suppose, propelled me into school debating. The school Literary Club was the debating society but was only open to third form and above. It was decided to form a Junior Lit Club for younger boys in the senior school.

The first debate was on 'the benefits of television'. I was told by my English master that I would be proposing the motion in favour of TV. You might have thought it would be relatively easy to persuade a schoolboy audience to support television. However, we lost.

I still have a copy of that first speech, made when I was thirteen. It is handwritten and three pages long. I point out that television gives pleasure and broadens the mind. I argue that TV encourages reading books rather than discourages, by getting viewers interested in learning more. I defend 'Westerns and gangster films' as they bring excitement to people's lives.

I conclude with a rousing declaration that 'anybody who says television is bad must be havering and out of his mind'. Perhaps it was this evidence of intolerance that turned my audience against me.

It was not an auspicious beginning to my future career, but I had got the bug. I found public speaking to be fun, stimulating and something I was reasonably good at. I had no hesitation in joining the senior Lit Club when I reached third form at the age of fourteen.

I have my notes for several of the debates that I took part in. On one occasion I made a passionate defence of monarchy against republicanism. I declared that 'royalty needs money to give it dignity and by giving itself dignity it gives dignity to the state it serves'. I made uncomplimentary references to President Kennedy, 'insulted and jeered at by his own fellow citizens', compared to 'our own widely admired Queen Elizabeth'.

Interestingly, while that speech is written out in full, on a separate sheet of paper I summarise it to its specific points. That must be because I was already trying to get away from reading a text and, with notes, wanted to address my audience directly and develop my oratorical prowess.

I have a copy of the minutes of the Lit Club for the session 1961/62, when I would have been fifteen. The minutes read:

> It was Mr Rifkind's duty to propose the motion, that we do not wish to join the Common Market. It was a task he tackled with obvious enthusiasm and Beaverbrook propaganda. He pointed out that economically and politically Britain would lose by entering the Common Market. This was the best speech [of the debate].

I am relieved the minutes said that it was my 'duty' to propose the motion. I cannot assist the reader as to whether that was also my personal view at the time. I suspect it was but I do not remember.

My most revealing speech, in retrospect, was my contribution to the mock election debate when I must have been fifteen or sixteen. I invented my own political party with the rather fascistic title of British United Loyalists. Although my rhetoric was jingoistic, my policies were mainstream.

Some of my programme anticipated my future beliefs. I supported spending more on defence and was against unilateral nuclear disarmament. I doubt, however, whether the Ministry of Defence would have welcomed my call for the return of National Service. Nor would they have been impressed by my call for the removal of all American bases from Britain on the grounds that we should defend ourselves.

I am saddened to see that I supported capital punishment but proud that I called for the exclusion of South Africa from the Commonwealth because of apartheid. On another evening I made a similar fierce attack on apartheid, describing it as 'despicable'.

Finally, I quoted Palmerston with approval (as I did in my first speech as Foreign Secretary in 1995), called for Communist China to be admitted to the UN and stressed support for NATO.

The significance of the speech is not so much its content but the interest in politics it shows that I had developed at that age and, especially, its concentration on foreign policy and defence rather than domestic issues.

What was also happening around that age was my emergence from the shadows at my school. My academic performance was still middling at best and far from impressive. My sporting enthusiasms were limited to table tennis.

But I was ceasing to be invisible in the life of the school. It had begun with amateur dramatics, which led to *A Man for All Seasons*. Its main focus was debating and public speaking in the Lit Club. I was elected to the committee of the club when I was in the fifth form and was chosen as junior president (the president was always a master) at the end of my fifth form for the following session.

I never actually served as junior president, as, in the event,

I left Watson's for Edinburgh University rather than go into the sixth form. I was, however, invited back to the Lit Club for one of their debates evenings on Friday 22 November of that year. It was during that meeting that we heard of the assassination of President Kennedy.

In my fifth year I also became deputy editor of the Lit Club's magazine, *The Phoenix*. I wrote a short contribution to that magazine which I reproduce most of here, as it shows how both my writing style and political awareness had matured by the time I was a fifth former.

> Noah's Ark?
>
> 'Get out.'
>
> 'But I've nowhere to go.'
>
> 'That's not my affair ... Go away.'
>
> 'But, Christ, you're not going to leave me out here to get caught by that bloody radiation!'
>
> '... I couldn't give a damn about you. Alright I'm selfish, maybe I'm being inhuman but I can't let you in...'
>
> 'Daddy, who's that outside?'
>
> 'Never you mind ... IT'S ONLY A POOR HUMAN WHO FOR NO SENSIBLE REASON IS TRYING TO SURVIVE IN THIS MAD WORLD ... All right, man. Come in but for God's sake, make it quick ... Tell the whole world to come right on in. If we survive this bloody atom bomb the next one will get us anyway and if it doesn't? Then we can start all over again. Isn't it funny. First it was Adam, now it's Noah ... And in a few thousand years it will be somebody else. We'll rebuild the world, a world of peace, but soon there will return blood and strife until finally we have another nuclear war and we'll be right back where we started but somebody will always survive. Isn't it funny ... No, on the other hand perhaps it isn't.'

Although I was never a unilateral disarmer, it is these thoughts, expressed as a sixteen-year-old, that continue to influence my public life half a century later. In recent years I have spent considerable time working with Global Zero, with Senator Sam Nunn's Nuclear Threat Initiative and with other similar bodies that seek to advance the cause of radical multilateral disarmament to remove, or at least reduce, the nuclear weapon threat to the planet.

I owe a great deal to the encouragement George Watson's gave to debating and public speaking. It turned out to lead directly to my political career, but, even if it hadn't, it matured me, stimulated my interest in the wider world and gave me self-confidence in expressing myself.

If one can become relaxed at the age of sixteen when addressing an audience, one has a skill and an ability that will be of enormous value throughout one's life whatever one's chosen career.

If I had to choose between a school promoting a debating society or ensuring that its pupils were computer literate, I would always demand the former. Of course no such choice is necessary, but computer skills can be learnt at any age. Learning to speak in public when one is already an adult is much more difficult and for some is thought to be beyond their powers. It is a great loss.

My maturing in my middle teens also led to my enthusiasm for reading, an enthusiasm which has grown over the years.

We had books at home but never very many and I rarely saw my father or mother reading one. My own, as a youngster, were largely my schoolbooks, though visits to the public library became much more frequent in my teens.

My reading interests were whatever caught my attention. I devoured John Steinbeck's *The Grapes of Wrath* (which I reread last year) as well as Ernest Hemingway, including *For Whom the Bell Tolls*. I am not sure why but I worked through several of Ibsen's plays as well as Strindberg's.

My interest in books was enhanced when I visited my friend Peter

Farago's home. Peter's family were Hungarian, They, like many others, had fled Hungary after the Soviet invasion of 1956. His father was a professor of nuclear physics at Edinburgh University.

When I went into Peter's bedroom, I found one wall, with bookshelves from floor to ceiling, crammed with novels, plays and books on every subject. Books ceased, from that day, to be objects that you borrowed from public libraries. Every house we have lived in since then has been full of them and I could not consider it otherwise.

Peter also influenced my attitude to hierarchy within the school. Most unusually, but deservedly, he had been made a prefect in his fifth year. As a result, he wore the coveted prefect's tie and silver badge in his lapel.

I thought it would be rather agreeable to have that distinction in my sixth year and smartened myself up and was more agreeable to the masters and more attentive in class. It was never likely to have happened because of my lack of sporting or academic distinction, but as, in the event, I left school at the end of my fifth form, I will never know for certain.

There was, however, one splendid sequel. When, many years later, I was the guest speaker at the annual prize day, I said to the headmaster and the assembled pupils that Watson's had shown more judgement than Mrs Thatcher by never putting me in a position of authority, never having made me a prefect. When the headmaster thanked me at the end of the proceedings, he suddenly brought out a silver prefect's badge and pinned it on my lapel. Better late than never.

I had assumed that I would, in due course, go into the sixth form. I was, however, bored with the academic side of school and was greatly influenced by the success of my two closest friends, Peter Farago and Mark Sischy, in getting places at Edinburgh University for the following year. It was not unusual in Scotland for universities to accept applicants when they were seventeen, partly because the degree course in Scotland was four years rather than three as in England and Wales.

My parents had always made it clear that they expected my brother and me to go to university or college and have a profession. I was content with that but, at first, had no idea what discipline I would choose. I had an uncle and four cousins who became doctors, but that was not for me. Nor was anything scientific, nor accountancy.

By chance I had just been reading the light-hearted novels of Henry Cecil, such as *Sober as a Judge* and *Brothers-in-Law*. They were about the life of a young English barrister.

I had never been interested in becoming a solicitor, which I, wrongly, assumed to be a dull, deskbound occupation. I discovered that, in contrast, barristers were dashing fellows, in wig and gown, addressing juries and praised for their oratorical prowess.

I decided that the Bar was for me and so informed my father. He was surprised but raised no objection, on the assumption that it would be the Scots Bar and that I would live at home while pursuing my studies, thus keeping costs down.

I applied to Edinburgh University's Law Faculty but with little hope of success. It was several months after the closing date for applications, I was only in the fifth form and my Highers (the Scottish equivalent of A-levels, and less demanding) were mediocre to say the least. I had got three: two Bs, in English and History, and a C, in Latin.

At the end of the school year, I left for a hiking holiday in the Alps on the French–Italian border. It was my first trip abroad. I expected to return and still be a schoolboy when the new term began. I had asked my brother to telegram me whenever we heard from the university. A telegram duly appeared. To my astonishment, I had been accepted.

Nowadays, with my dismal grades, I wouldn't even have been considered by the Law Faculty. But this was 1963 and they had more places than applicants. I presume that my debating and public speaking activities influenced them, but it was astonishing nonetheless.

I have given considerable thought as to why my academic achievements at school were so mediocre when throughout the rest of my life, in profiles and in comment, I have often, to my pleasant surprise, been described as ferociously bright, highly intelligent, incisive and articulate.

Of course, a likely explanation is that these compliments are unmerited. I have often felt uncomfortable when reading these comments, conscious of my lack of glittering prizes at school and suspicious that my debating skills and reputation for speaking without notes might be giving a false impression of my intellectual capability.

I recall once having lunch with the broadcaster Robin Day at the Garrick Club. That morning, in an article in *The Times*, William Rees-Mogg had lamented the lack of intellectuals in the Tory Party, mentioning me as one of the few he could think of.

Robin Day told me that he had bumped into Rees-Mogg an hour before and had told him, 'Rifkind's not an intellectual. He's just a smart Edinburgh lawyer.' Sir Robin was always very perceptive.

Nevertheless I think I can offer some explanation for the contrast between my early performance and my later reputation.

One mistake I made was, at the end of my third form, to opt to concentrate on Physics and Chemistry for my Highers rather than French and Mathematics.

There was reason for this. At the time I was not considering the Bar as a profession and it seemed unwise to rule out all the careers associated with science. My French and Mathematics were reasonable. Chemistry and Physics, however, were poor, as my report cards for those years remind me.

But there is a more substantial explanation for my performance at school. Firstly, I was not stimulated by the teaching except, as I have indicated, by Robin Morgan in History, and to a lesser extent by English.

Nor was I under any real pressure from my parents to apply myself and deliver better results. They, of course, wanted me to do well but they did not have an academic background and had no reason to assume I had any exceptional talent. They took a proper parental interest in my grades and the comments in my successive report cards, but because I was middling and never did badly, they saw no reason to be concerned.

There is, perhaps, an even more fundamental consideration. My success in my public life and my reputation as someone who is highly intelligent is, perhaps, because such talents as I have are particularly helpful to a political and ministerial career. They are less relevant to passing exams and achieving high marks.

I gradually became aware of these talents. Since my teens I have found that, for me to understand a problem or reach a decision, I must first break down the matter into its component parts. I need to appreciate fully where we are and how we have got there in order to know where I wish to go. I have found this task quite straightforward, as I have reminding myself that I must not fail to see the wood for the trees. This approach has enabled me to reach decisions on difficult questions without too much difficulty or agonising thereafter.

It has also been of enormous benefit that I was born with, and have developed further, a retentive memory for what interests me or what I need to know. This inherent skill has been boosted by my insistence, whenever possible, in speaking without a text or notes.

In order to speak without notes one is greatly assisted if one has prepared one's thoughts in advance as a logical sequence of facts, argument and analysis.

Of course, one has to be able to improvise if one forgets one's next point. I received early advice not to worry about that. As long as what I said followed what I had just said, it did not matter if it was not what I originally intended to say. Nobody else knew that either.

It is no coincidence that in choosing my first profession I opted for the Bar. Barristers and advocates are like MPs and ministers. To succeed, they must be forensic, articulate, logical and pragmatic.

I may have developed as a fine speaker, but I am not an orator. That requires passion and emotion. Although I can be as passionate and as emotional as anyone else, I am uncomfortable about using passion as a substitute for argument. This is not a consideration that has ever deterred the great orators over the years.

So, it was not just my indolence or the lack of stimulation that led to my indifferent academic record while at school. It was also that such talents as I had remained latent and unknown both to me and to my teachers. Only when, by chance, I was drawn into debating and public speaking, where forensic skills are so relevant, did I and others discover that I might have something significant to offer after all.

I wrote to my headmaster, Roger Young, informing him of my acceptance by Edinburgh University. He did not know me well. Watson's was a large school and the headmaster could not be expected to be close to every pupil. He was an outstanding headmaster, a future chairman of the Headmasters Conference, and was, deservedly, knighted in the latter part of his career. He was probably as surprised as I was by my admission to the university but was generous in offering his good wishes for my success.

I had just turned seventeen. I did not have to continue wearing my school blazer and uniform. I was an undergraduate of Edinburgh University, one of Scotland's finest establishments.

I never looked back.

CHAPTER 3

A UNIVERSITY EXPERIENCE

A S I WALKED across the Meadows to my first lecture in the Old Quad wearing my new varsity scarf, I should have been asking myself why Scotland had had four universities for hundreds of years while England made do with Oxford and Cambridge until the middle of the nineteenth century.

While it may seem strange that a poorer, much smaller country should have provided more opportunities for higher education than its much larger and richer neighbour, it was, in fact, that poverty that was a significant part of the explanation.

Education was one of the very few ways by which a young Scot could escape from poverty. With a degree he could become a teacher, a lawyer or a clergyman. With learning he could choose to be a merchant.

Edinburgh University was unusual even in Scotland. Its origins, unlike Glasgow, Aberdeen and St Andrews, were not in the Church. It was founded in 1582 by Edinburgh Town Council. It is the sixth oldest university in the English-speaking world. It began its life as a college of law, a faculty of which I had now become an undergraduate.

Because the Law Faculty was as old as the university, it was situated in the Old Quad, the heart of the university complex. The building of the Old Quad had begun in 1789, to a plan prepared by Robert Adam. In 1792, Adam's death, the outbreak of the Napoleonic Wars and, curiously, the imposition of income tax slowed then halted progress until 1815.

William Playfair was chosen as architect to complete Adam's plans and by 1827 the building was virtually complete apart from the splendid dome added in 1887.

On the south side of the Old Quad was Playfair's magnificent library, while the Law Faculty occupied most of the north side. This was to be my place of work for the next three years.

I have always had an enthusiasm for classical architecture. The first home that Edith and I owned was in Drummond Place, in the heart of the Georgian New Town. It was a pleasure as well as a privilege that I now studied in one of Edinburgh's finest buildings. I was daily reminded of the university's history and traditions stretching back almost half a millennium.

In recent years, as president of the Edinburgh University Development Trust, I visited the Old Quad regularly for meetings in the Raeburn Room, so called because of the impressive portraits by Sir Henry Raeburn that adorn its walls. During the years that I was Honorary Colonel of the university's Officer Training Corps we had our annual Haldane Dinner in the Playfair Library.

So much of our lives are dominated, quite reasonably, by the present and the future. It is good, especially for younger generations, to be reminded of where we have come from, not just where we are going.

The Old Quad, in the 1960s, though no longer, was also the location of the Rectorial Battle on the day students were electing the Rector, who would represent their interests with the university authorities.

The Rector, whose office went back to the earliest years of the university, had traditionally been a public figure whose role was largely ceremonial. That came to an end when students stood, successfully, for the rectorship, most notably Gordon Brown in 1972. The Rectorial Battle, as a tradition, had ceased a few years earlier so Gordon, rather sadly, was never involved.

On the day of the election, dozens of supporters of the two main candidates would face each other in the middle of the Old Quad, with hundreds of other students observing the battle from the raised terraces at either side.

One group would occupy the west end of the Old Quad, where the war memorial had been covered up to protect it, while the other group would see its purpose to engage in battle and try to dislodge their adversaries from the war memorial frontage.

Weapons used were water, garbage, manure and various other unmentionables. The contestants were advised to wear two pairs of underpants as, if captured, they would certainly lose one. I recall, as an observer, seeing one student with a flaming torch. No one was seriously hurt except as regards their dignity.

On the night of the election in 1966, after the result was announced, the supporters of the new Rector, Malcolm Muggeridge, marched from the Old Quad to the Calton Hill to celebrate.

I was supporting one of the defeated candidates, Lord Birsay, and we decided, spontaneously, to have our own march to Edinburgh Castle. Security was minimal in those days and when we got to the esplanade of the castle we found, despite the late hour, that the main door to the interior was unlocked and with no one there to prevent us we entered the inner part of the castle.

Undisturbed, we got to the highest battlements overlooking the city and were rather pleased with ourselves to be amongst the few who have ever captured Edinburgh Castle.

Eventually our celebration was brought to an undignified end. Several of the soldiers, who used the castle as barracks, appeared. We were abused by a sergeant major and ordered off the premises. As we got to the front gate we discovered that they had called the police to help evict us.

I have heard of the police, in some countries, calling out the army to help them. This was the first time I had experienced the reverse.

When, both as Scottish Secretary and as Secretary of State for Defence, I had to host dinners in Edinburgh Castle, I judged it prudent to keep this youthful escapade to myself.

One of the consequences of progressing from school to university was that I formed a number of new friendships.

On my first day, walking home to Marchmont down Middle Meadow Walk, I recognised one of my new fellow students. He was Jimmy Gordon, who had just left Gordonstoun and whose family lived in Craigellachie in the Highlands.

Jimmy was good looking, debonair, full of fun and very engaging. We conversed as he made his way towards his digs in Bruntsfield and found that we liked one another and had common interests, including politics.

Through Jimmy I also became friendly with several other fresher students in the Law Faculty, and half a dozen of us got into the habit of seeing a lot of each other, searching each other out and having, to some degree, a joint social life.

One was Duncan Campbell, who had been at Glenalmond and who lived in Inverleith in Edinburgh with his parents and his brother, Neil. Neil went on to be a distinguished civil servant in the Scottish Office with whom I worked when I was a minister.

Duncan was known to have a crush on the actress Julie Christie, like many other people did. The difference is that, unlike the others, he not only met her some years later but, eventually, married her and lived happily ever after. He has had a successful journalistic career, including being editor of *Time Out*.

Other close friends in that group included a Gordonstoun colleague of Jimmy's, Bill Mactaggart. Bill's parents owned a holiday cottage in remote Glenfeshie in the Highlands which we all enjoyed on one memorable occasion. There was also Eddie Torgbor, from Ghana, the son of a tribal chief, with ceremonial scars on his cheeks to prove it. He became a distinguished judge, serving for a number of years in the Kenyan High Court.

Most of these new friends were public schoolboys. Although all were middle class rather than aristocratic, their background was a notch above mine. I was struck by their easy social manners and self-confidence without any of the arrogance that one can sometimes find in those who have had a public school education.

We not only socialised together. The Law Library in the Old Quad had three rooms. We all tended to gravitate to the same room to work in, and this became known to our fellow students as the Public School Room, which is pretty embarrassing when I look back on it, though it was not quite the Bullingdon.

Now I was a student, I was expected to attend lectures. We were fortunate in having some of the most impressive legal academics practising in Scotland at that time.

Prominent amongst them was Professor T. B. Smith, then Professor of Civil Law. Knighted in 1981, he became general editor of the *Laws of Scotland: Stair Memorial Encyclopaedia*, to which he invited me to contribute a section on the Scottish Office and government of Scotland.

He had published in 1962 a very large *Short Commentary on the Law of Scotland*, which became my bible for the next three years.

Tom Smith was a large, moustachioed, extrovert academic who commanded attention by the sheer force of his personality. He lectured on Civil Law, the derivation of Scots Law from Roman-Dutch and the Corpus Iuris Civilis, otherwise known as the Code of Justinian. (I recall he insisted on pronouncing the 'C' of Civilis as if it was a 'Ch', though how he knew how the Romans spoke I do not know.)

At that time, a knowledge of Latin was essential if one was to study law in Scotland and our first term examination had a chunk of Justinian's Code in Latin which we were expected to translate. The vast majority of the students were not competent classicists and as there were almost as many translations as there were students taking the exam, a decision was reached that, in future, our study of Justinian would be entirely in English.

T. B. Smith also had a mischievous sense of humour. His assistant was a much younger lecturer, Michael Topping. One day he informed the crowded lecture room that he had an important announcement to make. He wished to inform us that his friend and colleague Mr Topping had just been appointed as Professor to the Chair of Law at … he paused … 'the University of Haile Selassie in Addis Ababa'. A great cheer went up from the assembled students.

The Professor of Constitutional Law was the equally distinguished J. D. B. Mitchell, who published his authoritative *Constitutional Law in the 1960s* and subsequently became the first holder of the Salvesen Chair of European Institutions at the university.

Professor Iain MacGibbon gave me my first grounding in International Law, which proved highly relevant to my work as a minister and Secretary of State in the Foreign Office.

One other academic whom I recall, though not for the most cerebral of reasons, was the elderly Professor David Maxwell, who lectured on Mercantile Law.

On the first morning he deemed it desirable to give us a few tips on how we should prepare ourselves for his lectures. Without a glimmer of a smile, and in a rather high-pitched voice, he advised us to go to bed early the night before and get a good night's sleep. He also thought it important to remind us to have sharpened our pencils before his lecture began. Having just been congratulating ourselves on no longer being schoolboys, we were forced to consider whether we had been a little premature.

One memorable presentation of Scots Law was from a lecturer, Bill Wilson, who began his lecture by saying that he was going to inform us about the law of bastardy. There were, he said, three types of bastards under the law of Scotland. There were uterine bastards, adulterine bastards 'and, ladies and gentlemen, plain ordinary bastards'.

My time at university, from 1963 to 1967, coincided with what has since become known as the Swinging Sixties. I must confess that I was hardly aware of it at the time.

Of course, the first satirical TV programme, *That Was the Week That Was*, began in 1962 and was compulsory viewing for me as for all my generation. The Profumo Affair had erupted in 1963, sexual mores were changing and the British habit of deference to those in authority was eroding; a process which has continued to this day.

But Edinburgh in 1963 was not London, Princes Street was not Carnaby Street and the Law Faculty of Edinburgh University had little in common with the London School of Economics.

As law students, we were expected to attend lectures in jacket and tie. It being a local as well as an international university, many of us still lived at home, with all that that implied.

Politicians are often asked whether they ever took drugs while they were students. I can say, in all honesty, that I never did. But I should add that that might be because I was never given the opportunity. Edith, who was a student at King's College London, at that time, remembers that soft drugs were not unusual at parties for those who were interested.

One of the joys of student life was the opportunity to travel during the long recesses. I had no car and had little cash for train fares, but that did not matter. Hitch-hiking was my normal means of getting around Britain. Motorways were not yet widespread, motorists were often friendly and one rarely had to wait too long for a lift.

One Easter recess, Peter Farago and I hitch-hiked down to London. The plan was to get temporary jobs while we were there, work during the day and enjoy ourselves in the evening.

Temping, in those days, was not difficult. We went to an employment exchange in Tottenham Court Road and were told that the accountants Coopers & Lybrand needed staff to serve morning and afternoon tea to their employees.

Peter and I lasted as tea boys for one day. It was very boring. We took cups of tea into individual offices. Occasionally we were thanked, usually ignored. So much did I resent the discourtesy of not receiving even a thank-you for our efforts that I have, ever since, taken the trouble to thank anyone who has served me whether in a café or when, as Foreign Secretary, I was chairing a crucial meeting with ambassadors or other ministers when the tea was served.

Although we decided to move on after one day, there is a delightful sequel. Years later, after I left government, I worked for some years as a consultant to PricewaterhouseCoopers, who had absorbed Coopers & Lybrand.

Addressing one of their conferences, I rather surprised the partners by saying that I had worked for them at an earlier stage of my career, before confessing the circumstances.

Our next job was to be sent to Ladbrokes as adding machine operatives. When we explained to the agency that we had never operated such machines, they were dismissive and said that it would all be explained.

That was not how it worked out. On arriving at Ladbrokes we were taken into a large room of employees working with such machines, given a bundle of betting slips showing wins and losses for the previous day and told to add them into the system. Our boss was not interested in testing our skills.

I cannot be certain but I suspect that due to our incompetence Ladbrokes records may have shown a significant loss that day which was not in accordance with the information on the betting slips.

At any event, at the end of the day we were informed that our services would not be required any further.

My third job in three days was to be sent to a warehouse to assist the manager. When I arrived I was told that he had gone off sick and to find something to do until he returned. He did not return for two days and no one was able to use my services.

It was rather boring but I recall one specific achievement. The

Chancellor of the Exchequer had just made his Budget statement to the House of Commons the previous day. In those days, *The Times* used to report parliamentary proceedings at great length.

The whole of the Chancellor's speech, covering two pages of small print, was there, and I read every word. It was the first and last time I did. Even when, as an MP, I sat in the Chamber to hear the speech, my attention often wandered during the more abstruse comments on monetary or fiscal policy.

During that week in London, we stayed in a student flat in Chalk Farm that was occupied by a friend of a friend of Peter's. It was a miserable and uncomfortable experience. The flat has been described by both of us ever since as the Black Hole of Hampstead.

The flat was dirty, as were the other occupants. Litter was all over the place and I was reliably informed by those who know these things that the smells included that of marijuana.

We decided to leave earlier than we had intended. Peter wanted to visit a girlfriend whose family lived somewhere in Oxford. To avoid another night in the Black Hole, we got public transport to the outskirts of London and then sought to hitch-hike up the A40. It was 11 p.m.

By 2 a.m. we were two thirds of the way there but had been dropped by a driver at a junction on a moonless night. After about an hour, the first car that stopped turned out to be the police.

They asked us what we were doing and we said we were visiting a friend in Oxford. They asked us the address and we confessed that we did not know but her father was a local GP. They were a little suspicious and asked us what was his name. Peter replied that it was Jones, which made them even more suspicious.

Eventually they accepted that we were harmless students and took us to their police station on the edge of Oxford. As it was about 4 a.m. they offered us two beds in an empty police cell, which they did not consider it necessary to lock. They gave us breakfast at 8 a.m., by which time we had worked out the Joneses' address. It wasn't the night we had planned, but as bed and breakfast accommodation it was the best I have experienced and came at no charge.

Hitch-hiking often produced surprises. On the A1 once with Mark Sischy we successfully hitched a lift north in a Rolls-Royce. The driver said that he normally flew up to Scotland but as it was so damn expensive he thought he would take the Rolls instead. We agreed with him, explaining that that was why we were hitch-hiking.

In 1965, Mark and I decided to hitch-hike down to London for the state funeral of Sir Winston Churchill. We arrived at about 5 a.m. on the day before and went to Westminster Hall in the Houses of Parliament to pay our respects at the lying-in-state.

Because of the huge number of people keen to do the same, they had decided to keep Westminster Hall open all that night. When we arrived around 6 a.m., the queue already stretched onto Westminster Bridge. Men in bowler hats, women in head scarves, young people like ourselves all wishing to bid farewell to the greatest Briton of all time.

We spent the day in London and then travelled to St Paul's around 11 p.m. There were already people there but we were able to find an empty space on the pavement with an uninterrupted view of the front steps of the cathedral. There we spent the night.

The following day, we watched the spectacle as the long procession, with the gun carriage bearing Churchill's coffin, arrived for the state funeral. We had a grandstand view as the royal family and the Cabinet arrived as well as dignitaries including General de Gaulle.

I must be one of the few people who can claim to have attended both Churchill's state funeral and the similar service for Margaret Thatcher forty-eight years later in 2013. The only difference was that on the second occasion I was sitting inside St Paul's as one of her former Cabinet colleagues while on the first I was behind a barrier on the pavement.

It was during these visits to London, as a student, that I first sat in the Strangers' Gallery of the House of Commons. It was not a memorable occasion, being in the evening with few MPs in the Chamber.

What I most remember was how little security was thought to be necessary in those halcyon days. No search was required as one entered the building and no bulletproof glass screen separated the public from the politicians in the Chamber.

I do recollect one unfortunate experience during a visit to London at that time. We had been having a rather bibulous evening and, with some student friends, we were making our way down Whitehall rather late at night.

I was feeling the call of nature as we passed an imposing door in Whitehall with a brass plate that informed us it was the Office of the Privy Council. I declared that I had found a privy and had to be restrained from acting accordingly. As we passed Downing Street (which, in those days, was open to the public), I had a similar urge but, once again, was directed elsewhere. It was to be about eighteen years before I next entered Downing Street, this time with a more legitimate purpose.

My interests during my student days were not limited to academic and social pursuits. Peter Farago persuaded me to join the cast of the play he was directing for the university dramatic society. It was Pirandello's *Picnic on the Battlefield* and I had the grand part of being the second stretcher bearer. It did not turn out, however, to be my last thespian activity.

It is not widely known, nor will it be found in my curriculum vitae, that I have performed in professional opera. This would be of most surprise to my immediate family, who have heard me sing and usually beg me to stop.

It is, however, true. I was, for several weeks, a member of the Prague Opera Company and performed in *Dalibor* by Smetana during the Edinburgh Festival. This is the truth and nothing but the truth, but it is not the whole truth.

The Prague Opera Company had come to the Edinburgh Festival to perform *Dalibor* at the King's Theatre. *Dalibor* was a Bohemian monarch of the Middle Ages who came to a grisly end. The company had brought their singing cast. To save money, they had not brought the non-singing spear carriers.

For that purpose, they asked the musical director of the festival, Richard Telfer, if he could find them some extras. Mr Telfer's main occupation was as a music master at George Watson's, which we had just left. He asked Peter Farago and me whether we were interested and we jumped at the opportunity.

We became temporary members of the company, with membership cards of the Festival Club stamped 'Artiste'. We were required neither to sing nor to speak but were, quite literally, spear carriers needed for Act I and Act III.

There was a long gap between these two acts, including the interval. We were permitted to take off our costumes and leave the theatre but were not permitted to remove the substantial makeup needed for the performance.

We wandered down Lothian Road towards Princes Street and went into a pub for a drink. It was not a wise decision. This was Presbyterian Edinburgh in the early 1960s. The sight of two young men, obviously plastered with makeup, entering a men-only pub, froze the other customers. Within minutes we decided to leave and go for a coffee instead.

Years later, when I was a junior minister in the Foreign Office, there was a sequel to this event. I had to visit Czechoslovakia in the early 1980s when it was still a hardline Communist state that had never recovered from the suppression of the Prague Spring in 1968.

I disliked having to be polite to these unpleasant Stalinists. On the last day of my visit, a lunch was given in my honour by the Czech Deputy Foreign Minister. The Czech ambassador to London was also present. I was obliged to reply to the minister's toast.

I was feeling mischievous. I said I was always happy to be in Prague ever since I had been a member of the Prague Opera Company in the 1960s. My hosts froze. Their ambassador went white. Their not unreasonable assumption must have been that they were hosting a

Czechoslovak who had defected and, somehow, had ended up as a British minister. I left it a while before I shared with them my more limited association with the Prague Opera Company.

I had a further, unplanned, opportunity to reveal my operatic experience early in 2016. I was in Oslo with Madeleine Albright for a meeting of the Aspen Ministerial Forum, a group of former Foreign Ministers who meet twice a year.

After dinner one evening, our group was entertained by a Norwegian soprano with several splendid arias. In thanking her, Madeleine revealed that she had had, since her childhood in Czechoslovakia, an unachieved ambition to sing in opera.

I could not resist telling her, on the bus going back to our hotel, that she might not have succeeded in performing in Czech opera but I had. When I confessed the circumstances we both had fits of laughter for the rest of the journey.

Not surprisingly, my main non-academic activity while I was at the university was debating at the Union. Debating at Edinburgh was different to Oxford and Cambridge. While there was a debating chamber in the Union, debating was an incidental activity. The president and officers of the Union were elected by the students as a whole, few of whom had any interest in debating. The President of Debates, however, was elected only by those who turned up to a special meeting called for that purpose. There were rarely more than a hundred or so present, although many hundreds more might attend debates with great topical interest or well-known guest speakers.

I was active in debates from my first term at the university in autumn 1963. Some had a parliamentary format, such as a mock election or a Queen's Speech. Others were either humorous or concerned with whatever was newsworthy at that time.

At the beginning of my second year, in 1964, debating brought me into contact with James Douglas-Hamilton. He and his wife Susie, a granddaughter of the *Thirty-Nine Steps* novelist John Buchan, have remained amongst our closest friends ever since. He was already a rather grand figure, having just completed PPE at Balliol College in Oxford. More importantly, he had been president of the Oxford Union, Britain's foremost debating establishment. To add to his lustre, he was a boxing blue and the second son of the Duke of Hamilton, which made him Lord James.

James and I met and quickly became good friends. Some time later I was invited to his family home, Lennoxlove, to stay overnight with his parents, the Duke and Duchess of Hamilton. Amongst the guests was his uncle the Earl of Selkirk, who had been a Cabinet minister in Harold Macmillan's government.

James's parents and his uncle could not have been more friendly, but it was all rather heady stuff for an eighteen-year-old from Marchmont.

There was a general desire to capitalise on James's Oxford Union experience and within months he had become President of Debates. It was a wise decision.

In the months before the Rhodesian declaration of illegal independence, he decided to organise a teach-in on Rhodesia. Teach-ins were an American innovation that involved a series of public figures invited to speak throughout the day to the student body on a subject of great topicality. James was successful in persuading Garfield Todd, the former Prime Minister of Rhodesia and an opponent of Ian Smith, to come to Edinburgh for the event.

At the last moment the Rhodesian government, foolishly, banned him from coming, which was a great blow. James, however, invited Todd's young daughter, Judith, to speak in her father's place and deliver his message.

The media loved the idea of the young, attractive Judith Todd flying to Edinburgh in place of her banned father. The result was live TV coverage of the teach-in and wall-to-wall reporting in the press.

James has a rather shy, reserved manner. It was not, however, the first or the last occasion that he demonstrated steely determination, as I would discover when we served together both in Parliament and in government.

I spoke in many debates. In December 1965, I opposed a motion that called for trade unions not to come under new statutory controls. Sir Keith Joseph was meant to be the guest speaker on our side but had to call off because of illness and was replaced by a Conservative backbencher, Sir Edward Brown.

My speech was several pages long but my notes, which I still have, show that, on a separate page, I had condensed the remarks to ten points, which enabled me, as I had done at the school Lit Club, to dispense with a text.

In May 1966, I became President of Debates. Those who turned up to vote were not very many. I see I won by twenty-four votes to twenty-three, defeating Tom Hutton, the editor of the student newspaper.

Robin Cook became Secretary of Debates at the same time. It was the beginning of an extraordinary double act that continued for the next thirty-one years, until 1997, when he succeeded me as Foreign Secretary.

While we were students, I was president of the university Tory Club and he was president of the Labour Club. At my 21st birthday party, Robin showed considerable foresight in his choice of present. He gave me, a future Defence Secretary, a book on defence policy, entitled *Britain's Role Tomorrow*, by a Labour MP, Christopher Mayhew.

However, after Mayhew defected from the Labour Party to the Liberals I teased Robin with his choice of author. He asked, anxiously, whether he had written in the book and I enjoyed telling him that he had inscribed it, in his own handwriting, 'To Malcolm from Robin'.

Robin and I were both unsuccessful parliamentary candidates for Edinburgh seats in the 1970 general election. We both became members of the Edinburgh Town Council and were elected to the House of Commons for Edinburgh seats on the same day in 1974.

Thereafter he shadowed me in various ministerial posts and was my parliamentary pair until 1997. It was not quite Kane and Abel as in the Jeffrey Archer novel but it always reminds me of the unpredictability of a political career.

Robin was of exceptional political ability but political circumstances denied him even the most junior government office until he was fifty-one. I, on the other hand, had uninterrupted ministerial office for eighteen years until I handed over to Robin in 1997.

Whenever I am asked by young political aspirants whether they should consider a lifetime in politics, I do not discourage them but I gently point out that their success will not, as in most careers, be determined by their ability but will also depend on the complete uncertainty of the political world. Not only must their party win elections; they must find favour with the Prime Minister of the day if their talents are to be used.

During my term as president we had a freshers' debate on the theme 'that the world owes less to Marx and Lenin than to Marks and Spencer'. I began my own speech by remarking that Communists were once described as persons who, having nothing of their own, were very eager to share it with everyone else.

On Armistice Day, we debated 'that the best way to preserve peace is to prepare for war'. Julian Amery, a right-wing Tory MP and Konni Zilliacus, an MP from the Labour left, were the guest speakers. A photograph I possess shows the two future Foreign Secretaries, Robin and me, with our guests that evening.

On 25 November of that year, we had a mock election. I am pleased to see that in my speech I called for council tenants in Scotland to be given the right to buy their homes. Fourteen years later, as a Scottish Office minister, I had the privilege of taking the Tenants' Rights (Scotland) Act through Parliament, giving tenants just such a right.

Years later there was a profile on me on 5 Live in which Stewart Hamilton, who had been an SNP fellow debater at Edinburgh, compared me with Robin Cook.

He remarked:

> Malcolm was actually always a very well-prepared and incisive
> debater. He relied on intellectual persuasion rather than emo-
> tion. And in fact very much in stark contrast of his now adversary
> Robin Cook. If there was an intellectual argument to be won,
> Malcolm would always get there hands down. If it was appeal-
> ing to people's emotions, then I think he was a bit less successful.

In early 1967, I attempted to repeat the success of the Rhodesia
teach-in with one on whether we should be part of the European
Community; then as now a hot issue.

We had excellent speakers, including Jo Grimond, Lord Gladwyn,
George Ball, a former US Under-Secretary of State, and George
Thomson, a Foreign Office minister.

BBC radio covered the day's proceedings but the attendance was
much less than for Rhodesia. Sadly, on this occasion none of our
high-level speakers had been banned from attending.

Nor did we have any excuse to invite their attractive daughters to
represent them.

The main publicity was a complaint by the SNP Club that no
Nationalist had been invited to take part. That was true, as the issue
was whether the UK should join the EU, not whether Scotland should
join, and it hadn't been thought necessary to have a Nationalist. We
were entirely logical in making this argument, but I should have
remembered that logic is the art of going wrong with confidence. The
Nationalists proposed a censure motion on the Debates Committee,
saying we had been prejudiced. I am glad to report that the motion
was defeated.

Part of the fun of debating were the invitations received to visit
other universities. I went to Dublin to speak at Trinity College and
proposed that the Republic of Ireland should re-join the Commonwealth. We lost.

I also spoke in Newcastle on whether a regional accent was a social handicap. I do not recollect whether I was for or against but I remember borrowing James Douglas-Hamilton's kilt for the occasion, the only time I have worn one in Britain. I have worn the kilt in Vienna, Hungary and India but the reader must wait for the next chapter to find out why.

CHAPTER 4

PASSAGE TO INDIA

W E ALL HAVE events in our youth which, in retrospect years later, can be seen as defining moments in our life story. For me, one of those was my 'passage to India' in 1965. Until then I had had occasional visits to mainland Europe, including Florence, Paris and the French Alps, but I had journeyed no further.

In July 1965, I set out on an overland expedition, across Europe, beyond the Iron Curtain, south to Istanbul, Damascus and East Jerusalem. Then, we journeyed across the desert to Baghdad, on to Tehran, through Pakistan and, finally, to Delhi, capital of India.

It was no ordinary journey. I was one of 200 British students. We drove our own five single-decker buses. I sat at the front of our bus, helping with navigation and in charge of the radio that enabled each of the buses to remain in contact with each other.

Each bus had around forty male and female students from different parts of the United Kingdom. Mine consisted of Scottish students. The other four were from Oxford, Cambridge, London and Wales.

The expedition, known as Comex (Commonwealth Expedition), was the brainchild of a retired Gurkha officer, Lt Col. Lionel Gregory, known to us all as Greg. He had known Jawaharlal Nehru, India's first Prime Minister, as well as other Congress leaders.

He had a passion for the Commonwealth and wanted to bring young British students into contact with their Indian counterparts. He had persuaded Prince Philip, the Duke of Edinburgh, to be our patron, and various British companies with interests in India were covering the costs of our buses and other essential expenditure.

The rest we were expected to fund ourselves. I spent several weeks of my summer recess peeling potatoes and carrying out other catering chores in the kitchens of the Astley Ainslie Hospital in Edinburgh to fund my share. The Army helped us to learn to drive the buses and operate the radio equipment at their garrison at Catterick in Yorkshire.

The journey to India took us thirty-three days. The expedition was one of the few occasions that I have kept a daily diary. I have no intention of boring the reader with thumbnail sketches of each of the countries we passed through. What I will share are the more entertaining or unforgettable events of our journey and the impact of the expedition on my future life.

The Scottish bus set out from the City Chambers in Edinburgh on the evening of 29 July. We were not to return to Britain until 5 October and we did so by plane via Moscow.

That was not the original plan. We had intended to return the way we came, but some days after we had arrived in Delhi, India and Pakistan went to war with each other over Kashmir and the border was closed to normal traffic throughout our visit.

Having driven south from Edinburgh, we met the other four buses in London and crossed the Channel on 31 July. Arriving at Ostend, we travelled through Belgium and West Germany, reaching the American air base in Frankfurt, where we were staying the night.

We slept in the gym with male and female students segregated.

Officially, this was to keep the Americans happy. The real reason was to deny the *Daily Express* reporter travelling with us a titillating story. He had already described us, inaccurately, as on the road to Kathmandu, on the grounds that it sounded 'more romantic'.

Having travelled, the following day, through Germany into Austria, we spent the evening exploring Vienna.

Each of the buses had been asked by Greg to choose a cultural theme that we could offer as we travelled. The Scots had decided on Highland dancing and bagpipes, so we all had to provide ourselves with kilts. I had bought a second-hand kilt in Edinburgh but, not being familiar with this garment, I did not realise that I should have avoided the heavy woollen winter kilt. It turned out to be distinctly uncomfortable during the heat of an Indian summer.

The kilt's first outing was that evening in Vienna. Having had a convivial dinner, we ended up entertaining the Viennese to a Highland Fling and the Duke of Perth on the Karlsplatz.

The following day, we crossed the Iron Curtain into Hungary. The Communist border guards, instead of taking our passports collectively, insisted on checking each person. We got our revenge during the two hours that this took by the 200 of us singing, dancing and playing our bagpipes.

It was because we were travelling through Hungary that Peter Farago had decided he could not be with us, as his parents had defected from that country only eight years earlier. One of my friends, Eddie Torgbor, from Ghana, was with me and he contributed an African song, 'Baba Noma', which became the theme song of the expedition, sung, lustily, on many occasions.

After Hungary we continued south through Yugoslavia and into Greece, stopping overnight at Kavalla on the coast, which enabled us to swim in the sea.

Our time in Istanbul was disappointingly short but did include a visit to Hagia Sophia and the Blue Mosque before we crossed the Bosphorus into Asia. We travelled through Anatolia to Ankara and, after visiting Atatürk's mausoleum, travelled south towards Syria, seeing our first camel on the way.

Visiting the Middle East overland from Britain hardly happens today. It should be done more often. It reminds us of how much we miss when travel is merely flying from one airport to another. During our journey, each few days brought a new language, a new style of clothing and new cultures. We may be living in a global age, but what differentiates nation from nation and community from community is still profound.

We travelled to Damascus through Homs and Hama, cities that have become familiar to us in recent years because of the terrible Syrian civil war. We entered Damascus on the fourteenth day of our odyssey.

Thereafter, there was a planned detour to Jordan and East Jerusalem. We stopped at Jerash to see the famous ruins. I am impressed that in my diary of that day I show off my knowledge of the difference between Ionic and Corinthian columns.

Our visit to Jerusalem was one of the highlights of our journey. This was before the Six Day War, and the Old City was still administered as part of Jordan. Israeli Jerusalem was yards away but could have been on the moon, so little was the contact that was possible.

While I was walking around the town with a friend, an Arab boy asked us, in good English, whether there was anywhere we would like him to take us. I asked if he knew where the Western Wall was and he offered to show us.

The Western Wall is the one remaining part of the ancient Jewish Temple and is to Jews what the Church of the Holy Sepulchre in Jerusalem is to Christians or the Dome of the Rock to Muslims.

Today, one can view the whole of the remaining wall in a very large square which can accommodate thousands of people, but in 1964 most of it was hidden away by other buildings and only an area about the size of a large courtyard could be visited. When we got there it was completely empty.

There is a tradition that because of its past as part of the temple, visiting Jews sometimes pray at the wall with their forehead touching it. My friend, knowing I was Jewish, suggested that I do that and that he would film me.

Before I could respond, the Arab boy, who could not have been more than thirteen or fourteen and who did not know I was Jewish, intervened to say that this would be unwise. He explained that only Jews were supposed to do this and if my friend filmed me and showed the film to any Jewish friends we might have in Britain, they might be upset.

To this day I often quote that incident. If an Arab boy in Jerusalem could have been so sensitive to the feelings of Jews in Britain, there must be some hope that Palestinians and Israelis will be able, one day, to show full respect for each other and for their respective national aspirations.

We crossed the desert from Amman to Baghdad, and a more boring journey it would be difficult to conceive. The road, which ran alongside the oil pipelines, was featureless. At night, we put our buses into a Western-style wagon circle. Once again we were virtuous, with the girls sleeping in the buses and the boys in sleeping bags outside.

Eventually, within Iraq, we crossed the Euphrates and ended up in Baghdad, on the banks of the Tigris. This now felt like Mesopotamia of old.

On we drove, now in the twentieth day of our journey, well over halfway to India. Our convoy had been received politely, but only with modest hospitality and some curiosity as we worked our way across the Middle East. That all changed when we reached the Iranian border.

There we were addressed by the provincial governor, welcomed by the military commandant and given cold drinks and sweetmeats. An escort was provided to take us to Hamadan and, as I say in my diary, 'What a journey that was!'

I wrote: 'Villagers had been lined up on the road to clap us on, a bus was emptied of its passengers to cheer us through, there were even, at various stages, guards of honour who saluted and stood to attention as we passed.'

One possible explanation was that they had heard that Prince Philip was our patron and had assumed that he was travelling with us. Iran in the days of the Shah was well disposed to other monarchies and that, I suspect, is why we were the beneficiaries.

Having arrived in Tehran, we were lodged in a university hostel near the centre of town, in Roosevelt Avenue. Over the next day I spotted Queen Elizabeth II, John F. Kennedy and Winston Churchill, all with avenues of their own. I presume that none of them survived the arrival of the Ayatollahs after the 1979 Revolution.

The following morning I visited the British Embassy to see Air Vice-Marshal Moore, the Defence Attaché, to whom I had been given an introduction in London. Being rather scruffy, I had to wash a shirt, borrow a pair of presentable trousers from Eddie Torgbor and don a pair of socks.

Entering the British Embassy after three weeks wandering on various highways was a relaxation in itself, not least because of the quality and cleanliness of their lavatory compared to some we had been required to use.

We left Tehran, drove south through Isfahan and then east towards Pakistan. The road turned to a gravel track and the toughest part of the expedition so far began. The countryside was flat and desolate apart from a few shrubs. My diary says: 'Stopping in the dark to prepare an evening meal, we heard the tinkling of bells and soon a caravan of four camels and two Persians passed by. Coming out of the dark ... their entrance helped to convince the doubting that we really were east of Suez.'

On the twenty-fifth day of our journey we crossed into Pakistan, which of course had been part of British India and the Raj until only eighteen years before. The main evidence of this was that we suddenly found we had to return to driving on the left for the first time since leaving England.

Travelling north to Quetta and Lahore, we suffered our first serious accident when a lorry going at breakneck speed hit an open emergency door at the back of the Cambridge bus. Two of our colleagues were injured, one having to have a stay in hospital and then be flown back to Britain. Needless to say, the lorry did not even stop.

Beyond Lahore was Peshawar, and an opportunity to visit the Khyber Pass. Given how much Afghanistan and the Khyber has been part of British history both in the nineteenth century and in recent years, one could be forgiven for thinking that not much has changed.

Our Pathan guide the night before in Peshawar had to be persuaded before he would concede that his native South Waziristan was part of Pakistan and not an independent state.

We could not travel right through the pass into Afghanistan, but my diary makes clear the magnificence of the part we saw:

> The pass itself is a natural barrier, a defence par excellence. Twisting and turning through the lofty mountains and sheer hillsides, it makes it clear why Muslim invaders were defeated seventeen times before they finally broke through. The scenery is superb and on each hillside one can see a small fortress guarding the entrance. Plaques are found all through the pass commemorating the actions fought by British and Indian troops in the area, and one very large post, Shagai Fort, still controls the travel of the area.

On Day 33, 30 August, we crossed the border into India and were greeted by a 'Welcome Comex' banner, with Greg being garlanded with flowers.

That night, we arrived at Delhi at 12.30 a.m., only six hours behind our original target, agreed before we left the UK. That was not bad for a month-long journey across two continents and through fourteen countries. Indeed, Greg argued, unconvincingly, that we were actually punctual, as the target time had been based on Greenwich Mean Time not local Indian time.

The following day we went sightseeing in Delhi and had a reception at the British High Commission, where we met the High Commissioner, John Freeman, a former Labour MP and editor of the *New Statesman*.

He was well known for his pioneering TV interviews of prominent politicians on his programme *Face to Face*. Throughout the interviews, Freeman's face was never shown; only the back of his head as he faced his victim. It was a remarkable technique but has not been followed by other interviewers. I doubt whether Jeremy Paxman or Robin Day, enthusiastic for public acclaim, would have been attracted by an interviewing style that required their own anonymity.

The final event that evening was a forum with five Indian and five Comex students giving their views on 'University Students and Politics'. I was one of those taking part and because I did not have much to say I chose to use a rather declamatory style to entertain the audience. I was amused to hear later that a professor in the audience had likened me in my delivery, though not in substance, to a Communist agitator.

The following day, the President of India, Sarvepalli Radhakrishnan, gave a reception in our honour at Rashtrapati Bhavan, the Lutyens-built former residence of the Viceroy.

As we mounted the staircase, we were slightly surprised to see the walls still adorned with large portraits of British Kings and Queens as well as former viceroys. I had been amused to see that while the old Kingsway avenue had been renamed since the British had left, its new name, Rajpath, was, in fact, Hindi for Kingsway.

The Indians had an ambivalent attitude to the Raj. While they had fought for their independence, they took the view that the history of their country over the centuries had involved many invasions and occupations by foreign powers. The Mughal Empire was one such experience which they had never tried to erase from their history. The British Raj was another.

They recognised that British rule had brought major benefits to

India. Since independence they have enjoyed both a civil service that is politically neutral and armed forces that have never threatened India's democracy, unlike Pakistan, where the opposite has frequently occurred. The rule of law and the independence of the judiciary are genuine, unlike China and Russia, where there is little attempt to conceal that the judges and the courts are controlled by the politicians and their judgments have to be acceptable to their political masters.

This is not to say that the Indians are starry eyed or uncritical about Western political and cultural values. Gandhi, once asked what he thought about Western civilisation, famously replied that he thought it would be a good idea.

The following day took us to Agra to see the Taj Mahal. Before we arrived I was rather blasé, as we had seen so many fine buildings since our arrival in Istanbul and especially during our visits to Jerusalem, Damascus and Isfahan. I freely admit, however, to being bowled over by the Taj. Its white marble, the perfect symmetry of its twin minarets rising on either side, and the backdrop of clear blue sky are, quite simply, stunning.

The following day, our expedition split into five separate groups, with the other four visiting Calcutta, Madras, Lucknow and Bombay. We were the most fortunate, with Rajasthan our province to visit. That meant the pink city of Jaipur, Jodhpur, and the lake palace of Udaipur were our destinations.

But we were not just tourists. Our programme included a visit to Mayo College, the 'Eton of India' in Ajmer. Originally the school was exclusively for the children of maharajahs, but it now catered for all who could afford it.

The background of the pupils was evidenced by one I spoke to. He said that he spoke only English at home except when he was addressing the servants, when he used Hindi.

In Udaipur we had to sit on a platform of a vast open-air auditorium packed with students. When it came to questions, I was asked to answer why India's policy on Kashmir, which was 'legally and

constitutionally right', was so misunderstood in the United Kingdom. I gave a diplomatic answer the Foreign Office would have been
proud of.

I was influenced by the fact that we had just heard that Indian
troops had crossed the border into Pakistan that day and were apparently marching on Lahore. They had crossed at exactly the same
point on the border that we had used, in the opposite direction, the
previous week.

That night, in Jodhpur, a blackout was imposed because a
Pakistani raid was expected on the air training base nearby. We spent
the evening by candlelight listening to a radio broadcast of air raid
precautions.

My diary records that that evening: 'As soon as I got to bed I slept
all night and in doing so repeated an established Rifkind tradition of
sleeping right through an air raid,' just as my father had done during
the Second World War.

The following night we were woken by the air raid sirens at 2 a.m.
Our Indian student colleagues, rather sensibly, made straight for
the safety of the trenches while we, I reported my diary, 'made our
way leisurely outside and, with a mixed feeling of amusement and
curiosity, we made ourselves comfortable on the ground'. Four or
five Pakistani planes flew overhead and at least one large bomb was
dropped on the airport a mile away.

The final part of our official programme was a visit by the whole
expedition to Simla, in the foothills of the Himalayas, where the
Viceroy and his entourage had always moved during the heat of
the Indian summer. For part of the journey, from Kalka to Simla,
we transferred to a chartered train 'which chugged its way up the
narrow twisting line, ever higher'.

On arrival at the railway station, we had to trudge in darkness,
because of the blackout, one and a half miles to the old Viceregal
Palace, where we were staying. It was a strange way for guests to arrive
at a palace.

Our visit to Simla was a relaxing interlude, but I remember it most of all for one memorable evening. I quote from my diary:

> In the evening the Oxford Group put on a production of The Importance of Being Earnest at the local Gaiety Theatre. This was furnished in Edwardian style and perfect for putting on Oscar Wilde.
>
> The production was quite good and well acted but, unfortunately, was interrupted by a blackout due to the alert. The cast and audience broke into a repetition of the London Blitz with spontaneous singing.
>
> Then the farcical occurred. Having turned off all the lights, the local vigilantes decided that the clapping and singing might be heard by a potential pilot overhead and so they demanded virtual silence. Although the likelihood of a pilot roaring through the night hearing our puny voices was pointed out to them, they remained adamant and it was only after the all clear that the show resumed to a successful conclusion.

The following day should have seen our re-crossing the Pakistani border on our way home. This was impossible due to the continuing war, so we returned to Delhi, where we were all farmed out to Indian families for a fortnight before we were able to fly back to the United Kingdom.

I found myself billeted with a delightful family. The husband, Dr Verma, was a senior Indian civil servant. His wife was Scottish from Edinburgh. We had the opportunity of porridge for breakfast and curry for lunch. Dr Verma's brother-in-law was a Congress MP and he got me into the public gallery of the Lok Sabha to hear parliamentary exchanges. The subsequent afternoon debate was on a report by the Indian Coconut Committee, which I decided I could miss.

Our final night in India was a farewell reception where the guest of honour was Indira Gandhi. She used the occasion to lecture us on Kashmir. In my diary I, wrongly, predicted that she would not rise to the top of Indian politics. But I did write that 'the fire of her personality as well as the sentiment of her parentage will combine to make her a potent influence for years to come'.

My overland expedition to India was, of course, a fascinating and formative experience for a nineteen-year-old. It was, incidentally, the one occasion that I grew a beard. It did me no favours and came off a week after I returned to Edinburgh. It has never reappeared.

Travelling to India did not, by itself, create my lifelong interest in the wider world. That had already begun in my final year at school and had grown substantially during my first two years at university.

My first memory of international events was during the Suez Crisis in 1956, when I was ten years old. A map was put up in the school classroom showing the disposition of British forces in the region.

I also recall hearing on the radio in my bedroom both the advent to power of Fidel Castro in Cuba in 1959 and the culmination of the Cuban Missile Crisis in 1962 when Khrushchev climbed down and the risk of a US–Soviet nuclear clash was averted.

My diary covering the Indian visit has several entries of my views on the politics of the countries that we passed through, including the Kashmir issue, as well as my comments on the strengths and weaknesses of various Indian politicians.

So politics and international affairs were already entering my bloodstream. But because of that visit, together with the year and a half I spent living and working in Africa during 1967 and 1968, it became clear to me that my primary enthusiasm was for foreign policy and international affairs rather than for Westminster as such.

I was deeply interested in British politics and was beginning to consider whether I might one day try to be a Member of Parliament. But if at that time I had been asked what might, one day, be my dream ambition, I suspect I would have said Foreign Secretary, not Prime Minister, and certainly not Chancellor of the Exchequer.

The two months I spent travelling through Europe and the Middle East and around India helped convince me, as it has persuaded many British youngsters over the past 250 years, that Britain's vocation is international and that we have much both to give and to learn from the wider world. I was beginning to realise that I very much wanted to be part of that process.

My first formal step into the political world had been two years earlier, on my first day as a student, when, for rather different reasons, I joined the university Liberal Club. I had not been a Liberal for very long nor, as it turned out, did I remain one for very long.

My family background was not political. My father, I am reasonably certain, always voted Conservative. My mother usually did but indicated to me on one occasion that she did not rule out the Liberals getting her support.

Being middle class, my father being self-employed, owning our own home and attending a fee-paying school, I had never identified with the Labour Party, though my father's brother, my uncle David, made no secret of his Labour sympathies.

But if I had no instinctive reason to support Labour nor did I, as a teenager, have unqualified enthusiasm for the Tories either.

They seemed rather grand. While they received much of their support from ordinary people, that seemed to be partly from old-fashioned deference and partly from fear of the socialists.

They had also been in power for a very long time, since 1951, when I was only five years old. By 1963, Harold Macmillan had stepped down and been replaced by the Earl of Home, who had become Sir Alec Douglas-Home. They all looked rather out of date to this particular teenager.

Harold Wilson lampooned Sir Alec for his 'grouse moor image', which did Douglas-Home some harm. I do remember, however, the Tories getting their revenge. After Wilson became Prime Minister, a speaker at the Tory annual conference said he wanted to speak about Harold Wilson's grouse moor image. The audience were somewhat mystified until he added, 'Since Wilson became Prime Minister, people grouse more.'

The Liberals under Jo Grimond seemed to me more attractive and much more interesting. Their revival had begun after years in the doldrums and they were increasing their support especially in Scotland.

So I joined the Liberal Club and, eventually, was elected to the committee. But I must report that I found them seriously dull, though lovely people. Their parties were not nearly as good as those of the Tories and their speeches in the Union were earnest rather than inspiring.

At the beginning of my second year, I defected to the Conservative Club. There was no ideological conversion. I have always been on the liberal wing of the Conservative Party, which made me, if anything, more comfortable with the Tories than I had been as a right-wing Liberal.

Over the next two years I became secretary and then president of the Conservative Club. My predecessor as president was Donald Brydon, who has had a highly successful business career, including being chairman of Royal Mail and of the London Stock Exchange.

The Conservative Club was, at that time, the largest in the university, with 160 members. I wrote to Quintin Hogg inviting him to become our honorary president. When, but only when, he had accepted, I wrote again, inviting him to give what I called the annual presidential address, without feeling it necessary to add that this annual address would be the first we had ever had.

He obviously felt he had no choice but to accept. Knowing that he would be a great draw, we opened the meeting to all students and held it in the debating chamber, which could accommodate hundreds of people.

On the day, in October 1966, the chamber was packed with more than 700 students, including those in the upstairs balconies. Most there were not Tories; some were very left-wing.

As I led Quintin Hogg to the platform, I asked him what he would speak on. 'Oh, something will come. Something will come,' he assured me.

He then launched into a splendid, powerful speech. A bearded individual in the balcony started shouting, 'Hogg, you're a fascist!' but was ignored. He repeated his insult and on the third occasion Hogg stopped his speech, the audience fell silent and Hogg pointed to his accuser. 'Young man,' he said, 'I have the wounds of fascism on my body, which is more than can be said for you.' The audience roared their approval and the wretch in the balcony fell silent.

Later, during my presidency, Sir Alec Douglas-Home addressed a similarly packed, but more polite, meeting. I got to know Sir Alec well over the years. He sent me a complimentary, handwritten note after hearing my maiden speech in the House of Commons.

In his last years, I and Edith visited him occasionally at his home, the Hirsel, in the Borders. On his 90th birthday I drove to the Hirsel and presented him, on behalf of the Cabinet, with a fine book on British birds which, at my suggestion, the Prime Minister and every member of the Cabinet had signed.

The year 1965 saw my first letter to a newspaper, addressed to *The Scotsman*. In April, they published a letter from me calling for a conference between the South Vietnamese government and the Viet Cong to form a broadly based government.

On reading my letter, I see that my purpose in writing was to disagree with a Mr James S. Gordon, whose views had been published in an earlier issue. The James S. Gordon was almost certainly my close friend Jimmy Gordon, which suggests that my purpose in writing was mischief rather than to add to the sum of human wisdom.

Jimmy and I had become close friends. It was his idea that in 1965 we should become members of Pentlands Young Conservatives. A year later, I became chairman of the branch and got to know the local MP, Norman Wylie QC. I (and he) would have been astonished to know that, eight years later, in 1974, I would succeed him as Member of Parliament for Pentlands when he became a judge of the Court of Session.

My letter writing to *The Scotsman* was in danger of becoming a habit. I was published again on 3 June, disagreeing with Michael Clark Hutchison, the MP for South Edinburgh, as to the desirability of a Commonwealth Court. I argued that such a court would only be of value in determining disagreements between Commonwealth countries, not as some Supreme Court for all legal disputes concerning citizens of Commonwealth countries.

Whatever the merits of my letter writing, it demonstrates my increasing politicisation at the age of eighteen but it was also, perhaps, significant that both letters were on international not domestic issues.

My television debut came in 1967, when I was a member of the Edinburgh University team for *University Challenge* with Bamber Gascoigne. My colleagues were Tom Hutton, Bruce Tattersall and Ian Chisholm.

We beat St Hugh's, an Oxford ladies' college, in the first round, though we didn't expect to. In the dress rehearsal they had thrashed us. There was then a break of an hour and a half before the actual contest. We were encouraged to leave the studio and get some fresh air. We went into a pub feeling rather dejected and had more liquid refreshment than we should have. The effect, however, was to remove all our inhibitions when combat with the ladies of St Hugh's began. No longer did our fingers hesitate above the buzzer, and we ended victorious.

We then went on to trounce Essex 280–50 in the second round but were beaten in the quarter-finals by University College London.

I can say without undue modesty that I was the least impressive member of the team, but I did have one moment of glory.

The question was to name which other states shared a border with Senegal in West Africa. To the amazement of my colleagues, my finger was on the buzzer and I responded with Mauritania, Mali, Guinea and Guinea-Bissau. I then showed off by asking whether the question covered internal borders as well as external, as that would include Gambia, which is a virtual enclave of Senegal.

The reader may think I was trying to establish my credentials as a future Foreign Secretary. I had, it is true, become fascinated in my teens with the political map of the world. At that time I could name the capital city of every country and the President or Prime Minister of most of them. I am still pretty good on capitals; not so good on Prime Ministers.

I think this interest in my teens, when others were collecting postage stamps or kicking a football, was influenced by the disappearance of the British Empire, which was accelerating through the 1960s. Almost every month, it seemed, a new country left the Empire and joined the Commonwealth in Africa, the West Indies and the Pacific. I was fascinated at the time and thereafter. It was one of the reasons why I joined the Comex expedition to India in 1965. I have remained a strong supporter of the Commonwealth. I was appointed, a few years ago, as a member of the Commonwealth Eminent Persons Group, which made recommendations to the heads of government on the future of the Commonwealth.

In 1967, Bruce Tattersall and I were also part of the Edinburgh team for Radio 4's inter-university quiz *Third Degree*. On this occasion we won, defeating Birmingham University in the final.

But these events, exciting though they were, soon were of the past. Several weeks later, I was embarking in Southampton on the Union Castle liner *SA Vaal* to sail to Cape Town on my way to Rhodesia.

Africa was to be my home for the next one and a half years. The next stage of my odyssey had begun.

CHAPTER 5

OUT OF AFRICA

M
Y VOYAGE TO southern Africa in July 1967 was not part of some long-planned strategy but had its roots in choices I had had to consider two years earlier.

I had become a student in the Law Faculty of Edinburgh University with the intention, in due course, of being called to the Scottish Bar as an Advocate.

To become an Advocate required either an Honours Law degree, which at Scottish universities took four years, or a three-year Ordinary degree combined with a degree in the Arts or Social Sciences. Thereafter, one needed to work for months in a solicitor's office followed by devilling (apprenticeship) to an experienced Advocate before one could don the coveted wig and gown.

In my case, the decision as to which route to follow was even more complicated, as it was not just one but two professions that I had in mind. I wanted to become an Advocate but I was also seriously interested in one day being a parliamentarian as well.

These considerations had persuaded me, by 1965, to go the route of the second Arts or Social Science degree. I had had enough of academic law, while the possibility of studying politics or economics at degree level had its attractions.

This preference was made even more attractive by a suggestion put to me by James Douglas-Hamilton. Having come to Edinburgh on his route to the Scottish Bar, having already read PPE at Oxford, James urged me to apply to do the same in reverse.

I must confess that the attractiveness of this option was not just that I would benefit from Oxford's academic distinction. We discussed how my enthusiasm for a political career, which James shared, would be greatly assisted by developing my debating and public speaking skills at the Oxford Union.

In retrospect, I am slightly embarrassed to record that something as relatively superficial as the Oxford Union had such a major impact on my thinking. I can only say, in my defence, that I must have been rather embarrassed at the time as well, as I did not think it wise to mention the Oxford Union as a reason for my enthusiasm for an Oxford education in any of the letters I sent to several Oxford colleges.

I wrote to Balliol (James's old college, with strong Scottish connections) and several others. I received very friendly replies but all found themselves able to resist the temptation of offering me a place.

I do not blame them. Even in the 1960s Oxford had far more applicants than places. Although I had passed, at the first attempt, all my exams at Edinburgh and could have got Honours if I had remained for a fourth year, I had decided against. Oxford, quite properly, gave priority to those whose claims were far stronger.

I was disappointed but not desolate. I had already, in February 1966, been offered by Edinburgh University's Faculty of Social Science the opportunity to be admitted as a research student to study for the postgraduate degree of Master of Science (Social Science) for two years. My subject was to be 'The Politics of Underdevelopment'.

This was part of a new venture by the university to try to build links between the Social Sciences and established disciplines like

Law. I had received a letter the previous month from Professor Harry Hanham of the Politics Department saying that he had received recommendations about me from two of my law professors which were 'strongly favourable' and that he thought the University Senate would approve my application.

Accordingly, having graduated with a Bachelor of Laws in July 1966, I became a postgraduate at the start of the following session.

The first year of my Master's included the Sociology of Politics but, as part of the Politics of Underdevelopment, I concentrated on sub-Saharan Africa, which had caught my imagination.

This was partly because of the news coverage of the increasing concern over apartheid in South Africa and the Unilateral Declaration of Independence (UDI) by Ian Smith in Southern Rhodesia. But it was also because Africa represented the last major phase of decolonisation and the end of the British Empire.

The two-year MSc required the student to spend his second year writing a Master's thesis and I had decided that my choice would be on some aspect of African politics.

Professor Hanham, not unreasonably, suggested that if I was going to write a thesis on African politics, it would help if I had actually been to Africa. I agreed with him but explained that I had no private means and would only be able to travel to Africa and live there for any period of time if I obtained some employment. He, very generously, offered to see what might be possible.

A few weeks later he informed me that he had identified two possible jobs. The first was doing field work in the Sudan, several hundred miles south of Khartoum, in the middle of a civil war, with the temperature often over 100 degrees Fahrenheit. I reminded him that he had said there were two options.

The other was as an assistant lecturer in politics at the University College of Rhodesia, with income tax two shillings and six pence in the pound and with Salisbury, the capital, having one of the best climates in the world.

I had no difficulty in expressing a preference for the latter, especially as it would be an extraordinary opportunity to be a fly on the wall, seeing at first hand white Rhodesia's rebellion from Britain and the growing struggle of the African population for political rights.

I pointed out, however, that there would be little likelihood that a job as a lecturer in politics would be offered to a twenty-year-old with no degree in political science and only an Ordinary degree in Law. I did not know whether to feel encouraged or insulted when Professor Hanham told me not to worry as they were desperate.

It transpired that there had been few applicants for this post. This was probably because many academics thought of themselves as left-wing and felt that having Rhodesia, a pariah state at that time because of the illegal declaration of independence, on their curriculum vitae would not help their future careers. In addition, the university college had had a serious crisis in 1966 when a number of expatriate lecturers had been deported by the Smith regime because of their political activism.

These considerations did not deter me. I had no desire for an academic career and only intended to live there for one to two years. In any event, the University College of Rhodesia was multiracial, with black and Asian as well as white students. It was, at that time, linked to London University, whose degrees it could award.

The upshot was that in April 1967 I was contacted by the Inter-University Council for Higher Education Overseas and, in due course, invited to an interview in London.

I have the letter that I subsequently received from the University College of Rhodesia offering me appointment, from 8 July 1967 to 31 December 1968, as an assistant lecturer in the Department of Government. My salary, the first that I ever earned, would be £1,400 per annum, rising by £75 after the first year.

Curiously, the letter is dated 12 July, almost a week after I had arrived in Rhodesia. I do not recall but can only assume that they had signalled, a month or so earlier, to their colleagues in London their intention to offer me the job as, otherwise, the costs of my travel to Rhodesia would not have been authorised and I would not have already arrived.

The original proposal was for me to fly from London to Salisbury, but I insisted on being allowed to go by sea to Cape Town and then by rail to Rhodesia instead.

My reasons were threefold. It seemed more romantic and I assumed that it would be the only chance I was likely to have to travel the world on an ocean liner. Secondly, it would give me around eleven days on board which I could use to read and acquaint myself with the subjects on which I would be lecturing my students.

The third reason was that, having travelled overland to India, I had become firmly of the view that flying was cheating and that the only true traveller was he who went by land or sea.

I embarked on the Union Castle liner the *SA Vaal* just a few days after my 21st birthday. I was excited but also astonished and just a little nervous at the unexpected turn my life had taken. This was especially so as, having lived at home with my parents until then, apart from the relatively short Indian expedition, I was now travelling to a city and a continent where I knew absolutely no one, to live for well over a year.

We all share a strange feeling if we end up somewhere where no one knows us and we can potentially reinvent ourselves with whatever personality we decide. In practice, our past and our habits of mind travel with us and our options are not as unlimited as we may have fantasised.

Nevertheless, there can be little doubt that living and working in Africa changed me more than even Oxford would have done. I was thousands of miles from home, in an African country ruled by white 'settlers', a lecturer not a student, and expected to write my Master's thesis.

It changed my life in one other respect as well. It was in Rhodesia that I met Edith, who has been my wife since 1970.

The sea journey to Cape Town was very agreeable. Although my cabin was the most basic available, the *Vaal* had only one class of restaurant for all the passengers. This had to be of a standard of cuisine acceptable to the First Class passengers and, as a consequence, the rest of us dined off excellent fare.

I recall crossing the Equator for the first time but, thankfully, was spared any of the associated bizarre rituals that are often insisted upon on such occasions.

The relaxed sea journey was also very convenient. When I arrived at the University College of Rhodesia, I was to be responsible for lecturing on British and African politics. Unfortunately, I had at that time no degree qualifications that entitled me to do either.

The nearest I had to British politics was having passed the Constitutional Law examinations at Edinburgh. Likewise, I had completed the course on Africa in my first year for my Master's. I also had a reasonable general knowledge on both subjects, accumulated over the previous few years as an interested citizen.

Being on the *SA Vaal* and knowing no one as we sailed to the South Atlantic was an excellent opportunity for copious reading of the numerous books on African and British politics that I had crammed into my trunk.

When we arrived at Cape Town I had to board a train, later that day, for the long overnight journey of over 1,350 miles to Salisbury via Bulawayo.

On the train I met a young Rhodesian student, Erica Waxman, who was returning to Rhodesia from Cape Town University. She was extrovert, amusing and good fun. We became, and have remained, good friends. It was through her that I first met Edith some months later.

I arrived at Salisbury railway station on a Saturday morning in early July and was met by Professor Peter Harris, the head of the Department of Government, who took me to his home for lunch.

I was then shown to a room in one of the halls of residence which was to be my temporary accommodation. That weekend the whole of Rhodesia had closed down for the four days of the annual Rhodes and Founders Holiday. I felt very lonely in a strange country very far from home.

I went into the university library, which was, surprisingly, open. Looking for something to read I noticed *Mein Kampf* on a shelf and borrowed it. I never got past the first twenty pages, it was so turgid.

One of my first tasks was to purchase a car. Public transport in the country was very poor and rarely used by white Rhodesians. I purchased, for the princely sum of around £100, a splendid, cream Morris Minor that had already done around 90,000 miles. Instead of flashing indicators it had little arms that popped up on the right and left of the vehicle as required.

I had never owned a car in Britain and, indeed, had never driven since passing my driving test two years before. I drove out the garage at a funereal pace and slowly made my way the several miles back to the university campus at Mount Pleasant, a northern suburb of Salisbury.

The University College of Rhodesia (UCR) had been established in 1955 and was linked with London University. UCR was multiracial, with white, black and Asian students. There were, at that time, 700 students, of whom one third were black or Asian. The rest of the educational system, apart from a small number of independent schools, was exclusively for whites or Africans. Studying there was, therefore, the first, and only, opportunity that many young Rhodesians had of mixing with their fellow citizens of other races on an equal basis.

However, there were few personal friendships that transcended the racial barrier. The white students, with rare exceptions, either supported the Rhodesian Front or were indifferent to politics. The black students and Asians overwhelmingly opposed the regime and what it stood for.

Because it was a multiracial university and because most of the academic staff were presumed to be liberal in their views, UCR was distrusted by the Smith regime and dubbed 'the Kremlin on the

Hill'. This might have been true by the standards of white Rhodesia. Compared to the average British university at that time, UCR was an oasis of conservatism.

The Principal, until 1967, was Professor Walter Adams. He went on to be Principal of the London School of Economics and must have noticed the difference.

I do not remember most of my students, but two I do. One was a young white Rhodesian called Ian Rees-Davies. He asked to see me shortly after I arrived. When he came into my study, his first words were, 'I understand you are one of us.'

I had no idea what he meant until he mentioned that he had heard I had been president of Edinburgh University Conservative Club. He had assumed that, as a Tory, I would be a supporter of Ian Smith and Rhodesian UDI. He was unimpressed when I disabused him.

It was perhaps the first example of my pragmatic approach to politics. Some Conservatives in Britain supported Ian Smith because of 'kith and kin' considerations and because he was a strong opponent of Communism. I recognised these considerations but could not support the racial assumptions and policies of the Rhodesian Front, the political party Ian Smith led.

I had forgotten one of my black students until he wrote to me many years later, in 1979. His name was David Mukome. He wrote that he wanted to congratulate me on becoming a junior minister in Mrs Thatcher's government. He went on to say that, as I could see from his writing paper, 'I am now Foreign Minister.'

He served in this post for several months in the short, transitional government of Bishop Abel Muzorewa, which was never recognised by the international community. I gave him lunch once in London but his political career was as short as it was sweet.

When I became Foreign Secretary in 1995, I resisted the temptation to write to him to say that, as he could see from my writing paper, I was now Foreign Minister.

One lifelong friendship that began at this time was with Michael

Holman. He had been president of the student union at UCR but shortly before I arrived he had been restricted by the Rhodesian government to his home town of Gwelo (now Gweru), 138 miles from Salisbury.

Michael was a political activist and was a strong opponent of the Rhodesian Front and all that it stood for. But he was, and he remains, a man of gentle disposition and strong beliefs who would never have contemplated the use of violence.

I visited him at his home in Gwelo and, thereafter, we corresponded with each other, always conscious that his mail was almost certainly being tampered with. I was delighted to be able to arrange for him to be offered a place at Edinburgh University, where he was able to advance his studies.

Journalism has been his chosen career and he was for many years the very distinguished Africa Correspondent for the *Financial Times*.

Rhodesia was an extraordinary country during those years. Under Ian Smith, it had declared its independence in 1965, but its government was not recognised by a single other state, not even by apartheid South Africa.

It was subject to United Nations-imposed economic sanctions, which had limited effect because of the refusal of the Portuguese in Mozambique and the South Africans to implement them.

Both Salisbury and the rest of the country were peaceful and one could travel both in the African townships and around the countryside without fear. Indeed, on one occasion I hitch-hiked from Salisbury to the South African border. There was some African Nationalist guerrilla activity in the Zambezi valley near Zambia, but at that stage it was little more than a nuisance.

For one interested in politics, it was a fascinating opportunity to be living in Rhodesia and seeing one of the final acts in the drama of the British Empire.

UDI was a last, desperate attempt by a small, white settler community of around 250,000 (often compared in those days to the size of Portsmouth) to retain political power in an African country of over six million people.

Declaring their independence was a revolution but, in truth, it was a very British revolution. On the day they rebelled, no one was killed and there was no overt violence. I doubt if they had any tanks to put on the streets even if they had wanted to. Ian Smith and his Cabinet colleagues, who included the Duke of Montrose, professed their continuing allegiance to the Queen, who, we can assume, was not amused.

The Governor, Sir Humphrey Gibbs, not only declined to acknowledge that Rhodesia was now independent but refused to leave Government House. Ian Smith made no serious attempt to evict him but appointed one of his colleagues, Clifford Dupont, as the officer administering the government, with the Queen as head of state.

I played a small part in one event at that time which was more reminiscent of Alice in Wonderland than serious politics.

In 1967, the Governor, in true diplomatic fashion, declared that his Visitors' Book in Government House, on Chancellor Avenue, would be open on 11 November, the anniversary of UDI, for all those who wished to show their loyalty to the Queen.

Not to be outdone, Mr Dupont announced that his Visitors' Book in his office, which by a delightful coincidence also happened to be on Chancellor Avenue, would also be open for those who wished to show their support for UDI.

I climbed into my Morris Minor on the day to do my duty at Government House. I do not exaggerate when I say I can recall a police officer, on traffic duty, directing some to Government House and others to Mr Dupont's office. Only in the British Empire would a revolution have been conducted through a battle of Visitors' Books.

In other countries, they put you up against a wall and shoot you.

In truth, the situation in Rhodesia at that time was not so amusing as I might be implying, nor was the Rhodesian government so gentle. They could be cruel and were repressive. But by the standards of much of the world it is fair to record that there were many governments, in Africa and elsewhere, that were far more brutal in pursuing their objectives.

An early requirement for me was to find somewhere to stay during my time in Rhodesia. I was very fortunate to be introduced to Eileen Haddon, a formidable lady who had been editor of the liberal *Central African Examiner*.

She and her husband Michael were strong advocates of one-man-one-vote, knew the African Nationalist leader, Joshua Nkomo, well and loathed the Rhodesian Front. They had a long history of support for political reform and the repeal of racist legislation.

Michael was in prison at the time, having been sentenced to three years for some alleged breach of the law. It was widely assumed that the prosecution had been influenced by his and Eileen's political activism.

For the time being, Eileen needed a paying guest and I was happy to oblige for over a year. Through her, I met many of the leading white liberals who opposed Ian Smith. They included Guy and Molly Clutton-Brock, who had set up Cold Comfort Farm, a multiracial cooperative outside Salisbury, and Dr Ahrn Palley, an Independent MP who sat in the Rhodesian Parliament.

I also became friendly with Anthony and Ruth Eastwood. Anthony was a lawyer and son of a former government minister. Ruth was the daughter of Bram Fischer, a scion of an old Afrikaner family who had rejected apartheid, defended Nelson Mandela at the Rivonia trial and was himself serving a life sentence in a South African prison for terrorist-related offences.

Eileen's most important contribution to my time in Rhodesia was in my choice of a subject to research for my Master's thesis. I was uncertain at first, but had considered the history and background of the Rhodesian Front as a possible subject.

Eileen was dismissive. There was only one subject that needed to be studied and documented, and that was the history of land segregation and the Land Apportionment Act in Rhodesia. Not only was land the bedrock of the current political system, she emphasised, but, without fundamental reform, there could never be stability and equality of opportunity.

At first I did not think I would be qualified to deal with such an issue. I had little or no knowledge of rural or agricultural issues, had only just arrived in the country and would be unable to undertake full-time research because of my lecturing responsibilities.

However, discussing it with Eileen Haddon, and doing some preliminary research, convinced me that these deficiencies were not necessarily fatal.

So little academic work had been done on the subject that I realised that, if I restricted myself to a political history of land from the European arrival in the country in 1890 until the advent of Ian Smith and the Rhodesian Front in 1962, I would be able to deliver some potentially important research.

Although land segregation in Rhodesia had always been a deeply divisive and political issue, this was little understood throughout the years, even in Britain. This was not entirely accidental.

In the course of my research I discovered a revealing exchange in the Rhodesian Parliament in 1937 during a debate on land policy. When it was suggested that the Colonial Secretary in London would not be well informed about the land situation in Rhodesia, the Prime Minister, Sir Godfrey Huggins, replied: 'Well, that is all to the good. We do not want anybody messing about with our affairs who understands too much about them ... The less he knows, I think, the better.'

It was significant that he not only made these remarks but felt able to do so in an official speech which would be reported.

In the event, my thesis, approximately 66,000 words, was the first political history of land apportionment in Rhodesia and the first comprehensive account of land policies from 1890 until the 1960s. Although not published as a book, it has been referred to and quoted in many subsequent studies of Rhodesian history.

It was perhaps inevitable that my political interests, my own liberal beliefs, and my friendship with many white liberals in Salisbury led to an unintended and unplanned political activism during my stay in Rhodesia from July 1967 until December 1968.

On 13 February 1968, the *Rhodesia Herald*, the country's main newspaper, published a letter from me referring to the criticism there had been of the pressure by the British government on the Yorkshire Cricket Club not to visit Rhodesia. This introduction of politics into sport had been deplored by supporters of the Rhodesian Front.

I contrasted this, in my letter, with their silence now that the Rhodesian Front had banned multiracial sports in white government schools against the wishes of the parent–teacher associations.

A more serious involvement by me in Rhodesian political controversy was in March of that year. Three Africans, convicted of killing a white farmer, had been hanged in Salisbury in defiance of the Privy Council in London and the exercise of the royal prerogative of mercy. The issue, of course, was not just the fate of the three convicted men but whether the Privy Council and the United Kingdom still had any jurisdiction in Rhodesia since the Unilateral Declaration of Independence.

When it had been announced on the news that they were to be executed, I and five others went down to the prison to make a silent protest outside the gates. There were journalists there as well as the father, mother and sister of one of the condemned. They had been refused permission to make him a last visit.

An ITN news team was also present. I was interviewed and asked why I was there. I replied that we had 'come to protest against what we considered to be an inhuman and illegal act'.

In a letter to James Douglas-Hamilton the following day, I wrote: 'In Britain I would be the last person to take part in a demonstration, staunch Tory that I am. But here the injustice and the evil are so blatant that one cannot stand back and ignore it if one is to remain true to oneself and keep any self-respect.'

A letter appeared in the *Rhodesia Herald* on 8 March, with my name at the head and also signed by forty-two other staff of the university. It was restrained but unambiguous. It said: 'In this state of constitutional uncertainty, we cannot understand how men can take upon themselves the responsibility of carrying out these executions.'

At the same time, there was a peaceful protest by black and white Rhodesians outside the Parliament Building in Cecil Square in the heart of Salisbury. At one stage an angry white Rhodesian turned a hose on several of the demonstrators and soaked them.

I did not take part in this demonstration, but one of my colleagues who did, Linda Kirk, was drenched. Linda was an articulate and able history lecturer, a strong Anglican and a delightful person with an impressive sense of humour. She was, and remains, a close friend. She has lectured for many years at Sheffield University and her husband, Richard Carwardine, also a historian, is, at present, president of Corpus Christi College in Oxford.

In October of that year I was one of 300 students and lecturers at a protest meeting criticising the South African government for preventing an African lecturer from taking up an academic post at Cape Town University. The newspaper report said that 'Mr Rifkind made perhaps the most salient point of the meeting by pointing out that ... the South African government had gone above its own laws, which give absolute freedom to universities in appointing their staff' in banning the lecturer because he was black.

My most significant political act was, however, the public lecture I agreed to give on land apportionment in October 1968, two months before I was due to leave Rhodesia. It was reported, prominently, in the *Rhodesia Herald* under the headline 'Plea Made For Land Apportionment Act Repeal'.

My lecture was, in effect, a summary of my thesis. The press report highlighted my conclusion: 'As long as land segregation and the Land Apportionment Act existed, a society based on merit was impossible ... However, with elements in power in Rhodesia determined on retaining white supremacy ... and with armed fighters already battling in the Zambezi Valley, time is very short.'

Although Rhodesia became legally independent as Zimbabwe in 1980, with a black government and with the Land Apportionment Act repealed, this did not end the controversy. Six thousand whites continued to farm 70 per cent of the country's most fertile agricultural land while over half a million blacks farmed the rest.

The situation was fairly quiet in the early years but after 1997, as Robert Mugabe saw his popularity disappearing, land reform became his government's top political priority. This was carried out by the expropriation of white-owned land, which led to the collapse of the highly efficient and profitable tobacco industry. The methods used to implement land reform involved considerable violence and thuggery. Some white farmers were murdered; many others were harassed and intimidated. Some of the best land was transferred to Mugabe's cronies rather than going to peasant farmers as had been promised.

My judgement, in my thesis, that land reform was the crucial political issue in Rhodesia was correct. Many black farmers have undoubtedly benefited from the radical reforms of the past twenty years. But the farms and estates handed over, for no payment, to Mugabe's friends and colleagues, and the expropriation without compensation suffered by white farmers, must lead to the conclusion that, so far, one injustice has been replaced with another.

During one university recess in 1968, an academic colleague, Tony McAdam, and I travelled, in his car, from Rhodesia through Mozambique to Malawi, then to Zambia and finally crossed the Zambezi on our way back to Salisbury. It enabled us to see a bit more of Africa, but at one stage in our journey I had reason to be concerned that my budding career might be coming to a premature end.

In order to get to Malawi, we had to drive through the north-west of Mozambique, which at that time was a Portuguese colony.

Frelimo, the African Nationalist guerrilla group, were active in various parts of the country, fighting the Portuguese and those thought to be supporting them. We had enquired before we left Salisbury but had been advised that there had been very little Frelimo activity in the area we were to be travelling through. As crossing that part of Mozambique would only take us eight or nine hours, we decided to go ahead.

We had been driving for around three hours on an empty dirt road when, suddenly, as we turned a corner, we came across a dozen blacks in battle fatigues and carrying weapons, who gestured for us to stop.

They said something to us in Portuguese which we could not understand and then gestured to us that we should drive the vehicle into a corrugated iron shack that was nearby. As they were armed, we had no choice but to comply.

When we had entered the shack and stopped, they closed the doors. We had no idea who they were but given that they were black and armed, we feared that they might be Frelimo guerrillas and that we were about to be dispatched. It was not a pleasant feeling.

However, a few moments later one of them produced some equipment and started spraying our car. It turned out that the black men with guns were Portuguese soldiers protecting health ministry staff who were trying to eradicate insect threats to cattle in the locality. The spraying having been completed, we were free to leave.

I recall our time in Malawi as it was my first exposure to President Hastings Banda, whom, years later, I entertained at Edinburgh Castle.

Banda, an Edinburgh-trained doctor and adherent of the Church of Scotland, was an autocratic President. Having just sacked several of his Cabinet and appointed himself to their posts, he was being (privately) described in Malawi as a 'one-man Banda'.

State-controlled Malawi radio reported, while we were there, the President's recent visit to Wales, where, it said, 'he had been welcomed affectionately by the people'. It was harmless but I had my doubts as to how affectionate the Welsh had felt.

It was Rhodesia I have to thank for my meeting Edith Steinberg. It all happened during the interval of a concert in Salisbury in, I think, April of 1968. We were engaged in 1969 and married in 1970, both at the tender age of twenty-three.

Edith had been born in Colne, in Lancashire, on 23 October 1946. Her parents were both Polish. Her mother, Roma Likierman, from Lodz, had come to England in the 1930s and was living with cousins who owned a Lancashire textile mill.

Edith's father, Joseph Steinberg, from Kraków, had been in the Polish Air Force when the war broke out in 1939. He was not a pilot but an engineer, having studied at both Polish and German universities.

When Hitler invaded Poland from the west in September 1939, Stalin, a temporary ally under the Molotov–Ribbentrop Pact, had sent Soviet troops across Poland's eastern frontier. The territory occupied was annexed by the Soviet Union.

Edith's father was deported, together with many thousands of other Polish military prisoners and their families in the Polish territory occupied by the USSR, to labour camps in Siberia.

At that time he was already married to his first wife and had a baby daughter. The deportees in the camp they were sent to were used as labour for the felling of forest trees. The living conditions and medical facilities were primitive and both his wife and child died from typhus.

When Hitler invaded the Soviet Union in June 1941, Stalin desperately needed assistance from Roosevelt and Churchill. One of the conditions the Americans and British insisted on was that all the Polish prisoners would be released. Stalin agreed and, with typical generosity, gave them the choice of either joining the Red Army or being allowed to leave the Soviet Union and join the Polish forces in exile in the United Kingdom. Not surprisingly, the vast majority chose the latter.

My future father-in-law travelled across central Asia to Palestine and then went on by ship, spending one night off Durban and then sailing round the Cape before reaching Britain. He had decided not to join the Polish forces but had joined the Royal Air Force, instead, in Palestine.

He had also decided that he would not return to Poland after the war. His family was Jewish, as was Edith's mother's. The disaster that engulfed Polish Jews under the Nazi occupation was already known. Some of his close relatives perished in the Holocaust, as was the case with Edith's mother's family.

Having met, Edith's parents married in England after the war. In 1946, my father-in-law was offered a job in South Africa. All he knew of that country was having spent one night with the bright lights of Durban after years in a Soviet labour camp.

He took the job and travelled to Johannesburg. His wife and Edith, his baby daughter, only a few months old, followed some weeks later.

They lived ten years in Johannesburg, where my father-in-law worked for a hospital equipment firm, Protea Medical Services. He was then offered promotion to be in charge of their business activities in Salisbury, covering Rhodesia and what became Zambia and Malawi.

Edith attended school in Salisbury until she was fourteen. She was an only child. Her parents judged that there was unlikely to be a long-term future for a white woman in Rhodesia and it would be better if she got to know her cousins and other family in England. She was sent, with little enthusiasm on her part, to complete her education as a boarder at a girls' public school, Huyton School for Girls, near Liverpool, and to stay during the school holidays with family who lived in Cheshire and Lancashire.

On leaving school, she went to King's College London, where she graduated with a BSc in Zoology. She then returned to Salisbury, partly to be at home and partly because she needed to repay the grant she had got from the Rhodesian government, which she did by working for their Veterinary Services Department.

After we had met at the concert, we met a second time playing tennis with friends. That evening, while we were all having a steak dinner at Guido's in central Salisbury, Edith and I spent most of the time conversing with each other. We felt we had a lot in common, both having been to school and university in Britain and sharing various ideas and values.

The following night, I phoned to invite her out to dinner at Le Français, a more upmarket restaurant in downtown Salisbury. It was a great evening and we both knew we would want to see more of each other.

A few days later, Edith received a phone call from a lady friend of her parents. This friend had heard we were seeing each other and warned Edith off relationships with overseas visitors who would come into her life and then depart. She then, suddenly, asked Edith, 'My dear, are you going to marry him?' Edith was so annoyed at being asked that she said, 'Yes, I am' and put the phone down.

Edith, not surprisingly, didn't think it necessary to tell me about this conversation at the time. However, it seems that even in these first days we both felt that something long-term might be evolving.

That was certainly my view. Although I had taken girls out on several occasions, both while I was a student and since, until I met Edith I had had no serious relationship. With Edith, I was finding someone with a similar background and many common interests, someone highly intelligent and good fun to be with. We spent increasing time together, including a day trip to the Victoria Falls on the Zambezi River.

In autumn 1968, I flew back to Edinburgh for my brother Arnold's wedding to Hilary. At the airport I was stopped by police officers at the departure desk who said they wanted to search my luggage. I suspected this was because of my association with the university and my known opposition to the Rhodesian Front.

In my luggage, they discovered a camera that Michael Holman, my friend restricted in Gwelo, had asked me to return to its owner in the United Kingdom. I thought it best not to mention that it was Michael who had given it to me. The police officer asked me if there was any film in the camera. I hadn't the faintest idea but said to him that I could not remember. This made him more suspicious and he said they would take the camera away, take out any film and find out what was on it.

Off he went. When he returned, he was looking even more irritated. 'There is no film in the camera,' he said, and lost interest in me.

On return to Rhodesia, I only had two months before my final departure. I had completed the first draft of my thesis, though it would still need considerable revision.

Edith and I decided to have a holiday together and explore South Africa, Swaziland and southern Mozambique before I returned to Britain. Her father was a bit nervous about approving this trip. He appeared to like me but knew I was leaving in December and that there was no guarantee that my friendship with his daughter would survive our separation. Edith did not appear to share this concern.

We had a splendid trip in her Fiat through South Africa to Lourenço Marques (now Maputo), the capital of Mozambique, to the tiny kingdom of Swaziland and back to Salisbury. It was a very successful holiday and persuaded us both of our deep attraction to each another.

It could, however, have been a disastrous trip for another reason. On our journey south, we had noticed that we had to refill the petrol tank of Edith's car more often than should have been necessary. By the time we reached Lourenço Marques, we were seriously concerned. By an extraordinary coincidence, Fiat's only dedicated service garage in the region was a few hundred yards from where we were staying.

The garage informed us that throughout our journey from Salisbury we had had a petrol tank that had shrunk to a fraction of its normal size. This was because the petrol pump was defective but had continued working, though that wouldn't have lasted much longer. We were very lucky that the car had not broken down anywhere else in that part of southern Africa, as that garage was able to supply us, right away, with a new petrol tank. The gods were with us that day.

On our way back to Salisbury we made a detour to stay over-night with the former Rhodesian Prime Minister Garfield Todd and his wife.

Having crossed into Rhodesia, we had to leave the tarred road and journey to his farm over many miles of dirt track. Unfortunately, a stone had sprung up from the dirt and smashed our windscreen. For most of the journey we had no protection from the dust and flies, and arrived at the former Prime Minister's home looking like a pair of dirty and dusty tramps. They could not have been more hospitable.

Shortly after our return to Salisbury, I flew out of Rhodesia on my journey home to Edinburgh. I spent a short time in Nairobi, and then in Addis Ababa, in Ethiopia, before my flight to London.

Edith and I had agreed that she would come for a holiday to Edinburgh some months later. It was understood, but unstated by either of us, that we would be likely to decide our long-term future at that time.

As I flew out of Salisbury Airport I hoped that while the life I had had in Rhodesia had now concluded, another, equally intriguing, might now be beginning. I need not have been so concerned.

CHAPTER 6

BACK TO EARTH

R ETURNING FROM RHODESIA to Edinburgh in December 1968 was not just a change of residence. It soon became apparent to me that it was a considerable change in status as well. In Salisbury I had been a member of the academic staff of a university, receiving a good salary, giving public lectures and being a young man of some modest but real consequence.

For the next six months I was to be a junior Bar apprentice in a solicitor's office, sharing a room with the secretarial staff and receiving wages, quite rightly, much lower than theirs.

This was the unavoidable first stage in my becoming a member of the Faculty of Advocates and being called to the Scots Bar. I had to learn how the Scottish court system worked, learn how to draft various legal documents and be a bag carrier to the senior partners.

The firm was Courtney & Co., who had their offices in Edinburgh's West End. The senior partner was the eponymous Bill Courtney, who received me in a friendly, if rather distant, manner. Most of my time was with his colleague Bill Hailstones, bespectacled, conscientious and very likeable.

Although my wages were in the hundreds rather than the thousands, I am not certain that I earned them during those months. Most of the work in the office, not unreasonably, was the daily bread and butter of the solicitor, only some of which involves the law courts and the advocacy side of the profession.

My knowledge of Scots Law and legal procedure had been reasonable as a result of my three years as a law undergraduate at the university. But it had never been impressive and I found the drafting of documents and the somewhat arcane procedures of the Court of Session not very stimulating.

What made it much worse was that for the previous year and a half I had had all the stimulation of living in a rebellious African colony, involved, even if only at the margins, in its politics and controversies. I had moved from an exciting environment to the worthy but relatively humdrum world of the Scottish legal profession. I got on well with my employers but they were aware of my political interests and sensed that I was not destined to a life in the law.

After six months I left Courtney's to begin my devilling. To 'devil' is defined in *Chambers Dictionary* as to do another person's drudgery or to do very menial work. This is an excellent description of what awaited me.

Devilling in Scotland is quite different to that in England and Wales. In England, one's devilling begins after one has become a barrister. One works with a senior barrister, assisting him and learning the ropes.

In Scotland, one devils to a practising advocate before one is called to the Bar and dons wig and gown. Because I wanted experience in both criminal and civil law, I had two consecutive devil masters, both for around six months.

The first was Charles Macarthur, who, the following year, became a successful Queen's Counsel and then, in 1974, a Sheriff on the Bench in Lothian.

He had served during the war in the Royal Navy and practised for several years as a solicitor. By the time I worked with him, he was a successful and busy advocate specialising in criminal cases in the High Court of Justiciary.

In those days, the High Court went on circuit and by far the busiest courts were in Glasgow. All appeal cases were heard in Edinburgh in Parliament House, which also housed the Court of Session.

Charles was an excellent advocate to train with. He was practical, considerate but also very professional. He did not go in for great flights of oratory but his forensic skills were, nevertheless, usually to the benefit of his clients.

For the second part of my devilling I worked with David Edward, who is one of the most successful and impressive advocates Scotland produced in the late twentieth century.

Born in 1934 in Perth, he was educated at Sedbergh and University College, Oxford, as well as Edinburgh before being called to the Bar in 1962. Five years later he was Clerk of the Faculty of Advocates and by 1970 he was Treasurer. If he had wished, he would undoubtedly have become Dean of Faculty and then a judge of the Court of Session. Few would doubt that he would have ended as Lord President, the head of the judiciary in Scotland.

But David chose a very different career path. He has always been a committed believer in the European Union and has made a major contribution to the development of European law both as an academic and as a judge of the European Court of Justice from 1989 to 2004. He was knighted in 2004 and became a Privy Councillor the following year.

He supervised my instruction in Civil Law litigation and allowed me to examine the many erudite opinions he was asked to write. I was in awe of him and loved going to his New Town home in Heriot Row, where he worked in a book-lined study with a glowing fire for company.

He and his splendid wife Lizzie have been good friends of ours ever since. Our only regret is that we have not seen as much of each other as we would have wished.

He had few illusions about whether I would stick to law as a life-time career. When, in the 1980s, I was a government minister, I was invited to 'take silk' and become a QC. David wrote to congratulate me. After some friendly words, he added that perhaps, in the circumstances, I could best be described as artificial silk.

He was quite right. I had only four years of full-time experience as an advocate, and thus taking silk was more an honour than a recognition of my legal skills. Nevertheless, only one's devil master would have felt entitled to cut me down in that way.

I was called to the Bar in 1970. There were two parts to the ceremony. The first was in the Faculty Room at the end of the Advocates Library, where, in the presence of many advocates, I was admitted as a member of the Faculty, which had been established in 1532.

I then had to proceed to one of the courts in Parliament House, where whatever case was being heard would be interrupted so that I could take the oath before a Court of Session judge. This was required as advocates were deemed to be officers of the court and were privileged to plead in all civil and criminal cases.

This ceremony usually took place on a Friday, when most courts were dealing with undefended divorces, which in those days needed to be granted by a judge, having heard the evidence in open court.

The pursuer (or plaintiff) would usually be the aggrieved wife. She would have been assured that although her case would be held in open court, there would be no one interested enough to be there apart from the judge and the lawyers.

Suddenly, the new advocate would be ushered into the courtroom, accompanied by a dozen friends or other advocates who had come to watch the spectacle. The poor woman giving her evidence of her marital problems would be expected to continue until the judge interrupted her in order to administer the oath to the new advocate.

In my case, the judge was Lord Hunter and the ceremony went very smoothly. Nowadays, undefended divorces no longer require a court appearance and so this insensitive ordeal for litigants is no more.

Advocates, like barristers, wear wig and gown, but otherwise there are subtle differences in dress. The Scottish advocate, under his gown, wears an evening tailcoat, a white bow tie and a wing collar.

For my calling ceremony I did not possess such a tailcoat and knew them to be expensive. I had been advised by a friend to go to Armstrong's, then in the Grassmarket, a second-hand clothes dealer, who was known to have several for sale. As it would be worn under my gown, it would not matter if it was not in perfect condition.

I had entered the shop hoping that no one would have seen me. A helpful sales assistant found me a tailcoat which fitted perfectly and was being sold for a pittance. As I was about to leave, very pleased with my subterfuge, he said that he hoped I wouldn't mind him asking but was I 'Bar or hotel trade?' When I, rather crestfallen, replied that I was Bar, he responded that advocates and waiters were the only people nowadays buying such a garment.

That put me in my place, but I can hold my head up high. The last time I wore that tailcoat was at a diplomatic reception in Buckingham Palace before my expanding waistline required me to invest in a new one.

Immediately after the ceremony, I went to the polished wooden box, with my name on a brass plate, which had now joined those of all the other advocates in the corridor adjoining Parliament Hall. Solicitors who wished to brief an advocate would leave the papers in these open boxes.

There was a tradition that every new advocate would find his first brief in the box immediately after he had been called to the Bar. Sure enough, there was a slim brief tied with a pink ribbon from Courtney & Co. I was instructed to draft the divorce summons for one of their clients and represent her interests. For this task I would be paid the standard fee of six guineas. I was on my way.

Being an advocate, I had to dress each day in the required manner for my journeys to and from the courts. That was black jacket and striped trousers, a costume which even in 1970 was rarely seen except for lawyers, bank managers and undertakers.

I did have one minor rebellion. Although I have no difficulty wearing hats, and possess several, I refused, point blank, to wear a bowler hat, which at that time was part of the uniform. I thought I would look ridiculous and have never changed that view.

A more traditional legal colleague solemnly warned me that if I did not conform I would never reach the heights of the legal profession. In view of what happened over the years, his prediction was undoubtedly proved accurate.

In 1970, the Faculty of Advocates had just over 100 practising members, of whom only a handful were female. Today, there are over 300, almost evenly divided between men and women.

A surprising number of my new colleagues were advocates who ended up with successful political careers. They included John Smith, who became Leader of the Opposition and would have been Prime Minister but for his sudden death.

There were also Menzies Campbell, future Leader of the Liberal Democrats; Lord Mackay of Clashfern, who was our most eminent recent Lord Chancellor; and Nicholas Fairbairn, a colourful dandy but also a brilliant advocate. My close friend Michael Ancram, who was a highly successful Northern Ireland Minister and Deputy Leader of the Conservative Party, was at the Bar with me, as was James Douglas-Hamilton. Peter Fraser became Lord Advocate and Alex Pollock an MP.

I worked full time as an advocate for just under four years until I became an MP in February 1974. In my first year I earned about £800 and thereafter it rose to a more respectable level.

I did a considerable amount of criminal work, including defending several clients accused of murder in the High Court in Glasgow. Even without the death penalty, I will never forget the tension for lawyers as well as the accused as we waited for the jury to complete its deliberations and reach a verdict.

I was also involved in civil cases as well as planning inquiries. The most prominent of the latter was being junior counsel to James Mackay, representing the local residents in Shetland in the deliberations that led to the construction of the Sullom Voe oil terminal and Shetland's oil bonanza, which has lasted until this day.

The SNP like to talk of Scotland's oil. That is not how they see it in Shetland. With their Norse heritage and distinct traditions, the Shetlanders often see themselves as a separate people. One islander I spoke to said he would be going to Scotland for his holidays. Another assured me that if North Sea oil wasn't British then it wasn't Scottish either, but belonged to Shetland.

I enjoyed working as an advocate in criminal cases. I often got the verdict I wanted for my client, but not always. I had a client who was charged with reset, the Scottish term for receiving stolen property. A stolen television had been found in his sitting room. Under the law of Scotland, possession of a stolen item was not sufficient to establish guilt. There had to be some evidence that showed that you knew it had been stolen.

I had to cross-examine the police officer who had discovered the television in my client's living room. My tactic was to try to establish that the accused had not known the television was stolen.

The police officer agreed that it was a perfectly normal television in a room where you would expect a TV to be. So far, so good. I then made the classic barrister's mistake of asking a question to which I did not already know the answer.

I asked him to confirm that there was nothing else in that living room that made him suspicious. 'Oh, yes there was,' he replied. When I asked him what that was, he replied, 'Two other television sets.'

The accused in criminal trials can sometimes be their own worst enemies. I represented a young man, Willie Wallace, who was accused of a sexual assault on a young woman in a dark street in Glasgow.

The victim had confirmed that she had not known the assailant, that it was dark at the time, that it was all over in less than a minute and that she had not seen him since, except when she identified him in an identification parade in the police station.

I tried to suggest that she was mistaken in saying the person responsible for the assault was the young man sitting in the dock. I reminded her that he was unknown to her, that it was dark and all over in less than a minute. Might she not be mistaken, I asked her and, if not, why not?

'Because', she replied, 'after the assault I told him that I was going to tell the polis [Glaswegian for the police] what he had done. He replied, 'I'm not scared of you. My name's Willie Wallace and I come from 14 Dalmally Street.'

I asked the judge for an adjournment to consult my client. The result was that he changed his plea to guilty. It should have been guilty but insane.

While I was working as an advocate, I was also enjoying the first years of marriage.

After I had returned from Rhodesia in December 1968, Edith and I had agreed that she would come on holiday the following summer. She did; we had a splendid tour of the Highlands and ending up informing my parents and hers that we had become engaged.

In May 1970, both aged only twenty-three, we married at the St Petersburg Place Synagogue in Bayswater in London. We chose London as most of Edith's family lived there and her parents flew from Rhodesia for the wedding.

Our first home was in Edinburgh's Royal Mile at 242/5 Canongate. It was a top-floor flat for which we paid an economic rent to Edinburgh Town Council. The flat abutted Chessels Court, where John Smith, the future Leader of the Labour Party, and his wife Elizabeth lived.

A year later we bought our first home at 1 Drummond Place in Edinburgh's New Town. It was a ground-floor flat with double doors that looked out on to Drummond Place Gardens.

Its location meant I had a pleasant walk to the law courts.

As advocates were supposed to have a place in the New Town where legal papers could be delivered, our front door now had a brass plate inscribed 'Mr Malcolm Rifkind, Advocate'.

We bought the flat in Drummond Place for the princely sum of £6,300. We had planned to spend no more than £5,000 and agonised over the additional £1,300 the seller demanded. It was a good investment. We sold it seven years later for around £18,000 when we moved to Duddingston Village at the foot of Arthur's Seat. By that time, with two children, Caroline and Hugo, we needed a larger house and wanted a garden.

My income was modest those first few years at the Bar but Edith helped keep us both in a manner to which we liked to be accustomed. She was lecturing at Napier College (now Napier University) in biology and her income was significantly more than mine.

When I was a youngster, my father liked to advise me that it was just as easy to fall in love with a rich girl as with a poor girl. I didn't quite manage that.

Edith's parents were neither rich nor poor. Her London cousins, the Likiermans, were delightful people. That side of her mother's family had owned a textile business, Qualitex, which was later sold to ICI.

When Edith introduced me to them, after we had become engaged, the first visit was to Dolly and Jules, who lived in a very grand flat in Kensington Palace Gardens. Their daughters Helen and Jo were Edith's bridesmaids and remain very close friends of ours.

At that time, my income was also supplemented by Edinburgh University appointing me as a part-time tutor in politics at the princely sum of £300 per year.

My Master's thesis on the politics of land in Rhodesia was accepted and I could add MSc to my initials after LLB. I was, however, unsuccessful in getting it published.

Oxford University Press thought about it for several months but then in December 1969 wrote to me to say they wanted to take a further opinion from an advisor in Rhodesia as to whether there would be 'impeded sales' of such a book in that country. That was the kiss of death.

The central theme of the thesis and the unambiguous conclusion was that the current division of land between whites and blacks was a rotten deal for the blacks and that until land segregation was abandoned there would be no real peace in the country. This was anathema to the Smith regime, which would have been quite capable of banning the book. This, I assume, is what OUP meant by 'impeded sales'.

But neither Africa nor the law was dominating my life. Increasingly, instead of concentrating on my legal career, I was becoming distracted by politics. That distraction has lasted rather a long time.

CHAPTER 7

CLIMBING THE FOOTHILLS

PEOPLE HAVE DIFFERENT motives for choosing a life in politics. For some, there is a genuine desire to change their country or the world for the better.

For others, there is a fascination in power; in obtaining it and in using it. That is not, necessarily, discreditable. It is how power is used that distinguishes the villains from the saints, with most of us being somewhere in between.

In days gone by, some worthies became Members of Parliament because their fathers had been MPs and their grandfathers before that. It was part of the duty of the local gentry to represent the county, and a few such dignitaries remained on the Tory benches when I first arrived in February 1974.

In truth, I cannot claim any of these excuses or reasons for my parliamentary aspirations. I did want to play a part in improving the country and the world, but there are many other careers that offer such opportunities. I have no problems with the exercise of power, but for me its use is a necessary means for getting things done rather than an emotional or psychological requirement in its own right.

What attracted me to politics and to Parliament as a young man was partly a deep interest in foreign policy; in how the United Kingdom, no longer the British Empire, could continue to make a distinctive contribution to resolving world problems, and whether I could play some significant part in that process.

But I was also influenced by a strong and clear feeling that politics, whether domestic or foreign, was an exciting and stimulating activity. Being part of that would enable me to feel I was living my life to the full. I did not wish to spend my best years simply as a private citizen, earning my living, enjoying my family, playing golf and watching those years go by.

I had no objection to any of these activities (except, perhaps, playing golf) but I felt that life and the world was offering me more than that. I had, at university, met some MPs and national politicians. Some I was hugely impressed by; others did not appear particularly remarkable. It did not seem impossible or unrealistic to believe that I could be an MP. The House of Commons was the stage on which the nation's destiny was determined. There seemed nothing grander than, one day, to be part of that.

My hero was, of course, Winston Churchill. Though I had never met him, I had, as I have recorded, attended his state funeral on the pavement outside St Paul's.

Churchill never concealed the stimulation and the excitement that the political world gave him. He had lived his life at the centre of events and had helped to shape them even before he became Prime Minister. I had no illusions about having his remarkable qualities. He had remarked that we are all worms but that he thought himself to be a glow worm. I hoped that a faint light might, one day, emanate from me.

Returning from Rhodesia, I resumed my friendship with Michael Ancram. We had first met in the months before I went to Africa. We liked each other and found that we shared a common interest in politics.

Michael, who is now the Marquess of Lothian, was from one of Scotland's most aristocratic families, with their home at Monteviot near Jedburgh. His father, Peter Lothian, had been born a commoner but inherited the title from his cousin, Philip Lothian, who had died, childless, while serving as British ambassador in Washington in 1940. Michael's father was a fine pianist and a gentle man. He served as a junior minister in both Alec Douglas-Home's and Ted Heath's governments.

Michael's mother, Tony, was the daughter of a Major-General who had married the daughter of an Italian Count. She was no conventional marchioness. She had six children and had been a working author, journalist and broadcaster. She befriended Valentina Tereshkova, a Soviet cosmonaut and the first woman in space. She either loved people or loathed them. For reasons I never fully understood, I found myself in the former category.

Michael was keen to create a group of young progressive Scottish Conservatives who could help ginger up what was seen as a weak and declining Tory Party in Scotland. I agreed with him and this led to the formation of the Thistle Group, modelled on the Bow Group in London but distinctively Scottish.

I had volunteered the name 'Thistle' as something that was both Scottish and uncomfortable to tamper with. The group's founder members also included future Scottish MPs such as Peter Fraser and Alex Pollock.

I then went off to live and work in Rhodesia. At the press conference to launch the group, which I could not attend, a journalist asked if the real reason for the Thistle Group was simply to help get Michael Ancram into the House of Commons. He was told, in reply, that the real reason was to help get all of us there.

The Thistle Group had no corporate view on devolution and whether there should be a Scottish Assembly, but that became the dominant issue for Scottish Tories in May 1968 when Ted Heath made his Declaration of Perth, accepting, in principle, the need for such an assembly.

I was in Rhodesia at the time and, as a committed Unionist, was unimpressed by Heath's declaration, which had come out of the blue. Heath appointed a Constitutional Commission under Sir Alec Douglas-Home to consider the whole question and, to our delight, the Thistle Group was invited to give evidence to the commission in 1969. I was part of the delegation that did so when they were taking evidence at Peebles Hydro.

By that time I had accepted that constitutional reform was a political necessity and supported a joint submission from the Thistle Group welcoming Heath's Declaration of Perth. We presented an eleven-page report which emphasised that we would prefer a federal solution for the United Kingdom as a whole, which we believed would be inevitable. In the meantime, we said, the proposed Scottish Assembly should consist of the seventy-one MPs representing Scottish constituencies at Westminster with additional members selected on the basis of party strengths in local elections in Scotland.

One of the commissioners, Lord Ballantrae, formerly Sir Bernard Fergusson and an erstwhile Governor-General of New Zealand, wrote to me in 1974, saying that he 'had the clearest recollection of your group giving evidence ... and being very much impressed by what you had to say to us and the manner in which you said it'.

One should never underestimate how polite compliments of that kind cost little and boost the confidence of young people at the beginning of their careers. I have tried to do the same since becoming what the press never tire of referring to as a 'grandee'.

I had no strategy for advancing my political life but it took a significant and unexpected leap when I received a phone call in early 1969. It was from Paddy Finlay, a senior official at the Scottish Conservative Central Office at Atholl Crescent in Edinburgh.

He asked me, to my astonishment, whether I would be willing to be drafted in as chairman of the Central Edinburgh Conservative Association. I pointed out that I was not even living in Central Edinburgh, as well as being only twenty-three, but was told that would not be a problem.

The post I was being offered was not as grand as it sounded. Central Edinburgh was a fairly safe Labour seat and the Tory association had only around a hundred members, many of whom were either inactive or quite elderly. Central Office were determined to get it moving and felt that a young chairman and executive might help to achieve that aim.

I was completing my Bar apprenticeship and beginning my devilling at that time. That should have been my undiluted commitment. But I was flattered and could not resist the offer. It was clear that Central Office were viewing me as a young man with serious political prospects. Who was I to differ?

I became chairman, got together a few younger colleagues and began to pep up the association with meetings and political campaigning.

We already had a parliamentary candidate for the next general election, Jim Glass, but then, suddenly, an extraordinary thing happened. Jim was offered the opportunity to become a senior officer in the voluntary wing of the party but told that party rules would make holding that office incompatible with being a parliamentary candidate. He resigned as candidate. We had to select a new one.

I did not need much persuading. With the support of colleagues, I stepped down as chairman and offered myself as the new candidate. Several aspirants were interviewed. I was selected. On Tuesday 5 August, I was formally adopted by Central Edinburgh as their prospective parliamentary candidate. At twenty-three, I was, at that time, the youngest Conservative parliamentary candidate in Scotland.

In my adoption speech, I spoke on national and local issues. I made some rude remarks about Willie Ross, the Labour Secretary of State for Scotland. Harold Wilson had described him as a model Secretary of State. I said that I agreed with him as what was a model but a small imitation of the real thing?

I then turned to local issues and developed what became a central theme of my campaign: that the heart of Edinburgh was dying as a residential area. In the previous eighteen years, the population had decreased by a third as a result of demolition of older properties and the movement of people to the suburbs. I called for a commitment to new housing, private and public, in the city centre.

As it turned out, my proposals came to pass over the next thirty years. The Old Town of Edinburgh became fashionable for young people to live in and the Georgian New Town escaped the fate of Dublin and remains a location where people want to live.

It is sometimes assumed that politicians are always calculating and that their political advancement reflects a carefully constructed strategy. I have no doubt that that does happen, but my own career owed more to serendipity than to calculation.

I became a parliamentary candidate because of the unexpected resignation of the existing candidate for personal reasons, shortly after I had become constituency chairman. It took General Galtieri to invade the Falkland Islands for me to be made a minister in the Foreign Office. It required Michael Heseltine to storm out of the Cabinet and be replaced by George Younger for me to become a member of the Cabinet when I was thirty-nine. I had not planned any of these events. I certainly benefited from them.

I was a vigorous parliamentary candidate between August 1969 and the general election in June 1970. I have a sheaf of twenty-two press releases I issued through Conservative Central Office. Many were speeches I made either in Central Edinburgh or at party events around Scotland. They covered local, national and international issues, including Rhodesia. A reasonable number of them were picked up by local papers.

In April 1970, I joined forces with Victor MacColl, our candidate for Glasgow Woodside, in producing a report, 'Two Cities', which highlighted similar problems in Scotland's two main inner-city districts.

One of the issues I highlighted was how Edinburgh was the sole part of Scotland excluded from development area status and the financial help associated with it. I got in touch with Edward Heath's office and asked for a letter that I could use to get publicity on the subject.

I have a letter from the Leader of the Opposition, dated 26 March 1970, promising, 'When we come to office we shall look at the special case of Edinburgh,' which was, helpfully, reported in the local press.

This was all reputable political campaigning. During the general election I was rather more disreputable.

The sitting Labour MP was Tom Oswald, a Labour veteran who had represented the constituency for nineteen years. He was, probably, conscientious but had been largely invisible to the public either in the press or in Parliament.

I had scoured Hansard for any references to him since the 1964 general election. He had made no speeches in the Chamber and his total reported comments were six interruptions during other MPs' speeches.

We printed a leaflet under the title 'The Silent MP' that reported this record and, for added mischief, quoted three of the interruptions. They were 'Lovely weather', 'Oh, I see' and 'Mr Deputy Speaker, may I—'

On 9 June 1970, during the campaign, I challenged him to come out with me on the streets of Central Edinburgh to hear what local people thought of the Labour government and of him. He replied to me the following day with a handwritten letter accepting my challenge if I apologised for the 'scurrilous and deliberate lie' that he had failed to speak out against the exclusion of Edinburgh from development area status.

We never did tour the streets together and if he had spoken out for Edinburgh he deserved an apology. I do not recall whether he received one.

The timing of the general election was earlier than had been expected and could not have been less opportune. Edith and I had arranged to be married in London on 24 May. On 18 May, Harold

Wilson went to Buckingham Palace. An announcement was made later that day that the general election would be on 18 June.

To put it mildly, that was not convenient and Edith was not pleased. It did not interfere with the wedding itself. Indeed, we got some good local publicity about the candidate stopping canvassing to go off and get married.

Having to cancel a two-week honeymoon in Florence and Rome in the middle of the campaign was another matter. Having got married in London on 24 May, we spent our wedding night at the Cavendish Hotel in Jermyn Street, and then two days in London with Edith's parents and other friends before her parents returned to Rhodesia and we travelled back to Edinburgh.

Poor Edith had to spend what should have been our honeymoon pounding the streets of Central Edinburgh. In years to come, she would say that she had not been too disappointed. She had assumed that politics was like the measles and that after the election I would be cured. It turned out that the disease was incurable, but we did have our Italian honeymoon in August and all the better it was for the enforced delay.

The campaign itself was great fun. We had the use of a large empty shop in Lothian Road, near Princes Street, with 'Vote Rifkind' plastered on the windows. I decided to be unconventional and used purple rather than blue as my campaign colours. I had an excellent team of young friends and supporters campaigning throughout the election.

On the day, Labour held the seat, but their majority had slumped from 4,015 to 1,561. The Labour government was defeated and Ted Heath became Prime Minister.

I was elated not just by the national result but also by my local one. Conservative Central Office complimented us on an excellent campaign, and my prospects of being adopted for a winnable seat the next time around were much enhanced.

I had assumed that politics would then take a back seat for several years, but it was not to be. Later that year, Roy Wilson, a solicitor who occasionally instructed me and was also chairman of South

Edinburgh Conservatives, approached me in Parliament Hall, where advocates assembled each working day.

He wanted to know whether I would consider being the candidate for a by-election in the safe Newington ward for the Edinburgh Town Council.

I had never before considered municipal politics and my initial inclination was to decline. I eventually agreed to let my name go forward and did so for several reasons. My legal practice was still very modest and I had considerable time on my hands. Being a councillor would be excellent experience of representative politics and would help maintain my public profile in Edinburgh until the next general election. I was also aware that the sitting Tory MP for South Edinburgh, of which Newington was a part, was Michael Clark Hutchison, who might retire at the next general election, which would cause a vacancy.

But decisive was the helpful coincidence that the City Chambers, where the town council met, was literally across the road from the law courts in Parliament Square. I would only have to remove my wig and gown, put on my coat and walk 100 yards for council meetings.

The selection process by the Newington Conservatives turned out to be more form than substance. The chairman of the selection committee was a retired Lt Col., Aubrey Gibbon. He looked quite fierce, with a reddish complexion and mutton-chop whiskers. In fact, he could not have been more charming and became a good friend.

At the end of the interview he remarked that I was the first of the possible candidates that they had interviewed and they could not possibly come to even a preliminary view until they had interviewed the others. But, he added, subject to these considerations, would I be free to be adopted as the candidate on the next Tuesday?

And so it turned out. Within a few weeks I had been returned. As well as counsel, I was now a councillor in Scotland's capital city. I may have been the youngest of the City Fathers, but in my advocate's black jacket and striped trousers I was also the smartest-dressed.

At that time, Edinburgh was run by the Progressives, a group of local businessmen. The Progressives described themselves, without any sense of irony, as a non-political right-wing party. The contradictions of that identity were becoming apparent and I had become a member of the small but growing Conservative group whose purpose in life was gradually to replace them.

Our leader was Brian Meek, physically unprepossessing but shrewd, intelligent and with a splendid wit. He once attacked the Liberals as always placing themselves in the centre for tactical reasons to try to attract votes from everyone, left or right. He remarked that if Christopher Columbus had been a Liberal he would have discovered the mid-Atlantic. I borrowed that remark when I attacked Nick Clegg during the debate on House of Lords reform over forty years later.

My maiden speech in the town council was as memorable as I could have wished, but not for the reasons I had intended. We were debating whether the town council should give a grant to the Brook Advisory Clinic, which gave advice on contraception to young girls in order to try to prevent unwanted pregnancies. In those days such a service was considerably more controversial than it is today.

There was a free vote with no whipping and I spoke in favour of the proposal for a grant. The next speaker was Councillor Mrs Robertson Murray, an elderly Progressive councillor with very traditional views.

'I have been shocked, Lord Provost, by the speech we have just heard from Councillor Rifkind,' she declared. Then she said, 'It is people like Councillor Rifkind who are responsible for the spread of venereal disease in the city.'

If that was not enough, she went on to add: 'I believe, Lord Provost, that if young girls want sexual experience, they should go to their family doctor.' At this, Brian Meek was heard to remark, 'So that's what they mean by being under your family doctor.'

Newington, being largely a well-off part of the city, did not put large demands on its councillors, but there were pockets of considerable poverty. This led to one memorable event.

In March 1971, Michael Ancram, who was active with the housing charity Shelter, informed me that the Prince of Wales would be visiting Edinburgh and had expressed a wish to see some examples of sub-standard housing that was still being lived in. He wanted the visit to be entirely private, without any press awareness, to ensure informality.

Michael asked me if I had any examples of such housing in my ward. I was at that time dealing with such a case. A Miss May Stoddart lived in 7 Blackwood Crescent. She used only one room of a three-room flat because of serious damp and other defects in the other two rooms. In her room there was no electricity, only a gas lamp. She slept, cooked, ate and lived in this one room.

She was seventy-two years old and had lived there since she was two. She had no telephone or television and because of a leg injury could hardly get around.

It was agreed that the prince would visit her, but I was asked not to tell her who was coming in case it leaked to the press. I complied and only told her that it was a VIP who would be coming. The day before, however, I was nervous that she might be in shock when the Prince of Wales suddenly appeared. I got permission to tell her who her visitor would be the night before the visit.

When I did, her reaction was not what I had expected. Instead of being either excited or overwhelmed, she merely remarked that the Queen Mother had visited her parents in the 1930s and that she would look forward to meeting the prince.

On 27 March, Michael and I met at Dalkeith with the Prince of Wales, his equerry, Nicholas Soames, and his detective. The visit went well; the prince chatted with Miss Stoddart for ten minutes and expressed incredulity and anger when told that the landlord had not made any improvements to the flat. Some months later I had the satisfaction of getting her rehoused.

One sequel was that Edith and I were invited by Michael's parents to Monteviot for the weekend, where the Prince of Wales was staying with them. Edith's first meeting with Lady Lothian was as productive as it was agreeable. Lady Lothian gave her a crash course in how to curtsy, to prepare her for being presented to the Prince of Wales that evening.

By 1972, my main political priority was to try to find a winnable parliamentary seat for the next general election, which had to be held by June 1975.

The result in Central Edinburgh had enhanced my reputation, my work on the town council had kept me in the public eye and I was recognised as a good public speaker. In April 1971, I was invited to propose the motion on social security at the Scottish Conservative Party conference that year, which introduced me to a much wider audience of party activists.

My first attempt almost succeeded. Michael Ancram and I both applied for the Conservative candidacy in the Borders constituency of Roxburgh, Selkirk and Peebles, where David Steel was the incumbent Liberal MP with only a 500 majority.

To my surprise, I got through to the final two, but on the night was defeated by Stuart Thom, whom I knew slightly. His father had played rugby for Scotland, which, in the Borders, gave him a strong advantage.

But I also received an unexpected letter from the local Conservative agent, Eric Birnie, after the selection. He expressed the view that there was very little between me and Stuart Thom but that a possible reason for my failing to get 'a few essential votes' was 'because of your very professional manner and they have had difficulties with this in the past'.

I have puzzled over that remark. I suspect that the urban advocate was thought not to be quite right for such a rural constituency. But as Stuart Thom ended up as a first-class Mayor of Wandsworth, he must have been fairly urban too.

One delightful sequel was that the chairman of the local

Conservatives, who had rejected me, was Russell Sanderson, who became my Minister of State at the Scottish Office when I was Secretary of State in the 1980s.

He was slightly discomfited when I reminded him of the first time we had met, but cheered up when I pointed out that David Steel's majority had shot up from 550 to 9,017 at the February 1974 general election and the Borders had done me a great favour by not selecting me.

I was equally unsuccessful with North Edinburgh, who interviewed me but, very sensibly, chose Alex Fletcher, who in due course became an impressive Industry Minister at the Scottish Office.

I then tried Bute and North Ayrshire, as well as Berwick-upon-Tweed and Tynemouth, south of the border, but they felt able to reject me without even the inconvenience of an interview.

South Edinburgh did not produce a vacancy at that time, as Michael Clark Hutchison wished to continue. There was considerable opposition to him, as he lived full time in London and was not very active. At what was intended to be a merely formal vote of the executive of the local Tories to reselect him, the vote was carried but only by a majority of one. I was relieved I had voted for him, as Edith and I were dining with Michael and his wife, Anne, as their guests at the New Club that night.

These setbacks, in the event, worked to my benefit. In the latter part of 1973, it was announced that the Edinburgh Pentlands MP, Norman Wylie, who was Lord Advocate for Scotland, the equivalent of the Attorney General in England, was to be appointed to the Court of Session Bench as a judge and would be leaving the House of Commons.

Pentlands had always returned a Conservative MP but was very marginal. In 1966, Norman Wylie held it with a majority of only forty-four votes. I was active in Pentlands Young Conservatives during that election and we had responsibility for the campaign in Gorgie Ward. When I received, as did others, a letter from the MP thanking us for our support, we felt that our efforts in Gorgie, strong

Labour ward though it was, must have garnered at least the forty-four Conservative votes that he needed to win. In 1970, his majority went up to over 3,000.

There was a proper selection process when Norman Wylie announced that he was standing down. As it was already 1973, many of the other credible Scottish potential candidates had already been selected for Labour-held seats and few from south of the border chose to apply.

My main opponent was my old colleague Victor MacColl. He was very able and older than me. He suffered, at the final selection meeting, however, from being a Glaswegian and sounding like one. I learned later that the constituency chairman, Keith Mitchell, had voted for him but not most of those present.

I could have lost support through being an advocate. The constituency would not have wanted another lawyer who would end up as a Law Officer and be unable to be very political. However, because I was a mere twenty-seven, that scenario was implausible and so my youth worked to my advantage.

So, too, was the fact that not only was I an Edinburgh man but our surname was already well known in part of the constituency thanks to my brother. Arnold was by then the local optician in Morningside. On one occasion during the forthcoming election, one of my canvassers asked a lady on the doorstep whether she would support Mr Rifkind. 'Oh yes,' she replied. 'I am very pleased with these spectacles. I will always support him.'

I was chosen on 17 December 1973 as the Conservative candidate for Pentlands. Because of the miners' strike and the Prime Minister's decision to call a sudden general election for February 1974, I remained the candidate for less than two months.

On 28 February 1974, Ted Heath lost the general election but I became a Member of Parliament, increasing the majority from 3,183 to 4,602. I remained the MP for Pentlands for the next twenty-three years.

CHAPTER 8

UP AND DOWN

'GOOD MORNING, MR Rifkind,' said the police officer at
the St Stephen's Entrance of the Houses of Parliament.
It was my first day as an MP and I was both aston-
ished and impressed. As a 27-year-old stripling, I had expected some
difficulty in proving to the police that the person seeking admission was actually a Member of Parliament. It appeared that this
was unnecessary. I was already famous in London, not just in my
constituency.

That, sadly, turned out not to be the case. It was standard practice
for the police officers who provided security at Westminster to obtain
photographs of all new MPs and memorise them in the interval
between polling day and the opening of the new parliament. They
liked to make us feel important.

Nowadays there is a full course of induction for new MPs. In 1974,
we were shown where to hang our raincoats, given a locker with a
key in a Commons corridor and largely left to fend for ourselves.
Within a day or so, I had a desk in a building across the road, near
College Green.

My Scottish Conservative colleagues were very welcoming but my most traumatic experience was the collective meeting all the new Tory MPs had with the Chief Whip, Humphrey Atkins.

He explained that each week we would receive the whip, which was a printed sheet outlining the parliamentary business. Each item would be underlined once, twice or three times.

One-line whips meant we could do what we liked. A two-line whip meant we were expected to be in the division lobby and vote with the party unless we were paired with a Labour MP who would also absent himself. A three-line whip meant the business was important, no pairing was allowed and we were expected to be in the division lobby even if our granny was being buried that day.

'Any questions?' said Humphrey genially. I then proceeded to do my best to terminate my political career just as it was beginning. I thanked the Chief Whip and, innocently, asked him what was the procedure if one was thinking of voting against the party on a three-line whip.

There was an ominous silence which seemed to last rather a long time but was probably only three seconds. The Chief Whip thanked me for my question and, expressionless, informed me that if I was thinking of doing that, the whips would appreciate it if I informed them in advance so they could 'persuade' me not to. I do not recall making any other contribution during that meeting.

An early decision was a choice of a secretary to handle my parliamentary and constituency correspondence. I was very lucky in being introduced to Yvonne Willway.

Yvonne had started working in Parliament around 1950 for Lord Simon, who, as Sir John Simon, had been a senior Cabinet minister in the 1930s. She had stopped working in Parliament when her husband, Michael, an army officer, had been posted overseas. She now wanted to return and had expressed an interest in finding a backbench MP, not too active, who would ensure that she had a reasonably quiet life.

Instead, she got me and we liked each other immediately. In those days all the secretaries worked together in the bowels of Westminster and a Member had to make an appointment to see his secretary. Yvonne would arrive with the morning mail and usually with the replies that she had already drafted for me to sign. It was very spoiling. She and Michael retired to Bath, where Edith and I would visit and, sometimes, stay with them.

Parliament was very different in the 1970s compared to today. In 1974, I used to take a short cut to the Commons by walking across St James's Park, entering the rear entrance to Downing Street, walking past the single police officer outside No. 10 and then exiting into Whitehall.

It is not just the terrorist threat that has made that impossible today. Even if the terrorists disappeared, we now have a 52-week-a-year tourist industry, with thousands of visitors from home and abroad crowding Parliament Square, Whitehall and the entrance to Downing Street every day.

Another extraordinary change has been the explosion of TV cameras and broadcasting journalists covering Parliament and the national political debate. In 1974, an MP's contact with the media at Westminster was with a relatively small coterie of reporters from national newspapers and a significant number representing the regional press.

In order to do my first BBC radio interview I had to go to a small 'hole in the wall' at College Green in which one found a modest recording studio. That constituted the BBC presence at Westminster. Today, at Millbank, a short walk from the Houses of Parliament, we have hundreds of TV and radio journalists, many working for 24-hour news channels.

But some things are the same today as they were in 1974. A prime example is an MP's maiden speech. I decided to go through the ordeal of mine as soon as possible and did so during the Foreign Affairs debate on the Queen's Speech on 19 March.

Such speeches are expected to be reasonably short and not

too controversial. I had no difficulty with that but I decided I would speak without any text, or even notes. That does not mean I was speaking off the cuff. Rather, there was what has been described as well-prepared spontaneity.

Speaking in that hallowed Chamber for the first time, I was tense rather than nervous. I began by remarking that I was one of seven MPs from Edinburgh which ensured 'that all the deadly sins were well represented on both sides of the Chamber'.

I paid tribute to my predecessor Norman Wylie and confessed that I, like him, was an advocate. I went on to sympathise, but not agree, with Edmund Burke, who believed that the country should be governed by law but not by lawyers.

I then turned to foreign affairs, emphasising the links that Britain and France still shared with Africa and Asia despite the end of Empire.

My main comments were to refer to my experience in Rhodesia and to plead, whatever the controversies, that there should not be a cultural or academic boycott of Rhodesia and South Africa. It was necessary to encourage, by contact and dialogue, those in southern Africa who were working for peaceful, but fundamental, change.

I concluded my speech by quoting Robert Louis Stevenson, a one-time resident of my constituency, who had commented that politics was the only profession for which no training was thought to be necessary. I thanked the House for listening to me and hoped that I had not confirmed Stevenson's observation.

It being a foreign affairs debate, the Chamber was not full, but I was very pleased to get several handwritten letters from MPs on both sides of the House complimenting me on what I had said.

I was particularly delighted by a note from Sir Alec Douglas-Home, who had been sitting on the front bench during the speech. He wrote: 'It was a treat to hear you this afternoon in sparkling form…' Such courtesies between Members, sometimes from opposite sides, show the House of Commons at its best.

Choosing to make my maiden speech in a foreign affairs debate probably influenced my future political advancement. At that stage in a parliament, the whips are trying to identify potential future ministers from the new intake of MPs and to identify their prime interests. Not only had my speech been well received but it ensured that I was not typecast as a Scottish MP with only Scottish interests.

I was not hyperactive during my first year in the House. Most weeks I was back in Edinburgh from Thursday evening until Monday, both for family reasons and to nurture my new constituency. I held regular surgeries and responded to all problems that were referred to me. In these days before email, the demand was limited and many constituents assumed that an MP represented his constituents in Parliament rather than Parliament in his constituency.

Pentlands was a good cross-section of Edinburgh if not of Scotland. It was named after the Pentland Hills that fringe the south-west of the city. Although part of the Hills came within my constituency boundary, no one lived there apart from the odd shepherd.

It was entirely suburban, almost evenly divided between comfortable owner-occupied homes in Colinton, Fairmilehead and the like, and the massive Wester Hailes council estate with other municipal housing in Oxgangs and Broomhouse.

Although it always returned a Tory MP until the Blair tsunami of 1997, it never was other than a marginal seat. My majority was always in the low thousands.

The term 'marginal' is, of course, always relative. I recall Lord Hailsham once describing a constituency with a Labour majority of 12,000 as marginal. When asked how he justified this, he replied that all seats were marginal. The only difference was the size of the margin. Given the overnight disappearance of dozens of 'safe' Labour seats in Scotland in the 2015 general election, one can see what he meant.

On one occasion when I was the speaker in an English constituency, the chairman got confused and introduced me as the Member of Parliament for 'Penthouse'. I rather wish I had been.

In my first year in the Commons I achieved a splendid victory on behalf of one of my constituents.

In his Budget in 1975, the Chancellor, Denis Healey, introduced a 25 per cent rate of VAT on luxury goods, compared to the normal 8 per cent at that time. Luxuries were to include all fur garments.

I received a letter from an Edinburgh sporran manufacturer who protested that fur-lined sporrans were not a luxury but a necessity for those who wore the kilt.

I wrote to the Chancellor and organised a Commons Motion, signed by eight Scottish Conservative MPs, demanding a rethink. I was quoted in the press saying that if fur hats were not to be subject to the luxury rate of VAT then nor should 'something covering an equally vital part of the anatomy'.

To my astonishment, and to my constituent's delight, the Treasury crumbled within days and it was announced that fur-lined sporrans were no longer to be deemed 'articles of clothing within the scope of the Finance Bill'. The Treasury's logic was dubious, but they had bent the knee to the House of Commons.

I did not go in for many populist initiatives in those years, but I could not resist another opportunity in April 1978. The Labour government had decided that May Day, the traditional highlight of the socialist year, would become a public holiday. Many Tories were incensed.

I had discovered, by chance, that 1 May was also the day, in 1707, when the Act of Union had come into effect and the United Kingdom was created. I persuaded the *Daily Express* to publish a centre-page article by me under the patriotic headline 'Haul down the Red Flag, Hoist the Union Jack'. I am sure Mrs Thatcher approved.

The day I was first elected to the House of Commons was, of course, the day that Ted Heath lost power. The election had taken place in the middle of the miners' strike and had brought Harold Wilson back to Downing Street.

But although Labour was the largest party, it did not have an overall majority and the country faced a second general election in October of that year. Labour was returned with more seats but still without an overall majority.

The general election had been held on 10 October. Throughout the campaign, Edith was in an advanced state of pregnancy with our first child. We had no idea whether it would be a boy or a girl. My mother asked Edith whether she minded what sex the child was. Edith, who had studied zoology at King's College and had worked with cattle and sheep, replied that she did not mind at all. She added, absent-mindedly, 'As long as it is normal and has four legs.' My mother looked somewhat alarmed.

My chairman declined to let Edith sit on the platform at the eve-of-poll public meeting, just in case.

In the event, she gave birth to our daughter Caroline two days after polling, on 12 October. Given the election background, some kind friend suggested that she had 'lost her deposit'. Edith replied that she had been determined to 'beat labour'.

I was thrilled but also furious. Although I had been at the hospital, the old-fashioned doctor refused to allow me to be present at the birth.

Caroline made a huge difference to our lives. We were, of course, ecstatic and had further good fortune when Hugo was born two and a half years later, on 30 March 1977.

On one occasion when we were pushing Hugo in his pram outside our house in Drummond Place, with Caroline sitting on the pram, we met a neighbour, Kathleen Macfie, who was a colourful, delightful lady of Irish extraction and a local councillor. 'Ah,' she said, looking at our children. 'These must be the fruits of your passion!'

The big winners in Scotland at the general election had been the Scottish Nationalists. They had won seven seats in February and increased that figure to eleven in October, with 30 per cent of the vote.

I held Pentlands but my majority fell from 4,602 to 1,257, mainly because of a surge in the SNP vote supplanting the Liberals in third place.

Ted Heath had now lost three of the last four elections. He had never had a deep following in the party and the Tories do not like losers. The right wing of the party, under the influence of Sir Keith Joseph in particular, thought that Heath was too fond of state intervention in industry. Keith, and many of his colleagues, had become enthusiastic about monetarism in economic policy.

Margaret Thatcher became their standard bearer and in February 1975 defeated Heath in the first ballot, which led to his immediate resignation as leader of the party.

I had voted for Heath. I did so partly out of a sense of loyalty. I admired his ability and integrity but, like many, found him chilly and difficult to engage with.

When Ted had visited Pentlands, Edith had asked me to introduce her to him. She found it so difficult to converse with him that she made it clear that I would not need to repeat the exercise.

A couple of weeks before the ballot, I needed to have a bottle of House of Commons whisky signed by him so that it could be used for fundraising in Pentlands. I asked his aide, Sir Timothy Kitson, if he could get Ted to sign the bottle for me. To my surprise, within minutes, I was invited to the leader's room so that I could be present for the signing.

I was flattered but also naïve. It took me longer than it should have done to realise that the invitation was not for the pleasure of my company but because Heath knew that every MP, however obscure, had a crucial vote in his re-election. We had a brief but inconsequential conversation.

When Heath resigned, I had to decide how to vote in the second ballot. Willie Whitelaw and Geoffrey Howe were amongst the new contenders.

Being a liberal Conservative, I felt they were closer to me politically than Margaret Thatcher. She also, at that time, was thought to have limited horizons. She had shown little interest in foreign affairs. Jonathan Aitken had memorably quipped that she thought that Sinai was the plural of sinus.

Nevertheless, it was she who got my vote, and she got it for good pragmatic reasons. During the previous months, when she had led for the opposition in attacking Denis Healey's Budget, I had been impressed by her fierce, pugnacious style. She had a vitality that was not apparent in Whitelaw and the other male candidates.

I was anxious to support a Leader of the Opposition who would, in due course, lead us to victory. I also rather liked the idea of the stuffy old Tory Party being the first in the Western world to be led by a woman. I recognised that choosing Mrs Thatcher would be a risk. But the Tories had chosen Disraeli, of all people, as their leader in the nineteenth century and that had turned out to be inspired.

Minutes after her victory had been announced, she passed me on her way to address a meeting off Westminster Hall. I congratulated her and she responded how exciting it was.

A couple of days later I was appointed an opposition frontbench spokesman on Scottish affairs. At twenty-eight, and having been in Parliament for less than a year, to be on the front bench was no mean achievement. To be honest, however, there were only sixteen Scottish Tory MPs so the field of choice was rather more limited than for her other appointments.

My new boss, the shadow Scottish Secretary, Alick Buchanan-Smith, invited me to speak on constitutional affairs and devolution, which delighted me as they were the top political issues in Scotland.

After the October 1974 election, I had made a speech very critical of the Conservative Party's lack of coherence, which, I argued, had contributed to our election defeats both in Scotland and in the country as a whole. Speaking to East Edinburgh Conservatives, I suggested that we had 'lost the battle of ideas' and had 'tried to be all things to all people'.

These, I said, were 'bitter days' for the Conservative Party, especially in Scotland, where we had fallen behind the SNP in the popular vote and were down to sixteen seats compared with thirty-six in 1955.

My comparison with our vote in 1955, when the Tories in Scotland also won 51 per cent of the vote, was actually misleading, although it is often made by others, too. While technically true, it was achieved because in that year there were no Nationalist candidates standing and the Liberals only had candidates in six out of the seventy-one Scottish seats. If a voter was not Labour he had to vote Tory. By the 1960s, the Liberals were recovering strongly and the SNP had become formidable challengers. That, however, did not alter the fact that we were declining and in a mess.

In November 1974, when I was still a backbencher, I made a further speech on the Nationalist challenge that we were facing. In suggesting what should be our response, I put forward an argument that has been at the core of my beliefs over the past forty years.

'One of the great tragedies of the debate about devolution', I said,

> is that it has been conducted on the basis of the need for devo-
> lution from England. The need, however, is not and never has
> been for devolution from England but from the over-centralised
> power and control of London and the south-east. The inter-
> ests of Scotland and Wales are similar to those of the north of
> England, the West Country and the Midlands.

It has taken almost half a century for that to become Tory policy. I pay tribute to the Chancellor, George Osborne, a northern MP, for spearheading, over the past two years, major transfers of power from Whitehall to Manchester, Birmingham, Leeds and other English cities. At long last, the people of the United Kingdom are enjoying local power and not just for the benefit of the Scots, Welsh and Northern Irish. The English, too, are now recipients – and not before time.

These reforms are not just welcome in themselves. The United Kingdom, in a classic British way, is now stumbling into a new constitutional, quasi-federal system that will, in my view, persuade most Scots to remain in political union with their fellow citizens in England and Wales for the foreseeable future.

Having become a frontbench spokesman in February 1975, I concentrated on trying to give substance to the commitment the Conservative Party had had to a Scottish Assembly since Ted Heath's Declaration of Perth.

One of our proposals that was radical at that time was that any Scottish Assembly should be elected by proportional representation. That was to ensure that no one party could make irreversible changes in Scotland unless they had the support of at least half the electorate.

I do not normally support PR but my attitude to electoral systems has always been pragmatic rather than theological. The SNP were the main enemy and, at that time, and for many years thereafter, it seemed inconceivable that they could win 50 per cent of the vote in a four-party system. That assumption no longer holds, but PR has undoubtedly been preferable at Holyrood, not least for the Scottish Conservatives.

Being an opposition spokesman gives one much more public profile and more media coverage. On one occasion, at that time, I overdid it. I launched an attack on the Scottish press and on *The Scotsman*, the *Daily Record* and the *Scottish Daily Express* in particular.

I said that these newspapers should hang their heads in shame for encouraging electors to vote SNP while 'piously reiterating their opposition to separatism'. That was strong stuff but I then went over the top and compared their attitude 'to those who encouraged support for the Nazis in Germany in order to get rid of the Communists and in the naïve belief that the monster they had created would conveniently disappear thereafter'.

While there may have been an arguable parallel, I soon realised that, as well as being grossly unfair, it is the height of foolishness for politicians to make any comparison with the Nazis when attacking political opponents in Britain. It is never justified and is deeply offensive.

The response from the press was fierce. The *Daily Record* was splendid. Its editorial attacked me in the most virulent terms under the heading 'A speech we don't report', which made them almost as unfair as I had been.

My debut at the dispatch box, which was winding up, for the opposition, the first day's debate on devolution, was far more successful. I spoke for around thirty minutes. The *Glasgow Herald* remarked that 'by common consent the most noteworthy contribution came from Malcolm Rifkind … He delivered a stirring defence of the union without any notes. Only Michael Foot could have equalled such assurance.'

The *Daily Telegraph* was kind enough to quote the finale of my speech, where I had teased the Nationalist MPs by quoting Robert Burns at them. He had written, in his address to the Dumfries Volunteers, 'Be Britain still to Britain true / Amang oursels united.' I was enjoying myself.

There was a Tory commitment to a Scottish Assembly but it was only skin deep and by late 1976 we were in crisis. The government had introduced its Bill to create a Scottish Assembly. The opposition had to decide its response and the crunch question was how we would vote on the Second Reading of the Bill, which is normally considered a vote on the principle of what is being proposed.

Alick Buchanan-Smith and two thirds of the Scottish Tory MPs felt that we should vote in favour reflecting our support for an assembly. We should then try to improve the Bill and, if we failed, it might be acceptable to vote against at Third Reading.

The overwhelming majority of the parliamentary party, led by Willie Whitelaw, the deputy leader, did not support this view and wanted a three-line whip against the Bill throughout.

Not being in the shadow Cabinet, I wrote to Margaret Thatcher supporting Alick. She sent me a handwritten reply, which I still have.

Although not committing herself as to how we would vote, she wrote, 'We are committed to an Assembly and there will be an Assembly.'

I believe that she meant it at the time. The Lady, however, was for turning on this issue. She had no option given the strength of feeling in the Conservative Party. I wrote in a private paper at the time that since Heath's Declaration of Perth eight years earlier, we had been 'living a half-truth' committed to an assembly 'while the bulk of the UK party had been against it'. Once the party in England had begun to consider the issue, 'their reaction had ranged from the hostile to the very hostile'.

The Bill had been published on 30 November, St Andrew's Day, and Second Reading was to be on 16 December. During the intervening period there was a series of meetings between Francis Pym, who had responsibility in the shadow Cabinet for devolution, and the sixteen Scottish Tory MPs. Ten of the Scots Tories were pro-devolution, six were against.

Pym offered a reasoned amendment that we could all unite around if we then promised to vote against the Second Reading once the amendment had been defeated. We suggested, instead, that there should be a free vote so that all MPs could vote according to their personal beliefs.

Alick told me that he had little support in the shadow Cabinet, with only Ian Gilmour, Jim Prior and Norman St John Stevas on side and Geoffrey Howe trying to be helpful.

At a later meeting with the Chief Whip we were told that the shadow Cabinet had decided that all that was on offer to us was a reasoned amendment followed by a three-line whip against the Second Reading.

I suggested that a reasoned amendment might be acceptable if Margaret was prepared to say from the dispatch box that a Tory government would legislate for a directly elected assembly on the lines of the reasoned amendment if we came to power before an assembly had been created.

Francis Pym and the Chief Whip, Humphrey Atkins, said she couldn't do that because although she was sincere she couldn't deliver the goods. I, and others, replied that that was why we couldn't support a reasoned amendment. It didn't carry credibility.

That evening, it was announced that the opposition would vote against the Bill. Seven of us who had frontbench responsibilities met in Alick's room at 1 a.m. We all agreed that we were prepared to resign if necessary.

We met again the following morning and were told that the party in Scotland was very supportive but did not want us to resign. The possibility of abstention was raised. I argued strongly in favour as this would maintain our position of principle while reducing the damage that would be caused to the party in Scotland by mass resignations. There was support for this view and Alick agreed we should offer it to the Chief Whip.

We discussed with Humphrey Atkins whether we would be permitted to abstain on Second Reading as a way out of the crisis. He was impressed by our solidarity and determination not to vote against the Bill. A meeting was arranged with Margaret Thatcher for just after noon.

When we met, Alick presented to Margaret our joint position. In the private paper I wrote immediately after these events, I quoted her response as follows:

> Margaret stated categorically that she was not prepared to contemplate our mass resignations and that some compromise must be found ... She stressed that she still felt committed to a directly elected Scottish Assembly ... She remarked, laughingly, that if we had to resign she would appoint us again the following day if necessary!

She thought that a compromise should be possible and she recalled that Iain Macleod was not required to resign from the front bench even after he had refused to support his colleagues and vote against the Commonwealth Immigrants Act.

After this meeting I wrote that 'we felt that we had lost the battle but won the war'. I did, however, in the same paragraph, say: 'At the time of writing this might be premature and optimistic.'

Premature it turned out to be. The shadow Cabinet decided that abstention was unacceptable. In one sense they were right, at least as regards Alick and me. It is one thing to be allowed to abstain on an issue for which you have no official responsibility. But Alick and I could hardly have continued as the Conservative spokesmen on devolution after we had refused to follow the party line on just that subject.

On the evening of 8 December, Alick and I resigned. When I saw Margaret, to my surprise she offered me the opportunity to abstain and remain on the front bench as I was not a member of the shadow Cabinet. It was generous of her but I could not agree.

I issued a statement saying that the decision to vote against the Bill on Second Reading was 'a serious and unfortunate mistake'. Without referring to Margaret's offer to me to abstain and stay, I said that while I was not a member of the shadow Cabinet and not subject to its collective responsibility, I did not feel it would be 'appropriate' for me to stay a frontbench spokesman on Scottish affairs at that time.

My local party in Pentlands were very supportive and the Scottish press, not surprisingly, were very complimentary. A friend reminded me at the time of a comment attributed to Churchill that resignation was like adultery: the first time you do it is the most difficult. I can say without any fear of contradiction that I have no idea whether the second half of that comparison is true.

Despite the trauma of resignation, I had had an extraordinary debut in politics at the national level. The *Financial Times*, in a profile, commented on the contribution I had made as devolution spokesman. They concluded that 'without Rifkind's persuasive pressure the party would have been less likely to make even the minimal concessions it now offers to soothe the Scottish malaise'.

I had joined the front bench when I was twenty-eight. Now, at the grand old age of thirty, I had returned to the back benches. I could 'spend more time with my family', as the saying goes, especially my two-year-old daughter. It was quite a roller coaster.

Returning to the back benches also meant I could develop other parliamentary interests, especially as regards foreign policy. I became Joint Secretary of the influential Conservative backbench Foreign Affairs Committee and was appointed to the Select Committee on Overseas Development.

In January 1977, I received an unexpected invitation from the United States ambassador to visit America as a guest of the US government.

The embassy tried to identify young British MPs who might one day be senior ministers. The visit to the US was to enable us to get to know not just Washington and New York but the rest of that remarkable country as well.

They suggested that I chose a subject of interest to me and they would then construct a programme of visits around that. I must confess that I did exactly the opposite. I decided which parts of the States I wished to see and then chose a subject that would get me there.

This tactic worked. By choosing state–federal relations as my subject, which fitted in with my Scottish devolution background, they agreed that I would visit New York, Washington, New Orleans, Houston, San Francisco and Seattle. Getting to California, I was able to stop off in Las Vegas and see the Grand Canyon.

I travelled by myself. What was most memorable was not the official meetings and discussions during the day but the evening entertainment.

Rather than official dinners, they had arranged for ordinary American families to invite me to their homes for dinner around the family table. It was not only a relaxing end to the day but enabled me to better understand the American people.

Americans are as sophisticated and knowledgeable as anyone but sometimes, outside Washington, I have been disturbed by a limited awareness of what is happening in other parts of the world.

One of my meetings was with a speechwriter to a state governor. He asked me when the British were going to leave Ireland. I said that if the people of Ulster wanted us to leave we would. He said he wasn't just talking about Ulster but about Ireland as a whole.

I asked him if he was aware that most of Ireland was an independent republic. It turned out that he had not realised that. It was disturbing, to say the least, that he had such strong opinions on Ireland combined with profound ignorance of the political reality.

I have mentioned that I travelled to California via Las Vegas. In fact, I only changed planes at the airport and never went downtown. My visit was memorable, however, as I am one of the few who have left Las Vegas wealthier than when they arrived.

The airport was packed with one-arm bandits. When I found I had won a silver dollar on one of them I decided to quit while I was ahead and have been able to claim gambling expertise ever since.

1977 was memorable as our son Hugo was born in March of that year. I was in London when Edith phoned me to say she was being taken into hospital. It was too late for me to get a plane that evening so I said I would fly up to Edinburgh first thing the following morning. In the middle of the night Edith phoned me to say I need not rush. Hugo had arrived.

This addition to our family led to us moving home. We left Edinburgh's Georgian New Town for Duddingston Village, which is on the edge of Holyrood Park and which has retained a village atmosphere despite being within walking distance of Edinburgh's city centre. We lived there for twenty-one years.

In April 1975, I had revisited Rhodesia and South Africa with Richard Luce. Richard and his wife, Rose, have been amongst our closest friends for over forty years. I had first met Richard, the MP for Shoreham, the year before, when, accompanied by our wives, we had attended a conference on Africa with American colleagues at the Tides Inn, Virginia.

Richard and I would be ministerial colleagues in the Foreign Office in later years. In 1982, he resigned together with Lord Carrington over the Falklands War. After Richard had been completely exonerated by the Franks Commission, the Prime Minister showed her confidence in him by reappointing him to his old job.

Thereafter he had an extraordinarily varied career. He was a successful Minister of the Arts, and then left politics and became Principal and Vice-Chancellor of Buckingham University. As Foreign Secretary, I persuaded him to become Governor of Gibraltar. Just as he was preparing for retirement, the Queen invited him to become Lord Chamberlain. His public service has been recognised by the Order of the Garter.

On arriving in Rhodesia, we visited my old university campus. On our way to lunch with Rhodesian Front MPs, we saw Ian Smith, the Prime Minister, leaving his office. This was slightly surprising as we had been told that he wasn't available as he was out of town. I am sure my unhelpful political activism when I had lived in Rhodesia was the real reason he would not see us. The only time I ever met him was many years later when we were both changing planes at some airport in the United States and had an amicable exchange of views.

That afternoon we did have a meeting with the Foreign Minister, P. K. van der Byl. He was the last person we should have been allowed to meet if the Rhodesians wanted us to be more sympathetic to their point of view.

I wrote at the time that he was 'the complete stereotype of what the left believe the white Rhodesian to be ... He referred to Africans as having only recently come down from the trees and stopped brushing with the elephants.'

As we were leaving his office, he asked us whether we could do him a favour. He had been invited to a regimental reunion in London. Could we help get him permission to get entry to the United Kingdom? Sadly, we could not assist.

My views on Rhodesia remained robust. In September 1978, there was speculation that Ian Smith might invite the British to return to Rhodesia to supervise a transition to majority rule. I wrote to *The Times* suggesting that such a return should not await an invitation but be a Western initiative with, if necessary, a military component, that would remove the Smith regime, end economic sanctions and initiate political reform. In saying this, I clashed with Enoch Powell, who had called for Britain to reject any continuing responsibility for Rhodesia's future.

My travels were not limited to southern Africa. I joined a delegation visiting Western Sahara, a huge area annexed by Morocco when the Spanish left.

With the Overseas Select Committee, I spent time in Nigeria and the Ivory Coast, and visited Somalia in 1978, a time when it had internal tranquillity albeit under the despotism of President Siad Barre.

In 1976, I made my first visit to the Communist world as part of a parliamentary delegation to Czechoslovakia. Since the crushing of the Prague Spring by the Soviet Union in 1968, Czechoslovakia had had a hardline government. While we were well received and enjoyed the beauties of Prague, it was depressing to see such a lack of basic freedoms in the heart of Europe.

The most memorable overseas visit was to Fidel Castro's Cuba in January 1979. My companions were Richard Luce and two left-wing Labour MPs, Stan Newens and Martin Flannery. We were guests of the Cuban government.

We were in Cuba for a week. Our hotel in Havana had once been the Hilton and was now the Habana Libre.

Richard and I were surprised to find we were expected to share a bedroom, as were our Labour colleagues. We assumed this was because the rooms were bugged and they wished to hear our conversations. Richard and I decided to give them more than they would have expected.

'What do you think of Cuban democracy?' I would ask, sufficiently loudly to ensure they could hear. 'Not much,' Richard would reply. It wasn't very cerebral but I hope the Cubans were satisfied.

I would be fascinated to know what our left-wing Labour colleagues were saying to each other.

One evening we were invited to the official reception for Kurt Waldheim, the United Nations Secretary-General. We were introduced to Fidel Castro and his senior colleagues. He informed Richard and me that he had never before met British Conservatives but considered us preferable to the American variety.

On the following day we had a meeting with Castro at his office in the Central Committee building. His desk had a large cigar container and what looked like a jar of wrapped sweets.

Castro was in battle fatigues but they were very well pressed and well cut. His army boots were well polished and he smoked a large cigar. We were with him for just under two hours. He was polite and thoughtful throughout, gesturing with his hands though not excessively. The discussion ranged from the Cuban military presence in Angola to human rights and to South Africa.

The following day, we travelled out of Havana along the coast. Over lunch with local dignitaries, we had a conversation that somewhat disconcerted our Labour colleagues. We were discussing housing and mentioned that a future Conservative government would allow council tenants to buy their homes. It turned out that there already was such a policy in Cuba, which was very popular. Our Labour colleagues remained silent, if thoughtful, during this part of the conversation.

These overseas visits can be seen as agreeable perks that go with being a Member of Parliament. In my own case, they had an additional benefit. They gave me first-hand experience of countries, and their governments, in Eastern Europe and Latin America as well as in Africa.

A lot can be read from books or in official papers. There is no substitute, however, for spending time in other countries and meeting foreign leaders on their home ground.

Throughout this parliament, the Labour government, led by Harold Wilson and then James Callaghan, stumbled from crisis to crisis, ending with the Winter of Discontent, which destroyed their claim of being uniquely able to deliver industrial peace.

Scotland, which had taken up so much of my energy in the earlier part of the parliament, helped bring the government to a sticky end. On 1 March, there was the promised referendum on whether the Scottish Assembly should be established.

The form of devolution that Parliament had approved was not to my liking, as it proposed a Scottish executive as well as an assembly with greater powers than I would have preferred. Nevertheless, I voted Yes while Edith voted No. In this respect we were typical of many Scottish families.

Although there was a small majority for the Yes side, it did not meet the minimum 40 per cent requirement that the Act required, and the government, quite properly, refused to set up the assembly.

This led to a motion of no confidence in the government, which was to be held on 28 March. For once the Tories, the Liberals and the SNP all decided to vote against the government.

The Chamber was packed for the debate and there were some memorable flights of oratory. The Prime Minister, James Callaghan, was scornful at the SNP decision to vote with the Tories. He remarked that 'it is the first time in recorded history that turkeys have been known to vote for an early Christmas'. He was very perceptive. The Nationalists lost all but two of their seats at the general election.

Michael Foot was equally eloquent. Closing the debate, he attacked David Steel, the Liberal leader, describing him as having 'passed from rising hope to elder statesman without any intervening period'.

We all knew that the government could win or lose by as little as one vote. They made strenuous efforts to persuade Irish Nationalists to support them.

One independent Republican, Frank Maguire, who rarely attended Parliament, announced that he was coming. When he arrived, a journalist asked him how he would vote and Maguire replied that he had decided to abstain. When asked why he was bothering to come if he was not going to vote, he responded that it was such an important occasion that he had decided he should abstain in person.

The tension in the Chamber as the voting took place at 10 p.m. was more tangible than I have ever experienced. As we waited for the vote to be announced, a Labour whip appeared from behind the Speaker's Chair smiling and with his thumb up. The Labour MPs cheered but within a few seconds it turned out that their joy was misplaced. The government had been defeated by one vote, by 311 to 310.

The government immediately resigned, Margaret Thatcher won the general election and the rest, as they say, is history.

CHAPTER 9

CLIMBING THE GREASY POLE

THE WEEKEND AFTER a general election is a tense experience for the Member of Parliament whose party has been victorious and whose leader is safely ensconced in Downing Street. Each time the telephone rings he picks up the receiver wondering if it is a summons to a post in the new government.

As often as not it is some amiable relative or friend wishing to chat and assuming that, with the election safely behind him, the MP will have nothing else on his mind. Instead, the caller finds someone who wants to end the conversation as quickly as possible in order that the line can remain open for the only telephone conversation in which he is really interested.

I was by no means certain that I would receive such a call. If it came I assumed it would be for a post in the Scottish Office. But I was the youngest of the Scottish MPs and I had committed the cardinal sin of resigning from Mrs Thatcher's frontbench team and voting against the party whip in opposition. Although I had been in good company at that time, I had no knowledge as to whether the new Prime Minister had a forgiving nature.

In my case, the telephone rang five times that Sunday before, around 6 p.m., I found the Chief Whip at the other end of the receiver informing me that the Prime Minister would like me to be an Under-Secretary of State at the Scottish Office. I did not think it would be convincing to suggest that I wanted time to think about it and, in any event, if I had, she might have changed her mind. I accepted on the spot.

Little did I know that I was to remain a minister, climbing the greasy pole, for the next eighteen years without a break. It was probably just as well that I didn't know and even better that Edith didn't.

We assumed that I would be in the government for the whole of that parliament. If we were lucky there would be a second term and I might remain a minister for eight to ten years before the Labour Party had their turn.

It turned out that Labour was unelectable for four general elections in a row. By 1997, Edith was warning that if we won a fifth term she would ask for a recount.

Eighteen years is probably too long for one government to be in power in a democracy. But this long spate of electoral success also had family implications. When I became a minister, our daughter, Caroline, was four years old and our son, Hugo, was two. When I ceased to be a minister, Caroline was twenty-two and her brother was nineteen. For their whole childhood their father was a minister and for eleven of these years I was in the Cabinet, with the added public exposure that that created. For the final two years, as Foreign Secretary, I had armed bodyguards who accompanied us even when we had a family holiday in Austria.

This could have been ruinous both for my marriage and to any prospect of a normal childhood for our children. If it has turned out that Edith and I remained happily married and our daughter and son have become delightful and well-adjusted adults and parents, that has been through a mixture of good fortune and circumstance.

A wise decision was to keep our home in Edinburgh and not move to London. This enabled our children to see their cousins, to remain close to their friends and to enjoy less media intrusion in Edinburgh than might have been possible in London.

We were also fortunate that for around eight of those eighteen years I was Secretary of State for Scotland or a junior minister in the Scottish Office. That enabled me, most weeks, to be at home in Edinburgh from Friday morning until Monday evening, only being at Westminster from Tuesday until Thursday.

An added bonus was that as I had an Edinburgh constituency and we lived only twenty minutes by car from the Scottish Office, I spent more time at home, and less time travelling, than most of my Scottish colleagues. My successor, Ian Lang, for example, lived in Ayrshire, had his constituency in Galloway, in south-west Scotland, and had to commute each week to both Edinburgh and London. He deserved much more sympathy than I did.

By the time I became Defence and, then, Foreign Secretary, Caroline was eighteen and at Durham University and Hugo, then fifteen, was at boarding school at Loretto. As Loretto was near our home, I was able to pick him up from school every Sunday morning and he would spend the day at home before I drove him back in the evening.

All these considerations helped, but I must pay special tribute to Edith for juggling so successfully, throughout those long years, the varying responsibilities of being a wife and a mother and continuing, on a part time basis, her professional career. The more I think about it, the more I appreciate how fortunate our children and I were.

Our family life would, of course, have been different and more conventional if I had chosen another occupation. But, knowing myself, it is at least uncertain that I would have spent a huge amount of time either cheering from the touch line at my children's schools or being the hands-on, modern father that my grandchildren and their friends take for granted.

While Caroline and Hugo saw less of me than might otherwise

have been the case, that would have been as true if I had been in the Merchant Navy, in the armed forces or a business executive in some global company.

I think Caroline and Hugo did get what children most need: the sense of security that goes with a loving environment, parents who stick together through thick and thin, and a comfortable standard of living. They and Edith will give their own verdicts, which I hope are not too different from mine.

The day after my appointment, the well-oiled civil service machine quickly moved into action. My new private secretary rang the following day to arrange my first ministerial visit to the Scottish Office. On the Tuesday morning, a sleek, black government car arrived at my front door and, feeling acutely self-conscious and a slight fraud, I stepped in to be driven from my home in Duddingston Village, through Holyrood Park and thence to the concrete and glass mausoleum which was New St Andrew's House, the headquarters of the Scottish Office.

From that first journey I never ceased to be amazed that the entrance to the seat of government in Scotland was, at that time, through a narrow back street squeezed between the rear of a bus station on one side and the rear of the St James shopping centre on the other. The architect must have had a grudge against ministers and civil servants. That, at least, is the only charitable explanation I can think of. When I was Secretary of State for Scotland, I insisted on moving our offices back to Old St Andrew's House, an imposing building at the foot of the Calton Hill.

The first few weeks for a new minister are stimulating but nerve-racking. If one has served in a previous government, one at least knows what to expect and can concentrate, right away, on the policy issues that are one's responsibility. For virgin ministers like myself, there were more fundamental issues to be resolved.

My first misunderstanding arose when my private secretary asked me, in a rather embarrassed fashion, if I could give him £3. Thinking that he must be short and that civil service pay was clearly inadequate, I made some frivolous remark only to find out that the money was not for his own use but to pay for my coffee and biscuits. I hasten to add that this was not some new manifestation of the Thatcher government but was a sacred rule handed down from one government to another. I was solemnly informed that if I offered coffee to visitors who came to see me on official business, that was paid for by Her Majesty's Government. If I drank it in splendid isolation, however, I picked up the bill. If only Gladstone could have seen us, his heart would have swollen with pride.

The most difficult task of the first few days was to get the hierarchy of the civil service right. There is no obvious reason why one should have known that an under-secretary was senior to an assistant secretary or that the First Division Association was the trade union of the top civil servants rather than something to do with the football league.

Nor was it easy, at first, for me to get used to calling the Permanent Secretary, with thirty years' experience, by his first name while he would never dream of calling me anything but 'Minister'. What would have been strange for any raw new minister was exacerbated by the fact that I was a mere stripling of thirty-two.

Tony Blair famously had the same problem when, on his first day at 10 Downing Street, he invited the Cabinet Secretary to call him Tony and received the withering reply, 'No, that would not be appropriate, Prime Minister.'

On arrival at the Scottish Office, I was presented with a full brief which not only explained all the work of the department, but also made meticulous reference to our election manifesto commitments and the detailed ways in which many of them could be implemented. As there was no means by which these substantial briefs could have been prepared in the one working day which had elapsed since the general election results, I assumed that the civil service had been sensible enough to anticipate a Conservative victory and to prepare accordingly. It was with some disappointment that I subsequently discovered that the period of the general election campaign had been used to prepare two different briefs: one for a returning Labour government and the other for a Conservative administration. The civil servants were neutral after all.

Or were they? I subsequently learnt that when one of the junior ministers in the last Labour government first arrived at the Scottish Office, he was taken by a senior civil servant for a drink in a local pub. No such privilege was accorded to me or my colleagues and I can only assume that we appeared more intimidating than we felt.

The first few weeks are a crucial testing period for a new minister and for his civil servants. The minister, for his part, is anxious to come to an early view on the ability and reliability of those who are to advise him.

But the minister's requirements of his senior officials are not merely competence and intelligence. What he needs from them are political instincts, a nose for trouble and a willingness to subordinate their personal preferences as to policy to the aspirations and priorities of the government. A senior civil servant's need for political instincts is not in conflict with the political neutrality that is part of his professional creed. That neutrality requires him to ignore his own personal political prejudices when advising a minister and implementing policy. Without political instincts, however, he will be entirely unable to anticipate whether a particular option or possible initiative is politically acceptable to the minister.

I have mentioned the qualities that a minister tries to discern in his civil servants. It is, perhaps, not for me to speculate as to what they look for in ministers, but I suspect it is as follows.

Firstly, they want to know if the minister has the brains to understand what the civil servants are telling him in their beautifully presented papers. Ministers come in all shapes and sizes and are appointed for reasons not always directly related to their capacity to run a ministry. Their intelligence and ability are thus crucial considerations and not necessarily to be taken for granted.

Secondly, the civil servants want to know whether a minister's decisions will be taken on the basis of his instincts, his emotions, his reason, all three of them, or some combination thereof. Until that can be determined, they cannot judge whether a minister's first response to a departmental proposal is likely to be his last word on the subject or merely a prelude to discussion.

Finally, in the case of junior ministers, the civil servants want to assess the extent to which the junior minister enjoys the confidence of his Secretary of State or whether he is merely a transit lounge that must be passed through before the actual decision is taken on any matter of substance by the Secretary of State himself. If the Secretary of State is seen to prefer the judgement of the junior minister to that of the department, the message is soon taken and appeals to the Secretary of State become relatively infrequent.

The first few weeks will therefore be of considerable importance in establishing, for good or ill, the long-term relationship between a minister and his civil servants. For both, it is an education and an enlightenment as well as a dispeller of irrational prejudices.

A crucial member of the minister's staff is, of course, his private secretary. He or she is usually a young civil servant, considered by their superiors to be a potential high-flier, and assigned to the minister's private office to be initiated into the mysteries of ministerial life for one or two years before being thrust back to the anonymity of the department whence they came.

His function while in the ministerial penthouse suite is to be a cross between an éminence grise and a glorified ministerial luggage carrier. Like the Permanent Secretary, he has access to the minister whenever he feels like it and can deny access to almost whomsoever he wishes. Unlike the Permanent Secretary, however, he has only a brief experience of this civil service Valhalla and has to bear his own career prospects in mind whenever he contemplates telling permanent, deputy and assistant secretaries where to get off.

The formal duties of the private secretary are to look after the minister's engagements, ensure that there is a regular flow of minutes and correspondence to him for decision, and to ensure that these decisions are processed to the relevant officials for implementation. His informal responsibilities are to tell the minister what is really going on in the department and to warn his civil service colleagues whenever there is about to be a ministerial earthquake.

Ministers, of course, often use their private secretaries as sounding boards for new ideas or possible initiatives. If you do come up with what you think is a brilliant idea, your private secretary is naturally too polite and well-trained to tell you that it is the most hare-brained suggestion that he has heard since he joined the civil service. He will, however, if he is any good, be able to advise the likely departmental reaction and point to obvious problems (or advantages) associated with the proposal.

One of my best private secretaries was Jim Gallagher, who was in charge of my private office when I was Secretary of State for Scotland. The private secretary is at his best when, having read some ministerial decision scribbled at haste on top of a minute, he enquires, as did Jim, without the slightest hint of either sarcasm or irony, whether you really meant to say that. It is a brave minister who will stoutly reply that he did. Most will take the hint and be grateful for the advice.

The alternative is to let your proposal go to the department for comment and receive, in return, a ten-page closely typed minute tearing your proposal to shreds in the polite but unforgettable style that is peculiar to the civil service. This style is one that never dreams of using one word when ten will do. Nor will the minister's proposal be explicitly rejected. Indeed, it might actually be supported but with conditions and qualifications that ensure its early demise. I remember on one occasion being told that my suggestion was excellent but that the best way forward was the appointment of a committee to consider it, an extensive correspondence with other departments and a possible consultative document at the end. Such a procedure might have been justified if I had been proposing to abolish the Scottish

Office, but as my suggestion was rather more modest it did seem like the official playing for time.

Like most of my parliamentary and ministerial colleagues, I was a devoted fan of *Yes Minister*. One is often asked whether it was pure comedy or whether there was some truth in it. It was, of course, a splendid fantasy but, sometimes, truth is stranger than fiction. I give two examples of what I mean from my first ministerial years in the Scottish Office.

One day I received a letter from the Labour MP for Caithness and Sutherland, Bob Maclennan, requesting a speed limit in the village of Helmsdale in his constituency. Like all such correspondence, it was sent to the officials to consider and make a recommendation to the minister together with a draft reply that he might wish to send to the MP.

The recommendation that I got in due course urged strongly against accepting the request and attached a two-page draft reply that they wished me to send to the MP, explaining in detail why a speed limit in Helmsdale was neither necessary nor desirable.

They added, however, that the Chief Constable disagreed with them and if I preferred his reasoning they had attached an alternative two-page reply that I might wish to send, explaining why I was convinced by the MP's arguments and happy to accept them.

After due consideration, I decided that I agreed with the Chief Constable and minuted accordingly. The draft reply was taken away to be typed on proper ministerial writing paper for me to sign. It came back with several other ministerial replies, the contents of which I had already approved, so there was no need for me to read them again before signing.

Two days later, my private secretary came in to see me, looking rather agitated. He asked me to remind him what my decision had been on the Helmsdale speed limit and I told him I had agreed with the Chief Constable.

When I asked him whether they had sent the MP the right letter, he reassured me that they had. He then added, however, that they had sent the other one as well. The MP had received two ministerial replies from the same minister, one explaining at length why I agreed with him and the other explaining, at equal length, why I disagreed with him.

Aghast, I told him to get in touch with the MP's office right away to try to recover the offending letter. As he was a Labour MP, I had visions of both my letters adorning the front pages of every newspaper in the land the following day.

By extraordinary good luck, the MP was abroad; his secretary had been puzzled but was accommodating and the offending letter was in the shredder in no time. It turned out that although both letters had been sent, I had only signed one of them, but that would not have prevented the press and the opposition having enormous fun at my expense.

Another, equally true, tale was the letter I received from someone I slightly knew who had been a fellow student at Edinburgh University. At that time he had been Steven. The letter explained that he was now Alexandra.

She wanted a new birth certificate that would record her as female, as she might wish to get married in the near future and would not be able to if her birth certificate recorded her as a male.

I had some sympathy with her predicament and asked for advice. My officials said she could not get a new birth certificate unless the original one had recorded her as male in error. If it had been correct but she had had a sex change, that was her problem.

That seemed a bit bureaucratic and I was tempted to overrule them. I asked if anyone would be entitled to object if we did what she requested. They replied, to my astonishment, that the Treasury would object.

Calling in the Treasury in aid is usually the last argument that the civil service use when the minister is determined to reject their advice. Sorry, Minister, the Treasury won't let us.

What on earth has granting a new birth certificate got to do with the Treasury, I asked. They replied that it was the public expenditure implications. When I expressed scepticism that one new birth certificate would burden the taxpayer, they pointed out that the Treasury would be concerned because of the five-year difference in the pension age that then existed between men and women.

I asked them whether they seriously thought that if I granted this request thousands of men would seek sex changes in order to get their pensions five years earlier, but they still maintained the Treasury would be concerned.

Seeing that I was still unconvinced, the official decided to be conciliatory. 'You have told us, Minister,' he said, 'that this woman, who used to be a man, might wish to marry a man. If by any chance the man she might wish to marry used to be a woman and, also, had had a sex change, but in the opposite direction, they could both use their original birth certificates.' At this stage I gave up the unequal struggle.

Being a Parliamentary Under-Secretary, the lowest level of ministerial life, was an achievement I could be proud of, but, in truth, it usually involved little power and responsibility, with all real decisions being taken by the Secretary of State or, at least, the Minister of State.

In these pre-devolution days, the Scottish Office was a major exception. The Scottish Secretary had responsibility for Education, Health, Housing, Transport, Agriculture and Fisheries, Law and Order, and the Environment. Although Scotland was small in comparison to England, there was no way the Secretary of State could carry such a burden without using all his junior ministers, regardless of their seniority, for most of the day-to-day decision making.

In addition, I was fortunate in having George Younger as my Secretary of State. George had a relaxed manner, though he exercised real control over the strategic direction of the department. He won Margaret Thatcher's trust and usually got his way in Cabinet battles and he was determined to be kept informed as to all that was being done in his name. But he had no desire to micro-manage and all four of his junior ministers enjoyed real responsibility as a consequence.

He also decided that we should not, as in the past, be referred to simply as Parliamentary Under-Secretaries of State but should be given titles that described our actual remit.

I became the Minister for Home Affairs and the Environment. I was responsible for Police, Prisons, Housing, Transport and the Environment.

George also asked me to work with him on constitutional issues. That led to my first ministerial speech in the House of Commons, on 20 June 1979, a month after the general election.

The occasion was the repeal of the Scotland Act, which had provided for the establishment of a Scottish Assembly. The referendum having failed to deliver the necessary level of support from the Scottish electorate, it was sensible to repeal the legislation, which no longer served any useful purpose.

George, as Secretary of State, was to open the debate. He asked me whether I would be willing to wind up for the government. He was concerned that as I had voted Yes in the referendum I might be embarrassed by taking such a prominent part in the repeal of the Act and said he would quite understand if I preferred not to be the final speaker. I made clear that I had no such qualms.

Although I had supported the creation of an assembly, I recognised that there was, at that time, little or no support for devolution in England and Wales. I had, therefore, voted for the amendment that had required the Yes votes to be at least 40 per cent of the Scottish electorate if they were going to prevail.

I had made it clear that a tiny majority with a low turnout of voters would be insufficient to justify such a radical constitutional change which had strong opposition in the rest of the United Kingdom. In the event, 32 per cent had voted Yes, 31 per cent had voted No and 37 per cent had not bothered to vote or had deliberately abstained.

The MPs on both sides were on a three-line whip and the House was full when I stood up, at 9.56 p.m., to speak from the government dispatch box.

I was tense rather than nervous, as I always was when making an important speech. I had no written text but I had given careful thought to what I was going to say and had in my mind a clear structure for my speech.

But the House of Commons expects speakers and, especially, the minister winding up the debate to spend part of their time responding to those who have spoken before them.

In my case, I had an additional challenge. Winding up for the opposition was Michael Foot, the shadow Leader of the House and one of the most effective orators of his day.

As I had expected, Foot could not resist drawing attention to the fact that the minister calling for the repeal of the Act had voted for it and had, indeed, resigned from the opposition front bench in order to do so.

Foot's oratory, as on most occasions, had an unusual style as well as being very effective. He always spoke with power and passion but quite often his pauses for impact owed more to his breathing than to his syntax. That evening was no exception.

He declared:

> The minister who will wind up on behalf of the government did not need to be swung by oratory. He was there already ... All he will have to do when he speaks at the dispatch box tonight is to defend his principles. I hope that he will not find that too much of a strain so early on in his office.

It was good, legitimate stuff, but I was not ruffled. I pointed out that 63 per cent of Scots had either voted No or abstained. I reminded him that Scotland was also geographically divided, with Central Scotland voting, narrowly, Yes while the Highlands, the Borders, Edinburgh and the north-east had voted No.

But I also goaded Foot for claiming to speak for the people of Scotland on this issue. I said, 'We do not know what his credentials are for claiming to speak for the people of Scotland … We can only hope that they are slightly better than his credentials for speaking for the people of Wales.'

Michael Foot, like Jim Callaghan, was a Welsh MP. I went on, 'He and his Right Hon. Friend, the Leader of the Opposition, both representing Welsh constituencies, have suffered a rebuff unprecedented this century on a constitutional matter.' Wales had voted No by 80 per cent to 20 per cent. Foot remained silent and did not choose to intervene.

I concluded my speech by reminding the House that the people of Scotland had refused to endorse the Scotland Act and that it should, therefore, be repealed. It was, by 301 votes to 206.

I need to say something more about my own attitude to devolution and a Scottish Parliament during the Thatcher and Major years. As I was often reminded, I had resigned from the opposition front bench because of my support for a Scottish Assembly and had voted Yes in the referendum. I was accused of having done a volte-face when I became a minister. The charge was understandable; the truth was more complex.

Since 1969, I had been persuaded that there was a logical case for some form of Scottish Assembly or Parliament. I never deviated from that view. Scotland had a different legal system, we often needed separate legislation and it was increasingly difficult over the years to defend the Tories controlling the Scottish Office despite having less support at successive general elections than the main opposition party. In strict constitutional terms, there was no democratic deficit; the political reality was very different.

My support for devolution was from the head not the heart. It was intellectual rather than emotional. My Unionism, my belief in the continuing need for the United Kingdom, was, however, both head and heart. I felt very British. Scottish Nationalism in no way appealed to me.

When, therefore, the 1979 referendum showed that Scotland was evenly divided on the merits of an assembly at a time when England and Wales were passionately against, I concluded, and said, that there was no basis on which devolution for Scotland could go forward at that time. That was my genuinely held belief. It was not just a convenient formula.

That remained my view over the following eighteen years. What I had hoped to see was some form of devolution and decentralisation of government that could apply equally, though not uniformly, to England and Wales as well as Scotland, so that a new, more modern United Kingdom could come into existence.

I had to accept that neither Mrs Thatcher nor the Conservative Party, nor indeed English public opinion, had any interest in such a fundamental reform at that time and that it would have to wait for another government and another generation.

That fundamental reform was begun after 1997 by Tony Blair's government, when the Scottish Parliament and Welsh Assembly were created.

The current government, and George Osborne in particular, have been responsible for the major decentralisation of government and resources in England to the cities and regions, in particular in the north and north-west.

We are now seeing, in a very British way, the emergence of a new United Kingdom with decentralisation or devolution throughout these isles, including England. This new, quasi-federal Britain is one within which many Scots will, I believe, be content to remain fellow citizens with their English and Welsh neighbours.

CHAPTER 10

THE TORY IN THE WHITE HAT

WHEN I WAS appointed a minister, I was, of course, elated, but I was also a little apprehensive.

I had no idea whether I would be any good as a minister. I had made my mark in the House of Commons because I was a powerful debater, able to speak without notes. I could enthuse the party conference and handle myself well in TV and press interviews.

These are crucial skills for a successful minister but they are not his or her primary purpose. Ministers are appointed to run departments, take decisions, ensure they are implemented and provide strategic leadership for their part of the wider government programme.

My experience was as an advocate pleading my client's case, as a university lecturer trying to educate my students and as an MP representing my constituents. It was rare for me, in any of these roles, to have to take a decision, much less one that might impact on the lives of millions of people.

Sometimes successful business executives are made ministers in the belief that they will have no difficulty with running ministries, which cannot be that different to running a company. That is partly true, but, just as MPs have political skills but limited executive experience, so businessmen turned politicians often find they are hopeless with Parliament, are uncomfortable with the media and fail to impress the public.

In the event, I have found throughout my ministerial life that, far from having difficulty with taking decisions and accepting responsibility, I actually enjoy the intellectual challenge and stimulation as well as the satisfaction of seeing results delivered that, hopefully, improve people's lives or add some improvement to the world we live in.

Over the years I have become bored with and irritated by 'pure politics' and party political posturing, which is a poor substitute for the business of government.

I once heard Abba Eban, a former Israeli Foreign Minister, describe the difference between being in government and being in opposition. A minister wakes up in the morning and asks himself, 'What shall I do today?' An opposition spokesman wakes up and asks himself, 'What shall I say today?' Of course that distinction is unavoidable in democratic politics but that does not make it any the less frustrating.

I was fortunate in that the ministerial responsibilities that I had been allocated by George Younger corresponded to many of the political priorities for the government in Scotland. It gave me considerable prominence in Scotland for the next three years.

There were three major Scottish Bills over the first phase and I had to pilot all three of them through the House of Commons.

The first, and most important, was to implement in Scotland the government's commitment to give council tenants the right to buy their homes. If anything, this right was more urgent and necessary in Scotland than in any other part of the United Kingdom.

Not only did Scotland have fewer homeowners than the rest of Britain; it also had the highest figure for public sector housing in Western Europe. To my delight, I was able to point out to our critics that Communist Hungary had a higher proportion of homeowners at that time than did Scotland.

Nor was that because of any lack of demand from Scots to own their homes. In the months that had passed since the general election, between 20,000 and 30,000 council tenants had already applied to find out the conditions under which they would be able to buy their homes.

When the Bill was being drafted in my department, I asked what name was proposed for it and was told it was to be the Housing (Scotland) Bill.

I said that that was a very boring title and I wished it to be known as the Tenants' Rights Bill. I was told that was not possible as all housing Bills had the title they were proposing. I asked what was wrong with my alternative and was told that it was unacceptable as there would be a number of clauses in the Bill that would be about housing but not relevant to tenants' rights.

I am delighted to say that I was able to propose a suitable compromise that met the officials' concerns. The Bill was published as the Tenants' Rights etc. (Scotland) Bill. It is instructive how useful that 'et cetera' can be from time to time.

My determination to choose this title for the Bill had a serious underlying purpose. I not only wanted to get the Bill through the House of Commons; I also wanted to win the political battle for public and press support.

The Bill gave council tenants the right to buy their homes. It also contained a Tenants' Charter giving Scottish council tenants who did not buy their homes rights they had never had before, especially security of tenure.

Campaigning and voting in the lobby against something called the Housing (Scotland) Bill would not have been nearly so embarrassing for Labour MPs as having to campaign and vote against a Tenants' Rights Bill. When it was useful, I enjoyed being as party political as anyone else.

In making the final speech for the government during the Second Reading of the Bill in January 1980, I began by saying that that day's debate had been

> remarkable because the Labour Party, which for fifty years has presented itself as the champion of the council tenant, will shortly march in serried ranks through the No lobby to vote against a tenants' rights Bill – a Bill which by common consent does more to emancipate the council tenant than any measure during the last fifty years.

My peroration at the end of my speech declared that the Bill, together with that being brought forward for England and Wales, 'will make the single greatest contribution to the creation of a property-owning democracy that we have seen in this century'.

Throughout the subsequent committee stage and report stage, we found it fairly easy to discomfit the Labour Party and dominate the debate. Our efforts to win and hold public and press support had been highly successful, which was unusual for the Tory Party in Scotland.

Chris Baur, in *The Scotsman*, wrote that 'given his lack of ministerial experience [the Bill] might have sunk Rifkind in a messy ideological quagmire. But it didn't and he has emerged as a genuine 18 carat star. Indeed, it has been Labour who have been made to look flat-footed.'

The *Glasgow Evening Times* went overboard, describing me as 'fighting for the tenants' freedom' and as 'the Tory in the white hat. The good guy from the Scottish Office. The cross between Wyatt Earp and Robert Bruce who is going to ... free council tenants from their chains.'

Far be it for me to say whether these bouquets were deserved. The reader will understand why I have found it irresistible to quote them.

One of Margaret Thatcher's great qualities was that while she always saw the wood rather than just the trees, she recognised that the trees, too, needed to be nourished. She practised what she preached.

One day, during the committee stage of the Bill, while we were slowly working our way through clauses, sub-clauses and opposition amendments, the door of our room, on the Committee Corridor of the Commons, opened and in came, unannounced, the Prime Minister, with her parliamentary private secretary, Ian Gow, to sit on the public benches.

We were as astonished as the Labour MPs. Government backbenchers suddenly stopped doodling and dealing with their constituency correspondence and became anxious to intervene in the debate. Even the Labour MPs sat up as if in the presence of the headmistress. After twenty minutes the Prime Minister rose and swept away as silently as she had arrived. It was her way of emphasising the importance she attached to the right to buy and wishing to show that she was as interested in Scotland as in the rest of the United Kingdom.

Throughout the passage of the Bill, George Younger had over-all responsibility but was content to leave the day-to-day handling to me.

When the Bill had completed its Commons stages and had gone to the Lords, I received an unexpected letter from the Prime Minister. In it, she said, 'I have heard, on all sides, how superbly you dealt with this Bill during its long Committee Stage, and on the floor of the House … I wanted to send you my warm congratulations.'

I am as certain as one can be that the letter was the idea of Ian Gow, who was assiduous at keeping her in touch with junior ministers and backbenchers whom she would otherwise have rarely seen. The letter had me walking on water for several days.

Over the next seven years more than a million council houses were bought by their tenants throughout the United Kingdom. Homeownership rose dramatically in Scotland. We were able to say, convincingly, that homeownership was no longer just for the middle classes; it was available to the population as a whole.

I remain very proud of having spearheaded that social revolution north of the border. Indeed, in its impact on the lives of hundreds of thousands of people, it was one of my most important achievements in my public life.

It may not have changed the voting habits of the Scots but it improved their quality of life and that is about as satisfying as it can get when you are a minister.

No sooner was the Tenants' Rights Bill off to the Lords than I had to take the Criminal Justice (Scotland) Bill through the Commons. Here I was not on my own but had the invaluable support of Nicholas Fairbairn, the Solicitor General for Scotland and MP for Kinross and West Perthshire.

Fairbairn was Scotland's most colourful advocate and had concentrated his successful career on criminal cases. I had been his junior counsel on several occasions during my time at the Bar.

He lived in Fordell Castle, a Scottish tower house in Fife, painted with considerable skill, dressed like a Regency dandy, drank immoderately and could be either incredibly stimulating or a pain in the neck.

He was responsible for one of the best interventions in a debate that I heard during my years in the House of Commons. A Labour MP, Norman Buchan, had put down an amendment to a Bill to prevent judges and advocates wearing wigs and gowns. He argued that this dress code was archaic and that judges and advocates only wore wigs and gowns as 'a crutch for their dignity'.

Fairbairn intervened and asked why Buchan wore trousers. He suggested that Buchan wore trousers 'not as a crutch for his dignity but to add dignity to his crutch'. The amendment was defeated.

The Criminal Justice Bill was central to the government's programme in Scotland to improve law and order. It increased police powers to stop and search people suspected of having been involved in a crime. It permitted the police to detain suspects for up to six hours in a police station even if they had not been formally arrested.

There was an outcry from the civil liberties lobby and Labour pledged to do all in their power to block the Bill. I was able to discomfort them by pointing out that we had not dreamt up this Bill ourselves but had inherited a similar one from the previous Labour government.

The Labour Bill had proposed a power of four hours' detention rather than six, which had not caused any outcry. I remarked that 'no one is going to tell me that what is acceptable at four hours becomes an intolerable breach of civil liberties at six'.

Once again the Labour Party had misjudged the public mood. The *Daily Record*, Scotland's largest-selling paper at that time, and strongly pro-Labour and anti-Tory, gave the Bill strong support in their issue of 31 October 1979, no doubt responding to their assessment of their readers' views.

Under the headline 'The Crusader', they subtitled their article: 'Malcolm MP fights a one-man battle to make Scotland a safer place for the family'.

Referring to the many visits I had made to Scottish police forces and prisons during the parliamentary recess, they reported a conversation I had had with a double murderer at Peterhead Prison in Aberdeenshire.

I had asked the murderer what he did to while away the long hours in his cell. He liked to read, he told me. When I asked him what kind of books he most enjoyed he replied, 'Mostly escapist literature.'

The third issue that dominated my working hours was the ever stimulating subject of local government finance. In one form or another it was to be the challenge that Margaret Thatcher was least successful in resolving. Ultimately, in the form of the poll tax, it contributed to her political downfall and the end of her tenure in 10 Downing Street.

Domestic rates, paid by householders, were as controversial a means of raising revenue in England as in Scotland. They had become so because many of the electorate who were not householders received services from their local councils but did not contribute, directly, to the cost of them. The single pensioner paid the same as the household next door where there might be several adults, all earning, but with no individual liability.

Council tenants were liable for rates but many tenants were unaware of that because their rates were included in the rent paid and the tenants, as a consequence, did not have strong views on the system.

Scotland had a smaller middle class than England and far fewer homeowners. Domestic rates had a much higher profile with them as an unfair tax on the middle classes, and Conservative governments were subject to persistent pressure from their middle-class supporters to reform the system.

At the 1980 Scottish Conservative conference, George Younger had been pressed to protect ratepayers from local councils who were expanding their services despite requests to reduce their spending. His predecessor, the Labour Scottish Secretary Bruce Millan, had also sought to control council spending but had not been under pressure from his local activists, for whom high council expenditure was seen as a virtue not a vice.

George, as Scottish Secretary, had pledged reforms that would make Scottish local authorities more accountable to domestic ratepayers. A Local Government Bill was introduced, giving him greater powers to control 'excessive and unreasonable expenditure'.

Local authorities were ordered to reduce their spending, but by April 1981 only six had done so. Twenty-nine councils were exceeding government guidelines by more than 20 per cent. The worst offender was Labour-controlled Lothian Regional Council, which included Edinburgh. It planned to spend £62 million more than government guidelines and had increased the domestic rates by no less than 50 per cent to raise the necessary money.

Many of the electors who would benefit from the increased spending did not pay rates and were supportive of the council. Those who did pay were furious but felt impotent.

Battle commenced between the Scottish Office and Lothian Regional Council. George Younger, though mild mannered and ever courteous, was steely in his determination to prevail. He and I worked closely together. I dealt with the detail. He controlled the strategy.

It was very difficult for Lothian and the Labour councillors to portray George as a heartless and insensitive Thatcherite, despite his tough approach. I recall sitting with him at meetings he had with the Convention of Scottish Local Authorities. Most of the big councils were Labour-controlled and the meetings would begin with hostility and criticism in no small measure. Where I would have fought back, giving as good as I got, George's response was quite different but more effective.

He would listen quietly to all the complaints and then reply. 'Gentlemen,' he would say, 'if I was sitting where you are sitting, I would have made exactly the same complaints but let me share with you my problems.' Invariably they calmed down, the hostility began to evaporate and we had a more constructive exchange of views.

George Younger was the best example I know of that demonstrates that a politician can be invariably calm, courteous and cheerful. His success demonstrated that it is not necessary to be nasty or duplicitous to advance your political career. As Scottish Secretary he was tough on resisting threats to his budget without incurring the wrath of the Prime Minister, as I subsequently did. He achieved his ambition of being Defence Secretary and won the respect and admiration of the armed forces. He did so without being grand and with an occasional sense of mischief.

I was privileged in being asked by his wife Diana and their family to give the tribute to George at his memorial service in St Giles' Cathedral in Edinburgh in 2003.

In my address, I gave an example of George's sense of mischief that had been shared with me by his former private secretary Godfrey Robson.

On one occasion Godfrey was with George in the shuttle lounge at Heathrow when they became aware of a friendly wave and some-one heading in their direction. It was an elderly man who remarked, 'George, how are you?'

They had a little conversation and then George asked him, 'How is your mother these days?'

'Good of you to remember her,' he replied. 'I will pass on to her your good wishes,' and off he went.

The private secretary asked George who he was. 'I have no idea,' he replied.

'But you asked him about his mother.'

'Oh well,' said George. 'You have to take risks now and again.'

To return to Lothian Regional, the council made clear that they would not make any significant reduction in their proposed £62 million excessive spending and would not reduce their 50 per cent rates increase. The government retaliated by moving an order that would cut the rate support grant to the council by £47 million unless they changed their stance. They refused to do so.

The council then found they were losing £1.5 million a week in tax-payer-funded rate support grant and this would continue until they became cooperative. The government had made clear that the cut in grant would be reduced to £30 million if they became cooperative.

At first the council refused to budge. George Younger and I did a sort of good cop, bad cop routine. He was gentle in rhetoric though unbending in substance. I was less diplomatic. When asked what would happen if the council did not cut its spending, I replied, 'Quite simple. They would just go bust and they definitely would not be bailed out by the government.'

The council blinked first and agreed to cut current spending by £15.2 million and consider further reductions in their capital expenditure. The loss of £30 million in their rate support grant meant that total cuts of £45 million would have to be absorbed by them.

The council got little sympathy from the press. The *Glasgow Herald*, in an editorial, said:

Lothian region tried to wrong-foot the government but the reverse has happened … The Scottish Office, boxing quite cleverly throughout the contest, has scored most of the propaganda points; its patience and its readiness to compromise has shown up the region's intransigence … The council seems to prefer handing £30 million to the government to handing it to its own ratepayers.

The Times reported that the council's own officers had identified £26 million of cuts that could be made without a single redundancy. The *Daily Record* headlined their story 'Maggie's boys hit Lothian Labour rebels'.

The Guardian, too, was impressed by our handling of the battle, but they quoted Labour MPs describing me as 'a hardline Tory behind the well-cultivated liberal image'. That didn't do me any damage in Downing Street.

The three years I spent as a junior minister in the Scottish Office were a splendid baptism of fire. I had serious business to do and, by common consent, I was doing it competently and with some flair. David Scott, *The Scotsman*'s local government correspondent, wrote that 'the bulk of responsibility for local affairs has been delegated to [Malcolm Rifkind] by Mr Younger and he has quickly gained widespread respect as a minister in complete command of his subject'.

I was also working harder than I had ever worked before. So much so that I received a letter, out of the blue, from Jim Sillars, a former Scottish Labour MP and future leading member of the SNP.

Sillars and I were politically poles apart but had a friendly personal relationship. He complimented me on what I had achieved during that period but cautioned me against overworking and encouraged me to take it a little easier. It was good advice.

When in London, my office was in Dover House, a splendid classical building in Whitehall where Lady Caroline Lamb had entertained Lord Byron.

When I was Secretary of State for Scotland, we received a visit from the Prime Minister. She had never been to Dover House and remarked on what a grand building we had to house the Scottish Office.

I could not resist pointing out that Dover House was, actually, only our branch office, with our headquarters in Edinburgh. She had never forgotten my devolution sympathies and I doubt whether I did myself any favours by that remark.

Jim Sillars had advised me to slow down and take it easier. I had seen the wisdom of that advice. But politics and government are unpredictable. As it turned out, I was about to leave Scottish politics and join the world.

CHAPTER 11

HELPING TO END
THE COLD WAR

ON FRIDAY 2 April 1982, Argentina invaded the Falklands
Islands.

Within a couple of days the Foreign Secretary, Lord
Carrington, and two other ministers in the Foreign Office, Humphrey
Atkins and Richard Luce, had resigned. They acknowledged that this
disastrous event had happened on their watch and that the honourable response was for them to go.

Carrington's resignation also made it easier for the Labour Party
to support the government when the task force was sent to liberate
the islands.

On Tuesday 6 April, my private secretary rang me and said that
the Prime Minister wished to see me in her room in the House of
Commons that afternoon.

When I went in, she indicated, straight away, that she wished to
move me to the Foreign Office. She apologised that she could not

make me a Minister of State as there was a maximum permitted number of such appointments.

More surprisingly, she went on to say that she expected me to be a future Secretary of State for Scotland but that it would be useful for me to have wider experience in the meantime.

We talked briefly and she asked whether I was Jewish, as she recalled reading an article I had written in the *Jewish Chronicle*. When I said I was, she said she was delighted, as the Foreign Office had the reputation of being anti-Israel, which she wished to dispel.

She emphasised that this had not been the reason for my appointment, which had been decided on merit. This must have been true as otherwise she would not have needed to ask me whether I was Jewish.

I then left the Prime Minister. That evening I wrote in a memo that I was 'feeling delighted, exhilarated and disbelieving that it had actually happened'.

The Foreign Office was the department I had always dreamt of serving in and now I was one of its ministers. Some time later, a friend asked me whether it was a coincidence that a week after I had left the Scottish Office we were at peace with Lothian Region and at war with Argentina.

The following morning I left the House of Commons to attend a meeting of all the Foreign Office ministers with the new Foreign Secretary, Francis Pym.

On my way I met Ted Rowlands, a Labour MP who had been a Foreign Office minister in the previous government. He predicted that as I was only a Parliamentary Under-Secretary I would not be given any territorial responsibility, as foreign countries expected their bilateral relations to be conducted at Minister of State level.

I was deeply disappointed by this assertion. When we assembled in the Foreign Secretary's room, which is the grandest in the whole of Whitehall, Rowlands's prediction was confirmed.

While the Ministers of State were given the Middle East, Europe and Latin America, the new Permanent Secretary, Antony Acland, proposed that I should handle Economic Relations, the UN, the Passport Office and Migration.

Francis Pym asked if we were all content and I had the temerity to indicate that I was not. I wanted, I said, a territorial responsibility as well. Africa would have been my preference but, if that was not possible, I suggested, without any expectation of success, the Soviet Union and Eastern Europe.

I had assumed that I might get the South Pacific or Central America to console me. To my delight, the following morning I found that my first attempt in diplomacy had succeeded. I was to handle our relations with the Soviet Union and Eastern Europe.

In the light of what happened subsequently, it might seem strange that the most junior minister was asked to handle the Soviet Union. It was, in fact, entirely logical at that time.

Our bilateral relations with Moscow had been Arctic cold for several years because of the Soviet invasion of Afghanistan and the imposition of martial law in Poland. No British minister had made an official visit to Moscow since 1977. As far as Mrs Thatcher was concerned, if the Soviets were upset at getting a mere Parliamentary Under-Secretary to handle their bilateral relations with Britain, so much the better.

The following week, the British ambassador in Moscow, Sir Curtis Keeble, came to see me. He expressed the view that the West as a whole was lamentably ignorant of the Soviet Union.

In my note, written at the time, I recorded that he then noted that three of the Soviet leaders were in their seventies but one, Gorbachev, was only fifty and, clearly, would have a major role in the future but hardly a single Western politician had met him in recent years.

This was the first time I had heard of Gorbachev, but the ambassador's remark showed that the Foreign Office had their eye on the ball long before Mrs Thatcher showed interest in the men in the Kremlin.

Within a couple of weeks I had arranged to make my first ministerial visits to Hungary, Romania and Bulgaria later in the year.

The Falklands, of course, dominated these months. I had no personal responsibility in this area but it was the constant background to everything we did. Each morning, Francis Pym met with his junior ministers after the daily meeting of the War Cabinet. Often he would come in showing his exasperation with the Prime Minister. He wanted to explore every possibility of a diplomatic agreement with Argentina, accepting that this would involve some serious compromises.

Mrs Thatcher was not interested in such compromises and, in that respect, I was on her side. I thought it inconceivable that the Argentinians would leave the Falklands unless they were thrown out. I also thought it unwise of Francis to reveal his disagreements with the Prime Minister in front of his junior ministers.

One evening, the Prime Minister buttonholed me in the division lobby during a vote. She asked me whether I remembered my constitutional law and whether Michael Foot had been correct in suggesting that any international agreement with Argentina would need Parliament's approval before being ratified.

By one of those lucky chances I had been briefed on just this subject a few days earlier and could show off about the Ponsonby Rule, which permits a debate but does not require approval by Parliament for ratification. I wasn't often asked my advice by the Prime Minister, so it was nice to get it right when I was.

In June, I visited Hungary, my first time behind the Iron Curtain since I was on the parliamentary delegation to Czechoslovakia. Hungary was more relaxed than most of its Communist neighbours and was trying, step by step, to increase its independence from Moscow.

The Hungarians never lost their sense of humour despite the oppression of Communism. In some ways, humour and satire were the only ways they could deal with their loss of freedom.

On one occasion, while the Berlin Wall was still standing, I was asked by a Hungarian in Budapest what was the definition of an East German string quartet? He answered his own question by saying that

With my parents and brother, Arnold. Note my flowing locks and clutching tin of Johnson's baby powder, without which I refused to be photographed.

Dressed to enchant, with Arnold in more sober school blazer.

The nearest I got to Prime Minister. I am seated in my robes as Cardinal Wolsey in the school production of *A Man for All Seasons*. On my right is Peter Farago as Sir Thomas More; at the back, Gavin Hewitt, a future British ambassador; and on the right of the picture, Mark Sischy, a future Scottish sheriff.

Two future Foreign Secretaries. I was President of Edinburgh University Debates and behind me is Robin Cook. We are welcoming Julian Amery MP and Konni Zilliacus MP.

T.HUTTON | M.RIFKIND | I.CHISHOLM | B.TATTERS.

UNIVERSITY OF EDINBURGH

University Challenge, 1967. We got to the quarter-finals.

Edith on our wedding day in May 1970.

As a city father and town councillor in Edinburgh, 1973.

Practising as an advocate with Nicholas Fairbairn QC MP, outside the law courts in Edinburgh.

Margaret Thatcher meeting Mikhail Gorbachev for the first time, at Chequers. On the left, Denis Thatcher with Raisa Gorbachev. I am at the rear.

With the Prince and Princess of Wales at the Glasgow Garden Festival when I was Scottish Secretary. Turning round to watch the fireworks!

Picnicking with the Queen on Oronsay, Inner Hebrides, while cruising on HMY *Britannia* when Scottish Secretary.

Did not happen very often. Margaret Thatcher applauding me, at a general election rally in Scotland in 1987.

Hugo pretending to be Secretary of State for Scotland in my office in Dover House, Whitehall.

Margaret Thatcher meeting Caroline and Hugo at Bute House, then the official residence of the Scottish Secretary.

ABOVE As Defence Secretary, defending the realm, but not pretending to be a soldier.

LEFT Dropping in from a helicopter on the Royal Navy off Portland in the English Channel in 1992.

it was an East German orchestra that had just returned from a tour of West Germany.

In December 1982, I visited the United Nations and had a meeting with the Secretary-General, Pérez de Cuéllar. He expressed the view that meetings between Reagan and Andropov, or Schultz and Gromyko, should be so regular, and so taken for granted, that they would not be treated as failures because agreement was not reached on a specific occasion. The possibilities of such meetings should not be seen as sensitive or difficult; they should be taken as a matter of course.

That has always been my own view and it was good to hear it from the Secretary-General. Churchill's famous remark that 'Jaw-jaw is better than war-war' is as sound as ever. During the Cold War such dialogue had often been rare, as it has been in recent years with Vladimir Putin. The world is more dangerous as a result.

When I first went to the Foreign Office, I was concerned that our relationship with the Soviet Union was so dismal and minimal. I found that the diplomats I worked with shared my view. That was not altogether surprising. The Foreign Office exists for diplomacy. When there is no diplomatic activity and contact, there is little for them to do. But, that aside, there were obvious dangers in a prolonged absence of dialogue and contact between the West and the Soviet Union. To put it bluntly, there was more risk of the Cold War becoming hot, either through design or through misunderstanding. That could have led to military conflict, including the ultimate horror of a war involving nuclear weapons.

I had several discussions with Nigel Broomfield, then head of the Soviet and East European Department, who stressed that either Gorbachev or Romanov, the younger members of the Politburo, was likely to lead the Soviet Union one day and that we should get to know them now.

With the support of the department, I put up a submission to Francis Pym advocating restoring and improving contact between

Britain and the Soviet Union. Francis was responsive and liked our proposal for a gradual build-up of ministerial exchanges, including the possibility of a visit by himself or the Prime Minister to Moscow in 1983.

I was particularly in favour of the latter, as dialogue at the level of Mrs Thatcher would be reassuring in a year that was expected to see the deployment of Cruise and Pershing missiles. The Prime Minister's reputation as the Iron Lady and the victor of the Falklands would dispel any suggestion that we were going soft.

The Prime Minister was, at that time, unwilling to agree to any high-level ministerial visits to the Soviet Union. She was only willing to agree, and even then without much enthusiasm, that there should be contact at my level or below.

The outcome was that in February 1983 I welcomed Nikita Ryzhov, a Soviet Deputy Foreign Minister, to London for talks and the Russians were supportive of a return visit by me in April of that year.

It was interesting that Moscow wanted the visit to take place at that time, as we had just had a spate of tit-for-tat expulsions of Soviet spies operating from their embassy in London and British diplomats expelled from Moscow in retaliation.

We knew before my visit to Moscow that the Russians would keep it low-key and that I would not see the veteran Foreign Minister, Andrei Gromyko. That was at least in part for protocol reasons, as I was the most junior minister in the Foreign Office at that time. I had been tempted to call off the visit if there was no such access, but I had been rightly persuaded otherwise by my officials.

My visit was to be the first by a British Foreign Office minister to the USSR since 1977, when David Owen went as Foreign Secretary. My host was to be the Soviet First Deputy Foreign Minister, Georgi Kornienko.

Before I left for Moscow I was visited by the former Prime Minister Harold Wilson and Sir Fitzroy Maclean, who were active in the Great Britain–USSR Association.

Wilson looked the same as ever, sitting stolidly puffing his pipe. It was clear that he had deteriorated mentally. Each contribution he made to our discussion was little more than an anecdote about previous visits to Russia, including a television broadcast he had made in Moscow speaking, he claimed, in Russian with an Armenian accent.

I was in the Soviet Union for five days towards the end of April, including a visit to Leningrad. My talks with the Soviet minister covered arms control, Afghanistan and Poland. I also raised the case of Anatoly Shcharansky, the jailed Soviet dissident. Before I went I emphasised that one of my objectives was 'to try and see if there is a possibility of a proper realistic dialogue'.

The main talks were with Gromyko's deputy, Kornienko. He spoke in Russian but inadvertently revealed that he had excellent English. During a discussion on arms control, the interpreter had translated him as referring to 'military supremacy'. Kornienko interrupted him to say, in English, that he had said 'military advantage'.

When I raised human rights and the Soviet refusal to allow their dissidents to emigrate, he asked me how I would like it if he raised British immigration policy, which was also controversial. I invited him to do so but pointed out that the difference was that in our case people wanted to get in but in the case of the Soviet Union they wanted to get out. At this stage he lost interest in British immigration policy.

Lunch was at the ambassador's residence, directly across the river from the Kremlin. Our guests were Kornienko and Ryzhov. I could not help drawing Kornienko's attention to the portrait on the wall. He looked rather suspicious. He must have thought it was Tsar Nicholas II, though it was in fact the Tsar's cousin, George V.

That afternoon, we visited Lenin embalmed in his mausoleum on Red Square. The atmosphere was reverential. There were four Soviet soldiers standing to attention at the four corners of his bier. It was no easier to tell whether they were alive than it was with Lenin.

*   *   *

My time in Moscow included my first visit to the Bolshoi, where we watched a performance of *Iphigenia in Aulis* by Gluck. We sat in a box and were served caviar in a large silver bowl during the interval. It was very Russian if not very Communist.

My visit to the Soviet Union did not, in itself, change history, but it was the first public step and ministerial exchange that led to the seminar on East–West relations that Mrs Thatcher held at Chequers and then, the following year, to the Thatcher–Gorbachev meeting at Chequers, which I attended. That meeting undoubtedly kick-started a process which helped transform the relations between the Soviet Union and the West.

When I returned to London after my visit to Moscow, I said that Soviet–British relations were still 'at a low ebb'. But I added that 'if they were cold when I went there, they are cool now'.

The general election having been won resoundingly in June 1983, Geoffrey Howe replaced Francis Pym as Foreign Secretary and I was promoted to Minister of State for Europe. I discovered, to my delight, that Geoffrey shared my view that dialogue and contact with Soviet leaders was essential. Even more important, unlike Francis Pym, his relations with Margaret Thatcher were very good at that time. He had more influence on her than Francis ever had.

Geoffrey Howe was crucial to the success of the Thatcher government in its early years. Mild mannered, hesitant in speech, donnish in manner, he combined these characteristics with serious intellectual firepower, personal courage and great ambition.

He had shown these qualities as Chancellor of the Exchequer from 1979 to 1983. Denis Healey might have been entitled to describe being attacked by Geoffrey as like being 'savaged by a dead sheep' but it is less well remembered how Geoffrey got his own back. Several weeks after that barb, Healey had praised Geoffrey Howe across the dispatch box. Geoffrey sweetly replied that being praised by Denis was like being 'nuzzled by an old boar'.

Edith and I had lunch with Geoffrey and Elspeth at Chevening one weekend. After lunch we felt like a walk round the lake and offered to take the Howes' dog with us.

While Geoffrey was Chancellor, it had become known that the dog's name was 'Budget'. I asked him whether they had considered changing the name now that he had moved to the Foreign Office. With a twinkle, he replied that the dog had a new name reflecting that move. It was now called 'Fudge It'.

Margaret Thatcher was becoming more receptive to the need to improve relations with the Soviet Union. On 8 September 1983, she held a seminar at Chequers on East–West relations.

On the ministerial side there were Geoffrey Howe, Michael Heseltine and me. During the morning we were joined by eight academic experts as well as senior diplomats. After lunch, the academics left and the Prime Minister, ministers and diplomats discussed future policy.

They concluded that it was unlikely that any change in the Soviet system, in at least the medium term, would be fundamental. Nevertheless it was agreed that contacts between the UK and the Soviet Union should be built up, including a meeting between the Foreign Secretary and Mr Gromyko at the UN in September. The minutes also recorded that Mr Gromyko might be invited to visit the United Kingdom in 1984.

The possibility of Mrs Thatcher and Yuri Andropov meeting was not ruled out but the Prime Minister made it clear that she would not visit the Soviet Union. When she said this very firmly, I, knowing Andropov to be in poor health, whispered to Geoffrey Howe that she might go to Andropov's funeral, intending this to be a comment on Mrs Thatcher's dislike of Communists. In fact, it turned out, five months later, to be a very accurate prediction.

It was also agreed that it might be useful to invite potential successors to Andropov to visit London, and Mrs Thatcher confirmed that she would meet them if they came. This was a crucial breakthrough. It gave the Foreign Office the authority to start planning an invitation to Mikhail Gorbachev to visit London.

Also approved in the minutes was that further consideration would be given to a possible visit to Hungary by the Prime Minister. I knew that she might be open to such a suggestion despite a lack of enthusiasm for visiting Communist states in general.

I had helped persuade her to see the Hungarian Deputy Prime Minister, József Marjai, when he had visited London in March of that year. She did not normally meet deputy Prime Ministers and certainly not Communist ones. But our ambassador in Budapest had encouraged her to make an exception for Marjai as he was very different to most of his Politburo colleagues and was responsible for economic policy in Hungary.

When she met him, she asked him to explain his economic policy. He replied that his greatest problem was to persuade the Hungarian people that the government had no money of its own. Her eyes lit up. 'But that's what I'm always saying,' she declared. Mr Marjai remained in discussion with her for at least twice the time he had originally been allocated.

We were also seeing hard evidence of Hungary's desire for greater independence from Moscow. I received a message from Gyula Horn, a future Prime Minister of Hungary, but at that time in charge of the Foreign Affairs Department of the Central Committee of the Hungarian Communist Party. He wanted to visit me on a secret matter. We discovered that the French and the West Germans had received similar requests. An approach from the party rather than the government was almost unheard of.

When I saw Horn, he said that the Hungarians wished to establish direct relations with the European Community for the first time, rather than going through the Soviet-controlled Comecon. Before applying to Brussels they wanted to know whether we would support their application. We told them that we would and, in due course, they took this significant step.

In seeking to tempt Gorbachev to visit London, we had a problem. Our normal bilateral relations were with ministers. Gorbachev was not a minister but a member of the Communist Party's supreme body, the Politburo. Needless to say the relations between the Conservative Party and the Soviet Communist Party were not very fraternal either then or at any other time. A party-to-party invitation was not on.

The Foreign Office came to the rescue. They recalled that there had been, several years earlier, a British parliamentary delegation to Moscow. It was the turn of the Soviet Union to send one from the Supreme Soviet to London.

Through co-ordination with the House of Commons, an invitation was sent in February 1984 in the name of the British branch of the Inter-Parliamentary Union to the Supreme Soviet. Through diplomatic channels, we let it be known that if the invitation was accepted and if Gorbachev chose to lead the Soviet delegation he would be given extended personal access to Mrs Thatcher and other senior British Cabinet ministers.

There was radio silence for many months but then, in October 1984, we were informed that the invitation had been accepted, that Gorbachev would lead the delegation and that he would like to come in December of that year.

That his wife, Raisa, was going to accompany him was, itself, a mark that Gorbachev was different and that times might be changing. No one could recollect Mrs Brezhnev or Mrs Gromyko accompanying their husbands on official foreign visits.

When the acceptance of the invitation was sent by the Foreign Office to Downing Street, the Prime Minister's foreign policy advisor minuted asking the Prime Minister whether she would see Gorbachev in 10 Downing Street 'or invite him to your dacha?' The dacha was chosen.

What became the historic visit to Chequers was on 16 December and eight days later I wrote down my own recollections. The following are direct quotations from that document.

> The lunch [at Chequers] could hardly be described as a work-
> ing occasion ... with the PM keeping Gorbachev to herself

most of the time. Having their own interpreters between them encouraged this tendency. I could only hear snippets of their conversation, which, on her side, included the miners' strike and the control of the nationalised industries. [I was sitting with the Soviet ambassador on my right and Sir Percy Cradock on my left.] …

Gorbachev … was more interested in his conversation than his food. When the PM remonstrated with him he replied that man eats to live and does not live to eat.

After lunch, Gorbachev and the Prime Minister retired to have a private discussion. I had to help show Raisa Gorbachev around Chequers. She was a highly intelligent, rather cerebral lady. She professed her 'delight to be in England, the country of Hobbes and Locke'. This was not the kind of remark one would have got from many Soviet wives.

She had a good knowledge of twentieth-century English literature, having read, in Russian, Graham Greene, C. P. Snow and Iris Murdoch. I needed the help of Ian Sutherland, our ambassador in Moscow, when she asked who was the favourite contemporary Soviet novelist in Britain. The only name that came to my mind was Solzhenitsyn and he had not yet been fully rehabilitated.

The Prime Minister and Gorbachev, in due course, emerged from their discussions. Mrs Thatcher subsequently gave her verdict that Gorbachev was a man with whom we could do business. I recorded in my document: 'I believe they got on so well together because, essentially, they are two of a kind. Both hard as nails but also with a capacity to charm and a preference for frank talking.'

The next session of talks, the following day, was with Geoffrey Howe at Hampton Court. I was present. I wrote subsequently:

Gorbachev did not, unlike many of his compatriots, speak from a prepared text; he only occasionally looked at his notes and he used a personal notebook which appeared full of detailed notes in his own handwriting which he occasionally added to during the course of the morning ... His aides, especially Zamyatin, seemed free to intervene whenever they wished without any apparent resentment by Gorbachev ... During one esoteric discussion Gorbachev advised Geoffrey that they should not become too philosophical. He referred to the mediaeval dispute about how many devils one could put on the head of a pin. Geoffrey pointed out that, in our version, it was angels not devils and asked whether the difference might be significant. Gorbachev laughed and said we must blame it on the interpreters.

On the Wednesday evening, Edith and I took Gorbachev and Raisa to the English National Opera to see *Così fan Tutte*. We had prime seats in the royal box. Raisa asked me where the Queen sat when she came and I was able to answer, 'Where you are sitting.'

Some days later, I bumped into Edith's cousin Helen, who said she had been at the opera that night and had looked up at the royal box. 'Oh, there's Edith and Malcolm,' she thought. 'I wonder who they are with.' I was pleased she had got it the right way round.

We left the opera early because it had been a hard day for our guests and we were giving a supper party for them at Lancaster House. Conversation at the supper was very relaxed.

Gorbachev spoke of his childhood. He had been brought up by his grandparents, who were believers. As a result, he had been baptised. His grandparents had been cautious. Behind the portraits of Lenin and Stalin in their home were religious icons. When Gorbachev married Raisa in a civil ceremony, his grandmother had said to him, 'Mischa, you have forgotten God but I shall pray for you.' I was surprised, not that this had happened, but that he was keen to share it with us. With other Soviet leaders one rarely knew if they were married or had family.

The Chequers meeting was a success, though not because Thatcher and Gorbachev reached agreement. They agreed on very little. But they liked each other and they began to trust each other. That is a message very relevant to our current problems. Putin is no Gorbachev, but constant dialogue can help identify and make progress on areas of common interest and can narrow the gap where there is deep disagreement.

Gorbachev was a leader with special qualities. The West, and the Soviet Union itself, was lucky to have him at that time. It is very unlikely the Cold War would have ended and the liberation of Eastern Europe would have been achieved so peacefully without him.

After the Chequers meeting, I wrote: 'A negotiation with Gorbachev would be a difficult and intense experience. It would also be stimulating and refreshing. I can't help preferring him to the cold, wintry blocks of granite, muffled in their overcoats, on top of the Lenin mausoleum.'

In July 1985, I made a further visit to Moscow for talks with Kornienko. We had met three times in three years and I described our meeting as a 'prelude' to the Helsinki meeting later that week between Geoffrey Howe and Edward Shevardnadze, the new Soviet Foreign Minister. Britain now had as active a bilateral relationship with the Soviet Union as anyone in the West. Thanks to Mrs Thatcher, we were also having an unprecedented influence on Ronald Reagan, the President of the United States. Diplomacy was fashionable and the Foreign Office was in its element.

Moscow was very different in one respect compared to my previous visit. Not only was Gorbachev in power but one of his first reforms was to try to deal with the curse of Soviet alcoholism by a ban on vodka and other spirits at all public events.

The result was that our toasts were in apple or orange juice, and the caviar had to be consumed without vodka.

The one exception was when Edith and I visited the Russian Orthodox monastery at Zagorsk. The Archimandrite of the monastery gave us lunch and his table was groaning with vodka as well as food.

When I was at the Soviet Foreign Ministry the following day, I decided to tease my host. I asked Kornienko whether he realised that the only time we had had vodka since we arrived had been at the monastery in Zagorsk. His response was splendid.

'Of course,' he said. 'They gave you vodka at the monastery while we give you apple juice. Do you not realise that in the Soviet Union, Church and State are quite separate?' Game, set and match to Kornienko.

The month before the Chequers summit with Gorbachev, I had made what turned out to be a rather historic visit to Poland.

Poland was one of the last bilateral visits I made to Warsaw Pact countries although, normally, it would have been the first. However, General Jaruzelski had imposed martial law in December 1981 and that had not been lifted until July 1983. Solidarity, the mass trade union movement led by Lech Wałęsa, had been banned in October 1982 and remained illegal though active underground.

I was uncertain about how wise it was for a Western minister to visit Poland while Solidarity was still banned, even though martial law had been lifted. We did not wish to give the Communist government undeserved respectability.

I asked my officials to take discreet soundings from Solidarity to find out whether they would welcome or disapprove of a visit at this time. The exiled Solidarity activists said that they would welcome a visit as they did not want Poland to be boycotted.

What they most wanted, however, would be for a visiting minister to meet with Solidarity leaders in Warsaw. Jaruzelski's line was that Solidarity no longer existed and was irrelevant to Poland. A meeting with a visiting Western minister would demonstrate that the Polish government's strategy had failed.

I agreed that such a meeting should be part of my unofficial and unannounced programme while I was in Poland. And we planned on that basis.

I was due to arrive in Warsaw on Saturday 3 November. On 19 October, a Roman Catholic priest, Father Jerzy Popiełuszko, had been murdered by the Polish security service. He was a very well-known and outspoken critic of the Communist government. Whether or not the Polish government had ordered his killing, it was, rightly, assumed that it had been politically inspired. There was national outrage and the government was shaken.

By coincidence we were arriving on the very day of his funeral in St Stanislaw Kostka Church in Warsaw. We decided not to postpone the visit but on the plane I discussed with my aides what we might do when we arrived. The funeral would be over but we felt it appropriate that I should lay a wreath at the grave on behalf of Her Majesty's Government.

When we arrived, we were met by the British ambassador, John Morgan, who said that he had intended to recommend just such a gesture. It was agreed that we would lay the wreath the following morning.

He suggested that I might wish to make a private, unannounced visit to the church that evening and mingle with the crowds that were still present. Edith, whose parents were both Polish, travelled with me on the visit to Warsaw and accompanied me that evening.

It was a very emotional experience. It was estimated that around 250,000 had been present at the funeral earlier in the day, and thousands were still there.

From the top of the steeple of St Stanislaw Kostka's Church there draped the red and white of the Polish flag, but it was in the shape of the V for victory symbol of the banned Solidarity movement. The authorities had not dared interfere with it.

The following morning we returned to the church so that I could lay the wreath at Father Popiełuszko's grave. Thanks to the BBC World Service, the whole of Poland seemed to know what we were doing and approved. The Polish government, who, officially, were as outraged by the murder as the rest of Poland, were not in a position to complain.

Later that day, at the ambassador's residence, I met, as planned, four leading members of the banned Solidarity. The names of the four were at that time unknown to me, but they were to become leading statesmen in the post-Communist Polish government.

One was Tadeusz Mazowiecki, the first post-Communist Prime Minister. The second was Bronisław Geremek, who became a distinguished Foreign Minister. The third was Janusz Onyszkiewicz, who became Minister of Defence and a good personal friend. When I was Secretary of State for Defence, I welcomed him in London with a guard of honour in Whitehall. The fourth was Krzysztof Sliwinski, a journalist and advisor to Solidarity.

It was this meeting that really upset General Jaruzelski and his government. He refused to see me, and his spokesman, Jerzy Urban, accused me of treating Poland as if it was a former British colony. Thanks again to the BBC World Service, the meeting became known throughout Poland and made a significant contribution to boosting Solidarity's morale when the government was trying to marginalise and ignore them.

Most important, the meeting set a precedent for future visits by ministers from NATO countries. Hans-Dietrich Genscher, the West German Foreign Minister, was due to visit Warsaw. He had not intended to meet Solidarity representatives but changed his plans due to the overwhelming welcome for my own meeting. This became standard practice and helped force the Polish government to accept that Solidarity was not going to go away.

Solidarity was, of course, delighted with the upturn in their fortunes. On returning to London, I received a message of thanks, together with a brass 'Solidarność' medallion from their exiled leadership in the Netherlands. In 1998, I was decorated by the President of Poland with the Commander's Cross of the Order of Merit in recognition of my support for a free Poland.

Edith still had a few Polish relatives in Warsaw and we enjoyed seeing them again during our visit. We also travelled to Częstochowa, where we saw the Black Madonna, and Kraków, where Edith's father had grown up and where her grandfather had been a timber merchant.

While in Kraków, Edith went to the address where her father's parents had lived. There was a very old lady living next door who said she remembered the old couple who had lived there during the war until the Germans had taken them away. That was likely to have been Edith's grandparents. This combination of political and family engagements made those five days an emotional roller coaster.

Our visit to Poland had been successful. *The Times*, in an editorial headed 'Mission Accomplished', was kind enough to say that I had completed my difficult mission 'with admirable authority and skill'. They quoted the words that I had said at Father Popiełuszko's graveside:

> It is clear that Father Popiełuszko stood for many ideals with which the people of Poland identify, and the people of Britain want to share in their grief … we hope that the values that he stood for will continue to flourish in accordance with the wishes of the people of Poland.

This, *The Times* said, was a model piece of democratic statesmanship. They concluded by calling on Hans-Dietrich Genscher and other Western ministers who visited Warsaw to 'follow Mr Rifkind's example'.

Some months later, on 10 April 1985, Jacek Kuroń, a leading Polish dissident, wrote in *The Times* that 'Mr Rifkind [by meeting Solidarity and laying the wreath] … became a symbol of rapprochement between Western democracies and Poland – not just its government but also its people.'

These years between 1982 and 1985 were amongst the most fulfilling of my public life. Although only a junior minister, I had been fortunate in having an opportunity to press for new initiatives in British–Soviet relations as far back as 1982 and see this lead to the Thatcher–Gorbachev meeting at the end of 1985.

I was only a minor player in the relationship that was built up with

Mikhail Gorbachev. The credit goes overwhelmingly to Margaret Thatcher and most of the rest to Geoffrey Howe and the diplomats in the Foreign Office.

As regards Poland, however, I had a more substantial role. The visit to Poland at that time and my actions when I got there were my responsibility, though any credit needs to be shared with the senior diplomats and ambassadors who advised me.

I was in the Cabinet but not in the Foreign Office when the Berlin Wall came down in 1989 and when Communism disappeared from Europe two years later. I missed the birth of a new Europe, but I was privileged to have made some contribution to the conception some years earlier.

CHAPTER 12

FLYING THE FLAG

W HEN, IMMEDIATELY AFTER the 1983 general election, the Prime Minister had promoted me to Minister of State, I was given extended geographical responsibilities in addition to the Soviet Union and Eastern Europe. I succeeded Douglas Hurd as the Minister for Europe and, at my request, I took on sub-Saharan Africa, including South Africa.

Thankfully, I dispensed with the Visa Department, Economic Relations and the like, which, while important, were very much less stimulating. I was particularly delighted that my close friend Richard Luce had returned to the Foreign Office as my fellow Minister of State. He had resigned on principle at the time of the Falklands but had been found to bear no personal responsibility for the debacle. It was splendid to be working together.

To be the Minister for Europe was important but not as grand as it might sound. Our relations with the European Community were so fundamental to our national interests that Geoffrey Howe, as Foreign Secretary, quite rightly devoted much of his own time to European matters. He personally attended most of the Council of

Ministers meetings, as did the other Foreign Ministers of member states. Occasionally, I would represent him when he had to be elsewhere in the world, but that was not that often.

But even the Foreign Secretary had to make way for the Prime Minister on the most important European occasions. She, obviously, attended personally all heads of government councils.

Being Margaret Thatcher, however, she did not content herself with summit meetings. She also ensured that she was aware of much of the detail emanating from Brussels that might affect the United Kingdom and she expected to be consulted by Geoffrey before any changes of policy or concessions were announced.

This was not unreasonable. Not only was the evolution, and increasing powers, of the European Community an ongoing historic event; it was also an area of policy which, even then, was of intense interest within the Conservative Party both in the House of Commons and in the country.

Euroscepticism was not then as virulent as it has become amongst Tories. We were not deeply divided, as we are now, as to whether we should be in the European Community.

Indeed, it was the Labour Party, under Michael Foot, that had campaigned at the 1983 general election for us to leave Europe. It was that promise and others in their manifesto, famously dubbed the longest suicide note in history, that had helped convince the public that they were not fit for power.

So, as Minister for Europe, I saw all the submissions and could express my own views and help influence the policy. But the real power on European policy was with Margaret Thatcher and Geoffrey Howe.

This was particularly true as regards the controversy over Britain's contributions to the European Community Budget. The historic battle 'to get our money back' and secure the British rebate was Mrs Thatcher's victory, ably assisted by Geoffrey Howe. I was not involved in that but had the role of an admiring observer.

But one responsibility I did have on the British rebate was reporting to the House of Commons when an emergency statement was needed. There was such an occasion in July 1984, when the European Parliament for a time refused to authorise the repayments of the funds to which the United Kingdom was entitled. Mrs Thatcher condemned them as 'despicable'. Even President Mitterrand said their action was 'wrong and disastrous'.

I had to follow these reactions in my statement to the House. In doing so, I earned the approval of the *Daily Mail* columnist Colin Welch. He not only complimented me but went on to say that I

> had one of those high Morningside accents which recall the very prime of Miss Jean Brodie. Deployed with speed, emphasis and clarity, it is the sort of voice which greasy foreigners, beggars, bearers, gully-gully men, shady couriers, ill-intentioned Lotharios, cutpursers and seducers hear with alarm. They cringe and shrink away, muttering apologies.

It was great fun for me to read and just a little bit exaggerated.

In one important area I had direct responsibility. In 1984, the European Council established the Ad Hoc Committee for Institutional Affairs, which would consist of the personal representatives of the heads of state and government. I was asked by the Prime Minister to serve on the committee, which was chaired by a former Irish Foreign Minister, James Dooge, and inevitably became known as the Dooge Committee.

The heads of state and government had asked us 'to make suggestions for the improvement of the operation of European cooperation in both the Community field and that of political, or any other, cooperation'. This language was typically verbose but the intention was to lay the foundation for further major reform and integration within the European Community.

We were described as the personal representatives of the heads of state and government. Most of the committee members were either former ministers or senior diplomats. The most colourful was the Italian, Carlo Ripa di Meana, a future EU Commissioner. He was a handsome man whose reputation preceded him to Brussels. His aristocratic, thrice-married wife had published what she chose to call 'her sexual memoirs'. In them, she disclosed that her pet name for Carlo was 'Orgasmo'.

Most of the members of the committee were free to express their own opinions and make their own personal recommendations on reform. That was not my situation nor that of a minority of the other members.

Any recommendations that I wished to make and any endorsement of the final report of the committee would need the Prime Minister's approval. I did not object to that. The issues that were being discussed were of national importance. In any event, once it was known that I would need clearance from Margaret Thatcher before I could approve recommendations, it added to my negotiating strength on the committee. If they wanted a united report, they would need to accommodate not only me but her.

Nor was the official British position entirely negative. The most important issue to be discussed was a fully integrated internal market as envisaged by the Treaty of Rome. The United Kingdom was a fervent enthusiast of a proper single market. Indeed, Margaret Thatcher was persuaded that majority voting on the Council of Ministers would have to be conceded, as otherwise protectionists like France would be able to prevent a single market in services as well as goods from being achieved.

We met regularly in a grand Brussels palace. My main objective was, if possible, to get a unanimous report with recommendations that we could genuinely support. That was always unlikely, as there were some federalists amongst my fellow members who were inclined to express their own personal enthusiasms even when that went beyond the policy of their governments.

In the event, the report and the recommendations were as good as we could have realistically hoped. The most important recommendation was unanimous support for what became known as the Single European Market.

There was no explicit recommendation for the creation of a single currency. Instead, the language used was about forging ahead 'towards monetary integration' through co-ordination of monetary policies, liberalisation of capital movements, participation in the European Monetary System (EMS), 'provided that the necessary economic and monetary conditions are met', and increased use of the European Currency Unit (ECU). All of this was acceptable to 10 Downing Street.

I had objections to a small number of detailed recommendations, but these were met by footnotes at the bottom of the page. I had recommended this device as a means of avoiding the need for a minority report. It proved very popular and hardly a page of the report is without a footnote of reservations by one or other of my colleagues on the committee.

My main reservation was to an explicit recommendation that there should be an inter-governmental conference to draft a new European Union Treaty. I, along with my Dutch and Greek colleagues, dissented, saying that this was a matter for the heads of government to decide.

The most historic consequence of our report was the Single European Act, the first major revision of the Treaty of Rome, which had been signed in 1957. It was signed in Luxembourg in 1986 and provided for the establishment of the single market by the end of 1992.

At that time, the European Community had only eleven members. In March 1985, we completed the negotiations for Spanish and Portuguese membership. That session was memorable for me for two reasons apart from its historic significance.

The Greek Foreign Minister, Mr Haralambopoulos, made an impassioned speech about Spain. He spoke in Greek, which had to be translated for the other ministers. At one stage the interpreter, translating his words into English, quoted him as using the words 'putting a Spaniard in the works' as opposed to a spanner. The British fell about and, to this day, the Greek minister has no idea as to which of his serious remarks caused this hilarity.

One of the final issues to be resolved in the negotiations with Spain was whether the United Kingdom could continue to sell a product we called British sherry, which, of course, had nothing to do with the Spanish town of Jerez from which sherry gets its name. We had been told that the Spanish Cabinet had decided that the end of the term 'British sherry' was crucial to Spanish honour.

British sherry was a cheap, rather foul-tasting liquid that had no legitimate relationship to sherry and was drunk, I was informed, mainly by pensioners and alcoholics. It was, however, a 100-year-old industry and we were told that 2,000 jobs were at stake. We were successful at avoiding a discussion on the subject and British sherry won a short-term reprieve. I was not altogether proud of that victory.

My other responsibilities during those years were for British relations with sub-Saharan Africa. South Africa, Nigeria and Zimbabwe were the most important but I visited most of the other English-speaking countries as well.

Both during those years and when I was Defence Secretary and Foreign Secretary, overseas travelling became part of my way of life. There is no substitute for meeting one's foreign colleagues in their own capitals and, sometimes, in their homes, if one wants to develop the close relationships which are invaluable in helping resolve international problems. They do not, by themselves, bridge the gaps but they create a relationship of trust and friendship that can help find solutions rather than problems.

On some of these visits Edith accompanied me. They were hard work for her as well as for me. She would have her own programme, meeting the spouses of our ambassadors and diplomats working abroad.

Because of her medical background she would visit hospitals and clinics and help fly the flag. Her presence often meant that dinner in the evening would be at our host's home or official residence, with his wife also present. Just as Gorbachev's decision to have his wife, Raisa, accompany him to Chequers made the meeting with Margaret Thatcher warmer and more convivial from the start, there was a similar informality in my own visits which helped pave the way for the serious negotiations that followed.

I understand that in these more austere times it is now very unusual for spouses to accompany ministers abroad. There is much nervousness about accusations of freebies and additional cost to the taxpayer. It is a false economy. Ministers usually stay with the ambassador at his residence, not at hotels. The additional cost is limited to one air fare; the benefits can be substantial.

The first journey I made to Africa was an extraordinary visit, accompanying Prince Michael of Kent to Swaziland in September 1982 for the state funeral of King Sobhuza. What occurred could have been the subject of a short story by Evelyn Waugh.

King Sobhuza had reigned since 1899, when at the age of four months he had succeeded his late father. By Swazi custom, the King was to be buried, in a seated position, in a cave with his ancestors. Only next of kin were permitted to attend this ceremony but that, we discovered, involved a significant number of people given his seventy wives and 210 children.

We were to attend the state funeral in the capital, Mbabane, at a specially constructed stadium near the royal kraal.

When we arrived at the VIP section, the late King's senior wife, known as the Great She Elephant, was sitting, in tribal robes, in the place of honour. Prince Michael saluted her when he came before her but her only response was to raise one eyebrow.

We were seated with the other dignitaries. I noted the Vice-President of South Africa in his black Homburg hat sitting between the Zambian and Tanzanian Prime Ministers. Not a word was exchanged by them with him during the whole ceremony.

A few rows behind me was a splendid old man wearing nothing

but animal skins and with a red card pinned on his chest, with the word 'Press'. Whether he was from *The Times* or the *Daily Mail* I never discovered.

As the funeral cortège approached, the band played a slow version of 'Auld Lang Syne'. I thought that it should have been 'Will ye no come back again?'

King Sobhuza had been invested with the GCMG by the Queen when he was on a state visit to Britain. The gold insignia are valuable and should be returned when the recipient dies. I had been asked to bring them back with me. This proved to be rather difficult.

As the funeral casket approached, we saw what looked like a sedan chair. It was more than six feet tall and had a glass front and sides. Inside, clearly visible and in a seated position, was his late majesty, the King, in full military uniform and wearing around his neck the gold insignia of the GCMG. I had to report to London that, as His Majesty had been wearing it around his neck in his coffin, they would have to get it themselves.

I subsequently discovered how the new King was selected by the elders. They had little knowledge of precedent, as the last time it had been done was in 1899.

Primogeniture does not apply in Swaziland and there were dozens of sons to choose from. They decided on one of the sons, Prince Makhosetive, subject to the condition that he would have to satisfy them that he would be able, in due course, to produce an heir and continue the royal line.

The prince at that time was a fourteen-year-old schoolboy at Sherborne School in Dorset. It appears that he did satisfy them, as he is now King Mswati III. I presume his next school holidays were busier than they would otherwise have been.

In November 1983, I visited Zimbabwe and South Africa, two countries that were familiar to me.

In Harare, I had about an hour with Robert Mugabe. I began by complimenting him on what was then his policy of reconciliation with Rhodesia's white community. When I remarked that in 1967, when I lived there, no one in the Rhodesian Front would have believed that a government led by Robert Mugabe would be allowing Ian Smith to continue to sit in Parliament, he smiled and said that no one in his own party would have believed it either.

In visiting South Africa, I was the first British minister to be there for three years. As with the Soviet Union, I was determined that our deep political differences, in this case over apartheid, would not prevent dialogue.

Indeed, I took the opposite view; speaking to white South Africa was essential if there was ever to be a prospect of the peaceful end to apartheid. Lord Curzon, Foreign Secretary in the early twentieth century, once remarked, 'You may have action if you like, without diplomacy, but that action will be war. You may lay down the pen, but you are then bound to take up the sword.'

In South Africa, my main talks were with F. W. de Klerk, then Internal Affairs Minister, and the Foreign Minister, Pik Botha.

Given de Klerk's role as the leader who dismantled apartheid ten years later, it may be of interest to see my assessment of him in 1983.

I found him 'highly intelligent, slightly evangelical in manner and with considerable authority. He came over as a professional and articulate politician, pleasant in manner but steely in purpose ... One got the impression of a South African politician offering to the blacks any institutions or reforms that would not weaken white power.'

He was by far the most impressive of the South African ministers I met and he was already being spoken of as a potential future leader.

My conclusion on the prospects for fundamental change in South Africa was that I was 'intensely sceptical' of the government's 'desire or ability to contemplate fundamental reforms to meet black aspirations but we must wait and see before condemning any new institutions just in case the leopard has changed its spots'.

The leopard had not changed its spots in 1983. Thanks to de Klerk, it began to do so six years later, in 1989. De Klerk can be seen as

South Africa's Mikhail Gorbachev. Mandela deserves by far the most praise for the peaceful end of apartheid but without de Klerk it could not have happened.

In one respect, de Klerk's task was even more difficult than Mandela's. Mandela was receiving power. De Klerk had to persuade his own white community to give it up, and to do so before they had been defeated. That he succeeded showed that he had great political courage as well as remarkable powers of leadership.

Swaziland was not the only African monarchy to give me much to remember. In March 1984, I visited Ghana. While most of my discussions were with ministers in Accra, we were also asked by the High Commissioner to visit Kumasi for an audience with the Asantehene, the King of the Ashanti and one of Ghana's most respected tribal leaders.

We had been advised by Kevin Burns, the High Commissioner, that the Asantehene did not speak directly to mere mortals but through one of his elders, known as the Linguist. When we arrived at Kumasi Airport we were asked by one of the King's aides who my Linguist would be, as it was assumed that the minister, also being omnipotent, would use one. I volunteered my private secretary, Stephen Lamport, for this role, to his not inconsiderable consternation.

The Asantehene met us at his modest palace, dressed in a brilliant green, yellow and red toga-style garment. He had as many solid-gold ornaments on his arms and legs, around his neck and on his fingers as you would normally find in a Bank of England vault.

He welcomed us in Twi, the local language. This was then repeated by his Linguist in Twi and finally translated into English by an interpreter.

I replied in kind. Stephen, standing behind me like the family butler, repeated what I had said, which was then translated into Twi. It may have been because of this good experience of dealing with royalty that Stephen, later in his career, became a distinguished private secretary to the Prince of Wales.

I exchanged gifts with the Asantehene. As recommended by the High Commissioner, I handed over a crate of Scotch whisky and a bottle of Campari. I received a local wooden carving in return. After thirty minutes of these elaborate and not very informative exchanges, the Asantehene suddenly broke into perfect English and said, directly to me, 'Well, that's enough of that. Let's go and see some dancing.' It turned out that he was a London barrister, trained at the Inns of Court.

Anyone in Britain tempted to be amused by this ornate ceremonial that continues to be respected in the Court of the Asantehene should reflect on how our own State Opening of Parliament by the Queen must appear to those of republican tendencies.

Shortly after this trip, I had to choose a new private secretary. One of those who presented himself to be interviewed by me was Anthony Cary.

Normally, the interviewee, keen to be chosen, spends most of the interview agreeing with whatever the minister is saying in order to try to win his support. That was not Anthony's style.

I expressed a view and he interrupted to say that he did not agree with that. He did so on several occasions over the next half hour and, afterwards, confessed that he had assumed he had wrecked his chances. In fact, I chose him partly because he had been so provocative. A minister needs a private secretary who will speak truth to power, though preferably politely. Anthony finished his diplomatic career as a distinguished High Commissioner to Canada and ambassador to Sweden.

A Minister of State's life is never dull. Three months after my visit to Ghana, I was giving lunch to the new Nigerian High Commissioner in London. In my toast, I expressed my expectation that I would be seeing him again soon.

My wish was granted. The following day, he was summoned back to the Foreign Office and informed that he was being expelled.

While we had been having lunch, Umaru Dikko, a Nigerian

opposition politician, was being kidnapped on the streets of London. That afternoon, a crate, destined for Lagos, was opened at Stansted Airport and found to contain his drugged body.

Although they denied it, it was clear that the Nigerian government was responsible. The plotters had not been very clever. Although they claimed that the crate contained diplomatic bags, they had not described it as such on the documentation. The crate had therefore been opened without any breach of the Vienna Convention, which protects diplomatic material from being interfered with.

There was a curious sequel. A few weeks later, my private secretary said to me that we had a problem. Some freight had been identified at Heathrow which was destined for Nigeria. The authorities were suspicious.

When I asked him what kind of freight it was, he said it was a coffin with a body in it. When I asked if there was anything else that made them concerned, he said that there was. It was addressed to the Chief of Police, Lagos.

They were given permission to open the coffin. It turned out to be innocuous. The Chief of Police's nephew had been killed in a road accident. In that climate, we could not be too careful.

As Minister of State I was occasionally invited to Buckingham Palace when the Foreign Secretary was overseas. One such occasion was in 1985, at a lunch the Queen gave for President Nyerere of Tanzania. Amongst those present were the Prince and Princess of Wales.

After lunch Edith and I were in conversation with the Princess. I wrote at the time that 'she does not yet sound a royal – rather a pleasant young woman from good background. I doubt if she knows yet how to freeze you with a single glance!'

South Africa was, not surprisingly, the most difficult challenge the British government faced in Africa. We had a shared history and close family links with South Africa and we recognised the need for the continent's most powerful country not to descend into instability and chaos because of its own internal conflict.

At the same time, we detested apartheid, had acquiesced in South Africa's departure from the Commonwealth and, together with the international community, had imposed various sanctions.

In June 1984, Prime Minister P. W. Botha of South Africa was invited to Chequers to meet the Prime Minister. It was the first such meeting since 1961, when Dr Verwoerd met Harold Macmillan. Geoffrey Howe and I were the ministers present.

Geoffrey and I arrived at the same time but rather early. We had some difficulty in getting access to Chequers. We rang the bell twice to no avail. As we were beginning to wonder if we had chosen the wrong day, the door was opened by a disconcerted young lady assistant who was a bit flustered. Geoffrey's first words were, 'Good morning. I'm calling on behalf of the Conservative Party.'

When we joined the Prime Minister, she remarked, 'I'm not looking forward to this.'

When Botha's helicopter landed, Geoffrey and Denis Thatcher were sent out to greet him. There was press speculation that her decision not to greet the President at the helicopter was a political decision. In fact, her reason at the time was that the wind caused by the helicopter landing would wreak havoc with her hair.

P. W. Botha was tough and courteous but had little charisma. He looked rather like an old family doctor or solicitor. He was accompanied by Pik Botha, his Foreign Minister, and Dr Barnard, his head of intelligence.

The pre-lunch session concentrated on Namibia, Angola and the region. In the afternoon we discussed apartheid. Mrs Thatcher was excellent on the unacceptability of a colour bar. She said to the President that it was 'unacceptable that political rights should depend on colour of skin'.

The meeting was useful but it was clear that P. W. Botha neither could nor would dismantle apartheid. He did accept the need for reform but it would need a new leadership in South Africa before real change would begin.

In September 1985, I was representing the Foreign Secretary at a Council of Ministers meeting in Luxembourg which was to discuss a new basket of sanctions against South Africa. The Prime Minister and Geoffrey had discussed this the previous week and had decided that, at that meeting, I should seek to avoid isolation but also avoid agreement to any economic sanctions.

One new proposal that had been raised was that all European Community countries should withdraw their defence attachés from embassies in South Africa. Geoffrey gave me authority to concede that if it was necessary to obtain a package that excluded economic sanctions.

During the course of the Council of Ministers meeting, that became the package that was available but to my consternation I received a message from Charles Powell, the Prime Minister's private secretary, that Mrs Thatcher did not approve the withdrawal of our defence attaché and I could not, therefore, agree to the package. I was appalled. It looked as if our talks would collapse, with severe criticism of the British government both at home and abroad, over the relatively minor matter of defence attachés when we had achieved our main objective of avoiding economic sanctions.

The outcome that day was better than I feared. Instead of a collapse of the negotiation because of British obstruction, I was able to persuade No. 10 that I should say that Britain reserved its position on the attaché proposal to enable us to consider it further.

The British press were not, however, very impressed. The *Financial Times* headlined 'Britain blocks EEC line-up on sanctions' while the *Daily Telegraph* rebuked the Foreign Secretary for being in West Africa when he should have been in Luxembourg. They remarked that 'his hapless deputy waited for a message – any message – in faraway Luxembourg'. These remarks were unfair but entirely predictable.

I was feeling slightly bruised but Geoffrey, who was a marvellous boss, sent a message from West Africa thanking me for having been successful in 'avoiding the impression of a major row' in Luxembourg with our European partners.

On 15 September, the Prime Minister held a seminar at Chequers to discuss the Luxembourg package and our overall policy on South Africa. I drove down with Geoffrey in his car and as we were thirty minutes early he was uncertain whether to go straight in or drive around for a while. He decided not to wait but, given that he was Foreign Secretary, his hesitancy was significant. It indicated that even at that stage his relationship with Margaret Thatcher, while close and informal, was not as intimate or equal as it might, and should, have been.

During the informal part of the seminar we had what I described at the time as 'a splendid afternoon of the vintage Thatcher style with a furious row' over the proposed withdrawal of defence attachés.

After various explosions, the Prime Minister was willing to concede that we should accept the package. My personal note, written after the meeting, says: 'I remain unclear as to whether she knew she would end up there all along, whether she was battered into submission or whether she was simply enjoying herself and clearing her own ideas by this somewhat barbed and bloodletting procedure. I suspect that all these factors played their part.'

What was interesting and encouraging during the seminar, given her instincts and prejudices, was Mrs Thatcher's repudiation of apartheid and her acceptance of the need for fundamental reform. She also did not hide her pragmatism with regard to the need to involve the African National Congress and Nelson Mandela in any reform process.

At the end of September, Samora Machel, the President of Mozambique, came on an official visit and I had to sit in at his meeting with Mrs Thatcher.

When I saw the Prime Minister, and before Machel arrived, she was still angry about having accepted the package. She described the Foreign Office as 'gutless' and said it was just like 1939. It hadn't apparently dawned on her that if the rest of us were gutless in giving in to international pressure on this issue, so was she in giving in to her Foreign Secretary's pressure on the same issue.

President Machel then joined us and South Africa was raised. Later that day I wrote the following:

> We had a superb example of her ability to disassociate herself from HMG ... Discussing our view of sanctions she remarked, 'We have been applying diplomatic pressure. We do not sell them any oil. They [pointing at me] have decided to withdraw our defence attachés. I do not know what good that will do. He [pointing at me again] has a different point of view.

President Machel was somewhat nonplussed.

When you are a Foreign Office minister, you have to become skilled in diplomacy and the use of words. I had an early lesson with one of my first visits abroad in January 1983.

While in Pakistan, after a meeting with President Zia-ul-Haq, I visited a refugee camp for Afghans on the outskirts of Peshawar. I was required to address a hundred of them who were sitting on the ground in tribal costume and appeared to be armed to the teeth. I made a conventional speech wishing them well, hoping that the Soviet invaders of their country would be sent packing and that they would be able to return home to a free and independent Afghanistan.

My speech had to be translated into Pashto and seemed to be well received. The following day, the High Commissioner showed me the local English-language Peshawar newspaper. It reported my speech, but the reporter had clearly heard the Pashto version and had then translated it back into English. It had changed somewhat in the process.

I read that visiting British minister Malcolm Rifkind had called upon the Afghans to 'continue their jihad against the Soviet infidel'.

I was aghast. It was not the Pakistani papers I was worried about. I wondered how Mrs Thatcher would react to one of her ministers calling for jihad against infidels. Then I reflected that she might, actually, be quite impressed. Neither I nor the Foreign Office was as 'wet' as she had previously imagined.

Diplomacy deals with international issues by negotiation. But it also has procedures and protocol to deal with day-to-day issues. I had two splendid examples which illustrate the particular skills of our diplomats. As it happens, they both applied to exiled Balkan royalty.

One day I was asked by my colleague Julian Amery whether I would join him for coffee at his flat in Eaton Square to meet King Leka of Albania. I was intrigued and, as we had no serious relations with the hardline Communist government in Tirana, I decided to accept.

Not being used to meeting Kings, I asked for advice as to how I should address King Leka when I met him. He had never actually been King of Albania. He was one day old when Mussolini invaded Albania and his father, King Zog, had fled into exile, never to return.

The protocol department at the Foreign Office sent me unforgettable advice. There should be no question, they said, of the minister addressing Leka as 'Your Majesty', as he never had been King and was never likely to be. He should be addressed as 'Sir'. They went on to say that nor should I bow to him when introduced. However, in deference to the fact that he was the son and heir of King Zog, 'The minister should incline his head, but not too much, and only the first time.'

After the fall of Communism, Leka actually returned to Albania and persuaded them to have a referendum on the monarchy. He lost but got around a third of the vote, so it was just as well I inclined my head, even if not too much and only the first time.

A much more substantial figure was, and is, Crown Prince Alexander of Yugoslavia. He wrote to me at that time asking me to confirm that he was entitled to British citizenship as he was born in London, just after the war, when his father, King Peter, was in exile.

The Foreign Office lawyers said that, sadly, he was not so entitled as he was born in a suite at Claridge's which, at the request of his father, had been declared to be Yugoslav territory for the purpose of his birth.

However, they had done some research on his lineage and had discovered that he was the direct descendant of the Electress Sophia of Hanover and, under the Act of Settlement, all her direct descendants were entitled to British citizenship. So the answer was no but yes!

Edith and I got to know Prince Alexander and his wife Princess Katherine very well and they became, and have remained, close friends.

Prince Alexander refused to return to Belgrade while Milošević was in power. When democracy came to Serbia, he returned and was given official status and recognition. He and his wife live in the royal palace. While there is no proposal to restore the monarchy, they have an active public life, a considerable following and involvement in many charitable activities.

I have stayed with them at the royal palace and, in 2013, was invited to the state funeral of his father, King Peter, whose remains, together with that of other close family, were returned to Serbia and buried in the royal mausoleum with full honours. His dynasty, unlike other Balkan monarchies, were a family native to Serbia that had led the battle for liberation from the Ottoman Empire, which gives them a greater legitimacy than they would otherwise enjoy.

Being a Foreign Office minister meant I had to spend part of the parliamentary recesses in London. This even applied in August, when most of the inhabitants of central London seemed to be out of town on their holidays.

One day I had a free evening and decided to dine at Brooks's Club in St James's. I was not a member, but it had reciprocal rights with the New Club in Edinburgh.

When I entered the dining room, it was depressingly empty because of the time of year. Only one table was being used and the other diners were thirty years older than I was.

I joined them and, to my relief, the one empty chair was taken by someone of my age. It was Christopher Wilkins, a former Welsh

Guards officer who was now managing his own waste disposal company in central Scotland. He was amusing, stimulating and great fun. We spent the whole evening chatting to each other and have continued to do so over the subsequent thirty-six years. Christopher has, in recent years, been a very successful promoter of wind farms, especially in Scotland, as well as the author of a well-received history of England's last knight errant in the age of chivalry.

Edith and I are equally fond of his wife, Margaret Eliott, who is, amongst her many virtues, the Chief of Clan Eliott. She and Christopher live at Redheugh in the Scottish Borders, where we have often visited them.

By 1986, I had been in the Foreign Office for four splendid years. Throughout 1985, there was considerable press speculation that I would be promoted to the Cabinet to succeed George Younger, who had been Scottish Secretary since 1979.

The Prime Minister had indicated in 1982 that that was where she expected me to go and I felt ready for that challenge if it came. In March 1985, I had been asked by Downing Street to draft a passage on Scottish issues for the Prime Minister's forthcoming speech for the Scottish Conservative conference, which indicated that her thinking was still in that direction.

1985 came and went and nothing happened. Geoffrey Howe counselled me to be patient. It was good advice but it is always easier to advise patience than to practise it. I continued travelling around the world, reminding myself that I was only thirty-nine, far too young to despair.

CHAPTER 13

SCOTLAND'S MAN
IN THE CABINET

A DAY THAT WAS intended to be quiet, tranquil and an opportunity for recuperation from flu ended in a rather unexpected
fashion.

Mid-morning on 9 January 1986, while scrutinising Foreign Office
telegrams in my study at home in Duddingston Village, the phone
went. It was a BBC freelance reporter, Kenny McIntyre. He informed
me that Michael Heseltine had just resigned as Defence Secretary and
that the rumour was that George Younger was to replace him and I
was to replace George. Would I let him know if I received a phone
call from No. 10?

I told him that I had no idea what he was talking about but would
he please get off the line in case his forecast was correct.

Half an hour later the phone did ring and I was put through to
the Prime Minister. After initial courtesies about my state of health,
she informed me that her news would probably help me get better.
The Queen had just approved George Younger as Michael Heseltine's

successor at the Ministry of Defence and the Prime Minister would like me to succeed George. I said that I would be delighted and honoured to do so.

She said that she had spoken to Geoffrey Howe, who was 'devastated' that I was leaving the Foreign Office.

That evening I received another call from the private secretary at No. 10. I was concerned that the Prime Minister might have changed her mind but it was because she had forgotten to tell me that I would also become a Privy Councillor.

I rang Edith and asked her to come home as something important had happened that I could not discuss on the phone. I was being unnecessarily cautious. Edith jumped into the car, put on the radio and heard, courtesy of the BBC, of my appointment.

Although the timing was something I could not have predicted, being chosen as George's successor was not a complete surprise. Mrs Thatcher had anticipated it in 1982 and the press had predicted it.

But it was not entirely inevitable. In her memoirs, Mrs Thatcher wrote:

> Malcolm Rifkind was the heir apparent. But I appointed him with mixed feelings. He had been a passionate supporter of devolution when we had been in opposition. He was one of the party's most brilliant and persuasive debaters. No one could doubt his intellect or grasp of ideas. Unfortunately he was as sensitive and highly strung as he was eloquent. His judgement was erratic and his behaviour unpredictable.

The Prime Minister well understood that I was not a Thatcherite or 'one of us'. It is interesting that one of her concerns was that I was 'unpredictable'. It is another way of saying that I was pragmatic rather than a conviction politician. I had never suggested otherwise to her.

The evening of my appointment to the Cabinet, I wrote down my thoughts and noted that I believed that I could carry out my new responsibilities 'competently and effectively'. I added, 'What will be difficult will be getting used to being the centre of domestic controversy after the relative ivory towers of the Foreign and Commonwealth Office.' That turned out to be one of my better predictions.

Being Secretary of State for Scotland in the days before there was devolution and a Scottish Parliament was a powerful post for a Cabinet minister. I was not only a full member of the United Kingdom Cabinet; I also had real control over the Scottish Office departmental budget, with the discretion to vary spending on education, housing, transport, police or a range of other activities as long as the outcome could be accommodated within the overall resources available to me.

I could also amend or defer United Kingdom government policies in order to respond to specific Scottish requirements. This could include opting out of such policies if I deemed it appropriate, as long as I did not do it too often.

For example, in the late 1980s, the Home Office decided to introduce private-sector-managed prisons in England and Wales. Although a great enthusiast for privatisation in general, I took the view, and still do, that restrictions on a person's liberty should be the responsibility of officers of the state and that it was wrong, in principle, for the private sector to be invited to run prisons. I decided, therefore, not to replicate the Home Office initiative in Scotland and did not experience any resistance from Whitehall to this decision.

Such was the autonomy and discretion available to the Scottish Secretary (and, to a lesser degree, also to the Welsh Secretary, as Peter Walker demonstrated) that I once compared my office to that of a Viceroy.

There was some truth in the comparison, but it was a foolish one to make. I was referring to the discretionary power that I could exercise without obtaining Cabinet approval. My political opponents, however, were delighted to have the opportunity to point out that

Tory Scottish Secretaries, like Viceroys, had not been elected by the people of Scotland and owed their power and appointment to the government in London.

What I did believe, and what got me into trouble with Margaret Thatcher on several occasions, was that the Secretary of State for Scotland was as much Scotland's man in the Cabinet as the Cabinet's man in Scotland. The Prime Minister was enthusiastic about the latter but not so keen on the former.

Scotland, and its press, judged Scottish Secretaries by their defence, and advancement, of Scottish interests. To recognise that was not only politically wise for me but, if I was deemed to have succeeded, beneficial to the Conservative cause north of the border.

On the other hand, I had to use my judgement, constantly, to distinguish between Scottish interests and what the Scottish press and opposition politicians were clamouring for or resisting.

My appointment was well received in Scotland. This was no reflection on George Younger, who had been very impressive. But he had now done the job for almost seven years. He wanted a change and the public expected it.

The press concentrated on my being the youngest ever Secretary of State for Scotland, but even that was not presented as a problem. The Labour-supporting *Daily Record* described me as a 'hothouse whiz kid with all the experience of a seasoned veteran'.

The *Glasgow Herald* remarked that 'few Scottish Secretaries have enjoyed the warmth of welcome accorded to Malcolm Rifkind' but warned that I had 'appalling problems' to deal with in the steel industry, the teachers dispute and local rates.

They forecast delightful sparring in the Commons between me and Donald Dewar, the shadow Scottish Secretary. He talked even faster than I did. I liked and respected him.

The *Scottish Sunday Mail*, in a slightly critical mood, observed that my Scottish accent had become less noticeable in recent years. 'It's so the English can understand what I am saying,' I responded.

I joined the Cabinet just over halfway through Mrs Thatcher's eleven years as Prime Minister. It already had a very different composition to the Cabinet she had formed when she arrived in Downing Street in 1979. I, at thirty-nine, was the youngest member. The Lord Chancellor, Lord Hailsham, at seventy-eight, was the oldest. He, as well as Enoch Powell and Ted Heath, who still spoke often in the Commons, were the titans I had read about and held in some awe as a callow youth.

One of my first duties was to take the oath as the Keeper of the Great Seal of Scotland. This required me to attend a special ceremony in a packed Court of Session where Scotland's senior judge, Lord Emslie, the Lord President, and a full bench of judges presided.

I had appeared before most of these judges as a young advocate. This was an even more daunting experience. Edith, my parents, Caroline and Hugo, my brother and his wife and Edith's mother witnessed the ceremony from what was usually the jury box. It was as memorable for them as it was for me.

In early March, at my initiative, I and eight of my senior Scottish Tory colleagues held a wide-ranging policy and election strategy review at Michael Ancram's house, Monteviot, in the Scottish Borders.

Those present included my ministerial team, Michael Ancram, John MacKay and Allan Stewart, as well as my parliamentary private secretary, James Douglas-Hamilton. Also attending were the Lord Advocate, Kenny Cameron; the Solicitor General for Scotland, Peter Fraser; the party chairman in Scotland, Sir James Goold; and the Scottish Whip, Gerry Malone.

All of them were bright, energetic and good team players. Whatever the future might hold, I could not fault them as a formidable band of brothers.

We had no shortage of issues to discuss. When I arrived at St Andrew's House, three stood out. The most urgent was the ongoing disruption in the schools organised by the main teachers union, the Educational Institute of Scotland (EIS). The second was the reform of the domestic rates and its proposed replacement by the poll tax, which was a high political priority. In the longer term, the future of Scotland's main steel plant at Ravenscraig was rarely out of the headlines. On top of all that, a general election was likely the following year and the political omens in Scotland were not encouraging.

The continuing disruption in the schools was the most urgent issue for me to resolve. It had begun in the winter of 1984 and had continued throughout 1985. Teachers had withdrawn their involvement in supervising school sports and had boycotted new curriculum development, delaying the introduction of microcomputers into classrooms.

The issue was pay and the union demand for an external salary review, which had been refused by the government both in Scotland and in England and Wales. By early 1986, English and Welsh teachers had reached an agreement for the current year and had agreed discussions on pay and related matters under the auspices of ACAS, the arbitration service.

I would normally have been willing to continue a hard line on industrial disputes of this kind even if they had created inconvenience for the general public. But I was deeply concerned that the disruption in the schools was not just disagreeable and inconvenient to the public. It was also threatening the ability of pupils to be prepared for important examinations, which could do serious damage to their prospects for university admission and their future careers.

I discussed this with my Cabinet colleagues, especially the Prime Minister and Keith Joseph, the Education Secretary. We reached agreement that an external inquiry could be conceded in Scotland without inevitable consequences for the rest of the United Kingdom.

I made a statement in the House of Commons to this effect on 6 March but insisted that the external inquiry would not, as the teaching unions wanted, be restricted to pay but would also cover their conditions of service, the management of the teaching profession in Scotland and the affordability of any recommendations on salaries.

The EIS union grumbled about the breadth of the terms of reference, but teachers, with a sense of great relief, stopped their disruption and the schools soon got back to normal.

In the early stages of the disruption, while I was still a minister at the Foreign Office, I had, in an Edinburgh street, bumped into one of the senior officers of the EIS, whom I knew. Rather light-heartedly, I asked him whether he, and his union colleagues, believed the government's position to be a 'cock-up' or a 'conspiracy'. He thought for a moment and then said they saw it as 'a cocked-up conspiracy'.

The schools issue was resolved; the community charge, or poll tax, controversy had just begun.

Local government finance, and the domestic rates in particular, had been a preoccupation of Margaret Thatcher since she entered 10 Downing Street. Forty per cent of council spending was financed either by householders or by local businesses.

As I have indicated, a large proportion of people who voted paid no rates at all because they were not classed as householders. The consequence was that the elderly widow paid the same domestic rates as four earning adults who lived in an identical house next door. Council tenants paid rates but, as the sums were included in the rent bill, many were unaware that they paid rates as well as rent.

The inherent unfairness of the system was that certain high-profile, left-wing councils who were determined to increase their spending put the whole burden for paying for it on ratepayers and local businesses, assuming that most of them were not Labour voters anyway. That had been part of the problem when I was last in the Scottish Office and we were battling with Lothian Regional Council.

The problem was exacerbated in Scotland, where, unlike in England, we had a statutory obligation to have a revaluation of all property. That had occurred in 1984 and, while it was fiscally neutral, the revaluation severely harmed many domestic ratepayers and businesses.

Many ratepayers faced increases of 40 per cent, while Jenners, Edinburgh's premier department store, faced paying business rates double those of a similar store in Oxford Street in London.

George Younger had been an enthusiast for rates reform since his first day in the Scottish Office and had faced angry demands for fundamental reform from Tory activists and middle-class Scots as a whole. There was a similar, vigorous debate in London, especially after the 1983 general election. Increasingly, a poll tax was seen as the best (or least bad) alternative to the rates and Mrs Thatcher became convinced that it was the only way to control the spending of left-wing councils and ensure that they were accountable to ratepayers as a whole.

By an extraordinary coincidence, the proposed Green Paper, recommending a community charge or poll tax, was on the Cabinet's agenda the very day that Michael Heseltine stormed out of the Cabinet, resigned as Defence Secretary and was replaced by George Younger.

The item was the first to be discussed after the Cabinet reassembled. By that time, I was Scottish Secretary but was sitting in my study at home in Edinburgh. The Scottish position was presented by the new Defence Secretary, who warmly welcomed what was being proposed both for Scotland and for the United Kingdom as a whole.

I, like the public, was well aware that the government was moving towards supporting a poll tax as the alternative to the domestic rates. I was not unhappy with that, as, being a Scottish MP, I was fully aware of the anger of my own constituents at the unfairness of the rates and the consequences of the revaluation.

Even while I was in the Foreign Office I had been thinking about this issue. On 27 March 1985, nine months before the Cabinet approved a poll tax, and despite being a junior minister in another department, I had minuted the Prime Minister on local government finance.

In my letter I had stressed the need for change, dismissed a local income tax, and suggested that a poll tax was the only alternative.

I was acutely aware that the acceptability of a poll tax and whether it was considered fair or unfair would, to a considerable degree, depend on whether it was a small or a large sum that the individual would have to pay.

I suggested that it might be best to raise the Rate Support Grant to cover 90 per cent of local government spending rather than the current 60 per cent, in order to keep a poll tax at a very low level and more acceptable to those on modest incomes. I have no record as to whether I got a reply to this missive and, of course, my recommendation was not accepted.

It is technically correct that the commitment to a poll tax was agreed without my having any opportunity to oppose it in Cabinet. The truth, however, is that if I had been there my view would have been the same as George Younger's, though I might have argued, as I had in my minute to the Prime Minister the previous year, that the poll tax would have to be very small to win and keep public support.

As it happened, my first major appearance in the Commons as Secretary of State, on 30 January, was both to answer questions and to give a statement on rates reform and the Green Paper. My performance received mixed reviews. The *Daily Record* described me as 'Rambo Rifkind' and 'No More Mister Nice Guy'. Ron Brown, the hard-left MP for Leith, suggested I was 'the Governor-General for Scotland', which is, of course, less prestigious than being a Viceroy.

Donald Dewar attacked the proposed community charge as 'ramshackle and confused'. A Liberal MP, Russell Johnston, said it would leave a man of modest means paying the same as the richest man in the land. I retorted that under domestic rates, the richest man could have a permanent suite at Gleneagles Hotel and pay nothing at all.

We had announced that the legislation to abolish the rates in Scotland would be debated and decided by Parliament in the forthcoming session, unlike England and Wales, where the legislation would be deferred until after the general election.

Over the years, I have lost count of the times that opposition

politicians and sloppy journalists have alleged that Mrs Thatcher and
the government decided that Scotland would be used as a 'guinea
pig': they would implement the poll tax north of the border first in
order to test it before applying it to England.

The allegation is nonsense, as all serious studies of the history of
the poll tax have concluded.

The poll tax came first in Scotland because George Younger, the
Tories in Scotland, and Scotland's ratepayers were determined to get
rid of the hated rating system as soon as possible.

George did not want the abolition of domestic rates to be just
a manifesto promise. He wished to demonstrate the government's
good faith by getting the legislation on the statute book before the
general election. Although the English Bill would not be ready in
that timescale, there was no technical reason Scotland could not go
first. The half of Scotland that wanted to get rid of the rates were
vocal in expecting that that should be done. The other half, including
the opposition, were more concerned with the details of the poll tax
than the timing of its introduction.

Although I was not yet in the Cabinet when that decision was
taken, I supported it and had no difficulty continuing with it after
I became Secretary of State. Indeed, I would have had a massive
rebellion on my hands if I had tried to reverse it.

In retrospect, the timing was, of course, a serious political mistake.
As politicians we should have realised that the 'guinea pig' allegation
would be used again and again. Given the strength of the Labour
Party and the existence of a left or centre-left political majority in
Scotland, it was not too difficult for the guinea pig myth to take hold
in Scotland's political culture.

I was not entirely oblivious to this risk. I made clear again and
again that while we would get the legislation onto the statute book,
we would not implement it until after the general election and only
then if the government introduced similar proposals for England and
Wales. This major conditionality is firmly in the public record, but I

doubt if most people were aware of it or would have been influenced by it. Undoubtedly, we pleased our supporters and those who wanted reform by going ahead of England, but we paid a political price that was more burdensome, and lasted longer, than any advantage.

Throughout 1986, the government dominated the debate on rates reform, which produced few dark clouds. One of the political reforms that I pressed for when I became Secretary of State was that the Scottish Secretary should, for the first time, have a speaking slot at the annual party conference in Blackpool and Bournemouth. I wanted Scotland and the Scottish Tories to become more prominent in the Conservative Party as a whole.

I was successful and was invited to do the ministerial reply to the debate on rates reform. I spoke for twenty minutes referring to Scotland, but most of my speech was equally relevant to the rest of the United Kingdom.

Mine was the only ministerial speech made without a prepared text, but much good my fluency did me. As the *Glasgow Herald* remarked, 'Nobody realised that the Scottish Secretary was not using the invisible autocue which gives the appearance of effortless oratory to party platforms these days.' The result was that although I got a standing ovation, it came 'by instalments and in patches'. Quite correctly, it was referred to as a creeping ovation in one report.

My colleague Nicholas Ridley, who was responsible for rates reform in England, was not impressed by my habit of speaking without a text. He was asked by journalists for his response to what I had said about abolition of the rates and protested, not unreasonably, that he could not answer as he had no idea what I had said. That can sometimes be an advantage for a minister but not, I concede, on this occasion.

The third issue I inherited was Ravenscraig and the future of the Scottish steel industry. Not closing Ravenscraig had become, for the opposition and the press, the litmus by which the government's commitment to Scotland would be tested.

George Younger had been successful in meeting that challenge and, as recently as 1985, Ravenscraig had been promised at least a further three years.

I hoped that Ravenscraig would stay open but I knew that was unlikely in the long term as, efficient though it was, its location made it very difficult to compete with south Wales and other steel plants in England.

The steel industry was due to be privatised and my strategy was to help ensure that it would be privatised without the closure of Ravenscraig. Its future would then be determined by the industry and not by the government. In the event, it remained open for another six years, until 1992.

In May 1986, only four months after I had joined the Cabinet, I had my first serious confrontation with Margaret Thatcher. It was at a Cabinet committee where I was in a minority of one. On 28 May, after a meeting of the full Cabinet, she chaired a meeting to discuss territorial expenditure and, in particular, that of Scotland vis-à-vis England.

This was a long-running issue that continues to this day. Scotland had, and still has, public expenditure which is, per capita, significantly higher than that for England. That is true for Wales and Northern Ireland as well, but it is Scotland, because of its greater size, that has attracted most of the attention.

It is also true for the north of England and for other poorer English regions outside the prosperous south-east and the Midlands. It reflects the lower average income, higher deprivation and higher unemployment of most of these regions.

In Scotland, it is also the consequence of sparsity of population outside the Central Belt, including Glasgow and Edinburgh, where around 80 per cent of the population live. Much of Scotland's landmass is the Highlands and Islands, the Borders and other rural areas where the cost of providing housing, health, transport and other services is much higher because of the many small and widely separated communities.

The Prime Minister had commissioned a Cabinet paper to get a factual basis for our discussions. I was pleased with this paper, as it confirmed that the formula for determining how much Scotland received had worked, since it was introduced, as expected. It also confirmed that Scotland's economic performance compared to England had not improved since 1979 and that there were no economic criteria available that would justify a reduction in Scottish resources.

However, the Chief Secretary to the Treasury, John MacGregor, opened the discussion calling for a substantial cut of £100 million in the Scottish baseline. I spoke next and pointed out that the Cabinet paper showed that Scotland's economic performance had not only not improved compared to England but had actually deteriorated in the three areas selected, unemployment, GDP per capita and disposable income. The Prime Minister intervened to say these were statistical aberrations caused by the City of London inflating the English figures. I gently reminded her that these were the figures used by the Cabinet Office, not by me, in order that we could have an agreed factual basis for our discussions.

The only concession I made was to acknowledge that Scotland's population had fallen since 1979, but this had only been by a total of 30,000. To adjust Scotland's resources to take account of this would result in an insignificant reduction.

I also, perhaps rather smugly, pointed out that the Goschen formula which, in 1888, had given Scotland 13.75 per cent of the combined English and Welsh resources was the same proportion as in 1970 and 1985. In other words, the Treasury were trying to upset not some recent advantage that Scotland had obtained but a system that was almost a hundred years old.

Far from being impressed, the Prime Minister rebuked me for my unhelpful response. She said that she had come to the meeting intending to help me by opposing a Needs Assessment Study (NAS) but if I was not prepared to accept the proposed cut of £100 million she would change her view and support an NAS.

A Needs Assessment Study would have been a lengthy study of all the regions of the United Kingdom to see which deserved more public expenditure and which less. There was an assumption that that would be more harmful to Scotland.

I made it clear that I would prefer a NAS, which would be a reputable analysis of the needs of the different regions. Whatever the outcome, it would be more defensible than an arbitrary cut in Scottish resources not paralleled elsewhere in the kingdom.

Willie Whitelaw appealed to me to think again. I declined for two reasons, only one of which I declared. For me to accept a significant cut in Scottish expenditure when no corresponding cut was being made in any other part of the country would be political suicide both for me and for the Tory Party in Scotland.

My unstated reason was that I was convinced that the Prime Minister and the Treasury did not want a Needs Assessment Study any more than I did. It would take two years, would be highly controversial and would open up differences within England as well as between England and Scotland. As a result, the Treasury might end up with none of the net savings that it yearned for.

In the contemporaneous note I wrote about the threat of a Needs Assessment Study, I remarked, 'The possibility of execution in two years is preferable to the certainty of amputation tomorrow!'

The Prime Minister was pretty fed up with me by now. She remarked on the weakness of the party in Scotland and said that if it was not for Tory victories in England, 'you would not be here'. I replied that if I agreed to the proposed Scottish cuts, not replicated elsewhere, I would soon cease to be here anyway.

Mrs Thatcher then referred to her speech at the Scottish conference in Perth, when she had described how much extra spending the Scots got. There were a few chuckles when I quoted from the same passage in her speech, which showed that she had given these statistics to refute the argument, often heard, that London was not interested in Scottish needs.

The meeting concluded without a decision. Throughout, the atmosphere had been frigid and a little bad-tempered. The dispute rumbled on for eight months but never leaked to the outside world.

It re-emerged in February 1987 during the wider public expenditure discussions. I remained as stubborn as ever and it went to the final court of appeal, the Star Chamber, where Willie Whitelaw presided over a committee of senior ministers to adjudicate between the Treasury and unhelpful departments.

Again, I was in a minority of one, and Willie summed up accordingly. It was assumed I had no choice but to submit, but I then used the last arrow in my quiver. I requested that my dissent be recorded in the minutes.

This meant that the dispute would have to be referred to the full Cabinet, which was very rare. Willie Whitelaw, who had been no ally but was very wise, took this as a clear signal that I was prepared to go all the way and had a conversation with me after the meeting had finished. Thereafter, the proposal for a unilateral cut in the Scottish budget was quietly dropped apart from a minor adjustment as a result of population change, which I had no difficulty in accepting.

This had been quite a baptism of fire for a new Cabinet minister. Defeating the Treasury and resisting the Star Chamber is a painful and fractious experience. I used up a considerable amount of goodwill and my credit with my Cabinet colleagues was low in the immediate aftermath.

But although Mrs Thatcher was angry with me and felt that I was being extremely unhelpful, part of her may have recognised a kindred spirit. Saying 'No, no, no' was, after all, a tactic that she was familiar with.

It was not all gloom at that time. One of the agreeable consequences of being Secretary of State for Scotland was that I became a temporary member of the royal household when the Queen was in Scotland. The Queen would usually spend a week at Holyrood

Palace, holding an investiture and a garden party, as well as visiting various towns or villages not too far from Edinburgh.

On these occasions I would be in attendance but with little else to do. During one visit the Queen was doing a walkabout in Linlithgow and the crowds and the press were out in force. The Queen's press officer gently, but firmly, asked me not to respond to journalists' enquiries, as the story of the day had to be about the Queen and not the Secretary of State.

In August 1986, the Queen was due to cruise around the west of Scotland on the royal yacht *Britannia* on her way to Balmoral. She had agreed to visit Ardnamurchan Lighthouse, which is at a remote point on the west coast mainland.

Because I would have to be in attendance, the Queen kindly invited me to join *Britannia* on the Saturday and sail with them, over the weekend, to Ardnamurchan on the Monday morning. I could then, after the Queen's visit, be driven in my car back to Edinburgh.

It was an unforgettable experience. The other passengers included the Duke and Duchess of York, recently back from their honeymoon, Prince Edward and the young children of the Princess Royal.

We cruised around the Inner Hebrides and on the Sunday passed through the Sound of Islay and berthed off Colonsay. That afternoon, we travelled by launch to the small island of Oronsay for a picnic.

Tables and chairs had gone ahead of us but in every other respect it was completely informal, with the Queen helping lay the table. At one stage during the afternoon I asked the Queen's permission for her lady-in-waiting, Mary Morrison, to take a photograph, with my camera, of me with the Queen.

I have it to this day. It shows the Queen, smiling, in trousers and a headscarf while I have my white slacks rolled up almost to my knees, no socks, white sandshoes and my hands in the pockets of my sports shirt. Behind us are the tables, chairs and debris from the picnic. I have had the pleasure of being with the Queen on many occasions over the years I was in the Cabinet. Never before, nor since that day, was I dressed in such a casual manner.

I did, however, at a later time, fear that my dress might get me into trouble on the improbable issue of the Prince of Wales's buttons.

I had bought a smart blazer with plain brass buttons. Seeing in a shop window some buttons with the Price of Wales's feathers designed on them, I acquired them and had them sewn on to my blazer. However, a colleague who noticed them pointed out that I should not be wearing the Prince of Wales's feathers without his permission.

Knowing the Queen's private secretary, Bill Heseltine, I had cheerfully confessed this gaffe to him but, in due course, received a reassuring letter that the Prince of Wales would be delighted for me to wear his feathers and that I could 'flaunt [myself] in this adornment in the knowledge that you will be one of the very few properly authorised to do so'.

More important issues dominated those days. The general election was to be held on 11 June 1987. Five months earlier, on 6 January, I had minuted the Prime Minister on the prospects for the government and the Conservative Party at the forthcoming general election, whenever it was held. I marked the minute 'Personal and Confidential'. There were only two copies: hers and mine.

I began by pointing out that there was an increasing assumption that the Tories were going to win a third term of office. I then said that while the national speculation was on the likely size of the Conservative majority, the assumption in Scotland was that we would be 'severely mauled' and 'could see a substantial reduction in [our] parliamentary representation'.

Unlike in England, where our numbers had soared in the 1983 general election, in Scotland we had remained static with 28 per cent of the vote. I said that 'if a general election were held now, I would expect that we would retain about thirteen or fourteen of our twenty-one seats'.

I pointed out that this estimate was highly speculative. Because we had a four-party system, with the SNP and Liberals our main challengers in the rural areas and the Labour Party in the cities, we could end up with 25 per cent of the vote but win as few as twelve or as many as twenty seats depending on tactical voting, local issues and personalities.

I warned that if, in Scotland, we were reduced to ten or twelve seats, this would result in 'a major resurgence of the cry that the government had no mandate in Scotland'. I went on to say that we would, in such circumstances, have a major political crisis even if not a constitutional one, with 'our authority severely truncated'.

We would, I wrote, also have political difficulties in demonstrating a sufficient degree of public support to justify the community charge, privatisation and other future reforms. 'Devolution would be presented as an essential concession if Scots were to be reconciled to Conservative governments in Westminster that they had voted heavily against on three successive occasions.'

I then said, 'The foregoing is not a prediction but a worst-case scenario. We need not assume it will happen but I would be failing in my duty if I did not alert you to the possibility that it might.'

I take no pleasure in the fact that this minute turned out to be a remarkably accurate prediction of what did happen five months later when our seats in Scotland (though not our vote) collapsed and I ended up having to deal with my worst-case scenario.

Chapter 14

Secretary for Scotland 'in a State'

THE GENERAL ELECTION of 1987 duly took place and resulted in a great victory for the Conservatives, except in Scotland. North of the border we lost eleven seats, were down to a rump of ten, and my worst-case scenario had materialised.

Our vote had not collapsed. We retained six out of every seven votes that we had won in 1983 and had 24 per cent of the popular vote compared to 28 per cent beforehand. The SNP had to be content with 14 per cent of Scotland's votes. But even our modest drop in votes resulted in a disproportionate loss of seats. The Labour Party now had fifty of Scotland's seventy-two seats, the largest number in their history.

Our political opponents revelled in our disaster but, in retrospect, our experience has not turned out to be unique in Scotland's recent political history. Both the Labour Party and the Liberal Democrats were to experience a worse collapse, reduced to one MP each in the 2015 general election. Even the SNP had crashed to two MPs when Margaret Thatcher first came to power in 1979.

That was of little comfort to me the following week, when Parliament reassembled. All my Cabinet colleagues were rejoicing, as was I, in the Tories having won a third term. In my case, however, I felt rather like Mrs Abraham Lincoln being asked, 'Apart from that, did you enjoy the theatre?'

Some days later, I was coming out of St Giles' Cathedral in Edinburgh. An elderly clergyman came up to me and said, 'I just want to tell you that if you ever feel a bit depressed, remember what my old father said to me: "*Ne carborundum illegitimi.*"' Forgetting my Latin, I asked for a translation. The old man growled at me, 'Don't let the bastards grind you down.'

My first task was to reconstruct my Scottish Office team. I had lost some of my closest colleagues, especially Michael Ancram and John MacKay.

Michael was particularly unlucky. He was my undeclared deputy. If he had survived, he would most likely have been my successor when I moved on from the Scottish Office. He did return to the House of Commons, for Devizes, in 1992 and became an outstanding Minister of State at the Northern Ireland Office, where he made a significant contribution to the peace process.

During our years in opposition, he rose to be deputy leader of the party. But he never got the opportunity to serve in the Cabinet and that was a loss for the country as well as a disappointment for him. Politics can seem very unfair and be very arbitrary.

I tried to persuade Alick Buchanan-Smith to return to the Scottish Office as Minister of State. Not unreasonably, he decided to remain on the back benches. The two vacancies were filled by my close friend James Douglas-Hamilton and Michael Forsyth.

Twelve days after the election, I minuted the Prime Minister on the implications of the political carnage that we had experienced north of the border.

I remarked that to understand what had happened, one had to bear in mind the 'persistent overall decline in our fortunes over the last thirty years'. I suggested that the basic problem was one of Scottish identity and that the Conservatives were seen, essentially, as an English party.

Although devolution was not a high-profile issue during the campaign, as we were the only party opposed to a Scottish Assembly this was an additional stick with which to beat us.

Significantly, in my six-page minute to the Prime Minister I made absolutely no reference to the poll tax, either favourably or as a reason for our loss of seats. Despite what has often been claimed, it was not a major issue during the election campaign. Those who wanted rates reform were content with the ending of the rates. Its opponents spent far more time on job losses, factory closures and the other economic difficulties of the previous four years. Over a third of manufacturing jobs had been lost in Scotland. That had been the dominant issue.

In my minute to the Prime Minister, I said that the election outcome in Scotland, while not a constitutional crisis, had created an unprecedented crisis of political authority for the government. I wrote: 'Our parliamentary system of government is largely determined by constituencies won and lost. Operating by these criteria at the United Kingdom level we cannot credibly ignore them at the Scottish.'

This problem was, paradoxically, exacerbated by the existence of the Scottish Office and the substantial administrative devolution that Scotland enjoyed. The Tories had just as weak a political base in the north of England but that was much less visible and much less resented as, unlike Scotland, the north of England did not have its own ministers nor separate legislation in many fields. The north of England being a region rather than a country, allegations of a democratic deficit carried no weight.

I warned that while the implementation of the government's defence, taxation or other UK-wide policies would not be any more difficult in Scotland because of the outcome of the general election, the 'fundamental problem' would be any specific Scottish initiatives that we might wish to embark upon. Unless they were very popular they would be condemned as an imposition by a government without a Scottish mandate.

The earlier introduction of the poll tax became, in due course, an albatross around our necks which, in hindsight, I concede we should have avoided. We already had the legislation. We could have deferred its introduction until England and Wales had caught up with us.

In the minute that I sent her, I probably upset the Prime Minister by suggesting that one response that might need to be 'reconsidered' was our attitude to devolution and an assembly. While the election campaign had suggested that there was no demand for a Scottish Assembly, it was 'difficult to deny that there is a desire for it'.

I continued by saying:

> The issue is not going to go away and another five years with the Scottish Office run by a minority party is certain to lead to very heavy pressure for proper democratic accountability. We may need to give further consideration whether the long-term interests of the Conservative and Unionist Party in Scotland will be best served by continued total opposition.

These remarks reflected my own views but they did not amount to an attempt to persuade Mrs Thatcher to change course. I was well aware that not only would she have refused to do so but, as I acknowledged in the minute, 'the feeling amongst active Scottish Conservatives is mainly hostile to any change in our policy…'

The political reality was that it was going to need a change of government before devolution would be resurrected. Although I continued to be aware of the logical case for some form of devolved Scottish Assembly or Parliament, I did not, as I have said, have the emotional commitment to devolution that galvanised many other Scots and was content, having mentioned the subject, to leave it at that.

Devolution was a unique problem where letting sleeping dogs lie might be necessary. Such an approach did not attract elsewhere. In the minute to the Prime Minister, I wrote that 'one favoured course of action for this parliament [in Scotland] might be to do as little as possible, try and keep the temperature down and hope that better times will lie ahead. It is not a course that I could recommend.'

It may be thought that I could not recommend it as I was aware that, if I had done, I would have had my head bitten off by Margaret Thatcher. That was not what influenced me, at least not on that occasion. I had not yet reached a firm view as to how I, as Secretary of State, and the Scottish Office should use the powers that we had over the five years ahead. I knew, however, that seeking a quiet life was not a serious option.

My first public reaction to the general election result was in a statement issued the following day. While I expressed disappointment at the Scottish results, I emphasised that our vote was almost double that of the SNP. I suggested that 'economic and employment issues' had been 'prominent in the minds of the electorate'.

I concluded that Scottish Conservatives were 'disappointed but not depressed' and that 'we are a hardy lot and have been around for a long time and we are used to earning our votes'. This seemed to me the right blend of realism combined with determination to rebuild our fortunes.

I had said in the statement that we were 'disappointed but not depressed'. It was the right thing to say even if it was not how I felt. For the first few days I was deeply depressed, both by the loss of so many Scottish seats and by the realisation that I would have to carry the main burden of taking forward the government of Scotland from such a modest political base and with few political resources to fall back on.

The Prime Minister would want to help but it was impossible to ignore that she was part of the problem as well as being essential to its solution. Most of my Cabinet colleagues were very sympathetic, but there was little practical help they could give. The buck rested on my shoulders. Never again glad confident morn? Around this time the Scottish comedian Rikki Fulton gently referred to me as the Scottish Secretary 'in a state' rather than as Secretary of State. He had a point.

I thought hard about how to deal with this crisis in my own life as well as in the political firmament. This was the most serious challenge I had yet had to face, either in my life so far or in my thirteen years in Parliament. I also had an obligation to my Scottish parliamentary colleagues and to the Conservative Party in Scotland to show leadership and the way ahead.

I quickly realised that my own demeanour, what I said, and how I said it, had to be positive, cheerful and determined, not only to influence Scottish public opinion but to enable me to cope and deal with the unprecedented pressures that I was now facing.

Fortunately, as Edith has often confirmed, I am an incurable optimist. This is not the same as being foolishly naïve. I have often felt that the pessimist is someone who believes that things couldn't be worse while the optimist knows that they could be. If there is a silver lining, I will find it.

The silver lining was that the British electorate had given us the opportunity to continue the transformation of Britain, including Scotland, for the better. I was privileged to be a member of the Cabinet led by a Prime Minister with an international reputation as one of the greats. And in Scotland, while the government was unpopular, I had experienced no personal hostility. Whether merited or not, I was seen as likeable as well as competent, which was a considerable relief not only for me but for my family.

The first test of whether we would weather the storm was Scottish Questions in the House of Commons. Our troops were outnumbered sixty-one to ten. The exchanges were recorded by Michael Jones, the political editor of the *Sunday Times*, who suggested that the day reminded him of the battle of Culloden, when Cumberland defeated

Bonnie Prince Charlie. While Jones was kind enough to say that I 'put on a display of parliamentary brilliance' and 'carried the battle to the enemy and won the day', I was less pleased when he added that 'the Duke of Cumberland would have been proud of him'.

Of course, we knew that while our numbers were modest compared to those of Scottish Labour, we could draft in the massed ranks of English Tory backbenchers to ensure that we won the votes. Being still in Viceroy frame of mind, I allowed myself to explain this advantage by remarking, 'Whatever happens, we have got the Gatling gun and they have not.' I may have found this quote from Hilaire Belloc, referring to the Second Afghan War of 1878–80, irresistible. Whether it was wise of me to use it was another matter.

But while we were doing well in carrying on as if we did not have a care in the world, I knew that my Scottish Office colleagues and I also needed a clear and principled strategy that would determine the policy we would pursue on purely Scottish matters during the course of that parliament.

I gave careful thought as to what that strategy should be. Most important, it had to be a strategy that would benefit Scotland, increase its prosperity and enable it to face the challenges of the modern world. Scotland would need institutions, resources and a legal framework that would enable the natural ability, entrepreneurial skill and accumulated experience of Scots and of Scotland to be fully realised within the framework of the United Kingdom.

In applying these principles, I was quite willing to support and promote Scottish solutions that might not be identical to those being applied by my Cabinet colleagues in England and Wales. But it would not be differentiation for its own sake but only where the facts and the evidence pointed to such variation being desirable.

Although I was not an instinctive 'Thatcherite' but had always seen myself more in the One Nation tradition of Conservatism, I had been impressed not only by Mrs Thatcher's energy and leadership but also by the evident success of the trade union reforms, the early privatisation measures, the reductions in direct taxation and the attempts to end the dependency culture with which she was identified. I had myself been instrumental in bringing to the statute book the right to buy for Scotland's council tenants, which was both radical and progressive in its nature.

None of these reforms were in conflict with Scotland's interests and many were, if anything, even more urgently needed north of the border than in the rest of the kingdom given the dominance of the Labour Party and its enthusiasm for high taxation, government control and bureaucratic regulation. I was convinced that much still needed to be done in Scotland if we were to achieve the prosperity of the south-east of England.

I decided to spell out the strategy that we were going to pursue in Scotland and did so in a series of speeches I made in the weeks and months after the general election.

On 1 September 1987, twelve weeks after the election, I spoke to the Scottish Engineering Employers Federation in Glasgow. I began my speech by saying:

> Quite consciously and deliberately we are determined to change many of the attitudes and policies that have dominated Scotland for years and which are responsible for much of Scotland's social, economic and industrial problems ... These attitudes and policies which have dominated Scottish life have been essentially paternalist ... Half of all Scots are dependent on local or central government for the very houses they live in. An educational system ... has ... denied the parents any meaningful involvement in their children's schools. A suspicion of enterprise and the private sector is fostered which has led many of our best businessmen to depart south to pursue their careers ... Our real disadvantage compared to the south-east of England is the anti-enterprise, paternalistic, quasi-socialist culture fostered in Scotland for so long.

Two months later, on 5 November, speaking to the Scottish Council for Development and Industry, I continued with, and developed, this theme.

I said that the hallmark of the government's first two terms had been to create incentives for the public to develop their skills, work harder and, thereby, benefit their families. Some in Scotland had suggested that, however appropriate this might have been in England, the Scots were 'less materialistic, more egalitarian and more attracted to collectivist social and economic policies'.

If they believed that, I suggested that they should welcome what would be the hallmark of our third term of government: the encouragement not only of greater powers but also of responsibilities for citizens. Thus, we would establish, for the first time in Scotland, school boards so parents could be actively involved in the state schools attended by their children. Likewise, those council tenants in Scotland's large peripheral council estates who were not buying their homes would be encouraged to form tenants' cooperatives and housing associations to help ensure that the community of which they were part managed the housing that they lived in rather than the bureaucratic local authorities.

A third speech I made, in February 1988 to the Confederation of British Industry in Scotland, was particularly important. I argued that the free operation of the market in Scotland could increasingly favour Scotland and the English regions, as the south-east of England was becoming congested with extra costs, high overheads and damage being done to the quality of life.

Scotland already had an indigenous banking, insurance and investment industry second only to the City of London. There was, I suggested, an urgent need to develop private enterprise in Scotland by more ownership and decision making in Scotland and with more company headquarters based north of the border.

That led me to the main point that I wished to make. We had the opportunity 'to create major new Scottish private sector companies through the privatisation of nationalised industries located in Scotland'.

I argued that 'it is ... difficult to exaggerate the contribution that privatisation will make to the ... growth of the enterprise culture in Scotland'.

Firstly, it would mean the transfer of control of Scotland's nationalised industries from London back to Scotland. No longer would the investment needs of the Scottish electricity industry or the Scottish Bus Group be decided by the Treasury, seeking to reduce the public sector borrowing requirement, but by these industries themselves.

Secondly, privatisation would result in the creation of major new Scottish companies, especially in the electricity and gas sectors, with vast assets and many thousands of employees.

Thirdly, these employees and the Scottish public as a whole would have the opportunity to acquire a stake in the ownership of Scottish industry by becoming shareholders as well.

These three speeches summed up my determination not to let the general election results in Scotland paralyse the government and end the prospects for radical reform in Scotland for the foreseeable future. The *Scotsman* newspaper understood my approach. In February 1988, in a profile, they wrote:

> The Scottish Conservatives might have been expected to crawl into a cave and inconspicuously lick their wounds. But that, assuredly, is not the Scottish Secretary's style. Rifkind's response to his party's electoral mauling has been to muster his small band of troops to mount an ideological offensive against the serried ranks of socialists in Scotland.

But results and real reform are not achieved just by speeches. Not all of the changes that my Scottish Office colleagues and I introduced were controversial. We created a dynamic new Scottish Homes agency by merging a number of government housing bodies that had been set up many years before.

Likewise, Scottish National Heritage was the product of

combining the Countryside Commission in Scotland with the Nature Conservancy Council. The Scottish Development Agency was replaced by Scottish Enterprise, which was, unlike its predecessor, decentralised to the Scottish regions and made much greater use of private sector experience and personnel.

I felt a particular responsibility for the needs of the remote communities of the Highlands and Islands. I was pleased to be able to fund the construction of a causeway between the small island of Vatersay and Barra in the Outer Hebrides. Without a causeway, Vatersay was likely to be abandoned by its small population. Even the cattle had to swim the channel to Barra when they were on the way to market.

The following year, after the causeway was built, I was in Barra and went to see it. I was accompanied by a Grampian TV crew looking for a suitable story for their evening bulletins. As I looked towards Vatersay, I saw an old man walking across and approaching where I was standing.

He recognised me and, with the cameras whirring, he declared, 'If you are remembered for nothing else in this world, Mr Rifkind, you will be remembered as the man who brought the causeway to Vatersay.' This was top of the TV news throughout the north of Scotland that night. Pure gold.

When it came to privatisation, the main candidates were the Scottish electricity industry and the Scottish Bus Group, which controlled many of the bus services throughout the country.

In one respect I was more Thatcherite than Mrs Thatcher. When we had been discussing our manifesto in the run-up to the 1987 general election, the Prime Minister said to me that she assumed that we could not privatise the North of Scotland Hydro-Electric Board as it was committed, by statute, to charging the same electricity tariff throughout the Highlands and Islands despite the much greater cost of providing electricity to sparsely populated Hebridean islands and mainland rural areas.

I disagreed and argued, successfully, that privatisation would still be feasible as long as the government was prepared to contribute an element of subsidy that would enable the company to maintain equal tariffs. This was done and was a successful precedent for the privatisation of the railways with continuing taxpayer subsidies for uneconomic rural lines.

Although our weak political position was a constant strain throughout that parliament, until the end of 1990, it did not stop Edith and me enjoying many of the responsibilities and opportunities that went with being Secretary of State for Scotland. One of these was our entitlement to use Bute House, a splendid Georgian residence in Charlotte Square, in Edinburgh, and now the official home of Scotland's First Minister.

We chose not to live there, as we preferred the privacy of our own home and garden in Duddingston Village at the edge of Arthur's Seat. We did, however, initiate a series of informal Bute House dinners, where we entertained many of Scotland's leading public figures, including senior opposition politicians, which helped soften the otherwise harsh political disputes that divided Scotland.

When the Prime Minister visited Scotland, she stayed at Bute House and we moved in, too, for the duration. On one occasion we arranged for our children, Caroline and Hugo, to stay there as well so that they would be able to meet the Prime Minister over breakfast at the kitchen table.

Mrs Thatcher was not at her best with children but she tried, valiantly, to converse with Hugo, who was shyer on that day than he has tended to be in more recent years.

In order to spark his interest, she said to him how much she had enjoyed the Scottish Cup Final that I had taken her to see at 'Ibrox' some months earlier. After breakfast we took the necessary photograph of the children with the Prime Minister and she then swept out to her first appointment of the day.

I asked Hugo what he had thought of Mrs Thatcher. 'Not much,' he replied, pointing out that she had not even remembered that she had been at Hampden not Ibrox for the Cup Final. That has been his sole recollection of his only meeting with Britain's greatest Prime Minister since Winston Churchill.

A welcome break from the political grind were the annual, very busy, royal weeks when the Queen was at Holyrood with multiple engagements.

On one occasion, the Queen was visiting Stirling Castle. She inspected its Great Hall, where major restoration and refurbishment had begun which was expected to take a good many years to complete. I was standing next to the Queen when she asked one of the workmen when the work was expected to finish. 'Oh,' he said, 'it won't be in your time, Ma'am.' The Queen was hugely amused by this prediction, which turned out to be wrong by a very wide mark.

The following year, the Queen and the Duke of Edinburgh were visiting Dunbar. The whole population were lining the streets to cheer and wave flags as the Queen and Prince Philip were driven slowly through the town in a Rolls-Royce with a glass bubble roof so that they could be seen clearly.

I was in the second, equally grand, Rolls-Royce with the lady-in-waiting, the equerry and the Queen's private secretary. The crowd were enthusiastically looking into our vehicle, hoping it would contain the Queen Mother or Princess Diana. Not surprisingly, no one recognised the other three occupants but some did recognise the Secretary of State for Scotland.

I happened to catch the eye of one lady in the crowd who had been cheering the Queen and who then looked into our vehicle, saw me and recognised me. She was obviously not a Tory, as she stopped cheering and waving her flag, put her thumb to her nose in a rather offensive manner and expressed her strong view that I had spoilt her day.

I was tempted to make the same gesture in return but ended up annoying her even more by smiling sweetly at her and giving her the 'royal wave', which consists of a gentle, circling move with one's right hand. I was rather pleased with that small victory.

By the time of the Scottish Conservative conference in Perth in May 1989, we had had two years of the radical reform that I had promised after the 1987 general election. Domestic rates had been abolished, competitive tendering in the health service and local government had been introduced, the private rented sector in housing was being revived, the Scottish Bus Group had been privatised and school boards and self-governing schools were going forward.

In my speech to the conference I said that there was now 'a need for a modest period of consolidation ... parents, teachers, tenants and the wider public need to be able to experience these new opportunities, school boards need to flex their muscles, tenants need to plan new housing cooperatives ... These will be the priorities for the immediate future.'

I also said that we must 'consult and listen to those who do not bear us ill will but who are worried or alarmed by government reforms or initiatives'.

At the time I did not consider that I was saying anything too controversial. It seemed common sense to have a period of consolidation, after such a torrent of reform and legislative change, and to be sensitive to constructive criticism from potential supporters.

That was not, however, how my remarks were interpreted. My more right-wing colleagues, such as my junior minister, Michael Forsyth, interpreted my speech as an indication that I was going soft on the Thatcher revolution, and Downing Street was so informed. *The Observer*, ten days later, reported that some of my senior party colleagues 'were not overly impressed by the tenor of his remarks'.

This reaction was partly my own fault, as I should have discussed with my Scottish Office ministerial team in advance what I was proposing to say. But it is also true that my instinctive preference for reform followed by consolidation exposed a fault line that existed in the Conservative Party north and south of the border.

One Nation Tories never felt comfortable with permanent revolution, while the whole essence of Margaret Thatcher's conviction politics was to press ahead with radical reform without any need to stop for breath. The champion of the latter view in Scotland at that time was Michael Forsyth, who, while only a junior minister, had his own lines of communication with the Prime Minister, and who, unlike me, was seen by her as a true believer.

This became obvious when, in 1989, she overruled my objections and made Michael chairman of the party in Scotland.

Although I tried to work with him, from that time on there were mounting strains between myself and Michael. My relationship with the Prime Minister, which had never been intimate, became more complicated.

In February of that year, during a Cabinet committee discussion on teachers' pay in England, chaired by the Prime Minister, I had allowed my mind to wander when I suddenly realised that Mrs Thatcher was addressing me. 'What about Scottish teachers?' she said, and then added, 'Ah, the smile on the face of the tiger.' Without thinking, I replied, 'Which one of us do you mean, Prime Minister?' I doubt she was amused.

My most serious rift with Mrs Thatcher was the following year, in March 1990, as a result of John Major's Budget. In it, he announced a major increase in entitlement to rebates against payment of the community charge or poll tax. The poll tax had not yet come into effect in England and Wales but it had in Scotland, the previous year.

When the Chancellor was announcing his proposal, Donald Dewar, the shadow Scottish Secretary, intervened to demand that it be made retrospective in Scotland. He got no such assurance. It was unprecedented for a Budget Statement to be interrupted in this way and this ensured that the whole issue got national prominence.

I had only learnt of the Chancellor's proposal in Cabinet that morning, as that is the normal custom with the Budget. The Scottish Office had had no opportunity to consider the implications and we were suddenly faced with a tsunami of protest from Scotland with the understandable demand that the Chancellor's concession should be backdated in Scotland to the introduction of the poll tax the previous year.

That evening, I drafted a minute to the Prime Minister and colleagues pointing out that the political nature of the concession did require it to be applied retrospectively in Scotland. A meeting at Downing Street was arranged for the following morning.

At that meeting, the Prime Minister and John Major were opposed to any retrospection for reasons of both principle and practicality. Their reasoning was persuasive and the discussion moved to an ex gratia scheme of compensation as an alternative. The Prime Minister had to leave to go to a lunch engagement but she indicated she might be prepared to accept an ex gratia scheme if it was funded by the Scottish Office from its existing resources, which was acceptable to me. I agreed with John Major that we would consider this further.

After discussion with my deputy Ian Lang and my other Scottish Office colleagues, we decided to support an ex gratia scheme as a way of resolving the crisis, but that evening I was shown a minute from the Prime Minister's office saying that she had already made up her mind and was of the 'firm view' that there should be no concessions nor any ex gratia scheme. That was inconsistent with the outcome of my earlier meeting with her and John Major, as the collective agreement had been to consider the matter in more detail before reaching a decision. Accordingly, I circulated my proposals to the Prime Minister and colleagues that evening.

I was very angry to learn later that evening that my confidential discussions at Downing Street had been leaked. Much worse was the Scottish press the following morning when it became clear that the leaker had been Bernard Ingham, the Prime Minister's chief press officer.

The Scotsman, which, at the time, was refusing to respect the normal anonymity of lobby briefings, reported the following morning that Ingham had given the Scottish media a colourful account of how I had been 'dressed down' by the Prime Minister and told that there would be no concessions.

I was furious at this breach of confidentiality, as any attempt to have private discussions with ministerial colleagues to reach an amicable outcome had been rendered impossible by the Prime Minister's own press officer's remarks.

The issue was no longer just the need for a fair resolution of the poll tax rebates controversy. It was now about the authority and credibility of the Secretary of State for Scotland, which had been undermined by 10 Downing Street. I concluded that if we did not reach some compromise that nullified Ingham's press briefing, I would have to resign. I discussed this with Ian Lang, who, although very concerned, agreed I would have little choice.

At my request, I saw the Prime Minister at 9.35 a.m. She was alone apart from her private secretary, Andrew Turnbull. We had a stormy thirty minutes with a curt exchange of remarks. I was angry and so was she. She said that she did not know how the press had learnt of our earlier meeting and that Ingham's quoted remarks were not accurate.

The Prime Minister repeated several times that she had thought carefully about an ex gratia scheme and could not accept it. I made it clear that, without an agreement, I would not be able to continue to do my job with any credibility or authority. At the end of thirty minutes, she said it would be desirable for me to speak to the Chancellor. Once she said this, I suspected that I had succeeded, as there would be no point in such a conversation unless she was willing to accept any agreement I reached with John Major.

Later that morning, an agreement was reached on an ex gratia scheme funded from the Scottish Office's own resources. This was announced later that day and the political crisis was over. I gave a statement at a crowded press conference and then had thirteen radio and television interviews before catching a plane to Edinburgh.

In a note I made at the time, I quoted Kipling's remark about meeting with triumph and disaster and treating those two impostors just the same.

I was under no illusions that my relationship with the Prime Minister was likely to recover from the confrontation that we had had. To avoid having to find a new Scottish Secretary, the government had done a dreaded U-turn in the two days since the Chancellor had announced his Budget. That would certainly not be forgotten and might not be forgiven either.

I compounded the problem by some foolish comments I made to the Scottish *Sunday Mail* in an interview that weekend. When they suggested that I had been forced to fall in line with Mrs Thatcher's judgement, I replied, 'No, on this issue she has fallen in line with my better judgement.'

As if this wasn't bad enough, I denied that my political future was linked to Mrs Thatcher's. I responded, 'I came into politics before Mrs Thatcher became leader of the Conservative Party and no doubt I will still be in politics when she is no longer leader of the party.' Even if the truth of this remark was obvious, I should not have said it. I was at risk of becoming a semi-detached member of the Cabinet.

This clash had taken place in March 1990, which was, of course, only nine months before Mrs Thatcher resigned as Prime Minister. None of us knew that her reign was coming to an end and I had neither a desire nor an expectation that her departure would occur in such a timescale. She still seemed impregnable, though she had already lost Nigel Lawson and had alienated Geoffrey Howe.

Over the next few months, the Scottish Tory Party was a microcosm of the growing fissure in the Conservative Party as a whole. Michael Forsyth and two or three of our small band of ten Scottish Tory MPs decided that I was insufficiently committed to Mrs Thatcher and let their discontent become known.

They had some, but very little, support amongst party activists as a whole. On the first day of the Scottish party conference in Aberdeen, there was a press report that Bill Walker, the maverick right-wing MP for North Tayside, was plotting for my removal as Secretary of State and my replacement by Michael Forsyth.

When I rose to address the conference, I received a standing ovation before I had uttered a word, not to a mention another one when I finished. It was 12 p.m. when I spoke and I began by remarking, 'It's High Noon and I am still here.' The press reported that I had been hailed as a hero and that 'Rifkind bounces back'. Mrs Thatcher, in her memoirs, wrote that she had contemplated choosing a new Scottish Secretary but, she wrote, 'I did not want to move Malcolm Rifkind who, for better or worse, had established himself as a major political force.'

Although Michael Forsyth had made himself a powerful figure in the Scottish Tory Party, his tenure as party chairman had become increasingly controversial. He was an immensely able man but at that time he was impatient and intolerant with those who disagreed with him. Since becoming chairman in 1989, he had alienated many party activists, not so much by his close relationship with Mrs Thatcher as by the style of his chairmanship, which was seen as authoritarian, conspiratorial and divisive.

I was on the receiving end of numerous complaints from party activists as to the way in which Central Office in Edinburgh was being managed. To my surprise, this included a number of senior figures associated with the right wing of the party. *The Scotsman* reported in August 1990 that 'most of the party is in revolt against Mr Forsyth'.

I was, at first, reluctant to act against him. I recognised his enthusiasm. I had found him an excellent minister even if a difficult colleague. So soon after the Budget controversy, I was also anxious to avoid what was bound to be another bitter disagreement with the Prime Minister if I requested his dismissal as chairman.

The matter came to a head when Bill Walker and two other back-benchers, Nicholas Fairbairn and Allan Stewart, tried to block a Law

Reform Bill as a means of showing their disapproval of my leadership of the party in Scotland. Michael, as chairman and as one of my junior ministers, should have given me his full support. It soon became obvious that he was failing to do so. Other colleagues told me that he was encouraging the dissidents and that I must act before irreversible damage was done.

In July, I sent a memorandum to the Prime Minister in which I said that Michael Forsyth had 'undermined efforts to persuade Bill Walker and Allan Stewart to support the government's legislation to end the conveyancers' monopoly on house sales'. I added that despite being a minister and party chairman, he had to be instructed by me before he would put out a public statement in support of the Bill. As the purpose of the legislation was to end a monopoly and encourage competition, the opposition to it from fellow Conservatives was clearly aimed at me and not because the proposal was insufficiently Thatcherite.

The Prime Minister decided to defer a decision on the party chairmanship until September. On 24 August, I had to send her another minute. By that time the senior executive at Scottish Central Office had resigned after only eight months in office.

This followed the departure of several other agents and officials of the party, disillusioned because of Michael's chairmanship. The deputy chairman, Bill Hughes, who was close to Mrs Thatcher, had given me permission to say that he, too, felt Michael had to go. So too did Jimmy Gulliver, the chairman of the Scottish Business Group, which raised funds for the party.

I also reported that Central Office had been issuing press releases in which party members attacked other party members, including ministers.

The Prime Minister was getting similar expressions of concern from Willie Whitelaw, George Younger and other senior party figures. I had a meeting with her and, by that time, she had realised that she had no choice but to dismiss him as chairman.

I knew that she would be bitterly disappointed at having to do this and, as he was a good minister, even if a poor chairman, I suggested that she might promote him to be a Minister of State so that he would not be humiliated. This she did. In her memoirs she either forgot, or chose not to remember, that her promotion of Michael to Minister of State was at my recommendation.

It was a huge relief that this was resolved. The press reported it as a victory for me. It was, but Michael's enforced resignation, while unavoidable, was a Pyrrhic victory. Anything that exposed our internal divisions was likely to be bad news for the government.

In her memoirs, Mrs Thatcher gave her forced dismissal of Michael from the party chairmanship a wider significance. She wrote: 'This combination of the left and the traditional establishment of the party to rebuff Thatcherism in Scotland was a prelude to the formation of the same alliance to oust me as leader of the Conservative Party a few weeks later – although I did not know it at the time.'

She was incorrect in this assertion. By the time of his dismissal as chairman, Michael had lost the confidence of right-wing Tories in Scotland as well, because of the authoritarian way he was running the Central Office and the party organisation. His right-wing deputy chairman, Bill Hughes, had urged his departure, as had others from the right wing of the party, and his chief executive had resigned.

This Scottish drama turned out to be a minor sideshow. It was September 1990. We were only weeks away from the most dramatic resignation in twentieth-century British politics: that of the Prime Minister herself.

CHAPTER 15

END OF AN ERA

MARGARET THATCHER RESIGNED as Prime Minister on 28 November 1990, but the clouds had been gathering for over a year.

In July of 1989 she had sacked Geoffrey Howe as Foreign Secretary. Although he was promoted to Deputy Prime Minister, she treated him with growing disdain, which deeply worried her Cabinet colleagues. Nigel Lawson resigned as Chancellor in October of that year. Geoffrey resigned as Deputy Prime Minister a year later. To have lost her two most senior colleagues by her own insensitivity suggested that she was losing her touch. She was in deep trouble.

She was also blamed for the unpopularity of the poll tax. Its introduction in England had far more serious political consequences than there had been a year earlier in Scotland. Non-payment was a serious problem on both sides of the border but the riots against the tax were overwhelmingly an English phenomenon, the largest being in central London in March 1990. Increasingly, her political judgement and acumen were being questioned.

It is worth remarking that while Scotland, unlike England, had not voted Tory and Margaret Thatcher was unpopular to a degree not found in most of England, opposition to her and her policies never led to any violent consequences.

Throughout my period as Secretary of State for Scotland, which was just under five years, I never required nor received police protection. My constituency surgeries were open occasions and I often walked in the centre of Edinburgh without incurring any personal hostility.

On one occasion, having taken my daughter, Caroline, on a private visit to the Glasgow Garden Festival, we were walking back to our car, which was parked in a deserted side street near the River Clyde.

Before we reached the car I saw, coming towards us on the other side of the street, a number of youths who appeared to be in their late teens. One of them was pointing towards me and I guessed that I had been recognised.

Glasgow, by the River Clyde, was not exactly Tory territory and I was a bit nervous, especially having my teenage daughter with me in an otherwise deserted street. I walked a bit faster towards the car. As they came opposite us, on the other side of the road, one of them shouted out, 'Hi, Malky.' They could not have been more friendly.

The only explicitly hostile act I experienced had an unexpected conclusion. During the height of the poll tax controversy, we found that someone was spray painting the garden wall of our home in Duddingston Village and doing it again each time the paint was removed.

After this had happened twice, the police put a camera on the house, which they hoped would help them catch the culprit. It did and, to our surprise, he turned out to be quite elderly. Apparently, he had a grudge as his daughter had been fined in court for not paying the poll tax.

The police asked me whether I wanted him charged but when I was told he had no previous convictions I said I did not. The police officer thanked me and said that I had no need to worry whether he would repeat the offence. When they had arrested him, they had taken him to his home and explained to his wife what he had been up to. She was furious when she heard that he had been spray painting the home of the Secretary of State. 'Just you wait until the police have gone,' she had told him, in a rather threatening manner.

After the 1987 general election, we discussed whether there were ways we could make Mrs Thatcher more acceptable to the Scottish public. It was always a long shot. She was a woman. She was an English woman. And she was a bossy English woman. The combination was impossible to overcome.

On one occasion, during a visit to Scotland, Michael Forsyth and I were briefing her before she did a long pre-recorded interview with Kirsty Wark. I had noticed, on previous occasions, that she sometimes said 'You in Scotland' during a speech or an interview. I suggested to her that it made her look as if she was visiting somewhere outside the United Kingdom. Could she avoid that phrase? She promised that she would.

She went in to do the interview and Michael and I watched on the monitor. To our horror, she started saying 'We in Scotland', which was even worse. She was slightly miffed when we pointed this out.

One initiative we welcomed was the invitation she received to address the General Assembly of the Church of Scotland, the Church's governing body. The Church of Scotland is as much the established Church in Scotland as the Church of England is south of the border. It is Presbyterian rather than Episcopalian and the Queen changes her religion as she crosses the border each way.

There are significant differences between the two established Churches. It has been pointed out that the head of the Church of England is the Queen while the head of the Church of Scotland is God.

The Prime Minister addressed the General Assembly in May 1988 with what became universally known as the Sermon on the Mound, the Mound being the artificial hill which unites the

Old Town and New Town of Edinburgh and the site of the Church's headquarters.

Mrs Thatcher paid even more attention to her speech than she did with most other speeches she made as Prime Minister. Much of the text was her own and reflected her personal religious beliefs and convictions. To a considerable degree, it focused on her strong belief that taking personal responsibility for one's life and one's family was not only compatible with Christianity but a proper expression of it.

I was present when she spoke and she received warm applause but amongst the hundreds of clergymen and lay people present there were a significant number who strongly disliked her and made clear their disapproval. They were determined to find fault and would have done so even if she had restricted her remarks to the contents of a telephone directory. It was right for her to have been there and to have said what she did. I doubt, however, whether she made many converts.

If it was right for her to attend the General Assembly, it was pretty silly for her to be persuaded by the party planners to go also to the Scottish Cup Final at Hampden in Glasgow. As I have recorded earlier, she would remember this event, even if she confused Hampden with Ibrox when conversing with Hugo.

Her visit was at the height of the poll tax controversy and although her decision to attend was not announced in advance, the Labour-supporting *Daily Record* got to hear of it and, on the day of the match, encouraged the fans to show what they thought of her.

When she arrived in the director's box there was considerable booing, but that subsided when the match began between Celtic and Dundee United. At half time we went into the director's hospitality room.

As we left to return for the second half, I saw that she had put on a bright blue overcoat because it had turned chilly. Celtic fans traditionally react to blue as much as bulls are supposed to react to red and I encouraged her to take it off. 'But Rangers aren't playing,' she said. 'It doesn't matter,' I responded. 'Take it off.' It was the only time I ever gave her an instruction as opposed to advice. Without a word she let the coat slide off her shoulders and it was not seen again.

I was still a little nervous as to what would happen when she presented the Cup to whoever won. As it happened, Celtic scored the only goal of the match in extra time. The fans were so ecstatic that she could have been the Pope given the cheering when she presented the Cup. We then got her out of the stadium in double quick time and sped away.

The saga of Mrs Thatcher's fall from power has been often recorded and I will only add my own involvement in those extraordinary days.

When Michael Heseltine challenged her for the leadership of the Conservative Party, I had no hesitation in voting for her. Although we had had serious differences, I admired her courage, integrity and leadership. These were the qualities that had persuaded me to transfer my support to her after Ted Heath had been defeated in 1975 and she was contesting the leadership against Willie Whitelaw and others.

I had, over the years since she became Prime Minister in 1979, not only seen the success of her determination to curb the power of the trade unions, reduce the burden of direct taxation and launch a major programme of privatisation. I had also witnessed, at first hand, a Prime Minister who had more influence than any British Prime Minister since Winston Churchill with the leaders of both the United States and the Soviet Union.

I did have reservations. She had become intolerant and even bossier than she had been in earlier years. Her humiliation of Geoffrey Howe was indefensible and her approach to her European Community colleagues was disagreeable and dismissive.

My own serious disagreements with her had developed from 1986 onwards, although she had known when she appointed me Scottish Secretary that I was not an instinctive Thatcherite and that I was more sympathetic to Scottish devolution than most of my Conservative colleagues.

I would have welcomed it if she had decided to retire. Deposing her was another matter. I voted for her.

I was surprised when it was announced that although she had won the first round of the ballot, Heseltine had won the votes of 152 MPs to Thatcher's 204 votes, with sixteen abstentions. She was four votes short of the majority required and a second round of voting was necessary.

What was clear was that almost half of her parliamentary colleagues no longer had confidence in her leadership and had made that clear to the world either by voting for her arch-enemy or by abstaining.

That evening, Tristan Garel-Jones invited a number of fellow ministers to his house in Catherine Place after the ten o'clock vote for an informal exchange of views. Present were some who had been critical of Mrs Thatcher, such as Chris Patten and me; but also some of her strongest supporters, such as Alan Clark and John Gummer.

Everyone there expressed their view, and it was clear that there was near unanimity, that her premiership was dead in the water, with almost half the parliamentary party having withdrawn their support. Most of the discussion turned to her likely successor, with little enthusiasm for Heseltine. John Major and Douglas Hurd were seen as the most attractive candidates.

To our astonishment, Alan Clark suggested Tom King. As Alan spent most of his time trying to discredit Tom, who was his boss in the Ministry of Defence, we could only assume that Alan hoped he might become the new Defence Secretary if Tom King moved to Downing Street.

There was no plot or conspiracy that evening in Tristan Garel-Jones's house. However, the near unanimity of the view that we felt that she had been terminally damaged by the vote was reported to the Chief Whip as part of the soundings we knew he would be taking.

The following day, the Prime Minister saw each of her Cabinet colleagues separately to help her decide whether to fight to retain her leadership.

As one of the more junior members of the Cabinet, I was one of the later ones to see her and had no idea of the advice given by her previous visitors. I saw her in her spacious room in the House of Commons, behind the Speaker's Chair, during the afternoon. She, not surprisingly, was subdued and there was no small talk. She began by reminding me that she had won three general elections and had never been defeated. Why, she asked, should she be expected to resign? This, I later learnt, was the same opening salvo she had used with most of her Cabinet colleagues.

I replied that there was no constitutional reason why she should resign. In her memoirs, she wrote that while she had not been optimistic about Ken Clarke's support, she had 'written off my next visitor, Malcolm Rifkind, in advance. After Geoffrey's departure, Malcolm was probably my sharpest personal critic in the Cabinet and he did not soften his criticism on this occasion. He said bluntly that I could not win and that either John or Douglas would do better.'

That is incorrect. I neither believed that nor said it. I said that, although I believed she would win if she stood in the next round of voting, her problem was that her authority in the country had been shattered by the public knowledge that almost half her MPs had refused to support her. It was, I said, like a ship being holed below the waterline.

She then asked me whether I would support her if she did stand. I had, of course, anticipated that question and I answered that I could give her an assurance that I would never vote against her. She wrote in her memoirs:

> Still, even Malcolm did not declare against me. When I asked him whether I would have his support if I did stand, he said he would have to think about it. Indeed, he gave me the assurance that he would never campaign against me. Silently, I thanked God for small mercies.

In indicating that I would abstain if she did decide to stand in the second round, I was aware that I could not expect to remain in the Cabinet if she continued as Prime Minister. Abstaining is not a glorious position to adopt in a major vote but it was, on this occasion, a principled position. I had concluded that it was time, both in the national and in the Conservative Party interest, for her to retire and I wanted her to realise that that was the view of her Cabinet colleagues. However, if she rejected that advice I did not want to be instrumental in assisting Michael Heseltine, to defeat her. I recognised Michael's considerable talents but I was not as pro-European as he was and I was not convinced that he was the right person to become Prime Minister.

By the following morning, as we assembled outside the Cabinet room we still did not have an absolute certainty as to the decision she had reached. We did not have long to wait. She opened the meeting by saying she had a short statement to make. Having told us that she had decided to resign, she broke down, but only very briefly. Having had a glass of water provided, she not only recovered but conducted her last Cabinet meeting as if she did not have a care in the world.

At the end of the formal business, tributes having been given, we remained in informal conversation with her. One of my colleagues suggested that as her decision to resign would be known, she would have an easy time that afternoon dealing with the motion of no confidence that Neil Kinnock and the opposition had tabled. 'An easy time?' she replied. 'I don't want an easy time. I want something that will get the adrenalin going!'

That afternoon in the Chamber, she was in splendid form. Nothing in her political life became her like the manner of her leaving it.

Much has been said about her legacy. I can only say that I feel very privileged to have been a member of a government and a Cabinet that, with all the necessary qualifications, was, because of Margaret Thatcher's leadership, the most successful that Britain enjoyed in peacetime throughout the twentieth century. Britain is a much more successful, self-confident and modern country today than we would otherwise have been and Mrs Thatcher deserves most of the credit.

I might be asked why, if that was the case, Scotland was not more grateful for her. It is a fair question. I have long felt that truly great leaders invariably have many faults and the greater they are, the more disturbing are their deficiencies.

One has only to think of Churchill or General de Gaulle. The qualities that made them great were the same qualities that also made them insufferable. Mrs Thatcher fell into that category. Like them, her self-belief, her convictions, her energy and her determination to ignore obstacles to realising what was necessary for her country led not only to historic achievements but also to deep mistakes. We could not have enjoyed the former without accepting the latter.

Margaret Thatcher never really understood Scotland. Scots have been determined, over the centuries, to retain their national identity and have resented any attempt, however rational, to assume that what is good for England must also be good for Scotland. It has been said that we are well balanced. We have chips on both shoulders.

Mrs Thatcher and the Tory Party seemed too English to Scottish opinion and, as the Tory Party was a minority north of the border, it could never, during those years, claim the electoral mandate that it could in England.

Margaret Thatcher was wrong, however, to devote a section in her memoirs to Thatcherism having been 'rebuffed' in Scotland. That was not the case. Although they did not like to draw attention to it, vast numbers of Scots bought their council houses, bought shares in the privatised industries, served on the new school boards, welcomed paying less income tax, were relieved that the militant trade unions could no longer cause mayhem and cheered victory in the Falklands.

It was not Thatcherism that was rebuffed but Mrs Thatcher and the Conservative Party. Such was the more left-wing political culture in Scotland and, at that time, the strength of the Labour Party that the same people who were enjoying Thatcher's reforms felt slightly guilty about doing so and were anxious to reassure their friends and neighbours that they had not changed their political allegiance.

In her memoirs, Mrs Thatcher was very disagreeable about me. Where she was wrong was in suggesting that my failure, on occasion, to agree with her was because I was, as she put it, 'proving his Scottish virility by posturing as Scotland's defender against Thatcherism'.

The record shows the opposite. I was enthusiastic about the right to buy, strongly (if mistakenly) defended the poll tax, took privatisation further than she had thought possible, and introduced, for the first time, school boards giving Scottish parents the opportunity to create self-governing schools in the state sector.

Where I disagreed with her, and Michael Forsyth, was on how fast these reforms could be introduced in Scotland and on the need to adapt them to the distinctive requirements of, for example, Scottish education or the Scottish legal tradition.

I also had to insist that I was Scotland's man in the Cabinet and not just the Cabinet's man in Scotland, which was how she saw my job.

The Scotsman summed it up in their editorial on her memoirs:

> Had she listened more to her Scottish Secretary then her own
> and her party's massive unpopularity in Scotland might have
> been reduced. For example, Mr Rifkind told her that there was
> no enthusiasm among Scots for the opting out of schools – 'but
> I knew otherwise', Mrs Thatcher writes. She was wrong.

I am content with Andrew Marr's verdict in his book *The Battle for Scotland*. Marr concludes: 'Thatcherism did happen in Scotland. George Younger and Malcolm Rifkind, displaying skill, good humour and loyalty, were the men who made it happen.'

These years, from 1986 to 1990, were a turbulent period of my political life. But they were also very important in my private life.

During my tenure as Scottish Secretary, my father died, aged eighty, in 1987. He had been ill with cancer of the oesophagus for some time and faced the end with courage and determination. Some weeks before he died, he expressed his desire to visit the synagogue during the Passover Festival. Although we took him there by car, he had to climb some steps, which he managed with great difficulty. We got him home, where he recovered some strength, but he knew the end was near.

My mother was five years younger and she lived until she was eighty-nine. Her last years were blighted by Alzheimer's. She did not recognise any of us but, at least, did not suffer, as she was unaware what had happened to her.

I tried to visit her in the nursing home each week but that was probably more of benefit to me than to her. There was no conversation but, curiously, a few months before she died she turned to me on one such visit and said, 'To be or not to be; that is the question.' She said nothing before and nothing after but, clearly, there must have been some thoughts in her damaged mind at the time.

Edith's father had died in the late 1970s and her mother moved to Edinburgh, where we found her a small flat near us, next to the Sheep Heid Inn in Duddingston Village. When asked, Caroline remarked that 'Granny lives next to the pub'.

Both Caroline and Hugo attended my old school, George Watson's College. Caroline was very happy there and had no desire to move. She did well and in due course went to Hatfield College in Durham University, where she read Economics.

Edith and I were very proud of her achievements. She had received the Gold Award of the Duke of Edinburgh scheme while at school and afterwards worked in a remote area of Zimbabwe with Raleigh International, of which I am a patron. While in Zimbabwe, she bungee jumped from the top of Victoria Falls, but, thoughtfully, did not tell us until afterwards.

Subsequently, she joined PricewaterhouseCoopers and has risen to become a director. She has always been a bright, attractive, tough and marvellous daughter.

Hugo, also bright but sometimes lazy at that stage of his life, found Watson's too large a school and was not being fully motivated. He expressed interest when we suggested that he might move school and, at the age of thirteen, was offered a place at Loretto, a fine public school in Musselburgh outside Edinburgh. The experiment worked as, in due course, he ended up at Emmanuel College in Cambridge, reading Philosophy.

Loretto was a boarding school and when we left him there on his first day I encouraged him to let us know how he was getting on. After several days, a letter arrived and we opened it, anxious to find out how he was doing. The letter began, 'I WANT TO COME HOME', which was rather disturbing, and then continued, in his normal writing, 'Ha, ha, only joking!', much to our relief.

I have never been much of a sportsman, but when I became Scottish Secretary in 1986, I decided that I must get some proper exercise. Golf did not appeal, but for several months I had horse riding lessons, as I had done some riding when living in Rhodesia. I, sadly, concluded that although enjoying it, I had left it too late, at the age of thirty-nine, to take up riding seriously. It had not helped when I had fallen off and hurt my foot.

By chance, I was on the phone speaking to a friend, Peter de Vink, whom I had known at university and who had his own shoot. He insisted that I join him one day with his gamekeeper and shoot a few clays to see if I would be comfortable with a shotgun. I was and he invited me to a pheasant shoot he had organised at Arniston outside Edinburgh.

Peter has created at Huntly Cot, on the outskirts of Edinburgh, in the lee of the Moorfoot Hills, a very fine shoot on what had been very barren ground. He drove me around his land, which had been badly neglected when he first acquired it. He likes to remind me how I looked perplexed and described it as a wasteland.

He has been exceptionally generous with shooting invitations ever since. I was hooked and have found shooting a splendid sport which

I have enjoyed for the past thirty years. Thanks to the generosity of a number of friends in both Scotland and England, I have shot pheasant, grouse, partridge and woodcock, as well as stalked stags in the Highlands and Islands of Scotland.

I enjoy shooting not only because of the exercise and the sport it provides but also because of the glorious countryside throughout Britain that I have visited and enjoyed. One could, of course, visit most such places as a tourist, but it would not be the same.

On a day's shooting, one mixes with the keepers, the beaters and other local people. One goes off roads and sometimes even off tracks, seeing wild areas not always available to the rambler. One becomes reasonably proficient in recognising the different species of birds while they are in the sky, one enjoys seeing the Labradors, spaniels and pointers working, recovering the birds on the ground. For some of those years we had a delightful and mischievous cocker spaniel, Rufus, who occasionally came with me when I was shooting.

We acquired him in a strange way. Edith and I had been on holiday in the Highlands and were returning to attend a concert at the Edinburgh Festival. On the journey down, Edith said that she thought we should have a dog and she would like it to be a cocker spaniel.

Three hours later, during the interval at the concert, we met a lady whom I had last met when shooting in Fife. Without my mentioning the conversation I had had earlier with Edith, she asked whether we might be interested in a puppy which was the last of a litter owned by a friend of hers. I asked what was the breed of the puppy and, to my amazement, she said it was a cocker spaniel. Within twenty-four hours we had visited the kennels in Perthshire and Rufus was ours. I had never, either before or since, been offered a puppy by anyone. It was a coincidence but an extraordinary one.

Field sports are also an activity where one's spouse or children can often accompany one and sometimes take part themselves. Thanks to a good friend, David Laird, Hugo shot his first grouse in an Angus glen when he was thirteen and has never forgotten it. We visited other friends, Oliver and Clare Russell, at their Highland castle at Ballindalloch on Speyside, walking on their hills and fishing, without notable success, at the famed Junction Pool, where the River Avon meets the Spey.

On one occasion, when I was Defence Secretary, Edith and I were staying at Ballindalloch. Amongst the guests were Eric Anderson, then headmaster of Eton, and his wife Poppy.

Eric and I were lingering over our breakfast one morning in the splendid dining room. Clare was anxious for us to finish as the castle was open to the public that day and the dining room would have to be cleared of the breakfast debris.

Mischievously, I suggested that she should let us continue our coffee and conversation. When the public arrived, she would have the opportunity to inform them that this was the castle dining room and these are the Secretary of State for Defence and the headmaster of Eton having breakfast. For a moment she seemed to be tempted but, sadly, caution prevailed.

I also enjoy game shooting because one is not in competition with one's fellow guns. Politics is, unavoidably, competitive and I prefer to relax when I am at leisure. No one comes first or last when you are shooting with eight or nine friends. I prefer it that way and not just because it means my limited shooting skills are not always revealed.

CHAPTER 16

ON THE RAILS

I N THE LEADERSHIP elections that followed Mrs Thatcher's resignation, I supported Douglas Hurd.

I had no animosity against John Major. Indeed, I had a high
regard for his ability and found him very likeable. But I had worked
with Douglas in the Foreign Office, he had formidable Cabinet experience and already had the stature required to represent the United
Kingdom on the world stage.

John's ascent, on the other hand, had been remarkably swift. He
had entered the Cabinet after me and had been Foreign Secretary for
a few short months before being catapulted into the Treasury after
Nigel Lawson's resignation. Perhaps I was a little bit envious of him.

In the event, he was by far the strongest candidate compared to
both Douglas and Michael Heseltine. Over the years that followed,
he became, and has remained, a good friend. He was a fine Prime
Minister. Following Margaret Thatcher was no easy task but I doubt
if we would have won the 1992 general election if he had not been at
the helm at the time. During his years in 10 Downing Street, I saw
at first hand how he had true prime ministerial qualities while never

suffering from the excessive self-esteem that can sometimes attach itself to those who achieve high office.

Immediately after he became leader of the party, I wrote to him congratulating him and assuring him of my support. I said that I had been Scottish Secretary for almost five years. I indicated that I would very much welcome a change in departmental responsibility and that Ian Lang had been very loyal during a difficult period and 'deserves his opportunity' to be Secretary of State.

I was asked to see the new Prime Minister the following day, when he invited me to become Secretary of State for Transport. I would be less than honest if I did not acknowledge that Transport would not have been my first choice though I was very glad to move to a United Kingdom department.

I was to be the eighth Transport Secretary in eleven years, which was particularly unfortunate for a department that had responsibility for the strategic planning of our transport requirements.

Any sensible decision by a Transport Secretary as regards roads, air transport or the railways takes years to materialise. But any fatalities as a result of a rail or air accident are of instant national interest, with demands for government inquiries and instant solutions to prevent their recurrence.

One of my predecessors, Paul Channon, warned me that the Secretary of State for Transport was the only member of the government who had to apologise when his visitors arrived late for one of his meetings. Invariably, their excuse was the tardy arrival of their train or congestion on the roads.

I have a delightful recollection of the first Cabinet meeting over which John Major presided as head of the government. Sitting for the first time in the Prime Minister's chair in the Cabinet Room in 10 Downing Street, he opened the meeting by saying to his Cabinet colleagues, 'Well, who would have believed it?' I doubt if Thatcher, Blair or Brown ever said the same.

John's manner of conducting a Cabinet meeting was the exact

opposite of Margaret Thatcher's. She would begin by indicating what issue needed to be decided, expressing her own conclusion as to what decision we should reach and then challenging her colleagues to agree or disagree with her. I am exaggerating but only just.

She would go round the table enjoying a robust exchange with anyone who held a different view. She did not resent opposition but would only be influenced by it if it was based on facts and not on caution or concern about controversy.

John, on the other hand, would go round the table hearing every view before expressing any opinion of his own. That usually worked well, but sometimes his colleagues would have welcomed more guidance from the Prime Minister as to his own preferences on a matter where they might not have had strong personal views.

However, on issues which John felt strongly about, he was not so relaxed as I might be implying. I can recall several occasions, for example when I was Defence Secretary and Bosnia was on our agenda, when he would reach agreement with Douglas Hurd and me before putting the matter to the full Cabinet. He was aware that it would be very rare for the Cabinet to wish to disagree with the three most senior ministers who had responsibility for the matter under discussion.

As Transport Minister, I had to move from the Georgian splendour of Dover House, which I had occupied as Scottish Secretary, to the grisly tower block, one of three equally ugly buildings, that then disfigured Marsham Street. The only pleasure of being in my office at the top of one of the towers was that I had an excellent view of London without being able to see the tower I was sitting in. Thankfully, they have been demolished and the modern Home Office now occupies the site.

The day I moved to Transport, I made a point of making a short journey on the Underground. I had been a minister for eleven years and throughout that time I had had a ministerial car and driver to take me where I needed to go.

I realised that at my first appearance at the dispatch box as Transport Minister I would be asked when I had last travelled on public transport. Fortunately, on many weeks I used the night sleeper train to get from London to Edinburgh and back. I judged it prudent to be able to make a similar claim for transport within London.

Within the department, I had a good group of ministers working with me. Two of them, in due course, became Cabinet ministers themselves: Roger Freeman, who was Chancellor of the Duchy of Lancaster under John Major, and Patrick McLoughlin, who is currently Transport Secretary under David Cameron.

My first responsibility as Transport Secretary could hardly have been more historic. Three days after being appointed, on 1 December 1990, I had to travel underground halfway across the English Channel to meet my French counterpart, who had travelled likewise from the coast of France.

The tunnellers had been moving slowly towards each other since 1988. It was crucial that they not only each excavated halfway across the Channel but that their two tunnels met at exactly the same spot.

They succeeded and when we arrived there was only a thin sliver of rock preventing the British and French seeing or touching each other. Two of the workmen, an Englishman, Graham Fagg, and a Frenchman, Philippe Cozette, were given the honour of creating an aperture and shaking hands with each other, thereby making the first land contact between Britain and the rest of Europe since after the end of the Ice Age over 8,000 years ago. Europe was no longer cut off from Britain.

A larger hole was created and I and my French counterpart, Michel Delebarre, saw each other, shook hands and embraced, as did various other dignitaries.

I have liked to suggest that my effectiveness as a Transport Minister had been demonstrated that day. The idea of a Channel Tunnel had been discussed since 1802. Within seventy-two hours of my becoming the Transport Secretary, the dream had been realised. For reasons

I have been forced to accept, no one else has been prepared to give me the credit.

Although Britain and France were united that day, the cultural differences between our two nations still manifested themselves. While we had a joint ceremony to celebrate, the French drank champagne and we had to make do with mineral water. On our side of the Tunnel there were numerous signs forbidding smoking. The French were happily puffing their Gauloises. Vive la différence.

These cultural differences sometimes have practical consequences. On another occasion, I asked my French counterpart to explain why France had been so much more successful in completing great transport projects for their roads and railways. Whereas we had ten years of public inquiries, at the end of which nothing happened, the French government appeared able to ignore its own public opinion and the new roads and railways tore through the countryside. How, I asked, were they able to get away with this?

Speaking in good English, my French colleague gave me a succinct reply. 'In France,' he said, 'if, *par exemple*, we wish to drain the swamps, we do not consult the frogs.' I have often wondered whether he fully appreciated the delicious ambiguity of his remark.

I recall an amusing comment by one of the journalists who was with us under the English Channel when we celebrated with our French colleagues. He said, 'Big change to when you were Scottish Secretary, Mr Rifkind. You are under the Channel now. When you were Scottish Secretary you were expected to walk on the water.'

The saddest duty of a Transport Minister was to make the statement to Parliament whenever there was significant loss of life as a result of a train or plane crash. Particularly with train crashes, there were always complaints that insufficient resources were being used to ensure maximum safety of passengers.

One accident during my time had occurred when a train driver had appeared to ignore a red light and the result was a collision with an oncoming train. New rolling stock had Automatic Train Protection

(ATP) installed and this made a train stop at a red light, or slow down at a speed restriction, without the intervention of the driver.

There was a controversy as to whether the government should provide sufficient resources to ensure that all existing trains had ATP provided. This would have cost many millions of pounds. Every study showed that, at best, only a handful of lives would be saved, compared to the many hundreds of people who would escape death or injury if comparable sums were used to upgrade our roads. I found that a compelling argument.

Aviation issues were equally controversial. I was a strong believer in the need for more competition. My earliest experiences of air travel had been in 1974, when British Airways had a monopoly on the Edinburgh–London shuttle. The service was unimpressive and basic. The passengers sometimes felt that BA thought they were doing us a favour by carrying us.

When British Caledonian applied to compete on the same route, BA protested that the demand was too little for two airlines and that BA might have to withdraw if there was enforced competition. Fortunately, their protests were ignored and the service improved dramatically, with both airlines offering their customers free coffee, meals and newspapers.

Shortly after I became Transport Secretary, I was faced with a request from Richard Branson that we should transfer to Virgin an unused slot for a flight from the United Kingdom to Osaka in Japan which was held by BA.

I took the view that BA had no right to hold on to an unused slot when another British airline was willing to offer an additional service to passengers. I agreed the transfer.

Lord King, who in every other respect was an impressive and admirable chairman of BA, went ballistic with rage and protested to the Prime Minister. Before No. 10 could consider how to respond, Lord King made clear, in public, that if my decision was not reversed he would stop financing the Conservative Party. I suspect Lord King

Visit of Warren Christopher, US Secretary of State, to Chevening during the Bosnian War. Also pictured are John Major, Douglas Hurd and Raymond Seitz, US ambassador to London. © Press Association

Coming home. First day as Foreign Secretary.

Addressing the General Assembly of the United Nations.

With ministerial red boxes in hall of Chevening.

ABOVE Cartoon by Peter Brookes in *The Times*, 1996, after my Zurich speech on 50th anniversary of Churchill's Zurich speech.
© Peter Brookes/*The Times*

As Foreign Secretary, visiting Sir Alec Douglas-Home at the Hirsel on his 90th birthday and presenting him with a gift on behalf of the Cabinet.

As Foreign Secretary, with President Bill Clinton at the White House.

In uniform as a member of the Royal Company of Archers, the Queen's bodyguard in Scotland.

Edith, having descended from ship to dinghy in the Galapagos in 2003.

Shooting with Hugo (and our cocker spaniel, Rufus) at Redheugh in the Borders.

With Edith, Caroline and Hugo at Buckingham Palace after being knighted by the Queen.

Addressing the House of Commons at the beginning of the 2010 parliament.

With Edith and Rufus on the steps of our family home, Eskgrove House, Inveresk.

Children and grandchildren. Caroline at back; her husband, Andy, in front with their son, George, in between. Hugo on right with Roma; his wife, Fran, on left with Ruby. (Caroline's second child, Charlie, not included as born on my 70th birthday, 21 June 2016!)

realised, as soon as he had said this, that he had made it impossible for the Prime Minister to overrule me even if he had been so inclined.

My saddest experience of aviation had occurred while I was still Scottish Secretary. On the evening of 21 December 1988, I was informed in the House of Commons that Pan Am flight 103 had exploded in the air over Lockerbie in Scotland.

The plane had been destroyed by a terrorist bomb just after 7 p.m. and all 259 passengers and crew were killed. A further eleven residents in Sherwood Crescent, Lockerbie were killed when a wing section of the aircraft crashed into their homes, exploding on impact and creating a large crater.

It was agreed that I would fly up to Prestwick that evening in an RAF aircraft. I invited the shadow Scottish Secretary, Donald Dewar, and the local MP, Hector Monro, to accompany me. When we arrived at Prestwick, we were transferred by helicopter to Lockerbie, arriving in the early hours. The United States ambassador was also there.

I was impressed how the emergency services were already active, especially helping local people come to terms with what had happened in their town. I was shown some of the debris lying where it had landed. There were not only parts of the aircraft. There were also the personal belongings of the passengers. I recall seeing a handbag and a single shoe.

The force of the blast had been such that some of the debris had landed in the Kielder Forest, miles away over the border. The most moving experience was visiting the deep hole in the ground in Sherwood Crescent, Lockerbie where several houses had existed a few hours earlier. Nothing remained of them.

At around 2 a.m., I had to give a press conference to the dozens of journalists and TV crews that had already made their way to Lockerbie. Although there was not yet any firm proof that the explosion had been caused by terrorists, it was seen as the most likely explanation.

It was a sombre experience and there was little I could say other than conventional words of sympathy but even these have a purpose and fulfil a need on such an occasion.

The following morning, the Prime Minister visited the site and I was able to see in daylight what I had already seen in the dark.

I have, of course, never forgotten that night. I have seen no reason to doubt that Colonel Gaddafi and his henchmen were responsible. When Gaddafi met a grisly end years later at the hands of his own countrymen, I could not bring myself to feel any sympathy for him.

My responsibilities at Transport also included merchant shipping. I had a baptism of fire. In my first few weeks I was to accompany John Major to a white tie and tails banquet at the Guildhall, where he was to address the General Council of British Shipping.

Early on the morning of the dinner, I received a call from the Prime Minister saying that he would be unable to be at the Guildhall as there was to be an urgent international meeting that he had to attend to discuss the forthcoming Gulf War. Would I be good enough to speak in his place at the Guildhall that evening? I would be provided with the speech he was going to make.

I had, of course, no choice but to agree. I read the Prime Minister's speech that morning. It said all the right things, but I was determined that if I had to make the speech that night I would do it my way, and that meant without a text in front of me or, indeed, any notes.

In making that decision, I was aware of the risks, but my decision was made not just to show off. When most people read a speech, it is assumed that they have at least written it themselves. When ministers read a speech, it is assumed, usually correctly, that it has been written by the department for the minister.

It was, in my view, important to get across to these several hundred leading figures of the British shipping industry not only that this new Transport Minister would seek to help them but that he fully understood their industry, their concerns and their aspirations. There is no better way of doing that, if one can, than speaking directly to one's audience rather than from a prepared text.

Accordingly, I spoke for twenty-five minutes on everything from the need for a strong merchant navy to the problems of flagging out and tax in the industry. This not only impressed my audience; it also delighted my civil servants, which I was always happy to do. Ministers should not treat their officials as 'Sir Humphreys' when they are, most of the time, only too willing to be part of a strong and committed ministerial team.

During my first few months as minister, I dealt with issues as they arose, but I also familiarised myself with road, rail and air as individual modes of transport and explored whether there were unrealised opportunities for a more integrated transport strategy for the country as a whole.

I was conscious of the belief in many quarters that the Conservative government since 1979 had been unsympathetic to public transport. Margaret Thatcher, in particular, was often alleged to be uninterested in the railways, seeing British Rail as a state-owned monopoly dominated by old-fashioned trade unions and impervious to customer needs.

The roads, in contrast, were seen as an example of the market in operation. Millions of motorists, in cars, vans and lorries, made their own personal decisions; there were no monopolies involved nor trade unionists to go on strike and inconvenience the public. Such considerations were important to Mrs Thatcher.

There was a core of truth in this approach but it also left a lot out of the equation. Our road network was being transformed, but not as fast as the exponential growth in road traffic. The result was, in town and country, increasing traffic jams, congestion and journeys taking far longer than should have been necessary.

Part of the problem was the distribution of population in the United Kingdom. France has a population very similar in size to that of Britain. But whereas in France that population is distributed fairly well throughout the country, in Britain it is overwhelmingly concentrated in the south-east of our island.

On top of that, virtually all the freight or motorists that are going to, or coming from, continental Europe have to travel through the south-east whether crossing the Channel by ferry or tunnel. In many cases, they have no choice but to travel south either round, or through, London.

Furthermore, much of the congestion on our roads is caused not just by motorists but by tens of thousands of lorries carrying freight, many of which consist of imports or exports needing to be transported over long distances.

It does not need rocket science to conclude that if a much larger proportion, especially of freight, could be persuaded or enabled to be transported by rail, the main beneficiaries would be the motorists themselves.

These were the considerations that led me to conclude that it was timely to promote a major change in the government's transport policy towards an unambiguous commitment to railway expansion.

It was one of these pleasant occasions when the personal, political and national interests all coincided.

At the personal level, I was keen to stamp my own ideas and beliefs on the ministry I headed and the government of which I was part. This was the first United Kingdom department of which I had been Secretary of State. Transport had often been seen as a graveyard for ambitious politicians and I was determined that this would not be my fate.

The politics pointed in the same direction. We had a general election coming up by 1992 at the latest, when we would be asking the electorate for a third term. Public transport had been seen, however unfairly, as a Cinderella during the Thatcher years, but Tories and floating voters, as much as anyone else, used rail services, especially as commuters in the south-east, as well as in the rural areas.

I had the strong support of the Prime Minister for my initiative, both because of its political significance and because he had a personal enthusiasm for a healthy rail network.

The outcome was that in May 1991, five months after becoming Transport Secretary, I made a major speech at the *Financial Times*'s Transport in Europe conference in London.

In my speech I said, 'I must declare myself, enthusiastically and unequivocally, as desiring to see far more traffic, both passenger and freight, travelling by the railways.'

Today one might not think that a memorable statement by a government minister. However, the *Financial Times* said that this was 'a remark which no transport minister would have uttered in the pro-road Thatcher years'.

I unveiled, in my speech, a series of measures aimed at encouraging freight to switch from road to rail and committed the government to ending British Rail's monopoly over passenger and freight train services. Any safe and competent operator would be allowed, in future, to operate freight or passenger services without British Rail's permission.

I also indicated the government's intention to privatise British Rail, support urban light railway projects and advocate more combined road–rail services.

John Prescott, the opposition's Transport spokesman, described the government's new enthusiasm for railways as 'a massive conversion greater than St Paul's on the road to Damascus'. Mr Prescott would, perhaps, have been on stronger ground if St Paul's conversion had been on the train to Damascus.

The press gave blanket coverage to my speech with predictable headlines such as 'Mr Rifkind builds up steam' (*The Independent*), 'Jam-Buster' (*Daily Star*) and 'Back on the rails' (*Daily Telegraph*).

There was a near-universal welcome, though *The Times* declared the speech 'All Things to All Men' and was sceptical as to how much would change. Many commentators had entirely reasonable caveats. Some pointed out that the proposed policy would be expensive and that I had announced no new financial commitments. Others suggested that in the absence of a detailed integrated transport strategy, declaring enthusiasm for the railways would have little practical effect.

The comment that I liked best was in the *Guardian* editorial. They described my comments as 'the most thoughtful transport speech made by any member of this administration'. They went on to declare: 'Mr Rifkind correctly says that neither private nor public transport are the prerogatives of right or left.'

The Guardian concluded that 'the true test of the government's conversion to the railways will come not just from yesterday's rhetoric, but from this year's public expenditure round in the autumn'.

It was a fair point and I must confess that at the time I made the speech I had no more idea as to what would be in the Autumn Statement than did *The Guardian*.

I need not have feared. When the Autumn Statement was published in November of that year, the headline in *The Times* was 'Rifkind and rail come out on top'. They went on to say: 'An increase of a quarter in his department's budget made Malcolm Rifkind the clear winner and British Rail the main beneficiary.'

In an interview with the *Financial Times*, under the headline 'Pragmatist still to be tested', I was asked my overall objective. I was reported as grinning as I replied that 'I would like to be remembered as the man who brought back a bit of fun into travelling'. This was a fine ambition though not yet entirely realised.

The key to increased railway use was not just rhetoric that encouraged the public to travel by train, nor securing more resources from the Treasury, essential though those were. The railways had to be sufficiently attractive, reliable and comfortable for people to want to use them. There also had to be an increasing rail network over the years. The curse of Beeching had to be reversed. To be realised, these objectives needed privatisation to be at the centre of our policy.

This was not the result of any ideological obsession with privatisation on the part of the Prime Minister and the Cabinet. Mrs Thatcher had never been enthusiastic about privatisation of the railways, believing it to be too difficult. Furthermore, some Tory MPs were concerned privatisation of British Rail would be unpopular with the public, with one of them, Robert Adley, predicting that it would be 'a poll tax on rails'.

We realised it would be difficult, as many of the rural lines and local services would need subsidies for the foreseeable future. Only the InterCity main lines were able to be profitable.

However, once one ended British Rail's monopoly and allowed private operators to compete, there was no logical or economic reason to retain British Rail as a state-owned industry.

British Rail senior management, under Sir Bob Reid, did not oppose privatisation of British Rail but they were vehemently against breaking it up and, in particular, against separating ownership of the track infrastructure from the operating services.

It was this issue which, in due course, divided the Cabinet and I have to accept prime responsibility for that division. The internal debate was not resolved before the general election and that led to us fighting the 1992 general election supporting the principle of railway privatisation but unable to say how we proposed to do it.

When I became Transport Secretary, I had no preconceived views about how British Rail should be privatised. I agreed with the Prime Minister and the Chancellor, Norman Lamont, that British Rail would need to be broken up in order to create the conditions for meaningful competition.

We agreed that the InterCity services could be hived off and separately privatised. It would not be acceptable that any subsidies needed to maintain local or rural services should be financed by cross-subsidy from InterCity. If subsidy was necessary for social reasons then it should be clearly identified as such and funded by the taxpayer.

We also agreed that the regions of the country should each have their own rail company or companies, which made particular sense in Scotland but also in various parts of England.

What divided me from my colleagues was the conclusion I reached after considerable work in the Department of Transport, and with British Rail, that it would be unwise to divorce an operating rail company from the track on which its trains operated. Infrastructure represented about 40 per cent of the costs of operating companies and to leave these companies with little or no direct responsibility for the rail track which was essential to their operations seemed illogical and unnecessary.

The Treasury took a different view. They argued that the objective was to have more than one railway company operating services on as many lines as possible, competing for the business of the public by offering lower fares or better services. This could only be achieved if no one railway company also owned the track thereby giving them an unfair advantage that would make competition impossible.

I acknowledged that that sounded logical but pointed out that it ignored the practical reality. The real competition that would force a railway company to lower fares or improve its services would not come from other railway companies operating on the same line. It would come either from the public preferring to use their cars and travel by road, or journeying by air where the length of the journey made that a real option.

I argued, further, that in the few cases where more than one railway company might wish to compete on a particular line, such as InterCity, the operator that also owned the track could be put under a statutory obligation to make the track available to other operators at a tariff that would be independently determined.

The debate dragged on within the Cabinet right up to the general election. The Prime Minister was anxious to have the matter resolved and supported the Treasury view that track infrastructure should be privatised separately.

There was considerable irritation amongst my colleagues with my continuing resistance to this option. However, the Prime Minister recognised that neither I nor the Chancellor was being unreasonable and that the structure of railway privatisation was too important for a decision to be rushed merely to meet an election manifesto deadline. My commitment to the desirability of privatisation was not in doubt and as Transport Secretary due weight had to be given to my views and analysis.

The matter was resolved after the general election by my moving to the Ministry of Defence and the appointment of John MacGregor as the new Transport Secretary. His views were similar to the Chancellor's and the decision was taken, in due course, to separate the ownership of the infrastructure from the operating companies.

The result was the creation of Railtrack, whose life was brief and whose fate was inglorious. After eight years Railtrack was wound up in 2002 and the infrastructure transferred to a new body, Network Rail, entirely owned by the government.

We thus have privatised rail companies using state-owned rail track. It is an unattractive hybrid structure which, one day, will have to be revisited.

In the meantime, what is clear is that more people are now using Britain's railways than at any time in their history, a few services closed by Beeching have been reopened, and the comfort and convenience of rail travel is reasonably good, though commuter services still leave a lot to be desired.

I use both InterCity and local services often. Each time I do, I help make the roads less congested than they would otherwise be. Letting the train take the strain is a pleasant experience and one that I recommend.

To my intense surprise, I had quite enjoyed being Transport Secretary, but not nearly as much as I did my next job.

CHAPTER 17

DEFENDING THE REALM

W HEN THE PRIME Minister phoned me at my Duddingston home, I assumed it was to tell me that I was
continuing as Transport Secretary. There was also a possibility that he was going to sack me because of my opposition to the
structure of railway privatisation favoured by the Treasury.

To my amazement and joy, he asked me whether I would agree to
becoming Secretary of State for Defence. I had not been aware that
Tom King was retiring and would not have thought that I would be
in the running for that job if I had.

Unlike most previous Defence Secretaries, I had never served in
the armed forces. At first I was concerned that the chiefs of staff
might resent that, but I could not have been more wrong. They were
entirely relaxed.

Indeed, I began to realise that they were slightly relieved. Some
of my predecessors, having done national service or a short service
commission and ended up as a lieutenant or a captain, assumed that
they knew as much about fighting a war as the Chief of the General
Staff. I had no such illusions. Just as the Health Secretary does not

need to know how to carry out a heart transplant, I did not need to know the finer details of military tactics. Secretaries of State have enough responsibilities without trying to second guess the professionals as to how they should carry out theirs.

My pleasure in my appointment to Defence was twofold. The job itself attracted me. Like most people, I had long admired the military and their 'can do' attitude to life. I had a soft spot for their traditions, their ceremonial and their camaraderie.

I was also delighted, after six years, to get back to my real love: foreign policy, global security and Britain's role in the world. Diplomacy and military capability are often complementary to each other and not alternatives. Frederick the Great once remarked that 'diplomacy without arms is like music without instruments'. That is not always true, but it is more likely to be when you are dealing with dictators, despots and villains.

I received a delightful letter of congratulation from Julian Amery, a senior MP and son-in-law of Harold Macmillan. He wrote: 'You will enjoy the Ministry of Defence. They spoil their ministers and make them feel heroic.' When I subsequently drove in a tank, flew in a Tornado and journeyed under the Atlantic in a Trident submarine, I knew what he meant.

My first challenge when I took up occupancy in the Stalinesque building in Whitehall that is the Defence Ministry was to decide how to distinguish the top brass from the civil servants.

Britain is probably unique in that generals, admirals and other ranks, when working in Whitehall, wear civilian clothes. I soon realised that all I needed to do to decide which was which was to look at their shoes. If they were highly polished, they were likely to be at least a colonel or an air commodore. If they were scruffy, they were a civil servant or a politician.

Although my office had no distinguishing features, its contents were special. They included an octagonal table that had been used by Winston Churchill when he was First Lord of the Admiralty.

There was also a splendid display cabinet with a serious crack in one of its lower wooden panels. The damage had been done by Winston when, one day, he had lost his temper and given the panel a savage kick. It had never been repaired. That is true fame. If I had kicked in a wooden panel I would have received the bill for its repair.

One of the consequences of my promotion was that Edith and I moved from our London flat in Dolphin Square into the splendour of Admiralty House at the far end of Whitehall. While the state rooms were only used for official luncheons and dinners, there were two excellent flats in the upper floors and one was to be our London home for the next three years.

Some months later, at a reception, I was talking to Mary Soames, Churchill's youngest daughter. She told me that she had lived in our flat with her father when he was First Lord of the Admiralty after the outbreak of the war in 1939. Churchill continued to live there when he became Prime Minister until Neville Chamberlain found alternative accommodation.

I asked Mary whether she had ever been back since 1940. She hadn't, but a few weeks later she came to tea and Edith and I were given an excellent tour by her as she explained which room Churchill had used as his study and which as his sitting room and bedroom.

As soon as I took over, I had a meeting with my new team of junior ministers. They were a formidable group: Archie Hamilton, Jonathan Aitken, Robert Cranborne (now Marquess of Salisbury) and my parliamentary private secretary, Henry Bellingham.

To my astonishment, I realised they were all Old Etonians. To meet someone who had been at my school, I had to wait until I was with Pierre Joxe, the French Minister of Defence, who had been at George Watson's on a school exchange from his French lycée when he was a boy.

During my time as Defence Secretary, I lost three of my ministers in one day. Jonathan Aitken, Robert Cranborne and Jeremy Hanley (who had replaced Archie Hamilton) were all promoted to the Cabinet in a reshuffle. I can claim no credit for this phenomenon but I was happy to bask in the reflected glory.

My first major challenge was an international battle to save the Eurofighter project. The Eurofighter, now called the Typhoon, is a multi-role fighter aircraft in service in the RAF and in a number of other countries. It was a major project, costing around £22 billion, bringing together Britain, Germany, Italy and Spain.

By 1992, my German colleague Volker Rühe was indicating that Germany might decide to pull out of the project both on cost grounds and because, it was argued, such a sophisticated fighter aircraft was no longer required given the end of the Cold War. If Germany had withdrawn, it would have been almost certain that Italy and Spain would have followed.

The Royal Air Force were deeply concerned at this risk, as was BAE Systems, the prime British contractor, with about 40,000 jobs which would have been affected.

I decided I had to fight hard to preserve the project. Firstly, I reminded my European colleagues that the aircraft would still be essential despite the end of the Cold War. The Eurofighters would be in service for many years and none of us, I argued, knew who would be ruling Russia in twenty or thirty years' time. I claim no fore-sight but given the sad deterioration in our relations with Putin's Russia over the crisis in Ukraine, it is just as well that Britain and Germany have such an advanced aircraft as part of our military capability.

My second main argument was that £5 billion had already been spent on the project and if we were to scrap Eurofighter and go for a less sophisticated but entirely European-built alternative, as Volker Rühe was advocating, there would be few savings and we might end up paying considerably more in development costs. If Rühe had felt able to argue that we should buy American aircraft 'off the shelf' he would have been on much stronger ground as to the savings available, but that was impossible for him for domestic political reasons.

The industrial and jobs arguments also helped me get the Labour Party on side. The shadow Defence Secretary, David Clark, agreed to lobby his Social Democratic colleagues in Germany, as did other Labour MPs such as George Foulkes.

George, with whom I had been at Edinburgh University and on the town council, was very complimentary as to my efforts after we had won the day. 'I give a lot of credit to Malcolm Rifkind,' he said. 'He has been like a terrier, he never let go. He never took his eye off the ball – keeping the Germans in.' As George was quite happy to put the boot in when I displeased him, I am happy to record his tribute on this occasion.

By the time of the NATO meeting in Gleneagles on 20 October, I was able to demonstrate that Eurofighter was the cheapest plane available. On 11 November, when John Major met Helmut Kohl, the German Chancellor, for the German–British summit in Oxfordshire, Kohl endorsed Eurofighter and made it clear that he wanted a European, not an American, fighter.

Winning this battle was good for the RAF and the British aircraft industry. It also reassured the Ministry of Defence that their new Secretary of State could fight and win when he chose to do so.

One of my first overseas visits was to Kiev, the capital of the newly independent Ukraine, which had left the disintegrating Soviet Union the previous year.

I had chosen Ukraine deliberately as I had always taken the view that the collapse of the Soviet Union was as important a historical event as the end of the Cold War and the coming down of the Berlin Wall.

The Soviet Union was the Russian Empire, the last such empire in Europe. For hundreds of years, Moscow had controlled the countries around the core of Russia and forcibly absorbed them into their empire. The British, French and other European empires had gone; only the Russian Empire remained.

Now the Russian Empire had also gone and fifteen new states had emerged to replace them, of which Ukraine was the largest, after Russia, and the most important.

On our first day in Kiev, I met my Ukrainian counterpart. On our side of the table were five of us; only one, the defence attaché at our embassy, a colonel in uniform. On their side there were five generals, including the minister, in full military uniform.

The minister welcomed me and said that the new Ukraine wanted to be more like the West and could I give him any advice. I responded by saying that in the West the armed forces always came under civilian control, in the interests of democracy, and I contrasted the civilians on our side of the table with the five generals on theirs.

The Ukrainian minister did not reply on this point, but for our second session of talks the following day, all five of them turned up wearing lounge suits. The minister smiled and said that they hoped we were impressed. It was progress, I conceded.

I also made an early visit to Saudi Arabia to see King Fahd and his brother Prince Sultan, who had been Minister of Defence for twenty-nine years. Saudi Arabia was important to us because of its strategic significance in the Arab world, its oil and the Al-Yamamah contract for the purchase of military equipment from the United Kingdom over many years.

I arrived at Riyadh Airport to be received by Prince Sultan and a Saudi guard of honour. This, I was beginning to realise, was standard practice for Defence Ministers, having already been welcomed by guards of honour on my visits to Germany and France.

A guard of honour makes one feel rather grander than one deserves, only one or two down from being a Prime Minister or a head of state. I don't recall receiving one when I was Transport Secretary. Now they were routine and I had to ensure that my own shoes were polished when I was inspecting such fine soldiers.

Our ambassador, Sir Alan Munro, informed me that the King had agreed to see me but it was likely it would be sometime during the night, as this was his usual custom. After dinner at the embassy,

I retired and said I could be woken if the call came. It did. We had to be at the palace around 1 a.m.

I was advised by the ambassador that when I met the King I should not try to exchange views right away, as he would want to make introductory remarks of welcome.

So it turned out. The King spoke of his father, Ibn Saud, and the long history of friendship between our two countries.

He then started speaking about religion and emphasised that there were three great ones: Islam, Christianity and Judaism. One day, he said, one of them would become universal, 'but we do not yet know which one'. It was a very tolerant remark, though not one that I had expected to hear.

The substantive discussion was about regional issues but also about the possible purchase of forty-eight Tornados by the Saudis for their air force. The King indicated that he was personally favourable to such a purchase, which was what we had hoped he would say.

I visited Kuwait at that time. I met with the Amir, who had been reinstated as ruler the previous year when Saddam Hussein had been driven out of his country.

The Amir was solemn and we had long silences. He only became animated when I said that I had first visited the Middle East in the 1960s on my way to India, when I had lived on bananas while crossing the desert. He got excited and said that he and his brother had had a similar experience, many years before, travelling from Calcutta to Bombay. They had shared their bananas with chimpanzees, which was not a claim I could make.

During the audience, one of his rather corpulent ministers kept falling asleep and snoring audibly. The Amir ignored him, which was more than Margaret Thatcher would have done during one of her meetings.

One of the perks of a Defence Secretary in these halcyon days was that I had the personal use of an RAF plane when travelling abroad. This was not a luxury I was used to. On the first occasion we were stuck in a traffic jam on the way to Northolt Airport and I asked my private secretary whether we might have a problem with the plane if we arrived late. He looked at me as if I was of little brain and patiently pointed out that that would not be a problem. It would still be there as I was the only passenger.

I was keen to revisit South Africa, where I had not been for many years. Mandela had become President and I was in Pretoria in 1994 as Defence Secretary. The High Commissioner gave a dinner for me and I had sitting beside me Ronnie Kasrils, the Deputy Defence Minister.

Kasrils was a white, Communist South African who had been educated at the London School of Economics. He had also been a former commander of Umkhonto we Sizwe, the militant wing of the ANC, and had been involved, during the armed struggle, in blowing up pylons and other act of serious violence.

I asked him whether he and his colleagues had been trained in the Soviet Union as the apartheid government had always claimed and he said that they had been, in Ukraine. Later I asked him why they had wanted to continue the armed struggle after Mandela had chosen the route of peaceful change. He said that he had always assumed that the white government would never surrender power until they had to and that armed struggle would be essential to that end. When I asked him if that was what they had taught him in the Soviet Union, he smiled and said no. It had been what they had taught him when he had studied at the London School of Economics.

Within the Ministry of Defence, I did not often get involved in matters involving individual regiments. That was best left to the generals or my deputy, the Minister of the Armed Forces. I recall, however, two exceptions which had my personal attention.

The first involved the elite regiments of the Household Division, which consisted of the Household Cavalry and the Guards regiments.

While watching the Trooping the Colour, I could not help noticing that there were no black faces amongst those taking part, despite the rest of the Army having many soldiers from ethnic minorities.

When I asked for an explanation, I was told that senior officers were also concerned about this, that an attempt had been made to recruit black and Asian soldiers for the Household Division a few years earlier, but this had failed because of resistance from elements within the regiments, with inadequate support from some of their non-commissioned officers.

I made clear that this was unsatisfactory and that they were fortunate that the lack of ethnic minority soldiers at the Trooping the Colour had not already been noticed by the media. I was asked by the Chief of the General Staff to let them resolve this as an internal Army matter, and they promised it would cease to be a problem if they could have a few months to push through the necessary changes. This promise was kept and the issue was resolved without public controversy.

A second problem was more complex. Most regiments in the Army had their own bands which were used on ceremonial occasions, to help with recruitment, and at dinners and regimental reunions. They were expensive and many of them could not attract all the musicians they needed because of limited career advancement prospects.

The Army decided that, outside the Household Division, the bands should be amalgamated into a far smaller number, which could be called upon by individual regiments as and when needed.

There was fierce resistance from many of the regiments and from traditionalists who were upset that their regiment would no longer have its own band familiar with its history and traditions.

Lobbying by the armed forces direct to ministers is not permitted but this ban does not apply to honorary colonels-in-chief and honorary colonels of regiments, who are free to do what they like.

I received a letter from the Prince of Wales, in his capacity as a colonel-in-chief, encouraging me to reconsider the proposal for amalgamation of the regimental bands. I already knew the Prince of Wales. We had corresponded on several occasions and I considered that he was perfectly entitled to write as he did.

To my surprise, I then received similar letters from several other members of the royal family who were also colonels-in-chief. This was unusual and I began to suspect that there might have been an element of co-ordination. I had no evidence of this until, years later, Jonathan Dimbleby published his biography of the Prince of Wales, written with his cooperation, in which the Prince of Wales admitted organising these various letters from his family that were sent to me.

Ministers and the Army chiefs were agreed that the amalgamations of the bands had to go ahead. However, I never resented receiving these letters. Not only was the Prince of Wales entitled to have his views made clear; he also had a duty, as a colonel-in-chief, to represent the concerns of his regiment.

A Defence Secretary, to do his job properly, has to become familiar with the equipment, vehicles and weaponry used by the armed forces. The Royal Navy, the Army and the RAF were all keen to assist.

I spent a whole day under the South Atlantic in the first of our new Trident nuclear submarines. It was carrying out tests including simulated firing of its nuclear weapons, for which it had to come to the surface. Greenpeace had learnt what the Royal Navy was up to and had sent a ship to the location in order to try to disrupt the exercise as a political protest.

The Trident submarine could not carry out the exercise safely with a civilian ship nearby and for several hours it looked as if Greenpeace might succeed in their disruption. The submarine captain then gave the order for the Trident, which was on the surface, to sail away as if it was abandoning the exercise. This ruse worked and after Greenpeace had disappeared, our boat returned and the exercise and test firing were successfully completed.

We then voyaged for several hours underwater towards Cape Canaveral. There were several British and American admirals as well as the British Defence Secretary in the captain's wardroom. We watched a movie: *Mutiny on the Bounty*. The captain assured me that this was not being shown elsewhere on the boat in case it gave the crew any ideas.

Incidentally, if the reader does not know why submarines around the world are known as boats and not ships, this has a British origin. Before the First World War, when submarines were first being developed for the Royal Navy, the older admirals were unhappy. Gentlemen did not sneak up on their enemy in secret, underwater. These submarines were not ships; they were mere boats. Submariners have since adopted this designation as a badge of pride, rather as Mrs Thatcher liked to be referred to as the Iron Lady, a term first used against her, as an insult, by her Soviet enemies.

Joining a training exercise with the Army was not so enjoyable. Being shown a mortar, I was invited to load it. I did so successfully. I was then in conversation with an officer and was asked to do it again so that the press photographer could capture the moment. I was not concentrating and began to put the mortar shell in the barrel the wrong way round. I was stopped in time but the photograph of my blunder was too good for the press not to use.

I was mortified (a rather appropriate word in the circumstances) but was comforted, a few days later, by a letter from a retired general saying he had done exactly the same when he was a cadet at Sandhurst.

The RAF scooped the other two services. I was invited to fly in a Tornado GR1, sitting behind the pilot as we dashed around the sky. I confess to being rather nervous when I arrived at RAF Marham for the flight on 2 March 1993.

I donned my G-suit, essential because of the very high acceleration force we would be subject to. The pilot briefed me, explaining that in an emergency he would pull a lever and we would both be ejected and would parachute to the ground. If he was badly injured, I was to operate the lever myself and be ejected from the stricken aircraft. 'Any questions?' he asked.

I pointed out that I had never been ejected from a fighter aircraft before, nor parachuted to the ground. I knew the Prime Minister would prefer to avoid a by-election. Did he have any advice? 'Yes, I do,' he replied. 'Relax.'

I got my own back before we took off. He asked me, through the intercom, if I had any final questions or comments. I suspected that when they flew politicians, the pilots liked to loop the loop and make their passengers feel sick as parrots. So I said to him that in the MoD we hadn't yet decided how we would divide the resources available for the armed forces and, in particular, how much the RAF would get. This would be influenced by whether I enjoyed this flight. There was silence and then he said, 'Got the message, sir.'

It was an unforgettable experience flying from East Anglia to Northumberland in less than twenty minutes followed by a mid-air refuelling with an air tanker, flying very close behind it but at a slightly lower altitude to make certain we didn't bump into it by mistake.

I also visited Sandhurst, our military academy, for a passing out parade of Army cadets. My favourite general was one who, on a previous occasion, was taking the salute on a day when one of the cadets passing out was his son. The general had to inspect the cadets and would be expected to stop and speak to a few of them.

There was great speculation as to whether he would stop and speak to his son or ignore him. He knew that whatever he decided, someone would criticise him. He came up with a brilliant solution. When he inspected the cadets, he stopped opposite his son, looked at him and said, 'I think I know your mother.' Honour was satisfied.

I had a rather similar experience when Hugo's headmaster at Loretto, Norman Drummond, asked me to carry out the annual inspection of the Combined Cadet Force. I agreed but forgot to tell Hugo. Some weeks before the day, I asked Hugo if he knew who was going to inspect the CCF. 'Some Army wanker,' he replied. 'Actually, it's the Secretary of State for Defence,' I said. He was absolutely furious, as neatness and tidiness were not amongst his most obvious virtues at that time and he rather disliked having to be in the CCF. I made amends when I inspected him by making no comment on the state of his boots or the smartness of his appearance.

As Defence Secretary, I travelled constantly, visiting both British troops overseas and foreign governments. One of my counterparts was General Pavel Grachev, the Russian Defence Minister. I welcomed him to London and also saw him in Moscow.

On the latter occasion I was invited to lecture an audience of around 100 Russian generals on NATO and Western defence policy. I think they must have been ordered to attend the lecture, as I rarely have spoken to such a surly and uncommunicative audience. The need for translation did not help but I think the problem was also that they were unreconstructed generals still nostalgic for the past certainties of the Soviet Union.

My visits to Washington were, not surprisingly, far more enjoyable. Dick Cheney was my host at the Pentagon for my first visit. At that time he was a tough, no-nonsense, US Defense Secretary but without the harshness and bellicosity of his vice-presidential years.

I got on with him well and Edith and I welcomed him and his wife Lynn to our home in Edinburgh when he was in Scotland for a NATO meeting.

Years later, he received me at the White House when he was Vice-President, but we agreed on much less at that time. When Clinton replaced Bush as President, Les Aspin became Defense Secretary but was ill-suited for the job and only lasted a short time. He was succeeded by Bill Perry, a Pentagon specialist, who, despite his quiet demeanour, gave excellent leadership during his tenure. I still see him from time to time.

It was Perry who agreed to sell us Cruise missiles despite the US being unwilling to sell them to anyone else. When I spoke to him on the phone, his only condition was that we allowed them to vet our announcement of the deal, as he was concerned that it should not give the impression that they would sell Cruise missiles to anyone else. As this was at the time when some were saying that the special relationship was being damaged by our differences over Bosnia, I have often quoted it as evidence that the US and UK can have a healthy disagreement without lasting consequences.

On one occasion, I visited the Gurkhas at home in Nepal. When we flew out of Kathmandu, we were given permission to divert our RAF plane to enable us to fly round the summit of Mount Everest at close quarters. Edith and I were in the cockpit behind the pilots, who were as excited as we were.

As Defence Secretary, I was invited to give the Annual Balfour Lecture in Jerusalem. My host was the Israeli Prime Minister, Yitzhak Rabin, who combined the post with that of Minister of Defence. The next time I went to Israel was when I accompanied John Major for Rabin's state funeral after his assassination.

I firmly believe that Rabin, if he had lived, might have achieved a historic deal with the Palestinians on a two-state solution. The day after his funeral, I travelled to Gaza to see Yasser Arafat. The meeting had to be kept short because Arafat was going to visit Rabin's widow in Israel to pay her his respects. That in itself was a remarkable tribute between old enemies, as was the presence of King Hussein of Jordan at the funeral.

During my three years at Defence, I worked with first-class chiefs of staff. Dick Vincent was Chief of the Defence Staff when I arrived. He was followed by Peter Harding of the RAF and then Peter Inge, now a Field Marshal. Jock Slater was a hugely impressive First Sea Lord and remains a good friend. Mike Graydon was a highly able Chief of the Air Staff and fighter for the interests of the RAF.

Charles Guthrie was Chief of the General Staff, in charge of the Army, during my time. He was unusual amongst his peers.

Most chiefs of staff, when they came to see me with a request, acknowledged that there might be political problems if I agreed but made it clear that that was for me to resolve, as they couldn't interfere in political matters. Charles Guthrie was more creative in his approach. He would acknowledge that there might be political problems, emphasise that they were for me and not for him, but would then offer a way through the difficulty that might satisfy both of us. He was usually right. I was not surprised when he ended up doing two terms as Chief of the Defence Staff.

Britain continues to be exceptionally well served by its senior officers. I am proud to count a number of them as good friends. Most of
the time I was happy to accept their recommendations. From time
to time I did not.

On one occasion, I felt unable to accept the advice from a particular chief of staff. He expressed his concern that I was willing
to overrule him on what he considered to be a military matter.
I resisted the temptation to tell him that if I never overruled the
advice I received from the chiefs of staff, he would not have received
his current appointment.

When I first became Defence Secretary, my contacts with the
chiefs of staff were on a one-to-one basis. I was surprised that there
appeared to be no forum where ministers, the chiefs of staff, the
Permanent Secretary and other senior officials could meet collectively
to have strategic and other discussions concerning the Ministry of
Defence and defence-related issues.

I discovered that there was a body called the Defence Council,
which rarely met and then only for ceremonial purposes. I decided to
revive and transform it. Under my chairmanship, it met several times
a year to have strategic discussions and as an opportunity for the
chiefs of staff, as well as individual ministers, to share both their concerns and their achievements with the most senior political, military
and administrative personnel responsible for the nation's defence.

The Defence Council still meets and I hope that it is used as pro-
ductively as it was in the 1990s.

A memorable evening was the dinner I attended as the guest of
the Victoria Cross and George Cross Association. There were around
forty people present and all, except me and the Chief of the Defence
Staff, had won either the VC or the George Cross. I felt insignificant
in comparison with these brave men and women.

During the dinner, the elderly gentleman on my right, who had
won the George Cross, asked me if I slept easily at night. I replied
that I always did. He expressed surprise and said that if he had been

Defence Secretary he would have lain awake all night worrying about the various decisions that had to be taken. He would have found it nerve-racking to live with the kind of responsibilities that I had.

I was interested in finding out how he had won his George Cross, so later on I asked him what work he had done before he retired. 'Oh,' he replied, 'my career was in mine disposal.'

How extraordinary. He was worrying how I could sleep at night! I was not exposed to physical risks, while throughout his working life he could have been killed, at any time, while handling unexploded mines. His was real courage even though he felt he was only doing his job.

CHAPTER 18

FRONT LINE FIRST

FIGHTING WAS AN option always available to a Defence Secretary. Winning was not so certain. The end of the Cold War in 1989 and the dissolution of the Soviet Union in 1991 had made the world a much safer place. It had also made defence unfashionable and the Treasury, and its counterparts throughout NATO, were anxious for their 'peace dividend'.

The main consequence in the United Kingdom was Options for Change, announced in 1990, which reduced the armed forces by 18 per cent down to 255,000, cut the Royal Navy's destroyers and frigates from forty-eight to forty and made similar reductions in the RAF's fighting capability.

In the 1993 Defence White Paper, I had the disagreeable task of announcing the further cuts in capability that resulted from the Options decisions. But I also had one easier announcement. I felt, very strongly, that the cuts in Army manpower had gone too far. After discussions with Peter Inge, the Chief of the General Staff, I was able to state that the proposed mergers of the Cheshire and Staffordshire regiments and of the Royal Scots and King's Own Scottish Borderers would not go ahead. It was a good tonic at the time though, sadly, in subsequent years these regiments have lost their separate identity.

The Options for Change reductions did not satisfy the Chancellor's ambitions and I was faced, in 1993, with a further demand for cuts to the Defence budget of £3.2 billion over three years. This was, to be fair, part of a Treasury assault on all government departments, but in our case we were already in the middle of implementing the Options for Change reductions.

The Defence budget is so large compared to most other departments that there are never many friends around the Cabinet table. Concessions to us meant higher savings would be expected from others.

The outcome was that I was required to find around £750 million in the first year, not a vast sum out of a total budget of £23 billion but a serious challenge if we were to maintain our fighting capability. I was also concerned at the effect of further cuts on the morale of the armed forces if they were faced with what would appear to be entirely Treasury-driven requirements.

Having discussed this challenge with my junior ministers and the chiefs of staff, I made to the Treasury a proposal which was the one they least expected. Instead of making cuts of £750 million I proposed that we would make cuts of £1 billion.

There was, of course, a condition. If I delivered £1 billion of savings, the Ministry of Defence would be permitted to retain the extra £250 million a year to be used for whatever front-line operational capability improvements we wished. So far as I am aware, the Treasury had never received such a proposal before, but the Chancellor agreed.

This made the exercise that we embarked on very much easier than it would otherwise have been. We were able to say both to the armed forces and to our civil servants that if they identified £1 billion of sensible savings, mainly in support services, we would retain a quarter of the cash to be used to improve the armed forces fighting capability. I gave the whole exercise the name Front Line First.

I also got agreement that in order to identify where the savings could best be made, we should, for the first time ever in the Ministry of Defence, invite proposals not just from senior officers and commanders but from middle-ranking officers and those civil servants who were involved in many of the administrative services and who were often better placed than the top brass to know where sensible savings could be made. The objective was that it would not be all pain and no gain. In the event we received 3,000 proposals from staff, many of which were endorsed.

Thirty-three defence costs studies were set up and I put Jonathan Aitken in charge of the day-to-day exercise. Under his chairmanship, it was a spectacular success. Three main conclusions came out of the review. Firstly, that management and command structures could be streamlined; secondly, that many defence support functions could be outsourced to the private sector; and, thirdly, that many command, training and support structures could be provided by the armed forces jointly rather than the Army, Navy and Air Force each having their own.

Some further major savings were made as a result of advice from my informal advisor, David Hart, who had experience of the property market as well as being very well informed on defence matters. We had decided that it would be sensible to transfer ownership of defence married quarters and other housing estate to professional housing managers in the private sector. David's estimate as to what we would receive from the sale of this property was around twice the department's assumptions. His advice turned out to be correct.

It was also David Hart who, with his defence expertise, had encouraged me to raise with the chiefs of staff the desirability of Britain acquiring a Cruise missile capability from the United States. There was a question of affordability but the extra savings we achieved through the Front Line First exercise resolved that problem.

David was a remarkable man. He was a colourful, stimulating, controversial buccaneer. At first, the chiefs of staff were concerned that he was giving me informal advice. They soon came to like and trust him, and several of the most senior officers became close friends of his. On defence issues, I respected his judgement and often agreed with him. On foreign policy, he was close to American neo-conservatives and we had, often, to acknowledge our differences.

He had been close to Mrs Thatcher and gave her important advice during the miners' strike as well as helping the non-striking miners develop their alternative union.

David was never braver than when he was found to have motor neurone disease many years later. He lived for several years with diminishing mobility but never lost his joie de vivre and steely courage. His youngest child, Amalyah, is my goddaughter. David was, and would be, very proud of her. We remain close to David's eldest son, Bim, and his wife, Tas, as well as others of their large family.

On 14 July 1994, I announced the outcome of our work on Front Line First to the House of Commons. I began by saying, 'I have no proposals to announce that would reduce the fighting strength of our armed forces.' That got a good cheer, as for four years the opposite had been the case in such statements.

I began by announcing a series of savings from headquarters, stores, infrastructure and other aspects of administration. Ministry of Defence staff in central London were to be reduced from 5,000 to 3,750, the procurement executive would have 500 fewer staff and there would be similar other cuts elsewhere, including the closure of seventeen depots.

For operational as well as cost-effective reasons, we were creating a Joint Service Staff College as well as other 'joint' facilities for the three services, which were overdue.

Having announced those and other savings, I was then able to inform Parliament of the improvements to front-line capability that were now affordable because of the additional savings we had achieved. I announced that we were ordering two new assault ships for the Royal Navy and placing an order for a further batch of minehunters.

Twelve Harrier aircraft from the reserve fleet were being moved to the front line and for the Army I confirmed an order for a further 259 Challenger tanks.

One of the most important enhancements I announced was our likely purchase from the United States of Tomahawk land attack Cruise missiles for the Royal Navy. This order went ahead in due course.

Not surprisingly, my statement was well received by my side of the House and there was little criticism from the opposition. There was considerable relief that for once military capability was being enhanced rather than reduced.

The savings we had identified were successfully achieved, but we had made at least one significant mistake. We had announced the reduction of service hospitals from three to one and the establishment of military hospital units in NHS hospitals. This change was severely criticised and, in due course, the mistake was acknowledged.

In preparation for the parliamentary announcement, I had offered to brief Lady Thatcher and had seen her the week before at her home in Chesham Place, Belgravia on 6 July. I had been concerned that without knowing the background she might be called by the press on the day and make critical comments of the savings side of the Front Line First exercise.

To see her was a wise decision. As I went through each saving, she made critical responses. She was angry about any further cuts to defence spending. When I explained that the chiefs of staff had agreed that what was proposed would not affect operational capability, she said that the ex-chiefs did not agree. As the ex-chiefs, at that stage, did not know what we were proposing, that was clearly a knee-jerk reaction on Lady Thatcher's part.

She then, rather perceptively, predicted that we would 'illustrate a lousy statement with announcing orders'. This, she said, was 'an old trick'. It would not, in fact, be a lousy statement but she obviously

remembered the kind of statements she had approved when she had
been Prime Minister.

At one stage she said that the problem with the Ministry of
Defence was that we had no friends. 'The Foreign Office', she said
'are not wet. They're drenched.'

Despite these observations, she was courteous throughout and at
the end of the meeting she escorted me downstairs to see me out.
Her final comments were: 'I remember that in 1939 we went to war
to save Poland. You', she said, poking me in the chest, 'weren't even
born yet.' 'That was not my fault,' I remarked.

Crispin Blunt, then my special advisor, now the chairman of the
Commons Foreign Affairs Select Committee, had accompanied me.
He had never met her before and found the meeting an unforget-
table experience.

Despite the frosty exchanges, Lady Thatcher never made a public
word of criticism of Front Line First so there must have been some
grudging acceptance that it wasn't too bad.

If Front Line First was a considerable success, Rosyth Naval
Dockyard was a great disappointment. Since 1984, Rosyth had been
the sole location for refitting the Royal Navy's nuclear submarine
fleet, work that it had been doing for some time. In 1986, there was
extensive rebuilding to facilitate this new role.

Plymouth, Devonport was the other major naval dockyard. By
the early 1990s, the Royal Navy had decided that with the reduced
size of the fleet it did not need two dockyards and that one should
be closed in order to save resources.

I was faced with this recommendation when I became Defence
Secretary at the same time as Devonport was mounting a fierce campaign that the refitting of the future Trident submarines should be
switched from Rosyth to them.

I took the view that regardless of which dockyard did the Trident
refitting work, it would be against the public interest for there to
be only one naval dockyard. The naval dockyards were about to be

privatised and if there was only one it would have a monopolistic advantage when tendering for naval business.

I therefore overruled my naval advisors and made it clear that whichever dockyard won the Trident refitting work, the other yard would have a free run, at least for several years, on all non-nuclear work for the Royal Navy.

Because of the competition between Rosyth and Devonport for the Trident work, both yards were invited to tender. In the event, Devonport's bid was marginally cheaper than Rosyth's.

I must confess that I was disappointed by this outcome. I knew that there would be an outcry throughout Scotland if Rosyth lost the Trident work when our nuclear submarines were based at Faslane on the Clyde and the nuclear expertise was with Rosyth at the time. My own parliamentary constituency was just across the Firth of Forth so there was a local dimension as well.

The politics, however, applied on both sides. The south-west was a crucial battleground between Conservatives and Liberal Democrats and Plymouth was contested territory.

As Defence Secretary, I could not be politically partisan and had to acknowledge that Devonport had won the tender, however marginally. Ian Lang, the Scottish Secretary, put forward a very powerful case for Rosyth. He had support from me in that I argued that as the two tenders were so close that other considerations should be taken into account and Rosyth's nuclear expertise and the capital investment that had already been made there to service the Tridents should give them the edge.

There was no support from the Prime Minister or others on the Cabinet committee for this view. As far as they were concerned, Devonport had won the tender and if the politics also pointed in that direction, so be it.

In making the public announcement, I was thankful that I could give assurance that Rosyth would, nevertheless, have a healthy future with non-nuclear Royal Navy work. But there was an understandable feeling of considerable resentment at the way the decision had been reached. I was heavily criticised by Scottish interests and the government did not win many friends on this issue.

Rosyth remains, to this day, a successful naval dockyard and will be responsible for the final assembly work with regard to the Royal Navy's new aircraft carriers.

Nuclear weapons issues did not feature large during my time at Defence. With the end of the Cold War, the threat of a Third World War with the ultimate horror of an exchange of nuclear weapons had dramatically receded.

But we still lived in a world where there were potential aggressors, some with nuclear arms. I was as hostile to unilateral nuclear disarmament as I had ever been. But I did not see why the number of nuclear weapons could not be dramatically reduced. At the end of the Cold War there were 63,000 nuclear warheads in the world. Today there are 15,000–20,000. That is a dramatic reduction but still far too many. Ninety-five per cent of all nuclear weapons are American or Russian. We all have a responsibility to do what we can.

As Defence Secretary, I was able to recommend to the Prime Minister that the United Kingdom dispose of all its free-fall nuclear bombs that could be dropped from aircraft and of our tactical nuclear weapons that could potentially be used alongside conventional weapons in a conflict. This we have done and today Britain's nuclear arsenal is restricted to its Trident submarines, the absolute minimum we require to defend these islands.

One further reform of which I am proud was the Reserves and, in particular, the Territorial Army. I discovered that under existing legislation we could only call out either the whole Territorial Army or none of them.

This meant that except in times of national emergency the reservists could never be used even if some of them had specialist skills or the units to which they belonged could have made a useful contribution to some military operation overseas. The TA was very frustrated at this restriction.

The law was changed, but this was only part of a much more radical reform over the past twenty years which has made the armed forces Reserves much more integrated with the Regulars and used constantly. This has created some real challenges for part-time reservists who also have their own careers but the overall change has been highly beneficial.

Active military operations during my three years as Defence Secretary were limited. The Gulf War was over and Afghanistan, Kosovo and Iraq were still to come.

Bosnia was the main operation and I deal with that in the next chapter. Otherwise, there was the defence of the Falklands, which I visited, the use of air power against Saddam Hussein when he breached the no-fly zone in Iraq, and the ongoing need for the Army to operate in Northern Ireland.

On one occasion, in Northern Ireland, I was helicoptered to Crossmaglen, where the Army had a sangar or watchtower. Crossmaglen is right on the border with the Irish Republic and was known as 'bandit country'.

Our helicopter came in to land, using a figure-of-eight manoeuvre as it descended to make it more difficult for it to be attacked from the ground. Once it landed, the engines had to be kept running while we ran to the Army sangar, where our soldiers were based. The return trip was much the same. The day was peaceful but what was an exceptional experience for us was then the daily life of British soldiers in part of the United Kingdom.

The only time my life was endangered in Northern Ireland was in very different circumstances. I was being driven around west Belfast, which is a Republican area, in an Army jeep. I was in the front with the driver. Behind me were a brigadier and a general.

The Army, when on patrol, don't use seatbelts, to enable an instant response to any incident. It turned out that my door had not been properly closed. As we swerved around a corner, it flew open. The brigadier, sitting behind me, with great presence of mind grabbed my collar before I could be flung out of the vehicle as it braked.

For the British Army to have lost their Secretary of State to the IRA would have been bad enough. To have lost him due to their own carelessness would not have been a good career move. I am glad to report that the brigadier who saved me, Alistair Irwin, in due course became a distinguished general.

In June 1994, I accompanied John Major to Normandy for the 50th anniversary of the D-Day landings in June 1944. After the ceremony, there was a VIP lunch hosted by the French government in the local *mairie* in Bayeux.

After the lunch, as I was leaving, a fellow guest, speaking English with what I assumed to be a French accent, called out, 'Hello, Malcolm. How are you?'

I returned his greeting but had no idea who he was. He then said, 'You remember. We met when we were both transport ministers.' I cheerfully agreed but still I had no idea who he was.

I assumed that he was a French minister and asked him what job he was now doing. He looked rather irritated as he informed me that he was the Prime Minister of Belgium.

I was deeply embarrassed. He was Jean-Luc Dehaene, who several months earlier had been vetoed by John Major as the next President of the European Commission, as he was thought to be too federalist for British tastes. My failing to even recognise him must have confirmed his poor opinion of the British government.

CHAPTER 19

BOSNIA

T HE ISSUE THAT more than any other occupied my time and my concerns during my three years as Defence Secretary was the war in Bosnia.

Throughout that time, we had British troops in that country. Although they were there wearing UN blue helmets, escorting humanitarian convoys rather than for combat, they needed to be armed and were subject to real risks at any time, especially from Bosnian Serb forces.

During those three years, Bosnia was discussed by the Cabinet on many occasions but most of the day-to-day decision-making was in the hands of a triumvirate of the Prime Minister, the Foreign Secretary, Douglas Hurd, and myself.

Throughout that time, I do not recollect a single major difference between the three of us on Bosnian policy. Douglas and I would meet, often once a week, and we would see the Prime Minister when any major decisions or new initiatives were under consideration.

The decision to send British troops as part of the UN force had not been uncontroversial. Both Michael Heseltine and Ken Clarke were very critical, fearing mission creep and our troops ending up in a combat role. They accepted, however, that the humanitarian case for British involvement in helping deal with an unfolding European human tragedy was very powerful.

The Bosnian War had begun before I went to the Ministry of Defence in April 1992. In September of 1991, the UN Security Council had imposed an arms embargo on the whole of former Yugoslavia. In February 1992, the United Nations agreed to send 12,000 peacekeepers to Bosnia. Britain and France were the main contributors. The troops were deployed in March, with Sarajevo as their headquarters.

By that time, Bosnia had declared its independence. The Bosnian government, under President Izetbegović, had been reluctant to leave Yugoslavia, recognising that the ethnic mix within their country would make the creation of a distinct Bosnian nationality very difficult to achieve.

They were forced to do so when Croatian independence was recognised by the European Community at the insistence of Germany, despite serious misgivings by France, Britain and the United States. Bosnians, not unreasonably, recognised that they could not remain, joined with Serbia alone, in a rump Yugoslavia.

But Bosnian Muslims, though the largest group in Bosnia, were only around 44 per cent of the population. Fifty-six per cent were either Bosnian Serbs or Bosnian Croats, whose aspirations were to merge with the new states of Serbia and Croatia. In that, they had the active support of Serbian President, Slobodan Milošević, and the Croatian President, Franjo Tuđman. Neither intervened directly, with their own troops, but they held the prime responsibility for the war, the suffering and the ethnic cleansing that followed.

This war in Bosnia and parts of Croatia from 1992 to 1995 was different, in many respects, from all the other conflicts since 1945.

It was fought with savage intensity, tens of thousands died, several millions were displaced and 'ethnic cleansing' became part of our political vocabulary.

The international community and the United Nations became heavily involved, with thousands of troops dispatched to the war zone. But from the beginning there was a fatal indecision and ambiguity about the proper role for the UN 'blue helmets'.

Humanitarian convoy support, peacekeeping, peacemaking and full combat are each very different, and incompatible, roles for any military force. The British and French, who were contributors to the UN force, and the Americans and Russians were never able to reach full agreement on what the military contribution should be, and were often locked in deep and sometimes bitter dispute both bilaterally and in the Security Council of the United Nations.

They started, however, with one judgement that all shared and which had profound implications. No government in Western Europe, nor the United States, nor Russia, believed that the Bosnian conflict threatened the security of Europe as a whole. Nor was it seen as a serious challenge to the West's strategic interests.

If it had been, there is little doubt that they would have reacted as with Saddam Hussein's invasion and annexation of Kuwait in 1990. NATO troops, both ground forces and air power, would have been mobilised and, with or without the express approval of the Security Council, military intervention would have been used to force Milošević to abandon his Serb hegemonic intentions and try to ensure the territorial integrity of the successor states of Yugoslavia.

Whether such a strategy would have worked; whether Bosnia would have been spared the agony of ethnic cleansing; and whether stability would have been brought to former Yugoslavia will never be known. The disintegration and anarchy that erupted in Iraq after the Americans' easy military victory in 2003 make us much more cautious today about any such assumptions.

The fundamental belief of the Western powers was correct. The conflicts in Bosnia and Croatia were, essentially, internal. They had profound implications for Serbia, Kosovo and Montenegro as former parts of the old Yugoslavia. But despite many alarmist warnings during the course of the Bosnian War, there was never any serious possibility of the conflict or the instability spreading to Romania, Greece, Bulgaria or Turkey, much less affecting Europe as a whole.

The reasons are not difficult to identify. The disintegration of Yugoslavia and the conflict that broke out had many of the characteristics of a civil war. Both Bosnia and Croatia were independent states but their independence from Yugoslavia had only just been declared.

Throughout the whole Bosnian conflict, the combatants were Bosnian Serbs, Bosnian Muslims and Bosnian Croats. Likewise, the attempt by the Krajina to secede from Croatia was a battle between Krajina Serbs and the Croatian government.

The Bosnian Muslims, for their part, were not ethnically diverse from their fellow citizens. They were not the descendants of immigrants from the Ottoman Empire. Overwhelmingly, they were communities from a Croat or Serb background who had converted to Islam centuries ago.

That, of course, is not the whole story. It may have been a form of civil war but prime responsibility for these events rested with Slobodan Milošević in Belgrade and his strategy of seeking to create a Greater Serbia that would incorporate all the Serb communities of the former Yugoslavia.

Franjo Tuđman, the President of Croatia, had similar aspirations for the Croats. While struggling to recover the Serb-dominated regions of his own state in the Krajina, he shared with Milošević the objective of dismembering Bosnia by annexing its Croat-populated territory.

Some commentators have rested on the fact that by the time the war began, Bosnia was an independent state, recognised as such, and that the conflict should have been seen by the international community as a classic act of aggression by Serbia against Bosnia. This, they have argued, should have led to unqualified UN support for the

Bosnian government, including the kind of military commitment that was used to expel the Iraqis from Kuwait.

There is, of course, an element of logic in such an approach but it would have been quite undeliverable and would have ignored both the historic and the political reality. Bosnia, it is true, was an independent, legally recognised state, but it had only been one for several weeks at the time the war began.

These factors had military as well as political implications. Neither the UN nor NATO could have expelled either the Bosnian Serbs or the Bosnian Croats from Bosnia without themselves being guilty of 'ethnic cleansing'. Furthermore, there were no 'Yugoslav' forces to fight against. Milošević's support was political, diplomatic and through covert arms supplies. Although his influence on the Bosnian Serbs was substantial, neither his own army nor his aircraft crossed the border to aid the Bosnian Serbs.

Although the West had no strategic interest in Bosnia, they neither could nor wished to ignore what was going on in that country. Europe had only just emerged from the Cold War. New democratic societies were being built in the former Soviet satellites of central and Eastern Europe. The Soviet Union had itself collapsed and was being transformed into fifteen new states. While there was conflict in the Caucasus and in Moldova, these were on the periphery and Europe as a whole seemed more at peace with itself than for many years.

The wars in former Yugoslavia were a major exception and it was natural that the European Community and the United States, as well as the wider international community, should wish to use intense diplomatic efforts to help resolve the crisis.

It had also become clear that, as with any such wars, major displacement of civilians was occurring, together with real risk of shortage of food supplies, shelter and medical aid. But, even more grimly, what became known as ethnic cleansing began in 1991, in the Krajina, when Croats were expelled from a largely Serb area as part of a deliberate Serb strategy to secure their control. In due course, around a third of Croatia was to be occupied with 500,000 Croats and 230,000 Serbs displaced from their homes. In the summer of 1992, ethnic cleansing became a major tool of Bosnian Serb paramilitaries in their determination to control as much of Bosnia as possible.

These events had a powerful impact not only on Western governments. Through television and intense media interest, public opinion throughout the Western world was deeply disturbed and governments were pressed to provide as much humanitarian assistance as possible.

It became clear, however, that if aid, in various forms, was to be delivered safely to Bosnian and Croat refugees, in the middle of such vicious conflict, the aid convoys would need to be protected. In December 1991, it had been agreed that an international military protection force would be sent to Croatia and Bosnia. This force, which became known as UNPROFOR, was the second largest that the United Nations had ever sent in its history.

I have mentioned that when we discussed in Cabinet a major British contribution to the UN military force there was opposition from Michael Heseltine and Ken Clarke, who feared mission creep. No one at that meeting suggested that we should offer combat forces to assist the Bosnian government against the Bosnian Serbs. The British public would not have countenanced such intervention and the Cabinet shared that view.

As Defence Secretary, I felt I had a personal duty not to send British troops into combat unless there was a clear British national interest that needed to be advanced or defended. On that issue, ministers and the vast majority of the public were agreed.

The decision to send a UN force was not, in itself, very controversial. But there were major defects in the way in which it was implemented and these defects had increasingly serious consequences as the Bosnian War proceeded over the subsequent three years.

Firstly, there was no peace to keep. The function of the UN force was to protect the aid convoys that were travelling through some of the most dangerous parts of the country. It was that danger that required the UN force to be present, but when soldiers are used they need to be provided with weapons and other military equipment to ensure the safety of those they are protecting as well as themselves.

For this, UNPROFOR troops carried personal weapons while British soldiers travelled in Warrior armoured personnel vehicles and had access to a range of other lethal equipment. As the war intensified, UNPROFOR commanders were given the right to summon air support in the form of ground attack aircraft if they judged it necessary to protect themselves and their convoys.

Such an armed force in the middle of a war zone clearly had a significant military capability. In addition, although the aid was intended to be for the benefit of anyone who needed it, in practice a very high proportion of it was used to give relief to Bosnian Muslim communities. There was, therefore, no way that Bosnian Serb forces were going to see UNPROFOR as other than informal allies of the Bosnian government. UNPROFOR and its contributor governments may have thought of the force as neutral in the conflict. The Bosnian government complained that they were too neutral. But Bosnian Serbs saw them, with some justification, as aiding their enemies and enabling them to resist the Serbs longer and more effectively through the civilian aid that they provided.

There were occasions when it seemed the other way around and when it appeared that the UN forces were acquiescing and, indeed, assisting with ethnic cleansing. In July 1992, UNPROFOR escorted 7,000 Bosnian refugees from north-western Bosnia to Croatia. They had been told by the Serbs that these were voluntary refugees wishing to be reunited with their families. In fact, they had just been ethnically cleansed from their villages. It may have been a tragic mistake by the UN but it emphasised the ambiguity and dangers of their role and mandate.

The overall dilemma was, to some degree, made more complicated by the national identity of the main contributors to UNPROFOR, the British and the French. As a result, French and British generals were the senior commanders of the force throughout its operations.

These officers would have felt themselves to be politically neutral, as they were under the command of the United Nations and not of their national governments, though in the case of the French that distinction was sometimes blurred and, at least on one occasion, completely ignored.

In any event, Britain and France were not seen by the combatants, especially the Serbs, as neutral. It was the British and French governments who, together with the Americans, were responsible for turning the screw on Belgrade and the Bosnian Serbs throughout the war. As permanent members of the Security Council, these three governments were instrumental in imposing a no-fly zone throughout Bosnia which effectively grounded the Serb air force. They were also responsible for imposing on Belgrade increasingly tough economic sanctions which, ultimately, were the fiercest and most comprehensive that the UN had ever imposed on any state in the course of its history.

Simultaneously, it was two British Foreign Secretaries, Lord Carrington and Lord Owen who, together with Cyrus Vance, were the principal mediators trying to pressure the Serbs into surrendering a large proportion of the territory they had conquered.

In retrospect, it was always unrealistic to expect the Bosnian Serb forces to divorce the British and French military who were providing humanitarian aid from the British and French governments who were imposing sanctions, applying diplomatic pressure and introducing no-fly zones.

These difficulties became even more acute in the latter part of the war when the British and French governments acquiesced, albeit without enthusiasm, in the increasing use of NATO air strikes, which often included British and French aircraft, against Bosnian Serb positions. The temptation, in such circumstances, to retaliate by taking UNPROFOR soldiers hostage was as irresistible as it was indefensible.

I visited Bosnia on several occasions as Defence Secretary. My main purpose was to see British troops in action but it was also an opportunity to have talks with the Bosnian government and to understand better the situation on the ground.

My first visit was to the Cheshire Regiment, stationed in central Bosnia, under the command of the colourful Col. Bob Stewart who, after he left the Army, would end up as a Conservative MP. We dined under canvas with the regimental silver displayed on the dining table. When I expressed some surprise, he said it had been brought with the regiment for a serious purpose.

He wished to impress upon the various Bosnian militias he had to deal with that the British were professional soldiers with a long history of high standards who would not involve themselves in local political issues. Bob Stewart was a good leader of men. Though he was invariably cheerful and often light hearted, he had a highly serious purpose.

On the several visits that I made to Bosnia during the conflict, I accompanied the armed convoys that were carrying food and medical aid. I was usually in one of the front Warrior armoured vehicles. Often we could hear gunfire and occasionally the guns appeared to be directed towards us.

During one such journey I asked the British commander in the Warrior with me about our assailants. He said there were two kinds of snipers. The first group were just showing off with their rifles. They were known in the British Army as 'fuck you's. The second group were more dangerous. They would be happy to kill us if they could. 'What were they called?' I asked. '"Fuck me"s,' he replied.

I would have liked to have included that in the statement I made to Parliament when I returned to London. I concluded, sadly, that the Speaker would rule me out of order.

That we were in a war zone was evident each time we flew into Sarajevo. Because of the possibility of being attacked by Bosnian Serbs with shoulder-launched missiles, we had to make what became known as a Sarajevo landing.

Instead of the aircraft slowly descending towards the runway, it would remain at an altitude out of range until the last moment, when it would suddenly dip into a very sharp descent. Thankfully I had been told what to expect and did not disgrace myself.

Being driven into Sarajevo city centre was an experience in itself. Large parts of the capital were encircled by Bosnian Serbs. One could never be certain that one would not suddenly be at the receiving end of their attention.

On a subsequent visit to Bosnia in August 1993, the convoy I was travelling with was subject to sniper fire. I was later flown by a Sea King helicopter to our aircraft carrier, HMS *Invincible*. I was invited to address the whole ship's company of around 600 people on our mission in Bosnia. At one stage while speaking I became alarmed when my audience started swaying in front of me. I had to remind myself that I was on board a ship in the Adriatic.

One of the most serious issues needing to be resolved was the diverging relationship between the countries of Western Europe and the United States on how to handle the Bosnian crisis.

When the disintegration of Yugoslavia began in earnest in 1991, Washington was content to leave its handling largely to its European allies. James Baker, George Bush's Secretary of State, remarked, 'We don't have a dog in that fight.' Jacques Poos, the Luxembourg Foreign Minister, notoriously declared, 'The hour of Europe has dawned.'

This relative American disinterest was fatal. It meant that, from the beginning of the Bosnian crisis, there was insufficient dialogue between the United States, Britain and France as to the ultimate limits of Western involvement. No American troops were contributed to UNPROFOR and, as a consequence, there was no day-to-day co-ordination with Washington as there was between the British, the French and the UN in New York about the role of UNPROFOR, its ability to deliver its objectives and the threats to its safety.

As the months passed and the situation in Bosnia deteriorated, President Clinton found himself under greater pressure, both from Congress and from the American media, to be more proactive and to apply American muscle to assist the Bosnian government.

There was no question of anyone in Congress or elsewhere advocating the deployment of US ground troops to Bosnia in a combat or any other role. That continued to be ruled out until the final stages of the conflict. The pressure from Congress was twofold. They wanted the arms embargo that had been imposed by the Security Council on the whole of Yugoslavia in September 1991 to be lifted from Bosnia. Secondly, the US government called on the UN to authorise NATO to threaten and carry out air strikes against the Bosnian Serbs in order to assist the Bosnian government and prevent further encroachment upon its territory.

There were perfectly reasonable arguments in favour of both policies if the political will existed. However, there was, and there remained, a fundamental incompatibility between UN troops being involved in a humanitarian role in Bosnia, supplying food, shelter and medical aid to whoever needed it, and that same UN permitting the sale of arms to one combatant and authorising air strikes against the other.

Either the UN, as in Korea or the Gulf War, could unambiguously support, with its military assets, one side in such a war or it could remain militarily neutral. It could not do both simultaneously.

Such a proposition sounds obvious and it seems reasonable to assume that if American troops had already been deployed with UNPROFOR on the ground in Bosnia there would have been little dispute that either all UN forces had to be withdrawn or the option of aggressive air strikes had to be dropped.

The issue came to a head in May 1993 when President Clinton sent his Secretary of State, Warren Christopher, to Britain and France to see if he could win support for a policy that became known as 'lift and strike'.

John Major, Douglas Hurd and I met Christopher at Chevening, the Foreign Secretary's country residence, on 2 May. He was accompanied by the US ambassador, Raymond Seitz, the only career diplomat who has been appointed to London as ambassador and one of the best we have had.

Warren Christopher had a rather dry though friendly manner. He was highly competent and professional but did not seem to us to have his heart in his mission.

He began by saying that the view in Washington was that there were four options. They were: continuing the status quo, perhaps with more sanctions against the Serbs; attempting a ceasefire by pressure and then enforcing it through NATO; lifting the arms embargo; and air strikes against the Bosnian Serbs. He suggested that a combination of lifting the arms embargo and deploying air strikes was the 'least worse' choice.

Christopher acknowledged that air strikes, by themselves, would not end the war and might, in the short term, embolden the Bosnian Serbs to resist. They were, he said, 'an instrument not a policy'. He emphasised that there was still no appetite for deploying any US ground forces. Lifting the arms embargo was, however, what the Bosnian government wanted.

Christopher was then subjected to some intense questioning by his British hosts on the implications that would arise if American proposals were accepted. I asked what would be the future of the UN military mission. Would they have the cooperation of the Croats? How would they get arms to the Bosnian government given that Bosnia is landlocked and many of the Bosnian forces were cut off from their colleagues? Douglas Hurd queried how credible it would be to ensure that arms supplied would only be used in self-defence?

Christopher responded by saying that the purpose of supplying arms was to achieve 'equivalence' between the various sides to the conflict. He also said that the embargo would have to be lifted from the Bosnian Croats, not just from the Bosnian Muslims, sidestepping the fact that these two groups were not always allies and there had been fierce battles between them.

Overall, he gave the impression that he was presenting the arguments without any expectation that they would be acceptable. We learnt subsequently that the response in Paris had been equally sceptical. Although 'lift and strike' remained a US policy, no serious pressure was put on us to drop our disagreement.

The White House understood that their refusal to have American troops on the ground, even in a peacekeeping role, seriously reduced their negotiating strength. But senators, congressmen and significant parts of the US media were unaware of, disinterested in or unimpressed by this dilemma.

I saw this myself when I made a visit to Washington and had a rather acerbic meeting with US senators including John McCain and Bob Dole. They were well aware that their reliance on air strikes alone would be more symbolic than effective, but they were frustrated with the continuing conflict in Bosnia and the refusal of the British and French to use their military for purposes beyond escorting of convoys.

I also met Senator Dole at the Ministry of Defence in London. Dr Brendan Simms, in his polemic on the Bosnian War, *Unfinest Hour*, suggests that I rebuked the senator, saying to him, 'You Americans don't know the horrors of war.' This is complete fiction. I was well aware that Senator Dole, disabled with a war injury, knew far more about the horrors of war than I ever would.

There were a few in Britain who supported the American call for air strikes and our military forces being used in a combat rather than just a humanitarian support role. One of those few was the former Prime Minister, Margaret Thatcher.

Mrs Thatcher made a series of interventions in the public debate. Her intentions were to her credit but her judgement was questionable. Quite rightly, she despised Milošević. But she seemed to have a soft spot for the Croatian President Tuđman. At the last moment she had to cancel a proposed visit to Zagreb when it became clear that the Croatian Serbs had been responsible for some major ethnic cleansing.

On another occasion I clashed with her when she suggested that British and other Western governments were 'accomplices to massacre'. I described this as 'emotional nonsense', which, indeed, it was.

The consequence of the deep disagreement between Europe and the United States was an attempt by both Europeans and Americans to square the circle and enable conflicting strategies to be pursued. Accordingly, the Europeans reluctantly agreed that air strikes could be carried out by NATO if UN convoys or troops were being threatened by Bosnian Serb attacks. That policy was later extended to allow air strikes to be used to protect Sarajevo from further attacks by Bosnian Serb artillery.

The Americans, for their part, conceded that if NATO was going to launch air attacks in Bosnia while UN forces were on the ground, a 'dual-key' system of decision-making was unavoidable if chaos was not to ensue. Thus air strikes could not take place unless approved not only by NATO commanders but also by the UN authorities. The UN was a party as to whether air attack could be used and also had to agree to the choice of targets.

Expecting NATO commanders to await UN approval for individual air strikes and choice of targets was absurd from a military point of view. It made a coherent strategy much more difficult. The delays that could occur risked degrading the whole operation and reducing the impact on the Serbs.

But the Americans, on this issue, had largely themselves to blame. Some kind of dual-key system was unavoidable as long as the state carrying out the air strikes had no troops on the ground and no formal responsibility for the safety of other countries' troops that were contributing to UNPROFOR. In these circumstances, with different countries involved, operating under different mandates and with separate rules of engagement, a single chain of command was impossible.

President Clinton was very sensitive to these problems. But many of the more vocal senators and congressmen were remarkably obtuse. It is not difficult to imagine how the Americans would have responded if their troops had been on the ground while British and French aircraft were bombing enemy targets nearby. These problems reflected the failure of Western governments, despite their good and honourable intentions, to get their act together with a single agreed political strategy and military mandate.

The problem was not just theoretical or hypothetical. As well as the significant risk of 'friendly fire' on UNPROFOR troops, there was the real concern as to the likely Bosnian Serb reaction if air strikes were undertaken.

These fears were subsequently seen to be justified. In April 1994, approval was given for air strikes in order to try to deter further Bosnian Serb attacks on the enclave of Goražde. Not only did these strikes have no appreciable effect on Bosnian Serb military activity; they also led to the Serbs taking 150 UN personnel as hostages, including thirty-two British soldiers, thereby compounding the UN's humiliation.

I prepared a note for the discussion in the Overseas Policy Cabinet Committee, which met to discuss our response. The Cabinet Office paper had proposed negotiation with the Bosnian Serbs to secure the release of the hostages. I said that this would be insufficient. The Bosnian Serbs and Milošević had to be warned that there would be severe military retribution if any of the hostages were harmed.

I also recommended that the Bosnian Serb leadership should be told that the lives of British hostages in Serb hands would be treated as a vital national interest and that we would act accordingly if they were in any way harmed.

We also had to consider withdrawing UN forces to central Bosnia, where they would not be at such risk. The French and other UN contributing countries were also coming to this conclusion.

In the latter stages of the conflict, the American pressure to use its air power intensified. Britain, France and other contributor nations to UNPROFOR had made it clear that in these circumstances their troops would be withdrawn, as otherwise they would be exposed to a triple danger from the air strikes themselves, from Bosnian Serb artillery response and from further hostage-taking. UN troops had neither the numbers nor the weapons capability to protect themselves fully in such changed circumstances.

Gradually, UN forces were pulled back from the more exposed localities in Bosnia and concentrated where their protection could be more assured. This, of course, also had the side effect of reducing their original role of ensuring the supply of aid to threatened towns and villages in remote areas.

Britain and France also announced, in June 1995, that they would send a Rapid Reaction Force of further troops to Bosnia who would have a much more aggressive military capability. There was a deliberate ambiguity as to whether the purpose of this force was to enable military attacks on the Serbs or to provide full cover that would enable the safe withdrawal of the UNPROFOR troops if that should prove necessary. It was, indeed, the latter that was the main preoccupation of the British and French governments at that time.

In early 1993, it was proposed that several Bosnian government-held enclaves should be declared safe havens by the UN, with the Bosnian Serbs warned that they must not attack them or endanger their inhabitants. The first of these was Srebrenica, declared a safe area in April 1993, followed by five others including Sarajevo and Goražde.

When these safe havens were first recommended, the UN Secretary-General made clear that for them to be effective there would have to be a significant additional contribution of troops to the UN forces in Bosnia. The United Kingdom, France and a small number of other countries did increase their contribution but most others did not.

Britain warned that it would be unwise to declare safe areas if the UN did not have the troops that it judged necessary to make the policy effective. Most governments, however, felt that the UN had to go ahead, notwithstanding, and seek to ensure by both carrot and stick that the Bosnian Serbs did not attack the enclaves.

This judgement proved to be disastrous. Srebrenica was attacked in July 1995. The lightly armed Dutch UN contingent were unable to resist and thirty of them were taken hostage. What followed was the worst massacre in Europe since 1945, with up to 8,000 Bosnian Muslims, most of them civilians, killed.

The Bosnian Serb leadership had realised that the UN forces did not have the mandate, the numbers or the weaponry to protect those who lived in the 'safe areas'. It must be a powerful reminder for the future that neither the UN nor individual governments should make either promises or threats if they do not have both the will and the means to enforce these threats or promises if the need arises. Otherwise, they not only betray others but they disgrace themselves.

The final phase of the Bosnian conflict was more sudden and rapid than anyone had predicted. The Croatian Army began an offensive that drove the Serbs out of the Krajina while the Bosnian government forces were effective in capturing back large swathes of their own territory. Milošević had felt it politic to disown the Bosnian Serbs sometime earlier.

In July 1995, having just become Foreign Secretary, I had to chair a Lancaster House conference, where agreement was reached with the United States and the Russians on a joint series of demands on Milošević and all the Bosnian parties. The result led to the Dayton Conference and the uneasy peace that has kept a single Bosnian state in existence but has conceded full autonomy to the Republika Srpska within its borders. Bosnia remains united in form but divided in substance.

The Bosnian conflict had many of the ingredients similar to those we have had to grapple with in more recent crises, especially Syria. There was deep debate and controversy as to whether Western military forces should have become more involved and, if so, in what manner and with what end.

The need not to repeat the mistakes made in Bosnia was often used, fairly or unfairly, by both Bill Clinton and Tony Blair to justify the NATO bombardment of Belgrade during the Kosovo crisis several years later. In particular, it motivated some politicians and academics to argue the case for humanitarian military intervention, regime change and a proactive foreign policy, which contributed significantly to the preoccupations of the Bush–Blair era.

It is worth looking at some of the main accusations that have been made against the United Nations, and Britain and France in particular, about their handling of the Bosnian crisis.

The first was the charge of 'moral (or amoral) equivalence'. This alleged that the conflict was seen as a civil war, that all the parties were seen as just as bad and that the West appeared indifferent both to Bosnia's territorial integrity and to its government's multi-ethnic aspirations. In support of this view is mentioned the arms embargo imposed by the UN against all the combatants; the inability or unwillingness of the United Nations to reverse the ethnic cleansing that had dominated the earlier part of the war; and the pressure that was put on Bosnian President Izetbegović, from time to time, to make concessions of territory or policy in order for a negotiated peace to be achieved.

While it is correct that the conflict was seen, in many respects, as similar to a civil war, the charge of moral equivalence is groundless.

Neither the UN nor the British nor the French ever doubted that the Bosnian government was the legal government of the territory and deserved full diplomatic and political support. This was demonstrated in practice. Humanitarian aid convoys operated almost exclusively in the areas controlled by the Bosnian government. Little went to the Serbs though there were many Serb refugees from both Croatia and Serbia. There was constant cooperation and dialogue with the Bosnian government at both ministerial and official level. There was virtually none with the Republika Srpska, the Bosnian Serb entity.

Economic sanctions were imposed and increasingly toughened on Serbia and on the Bosnian Serbs. They were not imposed on the Bosnian Muslims. Some military support was given to the Bosnian government to try to protect Sarajevo, and a 'safe areas' status was conferred on other Bosnian enclaves. Nothing of the kind was ever contemplated for any Bosnian Serb territory when it was under attack from either the Bosnian government or the Croats. The no-fly zone, imposed in October 1992, in theory applied to all sides but in practice harmed the Serbs, as they were the only combatants with a significant air capability.

The argument about the arms embargo was more difficult. It had been imposed by the UN Security Council in September 1991 after fighting had broken out in Croatia between Croats and Serbs but before the war had begun in Bosnia itself. Imposing it was not seen as controversial in itself but as a standard UN response when a war broke out.

At the height of the Bosnian conflict, however, it understandably became very controversial. The Bosnian government forces had little more than light weaponry both to protect themselves and to try to secure more territory. The Bosnian Serbs, however, not only had covert assistance from the Milošević regime in Belgrade. They also had control over many of the old Yugoslav Army arms depots which had been situated in Bosnia for many years and which had a range of heavy weaponry that might have been needed if Tito's Yugoslavia had ever been attacked by the Soviet Union.

Thus the arms embargo, in practice if not in theory, was of significant benefit to the Bosnian Serbs as it made it very difficult for the Bosnian government to build up credible and effective armed forces.

The Security Council, including Britain and France, were aware of this imbalance but felt unable to lift the embargo. Firstly, any such proposal would almost certainly have been defeated by a Russian veto. Secondly, it was assumed that lifting the arms embargo would simply prolong the war and lead to more deaths and suffering. Finally, it was felt to be impossible for countries like Britain and France to be providing humanitarian support through UNPROFOR while arming one of the combatants and thereby adding to the humanitarian catastrophe.

These considerations were held quite sincerely not just in London or Paris but even more passionately by the UN Secretary-General, whose views never wavered.

On one occasion, in a meeting with President Izetbegović of Bosnia in Sarajevo, the President expressed his support for the American call for 'lift and strike' and asked whether we would withdraw our opposition. I pointed out to him that as the President of Bosnia he could call for US air strikes without our agreement, and ask them not to observe the arms embargo. However, if he did so, it was inevitable, for reasons that he already knew, that UNPROFOR would have to be withdrawn as the UN had no mandate to support combat operations except in self-defence of its own forces.

President Izetbegović made clear that if he had to make such a choice, which he deeply regretted, he would prefer UNPROFOR to remain because of the many lives that were being saved.

While the arguments for the arms embargo were powerful and consistent with the previous practice of the United Nations, it is clear that it did far more harm to the Bosnian government than to its enemies. The fact that no attempt was made to rectify this, even when these consequences became known, was a significant error.

Over the years since the Bosnian War, I have defended the policy that we and other European nations pursued with the exception of the arms embargo. It was so one-sided in its consequences at the expense of the main victim and to the benefit of the main aggressor that we should have disowned it at the time. If we had done so, there would still have been a war but it would have been concluded more quickly.

A further charge has been the refusal of Britain and France to support a new strategy of NATO air strikes against the Bosnian Serbs when, rather belatedly, the United States President, under pressure from Congress, decided to call for them. The initial American proposal was rebuffed, though gradually agreement was reached that specific air strikes could be used, subject to the dual-key arrangement, if UNPROFOR was itself under threat or, eventually, to help Sarajevo and the 'safe areas'.

The opposition of the UN, Britain and France to the 'lift and strike' policy of the Americans was not capricious, nor maintained because of any affection for the Bosnian Serbs.

Firstly, there was fundamental doubt as to whether such a strategy would deliver the desired results. We were aware that air strikes linked to a ground assault was a powerful military tool with a proven history of success. But Washington was not contemplating any ground attack either by themselves or by UN forces.

There was at that time a school of thought in the United States that air power, by itself, can decide a military conflict and force a hostile regime to surrender or at least to negotiate from weakness. The history of the use of air power has not borne out this claim.

Neither in the first Gulf War nor in Kosovo nor in the Iraq War did sustained and awesome air bombardment, by itself, deliver victory. Both the Gulf War and the Iraq War were only resolved by a subsequent ground invasion. In the Kosovo War, Milošević did not surrender even after six weeks of sustained bombing of Belgrade. Only when there was a credible threat that ground forces would be used did he throw in the towel. Syria has provided further evidence of the limitations of air power.

Bosnia remains a deeply divided state to this day. The power of the central government is minimal in the Republika Srpska and there is little evidence that that will change in the years to come. But the killing and the ethnic cleansing stopped in 1995, Milošević has gone and Serbia today is more interested in joining the European Union than in expanding its own borders. We must be thankful for such progress. It has been better than what came before.

CHAPTER 20

COMING HOME

O N 23 JUNE 1995, Douglas Hurd confirmed his intention to retire as Foreign Secretary. That day, I was in St Kilda, the remotest island of the United Kingdom.

I was there with my military private secretary, Tim Laurence. Based on St Kilda were a small detachment of naval personnel who tracked the missiles being tested from the military station in South Uist on the Outer Hebrides.

It turned out to be very convenient that we were there. In the aftermath of Douglas's announcement, the media were anxious to get hold of me to find out whether I expected to succeed him. I did not wish to be interviewed. Even the most intrepid journalist did not try to travel to St Kilda.

Tim Laurence, who at that time was a Lieutenant Commander in the Royal Navy, had been chosen by me as one of my private secretaries when it had been suggested that I should have someone from within the armed forces in my private office.

I had already met Tim at Holyrood Palace when I was Scottish Secretary and he had been an equerry to the Queen. After he had married the Princess Royal, he continued as a serving officer and had a very successful career, ending as a vice-admiral.

Tim and I became close friends. We have seen each other often over the years both in Scotland and in the south. Through that friendship, Edith and I have also got to know the Princess Royal well. She is a remarkable public servant and is respected and admired throughout the country.

Douglas Hurd's intention to retire was announced the day after John Major had made his own decision to resign the Tory leadership and submit himself for re-election. It was a dramatic initiative made in order to quell the Eurosceptics and others in the party who had been undermining his leadership. He needed to demonstrate that he retained the overwhelming support of his parliamentary colleagues and of the party in the country. In this, he deservedly succeeded.

There had been considerable speculation that I would be Douglas's successor. On 19 May, *The Independent* said that it was a 'foregone conclusion' that I would be appointed, suggesting that I had been 'foreign secretary-in-waiting for a decade' since I had been Minister of State. After Douglas's announcement, *The Times* had said that I was the man 'most likely to succeed' while the *Independent on Sunday* polled Tory MPs, giving me support from twenty-five of them while Michael Portillo had twelve, Ian Lang six and Michael Howard three.

It was true that, as *The Times* reported, I had over several months made a number of speeches dealing with diplomatic and political issues that went wider than the strict brief of the Defence Secretary and helped remind Parliament and the public of my foreign policy credentials.

Perhaps the most important was a speech I made signalling my deep doubts about a European single currency. At the time, some assumed that I was sounding more sceptical than I felt in order to build support in the party. That was not true. Although I was, and have remained, strongly supportive of our membership of the EU, I had been opposed to a single currency from the moment the subject was first raised. I have always believed that a single currency cannot work properly without transferring economic, monetary and fiscal power to a single government. That, for me, was a bridge far too far.

In that respect, my views on Europe were very different from those of Michael Heseltine or Ken Clarke. I made the speech not because my views had changed but because I was concerned that, unless I made it clear, my colleagues might assume that my views were the same as Michael's and Ken's, who were supportive of Britain's involvement in a Eurozone.

I had also, as Defence Secretary, used several opportunities to impress on John Major that I had strategic views on British foreign policy as a whole and not just on its defence and security implications.

John Major held two Chequers seminars on British foreign policy, one in September 1994, the other in January 1995.

For the first, I submitted a paper that said very little about defence and a lot about foreign policy.

I suggested that the passing of the Cold War should be seen as the end of an aberration and a return to normality. That aberration had lasted since 1914, since when either Germany or the Soviet Union had sought the domination of Europe.

I urged that Britain should continue to have a world role 'for reasons that have nothing to do with delusions of grandeur or nostalgia for the past'. I supported Douglas Hurd's recommendation that we should expand our diplomatic representation and 'polish' those 'priceless jewels', the English language, the BBC World Service and the British Council.

On the collapse of the Soviet Union, I remarked that its 'truncated borders' would 'severely limit the options of any future aggressive government'. The key, I said, was Ukraine and I added that 'Russia without Ukraine ... is not and is unlikely again to become a global superpower'.

In a similar paper for the January seminar at Chequers, I argued for an 'Atlantic Community' that would draw the United States and

Europe closer together in areas beyond defence and security covered by NATO. I also suggested that while it was unrealistic for Russia to become a member of NATO, a new category of associate member could be created to meet Russian interest in closer integration with Western security.

Some of the press might have been assuming that it was a foregone conclusion that I would succeed Douglas. I did not share that view and, as it turned out, I only got the job by the skin of my teeth.

On 4 July, two days before the ballot on John Major's leadership, he asked me to see him in his room in the House of Commons. I had assumed that he wanted to ask me what I felt he should do if the result of the ballot was very close. He was looking tense and under pressure.

He had, however, other matters to discuss. He began by saying that there were two posts he was considering for my future. He recognised that I was 'easily the best qualified' to be Foreign Secretary but he wanted me to be party chairman. He needed 'a hard hitter' in that post.

I was taken aback and responded by saying that the chairmanship was not where my strengths lay. I could make a competent chairman but I would be a good Foreign Secretary.

He appeared to be unsurprised by my response. He said that he was considering two Cabinet ministers covering foreign policy, with one concentrating on Europe. Could I live with that if I became Foreign Secretary? I said I could if the other minister's views on Europe were the same as mine. He said that his own views and mine, so far as he knew, were the same on Europe. I agreed. I then departed without any certainty as to his intentions in the likely reshuffle. As he had discussed his thoughts on the future of the Foreign Office, I hoped I had weaned him away from the chairman of the party option.

In the event, John won the ballot against John Redwood easily and the night of his victory I went to a celebration party at 10 Downing Street.

The following day, the press speculation was mixed as to who would be the new Foreign Secretary. Michael Howard, who was being recommended by the Eurosceptics, was running strongly, with the *Financial Times* convinced it would be him.

I had been asked to go to No. 10 at 9.30 a.m. The early timing was an encouraging indication that mine was going to be one of the main appointments. At that time I was unaware that Michael Heseltine's appointment as Deputy Prime Minister would be the most significant of the reshuffle.

I saw the Prime Minister in the Cabinet Room. He was alone apart from Alex Allan, his private secretary. He said, right away, that he had decided he wanted me to be party chairman. He needed a hard hitter. There were only three who could do the job, Heseltine, Portillo and me. Heseltine would not do it and he did not want Michael Portillo as chairman.

I repeated what I had told him at our first meeting, that I did not think this was the right place for me. He said that foreign affairs would not help us win the election. I agreed but said it might make us lose it. I was, of course, referring to Europe and he did not demur.

He then said that Heseltine and I were the best orators in the government. I said our styles were quite different. He was a superb populist, whereas I used analysis rather than rhetoric, adding that my strengths were policy implementation rather than party political.

I concluded by saying that if he did not want me to become Foreign Secretary I would prefer to remain at Defence than become chairman.

He asked me to retire for five minutes while he reflected on what I had said. The five minutes became fifteen while I waited in the anteroom. I pondered with rather a heavy heart what I should do. My head asked me if I was being unreasonable; if I should be making the Prime Minister's job even more difficult. My heart told me I should hate being party chairman and should not take it. I resolved to press that I should remain at Defence if the Foreign Office was not to be.

When I re-entered the Cabinet Room, he said, to my intense relief, that I was to be Foreign Secretary. Instead of being irritated by my unhelpfulness, he then apologised for raising the chairmanship and said that I was to forget that he had ever mentioned it. He said this in a charming and amiable manner which was typical of him.

I asked him if he could tell me who the new Defence Secretary would be. He smiled and said that there were four Cabinet changes he would have to make to his original plans because of my resistance to becoming party chairman. I felt that it should have been me apologising to him, not him to me. We discussed other Foreign Office appointments and I was relieved that he had dropped the idea of a Europe Minister in the Cabinet.

I then left No. 10, apparently grinning broadly and, in response to the press, said, 'We have much work to do.' I felt elated but not as excited as I might have expected. I think the tension and uncertainty of the morning must have had its effect.

In a record that I made shortly after that morning, I wrote, 'I suspect that for years to come I will tremble when I consider what I would have gained and what I would have lost' if I had agreed to the Prime Minister's original wishes. I still do.

The following morning I arrived at the Foreign Office by the main entrance in King Charles Street. I shook hands with the staff at the door, met my new private secretary, William Ehrman, climbed the grand staircase and entered the Foreign Secretary's room.

I had been there often, the first time, thirteen years before, as a junior minister in 1982, but now I was taking occupancy as Secretary of State.

Sitting at the Foreign Secretary's desk, looking at the portrait of the Rana Prince over the marble mantelpiece, savouring the light from the tall windows overlooking Horse Guards and St James's Park, I felt a deep and tranquil satisfaction. It was like coming home.

Douglas Hurd came in a little later and expressed his pleasure at my appointment. He said he had been nervous. On Tuesday he had been told it was 90 per cent certain but on Wednesday he had been warned that this might not be the case.

Douglas and I were not close friends but we had worked extremely well together over the previous three years. When, in June, he had announced his retirement, I had written to him saying it had been a privilege for me to work with him. I admired his wisdom, clarity and selfless pursuit of the public interest.

He was, I believe, one of the finest, most professional Foreign Secretaries we have had in the years since 1945. I knew he would be a hard act to follow.

The reaction to my appointment was as good as I could have hoped. The *Financial Times* reported that 'relief swept through the Foreign Office', though this may have been because the diplomats had been told by the *Financial Times* to expect Michael Howard, a strong Eurosceptic. *The Times* remarked that my handling of the Front Line First review had shown that I had 'a steel will'. Other press reaction was positive.

On my first day, I issued a statement that I had drafted myself. After praising Douglas's tenure I said that I saw my duty as fighting 'for British interests both in Europe and elsewhere'.

I said that my priorities were the strengthening of the Atlantic Alliance and, secondly, a Europe 'that we are comfortable with'; one that recognises that 'Europe's strength is in its diversity not in a sterile search for uniformity'.

Le Monde responded by adding a new nugget to the French language describing me as a 'Eurosceptique modéré' or moderate Eurosceptic. The *Financial Times* referred to me as 'the sceptical Euro-enthusiast', which I rather approved of.

Not everyone was as complimentary. Writing a profile of me in *The Spectator*, Robin Harris concluded: 'This man is dangerous.'

He described me as 'spiky and pugnacious', accusing me of not having any fixed convictions, nor discernible principles, and of having been pro-Serb on Bosnia.

This was powerful stuff and I could have been upset. Just in time I remembered that Harris had helped Margaret Thatcher write her memoirs and would not have forgiven me for my ambivalent relationship with her. Nevertheless, I admired his polemical style.

My ministerial team within the Foreign Office were of considerable ability. In those days, Overseas Aid was not a separate department but had considerable autonomy. Lynda Chalker, who is now in the Lords, was in charge and was my senior Minister of State. It is inexplicable that she never became a Cabinet minister. She was the best and longest-serving International Development minister this country has had.

The other ministers were Nicholas Bonsor, David Davis and Jeremy Hanley, all of whom were effective ministers. Nicholas had been chairman of the Defence Select Committee. He was a strong Eurosceptic and an unapologetic traditionalist on many issues. He also had great integrity, never minced his words or avoided uncomfortable truths. He was the sort of colleague that Secretaries of State need. We still see him and his wife, Nadine, regularly.

Henry Bellingham remained my parliamentary private secretary. I tried to get him appointed as a minister but he had to wait until David Cameron sent him to the Foreign Office, where he was a successful minister responsible for sub-Saharan Africa.

I had two special advisors, Crispin Blunt, who had been with me at Defence, and Graeme Carter, who had been my special advisor at the Scottish Office and who had since worked on European issues. Graeme helped me on European policy, Crispin on the rest of the world. They were both invaluable and have remained very close to me over the years.

Becoming Foreign Secretary also required Edith and me to leave our tied flat in Admiralty House and move to even grander accommodation in Carlton Gardens. Until Ernest Bevin's appointment in 1945, it was assumed that the Foreign Secretary would have his own town house in London. Bevin did not and 1 Carlton Gardens was acquired for him and his successors to use.

Even grander was the Foreign Secretary's entitlement to the use of Chevening, a magnificent, mainly eighteenth-century country house and grounds. It was left to the nation by the last Earl Stanhope and is in the gift of the Prime Minister. Edith and I used it for the weekend every few weeks and loved being there. Edith arranged my 50th birthday party, which we held at Chevening. In my speech at my party, I remarked that when I ceased to be Foreign Secretary I would not lose Chevening. They would take it away.

In the first few weeks of our tenure, Hugo came to Chevening for the first time, from Cambridge. He arrived early on a Friday afternoon and knew we would not yet have arrived. He decided to explore the grounds but was not aware that he was being scrutinised by security cameras.

Within minutes he was being accosted by two policemen with sub-machine guns while he was having a fag behind a bush next to the lake. They took some convincing that this rather scruffy-looking teenager with a ponytail was the Foreign Secretary's son.

When I became Foreign Secretary, I pointed out to Caroline and Hugo the first page of a British passport, which says, 'Her Britannic Majesty's Secretary of State requests and requires in the name of Her Majesty ... to allow the bearer such assistance and protection as may be necessary.'

I encouraged them, when they were travelling or backpacking abroad, if they had any problems, to point to that page and say, 'That's my dad.' I don't think they ever did and, sadly, it is now too late.

Caroline and Hugo appeared to cope well with the burden of having a father who was Foreign Secretary. I hope I did not embarrass them and their privacy was rarely intruded on by the media.

One exception was when Hugo joined a demo against education cuts while he was a student. The *London Evening Standard* reported that he was spotted 'lustily singing "The Red Flag" on the streets of Cambridge'. I reckon this particular claim must have been journalistic invention as his politics have never been of that persuasion and he is unlikely to have even known the words.

Less agreeable than the perks of office was the 24-hour armed guard I was deemed to need as Foreign Secretary. When I protested that I had not required this as Defence Secretary despite British troops in Northern Ireland, I was told that the real concern was when I was travelling abroad.

We reached a rather artificial compromise whereby I was protected while I was in London and when I was travelling to or from Edinburgh at the weekends. The protection officers disappeared while I was in Edinburgh and reappeared for the journey south. Clearly, the Scots were deemed to be less of a risk than Londoners. The protection officers were great guys. Highly professional, they would keep themselves at a discreet, but safe, distance when Edith and I were on holiday with Caroline and Hugo.

My life as Foreign Secretary was extremely satisfying but was very much more demanding than any other job I had done in government over sixteen years. I have in front of me, as I write, a list of all the countries I travelled to as well as the meetings with Presidents, Prime Ministers, Foreign Ministers and occasionally Kings. These meetings might be in London, in a foreign capital, at the UN in New York, in Brussels for the EU or at an international conference.

The list records that in the just under two years I served as Foreign Secretary I visited fifty-six different countries as well as making numerous visits to Brussels and several to New York, Washington and Paris.

Transatlantic journeys enabled me to use Concorde on several occasions. No sooner had one finished lunch than one was told to prepare for landing in the United States. It is a matter of deep sadness that that remarkable aircraft is no more.

On one occasion I flew to Moscow and back in a single day in an aircraft of the Queen's Flight, including several hours of talks with the Russian Foreign Minister in between.

What made this possible was the frequent use of an RAF plane, which is far less likely to be made available to anyone other than the Prime Minister in these more austere days. Having my own plane enabled me to cover far more countries in the time available, including some, such as Mongolia, that had never been visited by a Foreign Secretary. The diplomatic benefit to Britain's interests and the goodwill created by visiting one's ministerial colleagues in their capitals should never be underestimated.

My first major responsibility as Foreign Secretary was to chair the Lancaster House one-day conference on Bosnia on 22 July. It was held in the aftermath of the terrible massacre in Srebrenica of thousands of Bosnian Muslim men and boys by Bosnian Serbs. We had called the conference to see whether there was a way in which the UN force could remain in Bosnia and whether there could be agreement with the United States on military action if it was necessary to protect the other 'safe area' at Goražde, which was being threatened by the Bosnian Serbs.

On the Monday of that week I had had meetings in Brussels with my German, Dutch and French colleagues as well as with Andrey Kozyrev, the Russian Foreign Minister. I was able to assure my Russian colleague that we had not become enthusiastic for air strikes but that they would be used, only as a last resort, if Goražde's safety was threatened. On that basis, Kozyrev agreed to recommend to Yeltsin that Russia should be represented at the conference.

The following day, I flew to Washington for similar meetings with Warren Christopher and Bill Perry as well as a discussion with Vice-President Al Gore. We made good progress in these talks and Christopher also agreed to come to London.

John Major opened the conference, which was also attended by all the countries contributing to UNPROFOR. The morning political and military sessions went well but in the afternoon I became concerned that opinion might move against our preferred strategy of keeping the UN in Bosnia and warning the Serbs that air strikes would occur if Goražde was threatened.

Hans van den Broek, the European Commissioner for External Relations, made a very helpful intervention and I sent a message to Warren Christopher encouraging him to intervene, which he did.

The latter part of the conference required some ingenuity to achieve a successful conclusion. When everyone at a diplomatic conference is agreed, one has 'Decisions'. When there is general but not total agreement, there are 'Conclusions'. When, however, there is a split which no one wants to admit to, one has a 'Chairman's Statement'. This was what we ended up with.

I knew the Russians could not expressly support the threat of air strikes but wanted to be helpful. Others had their reservations too. I therefore made my chairman's statement and then banged my gavel on the desk, thereby closing the conference before anyone could complain. The French Minister, Hervé de Charette, had wanted to speak, and was waving his arm, but I (fortunately) had not noticed him.

Given the hostility of the Russians, the unhappiness of the Ukrainians and the dire warnings of certain of the military commanders, the conference could only have ended either with no agreement or with a qualified conclusion. I was satisfied, and relieved, that we had achieved the latter.

I had a break over August. Late that month, I spoke with the Prime Minister. He had heard that I had been stalking deer in the Highlands. I told him that I had been prevented, quite properly, from shooting a royal. I did not, at first, explain that a royal is the term given to a stag with at least twelve points to its antlers. I merely said that it would not have looked good if it had been reported that the Foreign Secretary had shot a royal near Balmoral.

In mid-September, I visited Bosnia, Serbia and Croatia. I met Milošević, for the first and only time, in Belgrade. He was a smooth, persuasive operator but I did not trust him. His record had been awful.

During my visit to Sarajevo, the story in all the newspapers was that I had been almost shot by a Serb sniper. There were Bosnian Serbs about eighty yards away and I heard a shot but so far as I know it was not aimed at me. I was pleased that it was reported that I was 'unruffled' and that I had responded by saying that 'this was pretty small when compared to the suffering the people of Sarajevo have been going through'.

On 21 September, I made, at Chatham House, my first major speech explaining my approach to Britain's foreign policy.

I said that my starting point was Lord Palmerston's dictum that 'the furtherance of British interests should be the only object of a British Foreign Secretary'.

Quoting Palmerston always has risks for a modern British Foreign Secretary. While he has always been admired as a strong, brave and, usually, successful statesman, he spoke for Britain when it was the world's super power not a medium-sized European state.

Nevertheless, I had always admired Palmerston's clarity and his honesty in defining, in such a simple and straightforward way, the duty of the holder of the office that I now occupied. Indeed, I had arranged for a portrait of Palmerston to be hung in my room at the Foreign Office.

On one occasion the French ambassador had tried to please Palmerston and had informed him that if he had not been born a Frenchman he would have liked to have been born an Englishman. Palmerston gave a splendid response: 'If I had not been born an Englishman I would have liked to have been born an Englishman.' As a Scot, I am inclined to remark, 'Och, man. Have you no ambition?'

In my speech at Chatham House, I made clear that British interests in the late twentieth century required a very different policy to running the British Empire in the mid-nineteenth. Britain was now one of several global players and our strength and success were bound up with our participation in the UN, in NATO and in the European Union and with our relationship with the United States.

My most important argument in the speech was to emphasise the difference between interests and influence. One was often told that Britain would lose influence if we did not join some area of European integration. I did not deny that this could be true but suggested that we must remind ourselves that 'influence is a means and not an end in itself. Occasionally it may be appropriate to accept a loss of influence if that is the only way we can protect our interests.'

I used the example of General de Gaulle taking France out of the integrated military structure of NATO for many years. He knew it would result in a loss of influence for France but the alternative, in his view, would have been a far more serious loss of sovereignty which would be against France's basic interests.

The public reaction to my speech was mixed. It was welcomed by *The Times* as a 'realistic exposition of Britain's interests in Europe'. The *Daily Telegraph* referred to my comments on influence and interest and suggested that 'with surprising sang-froid' I had 'torn up and scattered a hallowed Foreign Office doctrine'.

The Independent was not so complimentary, referring to 'Mr Rifkind's not so grand illusions', while *The Guardian* wanted me to 'pursue a more genuine internationalism'.

Being Foreign Secretary is, of course, very different from being a Cabinet minister with domestic responsibilities.

Ministers in most departments can use their time in office by initiating new policies, implementing them, often through legislation or public spending, and, hopefully, see them produce beneficial results.

That is rarely available to a Foreign Minister. Foreign policy is like a conveyer belt. It is already moving when you arrive, you can influence it while you are on the conveyer belt, and it continues its journey after you have gone.

Furthermore, by its very nature, the policy you are dealing with is not private to the United Kingdom. Many other countries are usually involved and much of your time is seeking to persuade or co-ordinate policy with your Foreign Minister colleagues who have their own parliamentary and public opinion to satisfy. You spend so much time in their company that you sometimes end up knowing them better than your own Cabinet colleagues.

Hans-Dietrich Genscher was Foreign Minister of Germany for so long that the joke in Germany was that the difference between

Genscher and God was that while God was everywhere, Genscher was everywhere except Germany.

Lord Salisbury, in the nineteenth century, remarked,

> There is nothing dramatic in the success of a diplomatist. His victories are made up from a series of microscopic advantages: of a judicious suggestion here, of an opportune civility there, of a wise concession at one moment, and a far-sighted persistence at another; of sleepless tact, immovable calmness and patience that no folly, no provocation, no blunder can shake.

Harold Macmillan, who was briefly Foreign Secretary, put the challenge facing Foreign Ministers more succinctly. He wrote, 'A Foreign Secretary is always caught by a cruel dilemma – hovering between the cliché and the indiscretion. He is either dull or dangerous.'

Some, I fear, have been both.

CHAPTER 21

SECRET DIPLOMACY

MANY OF THE foreign policy issues I dealt with as Foreign Secretary were part of wider problems involving a whole region or several countries. Some were freestanding, dealing with problems or challenges specific to the United Kingdom.

That latter category, in my time, were three: the Falklands, Hong Kong and Gibraltar. Each was different but they had in common the rights and freedoms of British citizens and passport holders. Parliament and the public rightly took an intense interest in their welfare.

With the Falklands, we had shown that we had the military power, which we did not have with Hong Kong, to ensure that they remained British. Nor, unlike with China, did any treaty exist with Argentina giving them any legal right to the islands.

One of the consequences of the Argentinian defeat had been the overthrow of the military junta and the return of democratic government.

It was, therefore, possible for me to develop a relationship with their Foreign Minister, Guido Di Tella. He was a great Anglophile and was determined to improve relations with Britain and achieve a diplomatic resolution of our differences.

On one occasion he decided to show goodwill to the Falklands by phoning one of their councillors in Port Stanley to wish them a Merry Christmas. Unfortunately, he chose a very intemperate lady councillor who had a low opinion of all Argentinians, especially ministers. When she realised who she was talking to, she slammed down the phone.

Di Tella would have loved to have visited the Falklands, but with an Argentinian passport that was impossible. His daughter, who was a journalist, had a Swiss passport. While she was in Port Stanley she gave an interview to *Penguin News*, the local paper. She was quoted as saying that she had never realised how British the islands were until she had arrived in the islands. This caused a stir in Buenos Aires and an end to such symbolic initiatives.

I met Di Tella for the first time in July 1995 and had ten further meetings with him, most in the margins of international gatherings, over the next eighteen months. At one of those meetings he informed me that he had the authority from his President, Carlos Menem, to put forward proposals of a radical kind that he believed would end the feud between Argentina and the United Kingdom. These conversations, in due course, led to a very private weekend which I had with Di Tella and his officials at Chevening in January 1997. We had two days of very sensitive discussions to see whether a resolution of the Falklands issue was possible. This was secret diplomacy of a high order.

At our first few meetings, Di Tella had informed me that he did not have authority to share with me the details of what they had in mind but would be able to do so at a formal session of talks if that could be held either in the United Kingdom or elsewhere.

On 30 January 1996, at a meeting with Di Tella at Carlton Gardens, he indicated that Argentina was interested in a condominium solution for the Falklands. I said this would be unacceptable as it implied shared sovereignty.

He then indicated that, as part of their proposals, they might wish to advocate the decolonisation of the islands, which would make them virtually independent while still having an ongoing defence treaty with the United Kingdom. This was potentially more interesting if it would have enabled the Argentinians to withdraw their claim to the islands without too much loss of face.

I knew that Di Tella was an enthusiast for restoring good relations between Argentina and the United Kingdom. I was concerned that while he was speaking in good faith what he was saying might not have the support of his President.

I shared our conversations with the Prime Minister. We were both very sceptical but I was given authority to continue seeing Di Tella and encouraging him to be more forthcoming.

I was due to be in Brazil in April 1996 and I agreed with Di Tella that I would meet him on the Argentine side of the magnificent Iguazu Falls, which marked the border between Argentina and Brazil. That meeting was to be the first time a British Foreign Secretary had stepped on Argentinian soil since before the Falklands War.

I decided to give Di Tella a small gift. As he had a good knowledge of English literature, and given the location of our meeting at the Iguazu Falls, I chose the Sherlock Holmes novel of the great detective meeting with his arch-enemy Moriarty at the Reichenbach Falls. Di Tella enjoyed the comparison.

I had told Di Tella that if his initiative was to go any further we needed to be certain that he spoke with the full authority of President Menem. To meet that need, he arranged for me to speak with the President on the phone while I was at Iguazu. The conversation did not deal with any detail but the President confirmed that Di Tella did have his full authority.

I had discussed with John Major, and I made clear to Di Tella, that if there were to be any talks on a specific Argentine proposal we would have to take the Falkland Islands councillors into our confidence. We would not even consider any negotiation about their future without their full involvement. In due course, Di Tella said that they could agree to that. This impressed me as it could not have been easy for them to accept that the islanders and not just the British government would be their interlocutors.

The Prime Minister and I then agreed it would be sensible to share what was being considered with the two other most senior members of the government, Michael Heseltine and Ken Clarke, who both agreed it was worth finding out what the Argentinians had in mind.

We also considered it sensible to give Margaret Thatcher a private briefing on what was happening. I went to see her. As I was able to say that Falkland Island councillors would be present when we heard the Argentine proposals, she was very relaxed.

The outcome was a weekend I hosted at Chevening from Thursday 9 to Saturday 11 January 1997. There was snow on the ground and the lake was largely frozen. There were sheep rather than cattle in the fields, which would have helped make the two Falklands councillors feel at home.

The first decision I had to take was to instruct that Di Tella be given one of the main guest bedrooms and not relegated, with the rest of the Argentinian delegation, to the second floor as had been proposed. That had been an uncharacteristic lapse on the part of those who decide these things.

The two Falklands councillors, Mike Summers and Sharon Halford, arrived with the Governor, Richard Ralph, in time for our briefing meeting and joined us for dinner on the Thursday evening. The councillors had been impressive in respecting the confidentiality of the meeting, which was not known beyond the Islands Council itself.

On the Saturday morning, shortly before the Argentinians arrived, I wrote: 'I am very doubtful that these talks will succeed as I don't understand how Di Tella and Menem would sell to their own people a deal which leaves sovereignty with the UK and does not concede any substance to them.'

Di Tella and his colleagues arrived and that day we had a total of four and a half hours of discussions. The substance of their proposals was that the Falkland Islands should become self-governing rather than a British colony.

They suggested that while there would be a British 'Lieutenant Governor', there would also be an Argentinian 'Vice-Governor' and they should be allowed to fly the Argentinian flag in several places on the islands. They felt they were unable to remove from their Constitution their claim to the islands but it might be possible to say that it had been 'superseded'. I made it clear, in very blunt terms, that if their Constitution retained their claim to the islands we were wasting our time. Di Tella did not seem surprised and said that he would report our view to his President.

By the end of the day it was agreed that we would prepare our draft text of a possible agreement and they might produce theirs. The following day Di Tella said that our text was unacceptable. I said that we needed to see their alternative.

We knew that Di Tella's officials were unhappy about the talks and were worried that their personal positions might be compromised if it emerged back home that they had been party to talks about ending the Argentinian claim to the islands.

I made clear to Di Tella that we could not proceed further unless there was an Argentinian paper before us with their proposals. They were reluctant to put anything on paper, but that was too bad. Di Tella agreed to produce a draft.

At 5.30 p.m. on Saturday, Di Tella asked to see me alone. We went to the Tapestry Room and he handed to me their draft. What happened next was pure farce.

Di Tella acknowledged that at least four passages in their text would be completely unacceptable to the United Kingdom and to the islanders. He then identified them for me.

They all referred to Argentinian sovereignty of the islands, Argentine responsibility for the Falklands' external affairs and the like. Di Tella said that they had been included to protect him and his colleagues in case the document leaked. He expected me to reject them and when I did no further reference would be made by him to them.

I then went over the rest of the document with my team and with the Island councillors. We agreed that it was hopeless. In effect, it proposed an asymmetrical condominium with no reference to the end of the dispute or the dropping of the claim.

While most day-to-day decision-making would be in the hands of the islanders themselves, the British and Argentinian roles and powers were described as similar, with joint representation on an executive council.

To be fair to Di Tella, their proposals did represent a big change from the traditional Argentinian position. The islands would be self-governing on most issues; Britain would retain responsibility for defence and civil emergencies and Argentinian involvement would be largely symbolic apart from a veto on future constitutional development.

If we had not had the Falklands War, with the islands occupied and many killed in its liberation, some might have felt these proposals worth considering but, even then, I doubt if they would have been acceptable.

As it was, the Island councillors indicated that they could not continue the discussions and I fully agreed with them. A condominium, which implied shared sovereignty, was not on.

We met Di Tella and his colleagues in a plenary session, but this time without the councillors present. I said that the document that they had presented was inconsistent with some of his statements at previous meetings and that our discussions must be terminated. He accepted this.

The spirit remained friendly. The Argentinians joined us for dinner, as did the Falklands councillors. After dinner, the Argentine ambassador and one of the Falklands councillors played snooker. I did not enquire as to who won.

In conversation, Di Tella and I agreed to continue to keep in touch to see how tensions could be reduced. Di Tella acknowledged that perhaps he had been too ambitious.

As people were giving their goodbyes on the Sunday morning, one of the councillors, Sharon Halford, gave Di Tella a photograph of part of the Falkland Islands. She remarked, with a smile, that the photograph was 'the only part of the Falklands he is going to get'.

Hong Kong was the other major issue I had to deal with, which also involved very sensitive negotiations. Hong Kong was due to return to China in 1997. Geoffrey Howe, and then Douglas Hurd, had been very successful in reaching agreement with the Chinese on most of the issues involved in the handover. Deng Xiaoping's formula of 'two systems in one country' was agreed by Britain and China. Most of the people of Hong Kong accepted it as well but were nervous whether the Chinese would honour it in the spirit as well as the letter. This was understandable given the Tiananmen Square massacre and suppression of human rights activists in 1989.

The Chinese, for their part, had been angered by the democratic reforms within the colony introduced by Chris Patten, who had become Governor of Hong Kong in 1992. They claimed that they were in breach of the 1984 Sino-British Declaration. These reforms had not been approved by Beijing but were fully endorsed by John Major and the Cabinet.

By the time I became Foreign Secretary, the temperature had come down with what was, basically, an agreement to differ. The reforms to the Hong Kong Legislative Council (LegCo) were still in place but the Chinese had made clear they would not continue after the handover.

I had a very early meeting with Chris Patten when he was in London on 18 July. I fully agreed with his approach and we liked and respected each other. My first exchanges with the Chinese Foreign Minister, Qian Qichen, were also in London on 2 and 3 October. He was a career diplomat and had been Foreign Minister since 1988.

It was a getting-to-know-you occasion, rather formal at first, as the Chinese prefer long statements of position to be read out by both sides so they can identify whether there has been any movement, however microscopic, in previous policy.

A visit to both Hong Kong and China was agreed and took place from 6 to 10 January 1996. Edith accompanied me.

A very early issue that arose was the transliteration of my name, which was, apparently, necessary for Chinese publications.

The *People's Daily* in Beijing, announcing my appointment, gave me the name Li Fu Jin De (Li being the surname). I was informed by our embassy that this was 'inoffensive but meaningless'.

More encouragingly, the Hong Kong Chinese press gave me the name Li Wenjun, which, they said, conveyed 'the sense of a cultured gentleman'. It was recommended that the embassy should 'try discreetly' to encourage the Chinese to 'follow this more elegant form before the other takes root'. Such was at least one of the issues that preoccupied our diplomats in Beijing. I have no idea whether they succeeded.

I made a point of arriving in Hong Kong first before travelling to Beijing. The people of Hong Kong were worried about their future, and their elected representatives on the LegCo needed to be reassured that I was on their side and would, like the Governor, champion their interests.

For this reason, I requested that my meeting with LegCo should be held in public. This was unprecedented and was well received.

I had decided both to be very supportive of the people of Hong Kong and also to be very frank with the legislative councillors as to the limits of what Britain could deliver against any Chinese opposition.

This was appreciated. The *South China Morning Post* said that I had been 'refreshingly realistic' and 'honest enough' to admit that Britain had no power to stop the Chinese from dismantling the Patten reforms after 1997. They also remarked that the gamble of holding an open session with the legislators had paid off and that others, both British and Chinese, should 'follow Mr Rifkind's lead'.

The following day, we flew to Beijing. On the journey from the airport, the Mercedes provided by the Chinese blew a tyre and we completed the journey in a stretched Cadillac complete with mini-bar and television.

My three hours of talks with Qian Qichen went much better than we expected. The Chinese had decided not to let their anger at the Patten reforms hinder a smooth handover. Our ambassador, Len Appleyard, in his telegram after the visit, said that we had 'secured a harvest of practical progress'. Each item was either technical or pro-cedural but those who understood China much better than I did said that the agreements reached were a clear indication that the Chinese were now in a frame of mind to make progress right across the board.

This was confirmed when I had separate meetings with President Jiang Zemin, a great Shakespeare enthusiast, and with Prime Minister Li Peng. It was apparently unusual for a Foreign Minister to get that level of access, which cheered up our embassy.

We did not have much free time but we used it well. Edith and I were given a private tour of Beijing's Forbidden City, which we seemed to have entirely to ourselves.

We also made the obligatory visit to the Great Wall of China. When asked what I thought about it by the press contingent, I resisted the temptation to say that Hong Kong could do with one as well to keep out the 'barbarians'. One newspaper, having been denied that story, criticised the fur hat I was wearing that day. It turned out to be a Russian not a Chinese hat and I should have known better.

The previous night at a dinner, I was asked by a Chinese minister my views on a European single currency. I replied that while China believed in 'one country, two systems' Europe was grappling with 'fifteen countries, one system'.

It is now nineteen years since Hong Kong returned to China. There are serious doubts about China's respect for human rights and there has been little progress on democratic government in Hong Kong, but there remain two systems in one country. In that major respect the Chinese have kept their word.

The real issue for Hong Kong is not just democracy but the rule of law. When I put that to Qian Qichen, he replied that I should not worry. The Chinese government also believed in the rule of law. He rather spoilt this assurance by adding that 'in China, the people must obey the law'. When I pointed out that in the West it was not just the people but the government who were under the law, he found such a concept incomprehensible. The truth is that the Chinese government believe in 'rule by law' not 'the rule of law'. They are very different.

One postscript is relevant in the light of later controversies. In July 1996, I received the Dalai Lama and had an interesting discussion with him. The Foreign Office had been very nervous that such a meeting would create a hostile reaction from Beijing and endanger progress on Hong Kong.

I insisted on going ahead, but in deference to their concerns I agreed to see the Dalai Lama in my private residence in Carlton Gardens rather than at the Foreign Office, and not to invite any press.

There were ritual complaints from the Chinese side but no other repercussions. To be fair, China was a much poorer country and had much less clout than it does today.

I remain convinced that if China can have two systems in one country to meet the needs of Hong Kong and Macao, as well as their aspirations for Taiwan, they could have three systems in one country, with serious, genuine and substantial autonomy for Tibet within China. This would help ensure Tibet's unique cultural, religious and national identity. One day the Chinese will make this concession, and the earlier they do so the better.

With Gibraltar, there were no dramatic developments at that time. I did, however, decide that the difficulties with Spain pointed to having a Governor with political skills rather than the traditional retired general or admiral.

I asked Richard Luce to take on the job. He had ceased to be a minister or an MP some years earlier and was currently Vice-Chancellor of Buckingham University. He had never been seen as a partisan politician, had begun his career in Kenya in the Colonial Service and had great integrity and a very independent mind. His wife, Rose, was equally impressive and I had no doubt that she would be excellent as the Governor's consort. They accepted and were as successful as I had hoped.

The Spanish claim to Gibraltar was made with great force and robustness. They declared how unacceptable it was for part of historic Spain to be ruled by another country.

They were never very convincing. The only part of Africa that is not today ruled by Africans are the two tiny Spanish enclaves of Ceuta and Melilla on the coast of northern Morocco. While they are technically part of Spain and not colonies, as far as the Moroccans are concerned the Spanish ought not to be there. What is sauce for the goose etc.

I got on well with my Spanish counterpart, Abel Matutes. I tried to persuade him that the Spanish practice of being nice to the Gibraltarians one day and being beastly the next was winning them no friends.

While I doubted if the Gibraltarians would ever wish to be part of Spain, the only chance Spain would have of persuading them otherwise would be if they removed all restrictions and sanctions on a permanent basis and hugged the Gibraltarians with a loving embrace. It might still take them a hundred years but any alternative approach would carry no weight either with the British government or with the people of the Rock.

On the wider front, my main responsibility was to ensure the continuing health of the relationship between London and Washington.

I made several visits to the United States, where my main interlocutors were Warren Christopher at first and then Madeleine Albright.

I would also regularly have a meeting with the Vice-President,

Al Gore, at the White House. When I first met him, as Defence Secretary, the meeting was so relaxed that it ended with him passing to me the 'Talking Points' that had been prepared for him by his staff and which he had not had time to raise. I was interested to see that they were not very different from those my staff had prepared for me.

Madeleine Albright has become a very close friend and we see each other often on both sides of the pond. Before becoming Secretary of State she was ambassador to the United Nations at a time when the Americans were suspending part of their very large membership dues because of their disapproval at the way the UN was operating.

Although many of their concerns were justified, we were keen to persuade them to resume their payments to the UN. When I addressed the United Nations General Assembly, I allowed myself to have some fun at their expense. Referring to the dispute, I pointed out that the Americans had fought for their independence in 1776 under the slogan 'no taxation without representation'. Now they should realise that it was the other way around: 'No representation without taxation.'

To my surprise and delight, I read that when Madeleine Albright was giving evidence to the Senate Committee for her confirmation as Secretary of State, she referred to my speech the previous year at the General Assembly. 'Even our closest friends, the British,' she said 'used a sound bite they have been waiting 200 years to use. No representation without taxation.'

Kofi Annan, the Secretary-General of the United Nations, also quoted me in October 1998, adding, 'I think most of the member states share this view.'

When in Washington I also got to know President Clinton. I had first met him, very briefly, when I was Defence Secretary representing the UK at the opening of the Holocaust Memorial. I wrote: 'He looks even more youthful than I expected but there is a simple, confident style that is engaging and purposeful.'

At a dinner given for the Clintons at 10 Downing Street, I had Hillary Clinton sitting next to me. I did not for a moment envisage her as a future Secretary of State and candidate for the presidency but I was very impressed. She was articulate, good humoured and clearly a serious public figure in her own right.

Foreign Secretaries normally don't get a call on the President, but I asked our ambassador to see if that might be possible while I was in Washington. We got a well-crafted response.

The White House did not wish to create a precedent that would lead other Foreign Ministers to expect such treatment, so there would be no official meeting. But the President would 'drop in' during my meeting with the Vice-President.

This happened and, during the substantive discussion that followed, I was able to see Clinton's remarkable facility to absorb new information on subjects he was not familiar with, understand their significance and respond with highly relevant comments and observations. As that was combined with his legendary charm, it was easy to see why he was a political star.

Cyprus was an issue that no British Foreign Secretary could forget. A former British colony, it had been divided between the Greek and Turkish communities since 1974 with a 'Green Line' buffer zone through the centre of the capital, Nicosia.

Britain was one of the guarantors of Cyprus's independence and territorial integrity back in 1960 but mine was the first visit by a British Foreign Secretary, and it was devoted exclusively to the problems of the island.

There was a need for movement on the island's future. The United Nations had declared 1997 to be the 'Year of Cyprus' and the European Union was to open discussions on the island's application for membership.

To give added evidence of the seriousness of our initiative, I had announced the appointment of Sir David Hannay, a former ambassador to the UN and one of our most distinguished diplomats, as Britain's Special Envoy to Cyprus.

I visited the island in December 1996 and first saw President

Glafcos Clerides, the leader of the Greek Cypriot community. The meeting with Clerides went well, but that was not unexpected. He tended to adopt an optimistic and conciliatory tone but words were not always matched with deeds.

I then crossed the Green Line into the Turkish part of the island, where around 30,000 Turkish troops were based. I was the first Foreign Secretary to cross the Green Line since the division of the island.

The Turkish Cypriot leader, Rauf Denktaş, had a different personality to Clerides. I spent forty-five minutes with him; just the two of us without aides. He began, as I had been told he would, by being truculent and negative.

I decided on a slightly risky approach. I said to him that before the visit I had been told by my Foreign Office advisors that I would find Clerides very optimistic and helpful but that he, Denktaş, would be surly and unhelpful. Did he think, I asked, that they were entitled to make that prediction?

He looked at me and said that yes, they were. He then relaxed and we got on much better. It was right to make the visit and launch the initiative, but I cannot claim that it made any difference in the longer run.

Today, in 2016, the island remains divided and if we are told the omens are more encouraging than for some years I can only hope that assessment is justified. In my view, a big mistake was made by admitting a divided Cyprus into the European Union. The EU lost any significant leverage and has been paying the price ever since.

In the Middle East, I was responsible for one important development in the Israel–Palestine dispute. For the first time, the British government committed itself to a two-state solution, with a Palestinian state living next to the state of Israel. I made the announcement at a dinner of the Palestine Medical Society in London.

I still believe that that is the only solution to this long-running confrontation. It could have been achieved if Yitzhak Rabin had survived. Today, both Israel and Palestine are led by politicians not statesmen. When there are leaders of the stature and wisdom of

Rabin and Shimon Peres, King Hussein of Jordan or Anwar Sadat of Egypt, a breakthrough will be possible.

At that time, the mood was much more optimistic than it is now. After a visit to Israel I was due to travel to Dubai in the United Arab Emirates. The Emirati were apologetic that they could not yet permit us to fly our RAF plane direct from Israel to Dubai. Rather than make two journeys, we found an ingenious solution.

Our plane flew from Israel to an Egyptian air base on the Red Sea. We landed there, but only to allow our wheels to make contact with the tarmac. Without stopping, the pilot lifted the aircraft and we flew direct to the UAE. As far as our hosts were concerned we had come from Egypt. When people want solutions that is what they find. Then, they did. Now, for the time being, they don't.

It is said that an Israeli and a Palestinian asked God whether there ever would be peace between their two peoples. God apparently replied that there would be, 'but it won't be in my time'. Let us hope He is not infallible.

As part of my itinerary, I visited Mongolia on the way back from Japan, the first British Foreign Secretary to do so.

Although there had been little contact between our two countries, the Mongolians were well disposed to the British as we had been the only NATO country to have an embassy in Ulaanbaatar during the Cold War. They may have been unaware that this had been solely because it was convenient for the West to have a listening post between the Soviet Union and China, and diplomatic premises were ideal for that purpose.

On the night of my arrival, the Prime Minister gave a dinner in my honour and he toasted my health. I had to speak in response and I must confess I had not thought, in advance, what I would say.

As one does on these occasions, I suggested that Britain and Mongolia had a great deal in common. The Mongolians applauded vigorously and then waited to find out what we did have in common. I had no idea what I was going to say – and then it came to me.

I said that Britain and Mongolia had both once been great empires but Britain had never conquered Mongolia and Genghis Khan had never reached London. There was great cheering on the Mongolian side (and great relief on the British).

I had a near disaster during our visit to Brazil in 1996. We had spent the weekend in Rio de Janeiro and, because we had no programme on the Sunday, our ambassador had got hold of a small sailing yacht and we spent the day around the bay.

We were due, that evening, to fly in our own plane to the capital, Brasília, to start the official programme. As I was wearing an open-necked sports shirt, casual slacks and sports shoes, and Edith was similarly dressed, I asked the ambassador whether we should change for the flight and the arrival in Brasília. The ambassador, who was dressed as we were, said that it would not be necessary, there would be no formal reception at the airport and we could change for dinner at his residence.

We took off and, in due course, landed at Brasília. As we taxied towards the terminal, I looked out of the window and saw a red carpet, a guard of honour, a military band and ladies with hats on. I looked at the ambassador, who had gone white.

By this time, the plane had stopped opposite the guard of honour and the conductor of the band was waiting for the door to open before the band would start playing.

I showed serious qualities of leadership that day. I ordered the steward not to open the door until I gave permission. Fortunately, as it was our own plane our formal clothes were accessible. I told Edith and the ambassador's wife not to change but to stay in the plane. The ambassador and I donned suits and ties within two or three minutes but that must have seemed a very long time to our puzzled hosts standing, waiting patiently, outside.

In truth, it was not the Brazilians I was worried about. It was the British media, who would not be able to resist a photograph of the Foreign Secretary, dressed as a day tripper, inspecting a Brazilian guard of honour.

To be fair to the ambassador, he would normally have been correct in his advice. It turned out that the guard of honour and the band had been there to welcome the President of Italy, who had arrived on a state visit that afternoon. The Brazilians had decided that it would be a good idea to surprise and delight the British minister with such a grand welcome. They were right. I was surprised, though not delighted.

During a visit to the Caucasus, I had dinner in the presidential palace with the President of Azerbaijan, Geidar Aliyev, the father of the current President. At the end of the meal he invited me to come downstairs to his 'grotto' for coffee. We entered a large room full of stalactites and stalagmites made entirely of polystyrene with a bar area at one end. It was the ugliest room I have ever seen.

It turned out that he had commissioned its building when he was the party boss in Azerbaijan during Soviet times and wanted to impress Leonid Brezhnev, who was about to visit.

As I was leaving, the President asked me what I thought of his grotto. Being Foreign Secretary, I had to be diplomatic, but was determined to tell the truth. 'It is unforgettable,' I said, and added, 'I will tell people in London about your grotto for years to come.' I have kept this promise.

A unique occasion was a one-night visit Edith and I had made to Norway when I was Defence Secretary. Our retiring ambassador, David Ratford, had invited us to a dinner he was giving in his residence for the King and Queen of Norway. All the other guests were to be British and he hoped we could join them.

I was free that evening and we used an RAF plane to fly to Oslo. We landed at a military airport, were met at the steps of the plane by the ambassador's car, drove straight to his residence, enjoyed the dinner, slept there that night and flew on to The Hague the following morning.

I can say that Edith and I are probably the only persons to have visited Norway and to have neither spoken to nor been in the presence of any Norwegian during our entire visit apart from the King and Queen.

One of the pleasures of my job was that Edith and I accompanied our own Queen and Prince Philip on state visits. We had a joint trip to Poland and the Czech Republic and another to Thailand.

As when I was Scottish Secretary and the Queen was based at Holyrood Palace, these occasions were tranquil for me, as I was not expected to give interviews or press conferences or do anything that would distract attention from the Queen. We became temporary members of the royal household and enjoyed their company.

I also got to know Diana, Princess of Wales. After she and the Prince of Wales had separated, she asked me, in 1995, to lunch with her at Kensington Palace. I assumed it was not just for the pleasure of my company. She was wanting help and advice for a number of international visits that she was making as a result of her interests and the personal charities that she supported.

At the end of the lunch she came downstairs with me and when it turned out that my car had not arrived, she insisted on continuing our conversation until it did.

After the luncheon, I wrote to thank her. To my surprise, I received a letter in return. She had 'enjoyed our lunch and am in no doubt (if I ever was!) that yours must be the busiest in-tray in Whitehall'.

Princess Diana had many problems and challenges in her life but she could not be faulted on her courtesy and consideration.

CHAPTER 22

EUROPE

I T IS NOT just death and taxes that are unavoidable. It is also the
European Union if you are Foreign Secretary.

I was not unfamiliar with Brussels. I had been Europe Minister
under Geoffrey Howe from 1983 to 1986 and had been Margaret
Thatcher's representative on the Dooge Committee, which had done
important work paving the way for the creation of the single market.

Thankfully, the traumas over the ratification of the Maastricht
Treaty were behind us when I returned to King Charles Street. But
nature abhors a vacuum. It was the prospect of a single European
currency that was now dominating the headlines and dividing the
government as well as the country.

I had a reputation in the Conservative Party for being a pro-
European. It was, in many ways, an accurate description of my views.
I firmly believe that the European Union is a historic, extraordinary
and positive achievement.

Divisions, animosities, ambitions and old hatreds were the cause
of two world wars breaking out in Western Europe during the
twentieth century. Tens of millions perished as a result and whole

countries were devastated. Half of Europe was condemned to Soviet Communist totalitarianism for half a century as a consequence of the Second World War.

It is no exaggeration to say that the European Union deserves much of the credit, along with NATO, for the historic reconciliation of France and Germany, for the spread of the rule of law and democratic government throughout Europe to the borders of Russia, for an unprecedented single market in both goods and services, and for the potential that it has created for the continuing strength of European values and civilisation for the centuries to come.

You can choose your friends but you cannot choose your family. Britain is, and has always been, part of the European family not just by virtue of its geography and history but also by virtue of our shared cultural, social, religious and commercial ties, which are as important today as they have ever been.

Furthermore, it is impossible to imagine any strategic threat to France, to Germany or to Europe as a whole that would not also be a strategic threat to Britain as well. That is not new. It was why an attack on Belgium brought us into the First World War in 1914 and an attack on Poland into the Second World War in 1939. NATO has protected us superbly. As a military alliance it has been, and continues to be, essential. But the security of nations requires economic, political and diplomatic strength as well.

So Britain's membership of the European Union is as natural as it is sensible. However – and there is a however – the real debate in our times should not be whether the United Kingdom should remain in the EU but what kind of union is appropriate or, indeed, possible for a European Union of twenty-eight states with different histories, languages, economic circumstances and continuing national priorities.

It is because I have never believed in the desirability of a European government, and because I have never believed that a single European currency can work without, eventually, such a European government, that I am, as *Le Monde* once suggested, a moderate Eurosceptic.

Nor have I ever had any difficulty contemplating a European Union whose members have different levels of integration with each other where there is 'variable geometry' and where, to some degree, there is a Europe à la carte.

To a considerable extent, what I am referring to already exists. Half the members of the EU use the euro; half do not. Most are in Schengen; two are not. Four member states, Austria, Ireland, Finland and Sweden, are neutral; the others are members of NATO. The leaders of Europe should not apologise for this diversity or try to ignore it. They should applaud it as evidence of the uniqueness of the EU and of why it deserves to survive and prosper.

Where we should integrate is where there is convincing evidence that to do so will enhance our security, our prosperity or our quality of life. That test has been met in the case of the single market in goods and services. It is becoming increasingly true as regards the environment, energy and climate change. It already applies to important aspects of our foreign policy such as Iran and the Middle East and the battle against terrorism.

What we should not be attracted to is 'more Europe' just for its own sake. I recall when I was Defence Secretary and we had a naval blockade preventing arms being smuggled into Bosnia during the war in that country.

I received a letter from the Western European Union (WEU), who, at that time, were the main body pressing for defence integration in Europe.

They had noticed that there was a British frigate, flying a NATO flag, helping enforce the blockade. Could I provide another frigate, they asked, that would fly the WEU flag to demonstrate a European initiative on this issue?

We had no intention of contributing another frigate but, in a mistaken attempt at light-heartedness, I suggested that our frigate could fly the NATO and WEU flags on alternate months. To my surprise, I received a letter thanking me for my constructive response. It was a typical example of preoccupation with symbolism over substance.

With that discourse on my lifelong views on the European issue, I turn to the more prosaic matters that demanded my attention when I was Foreign Secretary between 1995 and 1997.

My first responsibility was to prepare a White Paper on the British approach to the EU intergovernmental conference proposed for 1996. Getting agreement to publish a White Paper had been no easy matter. Douglas Hurd had been against, believing that it would be bound to exacerbate Conservative differences on Europe. I took the view that, though there was that risk, we had to demonstrate that the government was governing and that we had a strong and sensible European policy to offer.

On 18 January, I got the Prime Minister's approval to proceed. That day, I spoke to Michael Heseltine and Ken Clarke. They both agreed to change their position and support a White Paper. Later, I got similar agreement from Michael Howard and Michael Portillo on the Eurosceptic wing of the government. The outcome was a unanimous endorsement from the Cabinet, which would not have been certain twenty-four hours earlier.

On 6 March, I made a speech in Paris on the issue of the Common Foreign and Security Policy. I praised the French recognition of the reality of the different national interests of member states in various areas. I compared this to 'some capitals' where there was 'a preference to use the language of European interests and rarely to refer to national interests for reasons that we understand'. That was code for Germany, as was well understood.

Six days later, I presented our White Paper, 'A Partnership of Nations', to Parliament. I had chosen the title and been intimately involved in the drafting.

The White Paper emphasised the British view that while the European Union was more than a free trade area, it should resist the temptation for 'more Europe', more centralisation and more uniformity.

It then put forward our own proposals for change. These included a single-minded concentration on the EU only doing at the European level what needed to be done there. The White Paper criticised health and safety directives also being used to advance social policy. It stressed the need to improve the quality of European legislation and expand the role of national parliaments. It emphasised that foreign and defence policy had to remain the responsibility of national governments, with no move towards majority voting in these areas.

The White Paper was generally well received in Parliament. The shadow Foreign Secretary, Robin Cook, was low-key in his response and there was significant all-party support for many of our proposals.

The Guardian commented that the response of Tory MPs in the Commons showed that 'the Conservative mood has become more disciplined' and that 'Mr Rifkind may have managed to unite the Conservative Party for a time'.

The Times reported that the White Paper had been greeted 'with mild relief' in Brussels because of our unambiguous commitment to the EU and the absence of any demands to repatriate powers. All in all, the decision to publish a White Paper had been the right one. It had reduced rather than inflamed tensions on the Tory benches while explaining both to the British public and to our European partners that we had a responsible and constructive strategy for European reform.

These calmer waters on European matters did not last for long: fifteen days, to be precise. On 27 March, the European Commission imposed a worldwide ban on all British beef exports because of BSE (bovine spongiform encephalopathy), otherwise known as mad cow disease.

The initial reaction in the Ministry of Agriculture was total fury. While they accepted there was a real problem with BSE, the reaction of the European Commission was seen to be over the top and grossly unfair. The implications for British farmers were very serious.

Thus began what became known as the 'Beef War'. The British press, the Eurosceptics and the farming industry were all calling for a tough British response, and public opinion, as a whole, appeared to be behind them.

John Major knew that the government had to be sensitive to the demands for action. The official advice that he was receiving from the veterinary scientists and other experts supported the view that the EU was being unreasonable.

The relevant Cabinet committee met. I was not present, as I was with the Queen in Prague during her state visit. The government decided that Britain would initiate a policy of non-cooperation at all EU meetings, blocking decisions and delaying progress on all EU business until a compromise was reached on British beef exports. There was a precedent. General de Gaulle had done something similar in 1965.

I was uneasy about this decision, though I realised that passions were high. I was aware that I was likely to be the minister who, as Foreign Secretary, had to implement it.

And so it proved. Not surprisingly, our European partners were furious about our blocking or delaying virtually every proposal that came up for decision regardless of its merits and even including some proposals that we supported.

At a meeting of Foreign Ministers in Luxembourg on 10 June, I was 'savaged' or 'faced the wrath' depending on which press report one preferred. I was said to have borne the brunt of the fiercest anti-British attack from Europe for years when I vetoed another package of measures. I let through some proposals where we felt there were good reasons to do so, but this did not curb the onslaught.

I am pleased to see that the *Financial Times*, reporting my 'mugging', said that I had appeared before 100 journalists at a press conference afterwards 'insisting with a twinkle in his eye that everything was going according to plan'. That may be how I appeared. It was not how I felt.

The Prime Minister had asked me to visit a number of European capitals as his personal representative. Between 4 and 10 June, I had meetings with the German Chancellor, Helmut Kohl, and President

Jacques Chirac, as well as the Italian, Spanish and Portuguese Prime Ministers. They were courteous and keen to help but did not move on the essentials.

There was some progress. The ban on manufactured beef products was lifted but not the general ban on the sale of beef. We were seeking to get a deal on a step-by-step lifting of the ban by the time of the European Council meeting, which was to be held in Florence on 21 June.

We had two problems. We were finding it more difficult to demonstrate that the scientific evidence was as helpful to us as we had believed. There was also a political problem of a familiar kind. While there was a powerful case that Brussels had overreacted, many governments, especially Germany, were anxious not just to follow the science but to restore public confidence in their own countries as to the wisdom of eating beef. That made them unwilling not only to drop the ban but also to agree when it should be dropped.

Our strategy did not succeed except over a long period of time. It was years not months before the ban was fully removed and there was a growing belief, even in Britain, that the drastic measures imposed may have been necessary. Our handling of this crisis did not do us much credit.

There were other times when the British preoccupation with the EU did not impress. In June 1996, I was in Iceland for the opening of the new British Embassy in Reykjavik.

We had agreed with the German government to construct a new building that would have our embassy at one end, the German at the other, with shared facilities in the middle. That was very sensible but, at the last moment, we had a crisis about flags.

All German Embassies flew the EU flag alongside their own. At that time, no British Embassy flew anything other than the Union Jack. The Germans, not unreasonably, suggested that, as we were sharing the building, we should fly our national flags at either end and the EU flag in the middle.

I had no authority to agree to that and it would have resulted in a huge, and foolish, outcry in the British media if I had. We ended up with the EU flag flying alongside the German and the Union flag flying in glorious isolation. Fortunately, because it was Iceland, the rest of the world didn't notice.

The Florence summit of the European Council on 21 June coincided with my 50th birthday. I was there with the Prime Minister and the Chancellor, Ken Clarke. We had discussions with Italian Prime Minister Romano Prodi and Jacques Santer, president of the European Commission, and reached agreement on some useful steps to resolve the beef crisis.

That evening there was a reception for the delegates at the Palazzo Vecchio. We were then able to take a private route, not available to the public, through the Uffizi, over the Ponte Vecchio and into the Palazzo Pitti without ever having to go outside. This route had been constructed by the Medici so that they could make the journey without being seen by the public. Medici we were not, but their preoccupations all seemed very similar to our own.

At the Palazzo Pitti, there was a dinner for the Foreign Ministers in a splendid round chamber with trompe l'oeil on the walls and ceilings.

As I entered, my fourteen colleagues, singing in English, gave me a spirited rendering of 'Happy Birthday', which metamorphosed into 'Happy Beefday'. I was rather touched.

In September, I was in Zurich, where I had been invited to make a speech commemorating Churchill's famous Zurich oration of 1946.

I was on the same marble podium in the same room where Churchill had spoken. I began by confessing that he was a hard act to follow. My arrival in Zurich had not been like his, a triumphant procession through cheering crowds. My car had not, like his, been flooded with flowers by adoring onlookers.

I then remarked that, at least my speech, unlike his, would not cause pandemonium in Paris. Churchill had said that 'the first step in the re-creation of the European family must be a partnership between France and Germany'. The French, in 1946, were not yet ready to accept that, but Churchill's words were prophetic.

Much of my speech was on the present and the future. I said that 2020 should be the world's target for global free trade. Along with Ian Lang, the president of the Board of Trade, I published a White Paper later that year committing Britain to that target. We will not have global free trade by 2020 but we are still making real progress in that direction.

On the European Union, I said, 'We should not proceed down a path of integration faster or further than our people are prepared to go.'

I also took them by surprise by quoting in support the words of Robert Schuman, one of the founding fathers of the European ideal, who said, 'Europe will not be made all at once or according to a single plan. It will be built through concrete achievements which first create a de facto solidarity.'

I then acknowledged that Britain's vision was different to many others. I said that we had 'a certain idea of Europe, if I may take a liberty with De Gaulle's words'. We believed that Europe would thrive as a partnership of nations, the same term I had used in our White Paper.

On the single currency, I pointed out that whether or not Britain joined, Europe would be divided into two groups of countries for the foreseeable future, as the twelve applicant countries, mainly from central and eastern Europe, would not meet the convergence criteria. Such a divided Europe was not, I suggested, what the founding fathers had had in mind.

It was this remark that caused a bit of a furore in some EU capitals although it was only one paragraph in a long speech.

But it was a cartoonist's response and not that of a politician which I most enjoyed. Peter Brookes in *The Times* had a cartoon of me next to Churchill. Under Churchill were the words 'Zurich 1946'. Under me were the words 'Zurich 1996'. Churchill is giving his famous two-finger 'V for Victory' sign. So am I, but in my case the fingers are reversed. It is the only time I have spent good money to buy an original cartoon. It hangs, proudly, in my loo to this day.

It is well known that Churchill's enthusiasm for a united Europe did not mean that he expected Britain to be part of it. But that is another matter.

In October, I had to make a major speech at the Conservative Party conference in Bournemouth. Europe, and the single currency in particular, was one of the big themes of the week.

On the Tuesday, there had been a large meeting on the fringe of the conference, attended by several hundred people, where John Redwood and Norman Tebbit had called for the Conservative Party to unite against the euro and for the government to get off the fence.

My responsibility was to try to persuade the conference as a whole that to do this was both unnecessary at this time and would be unwise. Party activists in all parties, not unreasonably, yearn for their party leaders to shun ambiguity or indecision and go for clarity and conviction. 'Wait and see' may be pragmatic but it is not exactly the kind of clarion call they like to hear.

In preparing my speech, I decided to eschew too much rhetoric and address the conference in a forceful and robust manner but with straightforward and clear arguments that would appeal more to head than to heart. As our party was in government, and wanted to stay there, that was easier than when one's party is in opposition.

I was heartened by a message I got from the Prime Minister before I spoke. He was sorry that he could not be on the platform for the debate but he had read my speech and thought that 'it is wonderful and it will be a great success'.

I admit to beginning my speech with some easy rhetoric. I quoted Pitt the Younger, who 200 years earlier had declared, 'England has saved herself by her exertions and will, I trust, save Europe by her example.'

I then added, 'Since 1979 Britain has saved itself by its exertions, and will now, I trust, lead Europe by its example. We have a modern vision of Europe. It is a vision of Europe as a partnership of nations, not a federal superstate.'

This got the requisite cheer, but I did not want them to expect an anti-European polemic. I added, immediately, 'We are part of Europe. Europe's future will influence our future. We must not be anti-European. We cannot be anti-European.' The audience began to listen as well as hear.

Into my speech, I said,

> So the debate is not about whether we should be in or out of Europe. The debate is about what kind of European Union is right for Britain and Europe. We know what we want to achieve in Europe. Protecting British interests does not mean we are hostile to foreigners. That is not the British tradition.

I then turned to my main theme.

> I know that some of you would like us to take a decision now to rule in or rule out British participation in a single currency. I respect these feelings. I understand the feelings behind them. I want to share with you the reasoning why the Prime Minister and the Cabinet believe that a final decision at this moment would be unwise and against Britain's national interests.

I pointed out that a single currency might never happen and could not happen before 1999 at the earliest. 'The nation therefore loses nothing by deferring a decision.'

But taking a decision ruling out the currency would damage negotiations on related issues that were currently taking place. That would damage British farmers, business interests and the City of London.

I went on to say that if the national interest required a decision now, we would have to take one 'regardless of the political implications for the party'. By this I meant, as was well understood, the Cabinet split, and the likely resignations that would have followed if we had rejected the euro.

I then drew attention to the argument of John Redwood, and those like him, that it was in the Tories' interests to differentiate ourselves from Labour and appeal to the country as the party committed to keeping the pound.

My response was that 'to force a decision now just to differentiate ourselves from Labour would be to put party before country, and I suggest, the country would not be impressed'.

I asked the conference to be patient. 'Tories', I said 'do not put party before country. The Conservatives will always represent the national interest.'

The conference approved. I received a three-minute standing ovation and the demands for an immediate decision rejecting the single currency faded away.

Douglas Hurd wrote congratulating me, as did Leon Brittan, then a vice-president of the European Commission. He said that what was most gratifying was that I had persuaded the conference 'not by rhetorical gimmicks but by sustained, convincing argument'.

Leon was a relative of mine and we had been friends since I contacted him in my student days, when he was already the president of the Bow Group, an association of younger, more progressive, Tories. During the war, his father, who was a doctor, used to lunch, occasionally, with my grandparents in Edinburgh.

For a brief period, Leon and I were in the Cabinet together until he had to resign over the Westland controversy. Thereafter, he had a distinguished career in Europe.

Like everyone else who knew him, I was appalled by the disgraceful slurs and accusations that dogged his final days. I visited him a few weeks before he died and he was robust though, naturally, subdued. His wife Diana told me that he had said to her that his conscience was entirely clear. I did not doubt it and shared in the delight when the accusations were found to be worthless and his reputation was restored. Diana has worked magnificently on his behalf and Edith and I greatly admire her.

In retrospect, I believe my Europe speech at the party conference was the most important I made, outside the House of Commons, during my eighteen years as a minister. Some were more entertaining and got more cheers. This one changed the party's mood and kept the Cabinet intact.

A less satisfactory speech on Europe, in consequence if not in content, was the one I made to the Konrad Adenauer Foundation in Bonn in February 1997.

It was a robust presentation of the alternative British vision of the future of the European Union. We should, I said, resist integration for its own sake, relish the cultural and political diversity in Europe and concentrate on integration only when it would enhance our mutual security, prosperity or quality of life.

Perhaps the most controversial comments were when I turned to the problems of legitimacy and democracy that resulted from moves towards greater uniformity and integration in the EU.

'The problem with what is proposed', I said, 'is that in almost every case it means taking power away from institutions which are more legitimate and giving it to institutions which are less legitimate.' I was referring to the European Commission and the European Parliament.

I went on to say, 'Every time a majority vote is taken, a democratically elected government is somewhere overruled.'

Rereading these remarks now, I concede that the problem I was referring to was, and is, more concerned with the democratic deficit in the EU rather than the legitimacy of its institutions, but the point was valid nevertheless. In virtually all EU countries, including Germany, national parliaments command more loyalty than their counterparts in Brussels.

I concluded my speech with a quote from Martin Luther that had been recommended to me. I not only used it but spoke it in German, a language that I am otherwise unfamiliar with. It was: 'Hier stehe ich. Ich kann nicht anders.' Here I stand. I can do no other.

Generally, the reaction of the Germans was negative but only because they saw it as another dose of British Euroscepticism. Interestingly, the exception was the Bavarians, who said that the speech put into words what many Germans had not yet dared to think through for themselves.

It was, however, three words in the *Frankfurter Allgemeine Zeitung* that caused an explosion in Britain from both the press and MPs. Michaela Wiegel, a young journalist reporting my speech, at one stage referred to me as 'the Jew Rifkind'.

It appeared, subsequently, that she had not intended this as an anti-Semitic comment but had been reacting to my decision to quote the Protestant Martin Luther. It was an attempt at intellectual humour but it led to a British journalist quoting Mark Twain, who had written, 'The German joke is no laughing matter.'

In any event, I should have remembered that Martin Luther was a virulent anti-Semite and the last person I should have been quoting.

There was outrage in the British press, with various newspapers, MPs and others saying that the Germans were once again showing their true colours.

Although I deeply regretted that the comment had been made by the German journalist, I said, 'I have no intention of pressing the matter, nor would I want anyone else to do so. It was a rather silly remark by a young journalist who herself has said that she is mortified by the interpretation that has been put on it.' The furore, rightly, subsided.

I was hugely amused, rather than concerned, by an article on the same speech that appeared in another respected German paper, *Die Welt*. The article was headed 'Not the way for a gentleman to behave'.

The writer, one Martin Lambeck, accepted that it was reasonable for me to make frank and critical remarks comparing the British and German views on European integration. His objection was that I had made them in public.

'Talks', he said,

> are held behind closed doors – as is customary amongst gentle-
> men – and people speak their minds ... All these points could
> have been discussed with the German government. But it was
> much worse than that. In a BBC interview Malcolm Rifkind
> proclaimed that he was hostile towards the euro ... To put it in
> British terms: Malcolm Rifkind did not behave like a gentleman.

The article was revealing, not just amusing. The writer clearly felt
that the future of the European Union was too sensitive a subject to
be debated in public. The elites of Europe must discuss these matters
behind closed doors and, only then, announce the outcome.

The speech in Bonn was one of several I made in a number of
European countries in early 1997. I said that I wanted 'the British
message to reach further than the chancelleries of Europe. This is a
debate for the peoples of Europe, not just for the governments.' I am
not sure that most of the governments agreed either then or now.

February concluded with a splendid row over Europe that was
entirely my own fault. I was being interviewed on the *Today* programme by John Humphrys. He had pressed me on the government's
'wait and see' position on the single currency and I had stuck to the
agreed Cabinet position that no decision had yet been reached.

At the very end of the interview, Humphrys riled me by saying,
'So, Foreign Secretary, you are saying that on the most important decision Britain will have to make, the government have no
view whatsoever?'

I was, of course, not inclined to agree with him and replied, 'That is
not true, Mr Humphrys. The government is on balance hostile to the
European Monetary Union but we have not yet reached a decision.'

This remark had the virtue of being true and I left the studio happy
with the way it had gone. But I had no right to be. True or not, my
words had gone beyond the agreed Cabinet line.

Journalists immediately rang the Chancellor, Ken Clarke, who, rather generously, said it must have been 'a slip of the tongue'.

More damagingly, my old boss Geoffrey Howe, when asked, said that he knew me so well; I was so careful with words and so clear in my thoughts that if I had said this I must have wanted to move the issue forward. He was, on this occasion, wrong. It had been a gaffe, plain and simple.

Because Ken and I were friends and wished to resolve the matter rather than let it fester, we met that night in my flat in Carlton Gardens with the Chief Whip, Alastair Goodlad. Over a bottle of whisky, we agreed a line that we were both happy with and the press story, deprived of oxygen, soon faded away.

The government had made it clear that if participation in a single currency ever became government policy, it would have to be subject to a referendum of the British people. That turned out to be unnecessary and few, if any, in Britain now recommend that we should join.

As I write these words, we are awaiting a referendum on the even more vital issue of whether Britain will remain in the European Union at all. We will soon know whether the future is what it used to be.

CHAPTER 23

THERE IS LIFE
OUTSIDE POLITICS

A S THE 1997 general election approached, I knew, as we all
did, that, barring a miracle, we were going to be defeated
and Tony Blair would enter 10 Downing Street.

I was sad but not depressed. Eighteen years is a long time in a
democracy for one party to be in power. Nigel Broomfield, later our
ambassador in Germany, has reminded me that I had told him that
if in 1979 I had known we were going to be in government until
1997 and that I would be a minister throughout, I would have settled for that.

If the truth be told, I was rather looking forward to resuming
control of my own life and having time to do other things. During
the actual campaign I recall counting off the days to the election,
when I assumed that I would be liberated.

Although I knew the government would be defeated, I did not
consider it inevitable that I would lose my own Pentlands seat.
It had always been marginal, but the Tories had held it in bad years

as well as good. We also had, in Scotland, four parties not three, so the anti-Tory vote was split between Labour, Liberals and the SNP.

All that did not save us or me. By the last two weeks of the campaign the national opinion polls were bad and the Scottish ones were terrible.

General election night was a miserable affair. The results, as they started coming in, were depressing and they got worse. When I saw that Michael Portillo, with a 15,500 majority, had lost his seat, I knew that I, with a majority of only 4,290, could not expect any better.

My Labour opponent, Lynda Clark, was a very pleasant but uninspiring advocate who would later end up as a Scottish judge. When the returning officer announced that she had won with a majority of over 4,800, she stood stock-still, either out of nervousness or out of shock.

I had to suggest to her in a kindly manner, 'Lynda you've won. You must make your victory speech.' When it was my turn, I thanked all my supporters for their tremendous help and warned the new Labour MP that she had a leasehold not a freehold on the seat.

By the time we got home in the early hours, it was clear not only that Tony Blair had a thumping majority but also that the Tories had lost all their seats in Scotland and Wales as well as a very large number in England. When in 2015 the Labour Party, long the dominant force in Scotland, lost all but one of their Scottish seats, I almost felt sorry for them. It is a cruel business when the people pass their verdict.

Back home, Caroline and my special advisor, Graeme Carter, were visibly upset. They told me I seemed very calm and it was actually how I felt. Such is my nature (and the way I deal with bad news or serious adversity) that I was already thinking of the silver lining that would follow my release from the burdens both of office and of Parliament.

The following day I was watching, on television, Tony Blair making his triumphal entry into Downing Street. His majority was so large that it was clear that Labour would be in power for at least two terms, total-ling up to ten years. In some ways I felt relieved that I would be outside the House of Commons, at least for the first few years, and spared the frustration and impotence of sitting on the opposition benches.

Over the next week or so there were a number of obligations to fulfil. I returned to the Foreign Office, where I had a short courtesy call on my successor Robin Cook and thanked my private office team for all the support they had given me. I noticed that in his first few days not only had Robin rearranged some of the furniture but my portrait of Palmerston had disappeared.

If there had to be a Labour government, I was pleased that Robin had become Foreign Secretary. Although we agreed on very little, I had known him since our university days and he had been my pair in the House of Commons. I admired his ability but with reserva-tions. In one debate when we faced each other across the dispatch box, I had accused him of having 'the charity of a Robespierre and the objectivity of Senator McCarthy'.

Edith and I had a short holiday in Florence, where we had had our honeymoon. We were also able to make a last overnight visit to Chevening, which was very pleasant but also sad. Edith had given me a splendid 50th birthday party there in 1996 with many of our closest friends and family. The trustees presented me with a rather fine print of the house, which today hangs in my sitting room, together with one of the Foreign Office given to me by my former private office.

I had a final private audience with the Queen to return my seals of office. I had been fortunate, over the years, in accompanying the Queen on many of her engagements. As Scottish Secretary, I was a temporary member of the household when the Queen was at Holyrood. As Defence Secretary, I attended the Trooping the Colour and other military ceremonials. As Transport Secretary, I travelled with the Queen on the royal train, where I had in my compart-ment a small but real bath, which I used as the train hurtled north. As Foreign Secretary, I had taken part in state visits overseas, along with Edith, as well as attending state banquets in Buckingham Palace and Windsor.

I saw at first hand the burden that the Queen and the Duke of Edinburgh carried. I felt in need of a rest after carrying out state engagements for eighteen years without a break. The Queen has done them, assiduously, for sixty-four years without a break and shows no signs of flagging. We are a very fortunate nation.

I retained a duty to attend upon the Queen by having become, three years earlier, a member of the Queen's Bodyguard in Scotland, the Royal Company of Archers.

The Archers go back several hundred years and membership, fortunately, does not require skill with bow and arrow, though some members would put William Tell to shame. We wear a green uniform designed by Sir Walter Scott with a bonnet adorned with an eagle's feather.

I have been on duty a number of times over the years but the most memorable was a few weeks after I ceased to be Foreign Secretary.

The Queen was holding an Investiture at Holyrood Palace and a number of Archers had to stand to attention, adorning the walls, throughout the ceremony. Two of us, however, were required to act as ushers.

Our job was to ensure that when the Queen had stopped conversing with the person she had just decorated, he or she would be guided to where they were to sit for the rest of the ceremony. They would have been told this but sometimes they forgot in the excitement of meeting the Queen.

This happened with a recipient who had just received the CBE. I was able to catch his eye and indicate to him to come towards me. When he approached, he recognised me but had never seen me in my Archers uniform before. 'Oh, is this what you are doing now?' he asked. 'Not all the time,' I replied.

How the mighty are fallen. I had been Foreign Secretary a few weeks before. Now I was ushering people to their seats.

I received a large number of condolence letters from friends and colleagues. An unexpected one was from Margaret Thatcher. The substance of the letter was almost certainly the same as she had sent to every Tory MP who had lost his seat. It ended by saying that she hoped I would be returned to Westminster very soon.

What surprised me was that she had added in her own handwriting, 'We need you and so does Scotland.' I doubt if that was a sentiment she would have expressed in 1990, but it was a nice and generous comment for her to make.

I met her three or four times over the next few years, including once for a whole evening at the home of Richard and Rose Luce. She was always friendly and agreeable and there was never a single word of recrimination for the irritation our disagreements must have caused her when I was in her Cabinet. I was happy to make a genuine, warm tribute to her in the Commons when she died.

The handing over of Hong Kong to China took place in July, just a month after the general election. I was invited to the ceremony but I decided to watch it on TV instead. I felt I had been living on long-distance aircraft for too long and decided I would have a better view watching this historic event from my sitting room.

The search for a new career did not take as long as I had expected. Within a day I received a message from someone I had known at university. Now that I was no longer Foreign Secretary, would I consider working with BHP, the Australian mining and petroleum giant? They wanted help at their London office with the political implications of potential oil and gas projects in the Middle East and elsewhere.

It was to be part time, which suited me as I knew I would try to return to Parliament at the next general election and this ruled out taking a major full-time job. It was at BHP that I first worked with Christine Shaylor, who would become my secretary and in charge of my office when I returned to the House of Commons. It was one of my best decisions.

Over the next few months I did receive several other approaches, which, I should make clear, were not firm offers. Would I be interested in being considered as Vice-Chancellor of Durham University or chairman of the European division of Boeing? The most unexpected was from headhunters interested in recommending me as chairman of Railtrack. As I had opposed the creation of Railtrack as Transport Secretary, becoming its chairman would have been a fitting punishment in the eyes of some of my former colleagues.

I did express an interest in one full-time job. In 1999, it became necessary to appoint a new Secretary-General of NATO. It was clear that a good British candidate would be acceptable to the United States and other members of the alliance.

I had been sounded out for this post in 1994, when I was Defence Secretary, to succeed Manfred Wörner. Peter Inge, the Chief of the Defence Staff, told me that General Shalikashvili, the chairman of the US Joint Chiefs of Staff, had said I would be acceptable to Washington. My private office had received a similar message from the Assistant Secretary at the Pentagon. At the time, I said I did not wish to be considered as I wished to remain in the front line of British politics.

In 1999, I would have been happy to do the job. There was no serious prospect of another Conservative government for at least six years. The press reported that I was not interested in the job and I wrote to Tony Blair saying that that was incorrect.

He sent me a very friendly reply saying that he knew of my interest and had considered it 'very carefully'. In the event, he recommended the then Defence Secretary, George Robertson, who did the job very well.

During the eight years I was out of Parliament, I also served on the boards of two small investment trusts and acted as a consultant to PricewaterhouseCoopers and a non-executive director of Aberdeen Asset Management, chairing their remuneration committee.

From 2002 to 2005, I was chairman of Alliance Medical, which provides imaging services for both NHS and private patients, and also chaired Armor Group, a private security company, as well as being on the board of Ramco Energy. In later years I served on the board of Unilever as well as returning to Alliance Medical as a non-executive director.

These were all part-time commitments. They were not all held simultaneously. They took up a significant proportion of my time but far less than the burden I carried when I was a senior Cabinet minister.

As well as providing my income, I found these new responsibilities very stimulating. It is quite healthy when circumstances require you to make a substantial career change. It helps to recharge your batteries and stop you becoming stale.

These years enabled me, in my fifties, to become reasonably comfortable for the first time in my working life. Sometime after I ceased to be Foreign Secretary, at the age of fifty-one, Edith and I reviewed our financial circumstances.

At that time we had no stocks or shares. We had, like everyone else, a mortgage on our home and owned no other property. Our total savings were around £15,000.

This is not a complaint. I had chosen this way of life and our standard of living had, in fact, been high for several years because of the tied housing that went with my job as Foreign Secretary and the car and driver and personal protection officers I was deemed to need.

I was not disappointed that I no longer required a car and driver. On my last visit as Foreign Secretary, to Hong Kong, I had been reminded of the downside of having them.

I was sitting in the back of the Governor's 'other' Rolls-Royce with my assistant private secretary, Fiona Mylchreest, a young Scottish lady who, much though I admired and liked her, was the most undiplomatic diplomat I ever worked with.

In response to some casual remark I'd made, she said, 'Don't be such a pompous prig.' I told her, 'You can't say that to the Foreign Secretary.' 'Well, you are,' she responded. The driver in the front seat was pretending that he was not listening but I could see his shoulders heaving, Ted Heath-style.

A car and driver are a great asset when you are a minister. Indeed, you know when you have retired. It is when you climb into the back of your car and it does not go anywhere.

From 1996, I had the fascinating experience of being, for eight years, the Honorary Colonel of a Territorial Army regiment, 162 Movement Control, which was part of the Royal Logistics Corps.

I had been approached when I was Foreign Secretary by their commanding officer, Diana Henderson, and asked whether I would take this on. I was flattered as the armed forces are usually very happy to see the back of ministers when they move on. I welcomed their confidence in me and the opportunity to help our Reserve forces in this way.

This appointment meant that I had to be kitted up in uniform, attend regimental dinners, inspect the regiment and help the commanding officer when problems arose.

From time to time they would need to ring me at home. On one occasion Caroline answered the phone and was asked if the caller could speak to 'Colonel Malcolm'. This is a normal mode of address in the Army on informal occasions. It respects the officer's rank but also acknowledges the camaraderie of the regiment.

My children, unaware of these traditions but aware of my lack of military credentials, were hugely amused. 'Colonel Malcolm,' one of them shouted, 'there's someone on the phone for you.' After this had happened on several occasions I had to instruct the regiment not to use this mode of address when they phoned me, as my children were teasing me and making my life intolerable.

I also, from 1998, became the Honorary Colonel of the City of Edinburgh Universities Officer Training Corps. There, I was number two, as the Duke of Edinburgh, who was Chancellor of Edinburgh University, was designated the Royal Colonel.

I also served briefly on the University Court of my alma mater and for ten years was president of the Development Trust, which administered the substantial private donations that the university received.

I was given an honorary degree by the university and also received one from Napier University, which was based in my old constituency. I was delighted when Edith, who had lectured at Napier for several years and had served on their court, also received an honorary degree. Hers was more deserved than mine. I also serve on the Dulverton Trust, a charitable foundation, as one of their trustees.

Shortly after the 1997 general election, I received a letter from John Major offering to recommend me for a peerage in his resignation honours. I thanked him but said that I preferred to seek to return to the House of Commons rather than go to the House of Lords.

I was very happy to accept the knighthood that I was then offered and I became a Knight Commander of St Michael and St George. This is the order normally available for diplomats and others who are felt to have made a special contribution to Britain's foreign policy and international interests. I was encouraged by a colleague to remember that 'once a knight is not enough'.

I had a sad responsibility in June 1999 when I gave evidence at the Old Bailey. My former colleague Jonathan Aitken had pled guilty to perjury and was due to be sentenced.

Some months earlier I had offered to give evidence on his behalf as to the very real service he had provided for the country when he was with me at the Ministry of Defence. His QC, Sir John Nutting, had felt that such evidence would be helpful in persuading the judge towards a lesser prison term.

On the day, I gave evidence from the witness box answering questions from Sir John and the judge. The prosecution did not cross-examine. Jonathan was sentenced to eighteen months' imprisonment, of which he served seven months. His counsel later informed me that he believed that the sentence would have been more likely two years but for my evidence.

Jonathan was, of course, the author of his own misfortune, which he has always been the first to admit. I have to say that I admire the way in which he has dealt with this disaster to his life, never complained and is today making a very substantial contribution, through his public and private activities, to the wellbeing of the community.

Shortly after my election defeat I decided that I would not seek a safe seat elsewhere in Britain but would try to regain my Pentlands constituency at the next general election.

I also felt that I had an obligation to the Scottish Tories. We now had no Scottish MPs and I accepted an invitation to become president of the Scottish Conservative and Unionist Party, which office I held until 2005, when I returned to Parliament. I was asked by William Hague, the new Leader of the Opposition, to attend shadow Cabinet strategy sessions whenever Scottish interests needed to be represented.

My main reason for sticking with Pentlands was because I felt a loyalty to them and to Edinburgh, which had been my home since birth. It also hurt to lose the seat that I had represented for twenty-three years. I knew, however, there could be no certainty that I would win it back given Tony Blair's extraordinary popularity and the serious weakness of the Tories in Scotland.

However, I was well respected in Pentlands, and my successor, Lynda Clark, had no significant personal following. I also assumed that I could mount a strong campaign and that, although Labour were bound to win a second term in government, there would be some significant fall in the national Labour vote given how high it had been in 1997.

My reasoning was partly right and partly wrong. We did mount a very effective campaign over the next four years with lots of helpers, surveys and canvassing and substantial press coverage. I was delighted and surprised to get a personal endorsement from *The Times*, which, in an editorial, described me as 'the best choice for the Union and the next parliament'.

This was very nice but I was aware that hardly anyone in Pentlands actually read *The Times*. Much more valuable was the editorial endorsement in the local paper, the *Edinburgh Evening News*, which said that I was 'that most rare of beasts – a politician who commands respect, even affection, right across the political spectrum'.

Sadly, even the *Edinburgh Evening News* could not move mountains. On the doorstep, too many people were saying that it was nothing personal but Blair deserved a second term. At the 2001 general election I reduced the Labour majority from over 4,800 to 1,500, which was a great result, but I was still in the political wilderness.

It also meant that I had ceased to be available as a serious candidate for the party leadership if a vacancy should occur.

While I was Foreign Secretary, my name was one of three or four that was regularly mentioned if John Major was to lose the election and resign as leader of the party.

I would have been a candidate if I had still been an MP after 1997 but I do not believe that I would have won. If I had held Pentlands, it must be assumed that Michael Portillo would have held Enfield Southgate, where his majority was three times my own. The real battle would have been between Michael as the candidate of the Eurosceptic right and Ken Clarke as the standard bearer of the pro-European One Nation tradition of the party. I would have been rather like Douglas Hurd in 1990.

My second defeat in 2001 meant that I was out of Parliament for eight years. William Hague was succeeded by Iain Duncan Smith and then by Michael Howard. As new Tory MPs replaced retiring ones, the green benches were increasingly occupied by MPs I did not know and who did not know me.

I did not mind very much. My ambition had always been to be Foreign Secretary, and that I had done. My hope was that I might do it again. I was once asked if I would like to be Prime Minister and my honest reply was that I would like to have been Prime Minister. Having seen from a close vantage point the unrelenting pressures that the job entailed, I was less attracted to it.

One unexpected invitation that I received was in 2001 from my former assistant private secretary, Dickie Stagg, who was now our ambassador to Bulgaria. He asked me if I would make a visit to Sofia to brief the new Bulgarian government on parliamentary democracy, handling the media and related matters. The new ministers were all very bright but mainly technocrats with little political knowledge or awareness.

The new Prime Minister was King Simeon, who had become monarch in 1943, at the age of six, when his father, King Boris, had abdicated. He had only reigned for three years and had then lived in exile until the end of Communism.

When he returned to Bulgaria, he was, at first, very popular and wanted to stand in the elections for a new President. He was prevented from doing so on a technicality and so, instead, created his own political party and, as its leader, fought and won the general election.

Simeon became Prime Minister but had a problem. He could not be addressed as King, as Bulgaria was still a republic. But he did not have an ordinary surname like the rest of us. He resolved the problem by using his dynasty as his surname and became Mr Simeon Saxe-Coburg-Gotski.

I met the new Prime Minister shortly after I arrived. He was very courteous and began by saying that he had never really wanted to be Prime Minister. Of course, what he wanted was to be King again.

I asked him if, nevertheless, he was enjoying the job. He said he was but it was very hard work. He was expected to answer questions in Parliament every month. I pointed out how light a burden that was compared to the weekly sessions of a British Prime Minister, but I do not think he was convinced.

That morning, I gave a seminar at the Council of Ministers on the technology of government. It was well attended, with seven ministers and five deputy ministers present. Afterwards I gave a lecture at the ambassador's residence.

Mr Saxe-Coburg-Gotski remained Prime Minister for four years but then his party was heavily defeated. He, in due course, retired from the political fray. It is never very wise for Kings, or even ex-Kings, to get involved in party political battles. They must be above that in the modern world.

During the eight years I was away from Westminster, I remained a very active contributor to the public debate. I gave lectures, wrote many articles in both newspapers and journals and was a frequent contributor, on foreign policy issues, on TV and radio.

The main crises during those years were Kosovo and Iraq. I opposed both the NATO bombing on Serbia and the Bush–Blair invasion of Iraq.

I had no difficulty supporting the removal of the Taliban from power in Afghanistan after the 9/11 attack on the Twin Towers by al-Qaeda. Al-Qaeda used Afghanistan as their sanctuary and head-quarters with the approval of the Taliban government. The United States, having been attacked, was entitled to respond and to have the support of its allies in doing so.

Kosovo and Iraq were different. There was deep injustice in Kosovo, with the Kosovar Albanians having been deprived of their autonomy and with a serious risk of ethnic cleansing by Milošević in Belgrade. But the human rights violations, though serious, were, sadly, no worse than in many other parts of the world.

Nor was there any direct threat to British, American or NATO interests that could justify a military attack, as opposed to sanctions, on Belgrade.

In some ways it was similar to the issues my colleagues and I had had to deal with over Bosnia. Indeed, it was because we had refused to become partisan combatants in that war that Bill Clinton and Tony Blair were determined to apply a different response over Kosovo.

Blair, in particular, was convinced that the West could deploy its overwhelming military superiority and invulnerability to resolve major human rights violations by using NATO air power to impose its will.

In one sense, they were right. The violation of human rights by the Serb President, Slobodan Milošević, was stopped by NATO going to war and bombing Belgrade. What they failed to do over Kosovo and, subsequently, in Iraq, was to take account of the law of unforeseen consequences.

NATO had given two assurances when the bombing of Belgrade began. Firstly, they assured the world that the bombing would only last a few days and then Milošević would sue for peace. In fact, it lasted sixty-eight days, NATO ran out of suitable targets and Milošević only conceded when the possibility of NATO ground forces was raised.

Secondly, the US, British and NATO authorities all made clear that it was no part of their strategy to see Serbia dismembered and the creation of an independent Kosovo.

If they meant that, they failed. The Kosovars, not surprisingly, realised that with NATO on side this would be the only opportunity they would ever have of becoming fully independent. They refused to settle for autonomy and they are now an independent state. Our problems with Russia today are in part because of NATO's decision to go to war without UN backing and without any justification of self-defence.

In a very real sense, the road to Baghdad began in Belgrade. The facts concerning the Iraq War are so well known I will mention them only very briefly.

As with Kosovo, but unlike Afghanistan, neither the US nor the UK was acting in self-defence. Saddam Hussein, ghastly though he was, was not an ally of al-Qaeda. As with Kosovo, Bush and Blair did not have the express authority of the UN Security Council.

Even if they believed that Saddam wanted to develop nuclear weapons, achieving that goal would not have been possible for years to come. Unlike the Gulf War, Turkey and the moderate Arab states declined to provide military help or become serious allies in the conflict.

Like many others, I did not doubt that the US military would destroy Saddam in days or a few weeks at most. But it was obvious that the real challenge would be what happened thereafter.

Saddam's Iraq was not just a personal dictatorship. It was the latest manifestation of minority Sunni hegemony over majority Iraqi Shias that had lasted for decades. By removing Saddam, dismantling his army and banning tens of thousands associated with his regime, a political vacuum was created which attracted the terrorists. By replacing Saddam's despotism with democratic elections, Sunni dominance was ended and Shia power ensured. It did not take a political genius to predict what would and, sadly, has happened.

I, and many others, made these arguments in speeches, articles and interviews in the months leading up to the war, most comprehensively in the Gallipoli Memorial Lecture I gave to the Royal United Services Institute (RUSI) in April 2002.

I would like to be able to say that if I had been an MP I would have joined those who voted against the government in the crucial vote in the Commons in March 2003. I am not sure I can.

By the time of that vote, the case for going to war was as poor as ever but there were over 200,000 US troops in the Gulf waiting to cross the border. They could not stay there indefinitely. They had to be either used or brought home.

If they were brought home, leaving Saddam in power, the United States would have been humiliated; their authority and credibility would have been seriously damaged for years to come.

In an article I wrote for the *Daily Telegraph*, I said that 'the Western world should not be forced to choose between a rock and a hard place'. With a heavy heart, and deep misgivings, I concluded that as almost a quarter of a million US troops were ready to move across the border when the order was given, they had better get on with it, and we had to hope and pray that the judgement of their political masters was correct.

That reasoning might have determined my vote if I had been in the Commons at the time. I do not know. What I do know is that

I admire my colleagues who voted against the government. History is on their side.

Those years outside Parliament enabled me, as the saying goes, to have more time with my family.

Edith and I, together with Caroline and Hugo, had, in the late 1990s, a great holiday in the United States and Canada. We hired a Chevrolet Blazer and drove from New York through New England and then north to Niagara Falls and Toronto, where we stayed with my cousin Aaron Rifkind, who had married Joyce, an American, and settled in Canada. On another occasion we met Hugo in Zanzibar and Caroline joined us.

Caroline had finished her studies at Durham University and had joined PricewaterhouseCoopers, where she has remained ever since. Hugo had completed his time at Emmanuel College, Cambridge and was beginning his journalistic career, which has gone from strength to strength, pleasing his friends and astonishing his parents.

But we had one major blow. In 1997, Edith was diagnosed with progressive multiple sclerosis on the left side of her body. After various tests, including a visit to the Mayo Clinic in the United States, we thought through the implications.

For the first few years they were not too serious. Edith was able to walk and drive her own car, which we had specially adapted. Gradually she became dependent on a walking stick, then began to use a mobility scooter and became unable to use her left hand and arm.

In 2002, she informed me that she wanted us to holiday in the Galapagos. As a zoologist, she had a natural interest in visiting them. She wanted to do so before she was too disabled to get from ship to dinghy, and land from the dinghy on each island, which was what one was required to do. Most of the islands were uninhabited and no harbours or proper landing places were permitted.

We paid a premium to the travel company and this enabled her to have a dedicated assistant who ensured that she did not fall into the Pacific Ocean when making these daily transits. I, and our fellow tourists, admired her courage and determination. She has shown these same characteristics on many other occasions over recent years.

We visited the Galapagos with Richard and Rose Luce, and Tommy and Jean Macpherson. Tommy, or Sir Thomas Macpherson of Biallid, was a Boy's Own hero, already in his sixties when I first met him in the 1980s. He was one of the most highly decorated veterans from the Second World War, with a Military Cross and two Bars, a DSO and a Croix de Guerre from General de Gaulle. He had escaped from more PoW camps than any other British soldier. He had been parachuted into France, behind enemy lines, after D-Day, and worked with the French Resistance.

I met him first when he offered me a bed for the night in his home in the Highlands after a speaking engagement. Edith and I, thereafter, saw him and his lovely wife, Jean, on many occasions, staying with them at Craig Dhu near Newtonmore and welcoming them to our home in Inveresk.

When Tommy died in 2014 at the age of ninety-one, I attended his funeral in Newtonmore. After the service we followed his coffin to a family graveyard on a Highland hillside where, with a guard of honour provided by the Newtonmore Shinty Club, with their crossed shinty sticks, and to the sound of the bagpipes, he was buried with his Macpherson ancestors.

I was invited to give the tribute at his memorial service to a packed congregation in St Columba's Church in London. I recounted how he had parachuted into occupied France, wearing his kilt, together with a member of the French Resistance. Those on the ground, seeing his kilt billowing as he descended, thought he was his fellow parachutist's wife.

I mentioned that Tommy liked to point out that he had escaped from more PoW camps than anyone else. His son Angus had received a letter from an old friend, after Tommy had died, saying how he had teased Tommy that if he had escaped more often than anyone else, he must have been recaptured more often than anyone else, as well. Tommy became a hero in his early twenties. The following seventy years were packed with public service, business appointments and everything that life had to offer him, including an old sky-blue Rolls-Royce that he enjoyed driving around the Highlands.

Edith and I still see Jean often. Well into her eighties, she remains as joyful and sparkling as ever. All rooms light up when she enters.

A big change in 1998 was the sale of our Duddingston home and acquisition of Eskgrove House in Inveresk, just outside Edinburgh.

Eskgrove is an eighteenth-century small manor house with several acres of garden and a sliver of woodland attached. Edith transformed the paddock at the back of the house into a wild flower garden which looked charming every summer. We lived at Eskgrove, either full time or part time, from 1998 until 2014, when Edith's increasing disability forced us to concentrate on our London home.

It has been sad to leave Eskgrove but being in London has enabled us to see Caroline and Andy, Hugo and Francisca, and our grand-children most weeks. We have no cause to complain.

CHAPTER 24

UP, DOWN AND UP AGAIN

T HE GENERAL ELECTION in 2001 had been a deep disappointment both nationally for the Conservative Party and for me in Pentlands. I had reduced the Labour majority from well over 4,000 to 1,700. That was some comfort but, in politics, a miss is as good as a mile.

I had to consider whether my desire to return to the House of Commons made it now necessary for me to look elsewhere. The decision I reached was made much easier by the Boundaries Commission, which, in its wisdom, so changed the constituencies in Edinburgh that Pentlands effectively disappeared.

I discussed with Edith what I should do and we agreed that I should only express interest in a constituency that was in or very near London. The reasons were entirely practical. Inveresk remained our home though Edith was very happy also to be based in London, where Caroline and Hugo lived.

If I became an MP for a seat anywhere else in Britain, I would have to do a regular commute between London and the constituency every weekend. Edith's health and mobility was such that that would not have been sustainable. Nor did I want to. I had done the weekly commute for twenty-three years. I did not want to start it again, especially to a part of the country that I might be unfamiliar with.

I fully recognised that this self-imposed restriction might mean that I might not become an MP again. I was relaxed about that. My political and ministerial career had already taken me to heights that I could only aspire to when I began in the 1970s. In any event, Blair was still in power with a very large majority. It was very unlikely there would be a Conservative government before I was well into my sixties.

The first seat that I was seriously interested in was Windsor. The sitting MP, Michael Trend, had announced in 2003 that he would not be standing again at the next general election. There was considerable press speculation and I was asked if I was interested. I acknowledged that I was but made a point of saying that I was not taking anything for granted.

That turned out to be more perceptive than I had expected. Not only did I not become the candidate for Windsor, I was not even interviewed. To add insult to injury, I received the standard letter sent to the dozens of unsuccessful hopefuls explaining that they had had many able applicants and wishing me well in my future political career.

To be fair to Windsor, they had decided that they wanted someone who would be a good, local Member to help them in their local battle with the Lib Dems. A national figure was not deemed to be a great asset for that strategy.

I had better fortune with South West Hertfordshire, where I was put on the shortlist and invited for interview. However, on 7 November 2003, I was being driven by Andrew Mitchell to his constituency dinner in Sutton Coldfield, where I was to be the main speaker. He informed me that Michael Portillo, MP for Kensington and Chelsea, had just announced that he would be standing down at the general election because he had decided to leave active politics and pursue another career.

After Windsor, I made no assumption about my prospects in Kensington and Chelsea. However, the omens began well and, in reality, I never looked back. The following day, at a performance of *The Valkyrie* in the Theatre Royal in Glasgow, I was approached by a Kensington Conservative who encouraged me to stand.

I started getting press enquiries but, unlike with Windsor, I refused to give any indication of my intentions. I decided to become a Trappist monk and for the next three months refused to confirm, publicly or privately, that I was going for the seat. This not only prevented unwanted publicity but led to a series of approaches from party activists in Kensington and Chelsea encouraging me to apply.

I received a letter from Barbara Campbell, a local councillor and Deputy Mayor for that year. She encouraged me to put my name forward and I got similar messages from people who lived in the constituency over the following weeks.

Virginia Bottomley arranged a small supper party for me to meet Shireen Ritchie, the chairman of the local party. Shireen gave nothing away but was clearly keen to size me up.

Shireen was a superb local councillor and there had been speculation that she might put herself forward. If she had, I would have had a much more difficult task. She had the added fame of having Guy Ritchie and Madonna as her stepson and stepdaughter-in-law.

Although it was risky, I wrote to Hertfordshire South West and withdrew my name from their consideration. I did not tell them why but I am sure they guessed.

Kensington and Chelsea was seen as the plum seat in the country. The local Conservative association had around 2,000 members and the Tories had permanent control of the council. At that time, the Member represented Chelsea and the southern two-thirds of Kensington. There was not a single Labour councillor elected from that part of the royal borough.

The calibre of the councillors was very high. In addition to some retired people and several young aspirant MPs, there were a large number with a serious professional or business background. They were able, undogmatic and felt a considerable obligation to North Kensington, which had serious poverty and unemployment and a considerable immigrant community. Many of the residents hailed from the West Indies and had created the highly successful, annual Notting Hill Carnival.

The selection process began at the end of January 2004. There were 206 applicants. They were sifted and twenty of us were invited for interview. I thought hard about what I would say. I hardly touched national or international issues. I assumed they would want to know whether I would be a good and active local constituency MP. I also knew that I must not come across as grand but as someone with whom they would enjoy working.

With that in mind, I began by saying that I was feeling more nervous than I had been for years. The first question was from a local councillor, Barry Phelps, who asked how I would respond if he asked me a very hostile question. I replied that I would be more nervous if he asked me a friendly one. The chairman then asked him, 'What is your question?' 'That was it,' he replied. It was a relaxed and friendly interview and I left in good spirits.

The next stage was when the remaining seven of us were interviewed by the full executive. That, too, went well and we moved to the final selection by the whole association in Kensington Town Hall.

There were 617 members present and Andrew Neil had been invited to cross-examine each of the final four. My rivals were Nick Hurd, Douglas's son, and two excellent local councillors, Warwick Lightfoot and Mary Weale (whose father, Alan Glyn, had been MP for Windsor when I first entered the Commons).

I began by quoting Henry VIII, who had said to each of his wives, 'Don't worry. I don't intend to keep you long.' That got a good laugh. The session with Andrew Neil was tough but, unlike the other candidates, I had been interviewed by him often before.

He suggested that I was a carpetbagger down from Scotland and I pointed out that that was what people had said about him as well. The audience were friendly. One question from the floor that I could not hear because of poor acoustics turned out to be about noise pollution.

After we had all performed, we retired while the ballot was taken. I won on the first round with 372 votes; Warwick Lightfoot received 93, Nick Hurd 78 and Mary Weale 74. My 'wilderness years' were over.

My ten years as the MP, first for Kensington and Chelsea and then for Kensington alone, including the north of the royal borough, were extremely happy and fulfilling.

I liked the constituency office bearers, some of whom became good friends. The agent, Jonathan Fraser-Howells, was excellent. In the House of Commons, I had Christine Shaylor as my secretary. She had first worked for me after 1997 when I was with BHP. She is, by far, the most impressive and professional secretary I have had in over forty years in public life.

As a result of my selection, we bought a larger new flat in Westminster. We had been staying in Tufton Court but moved to Marsham Street. Both Winston Churchill and Margaret Thatcher had lived there briefly, but as neither of them has a plaque recording the fact, there isn't much chance for the rest of us.

The general election campaign was very gentle in Kensington and Chelsea. One Saturday morning I was accompanied by a *Financial Times* reporter and decided to canvass Tony Benn, who lived in Holland Park Avenue. I pressed the intercom and when Tony answered, I pretended not to know it was him and asked for his support. 'You do realise whose house this is?' he answered over the intercom. 'Of course, I do,' I giggled. He was about to invite me in for a coffee when he realised I had a journalist with me. I never got that coffee.

I returned to Parliament at the general election in May 2005. Tony Blair had been elected to a third term. Michael Howard had fought a vigorous campaign and had given good leadership to the Tory Party. However, we had only dented Labour's majority.

I had expected a tranquil period but, to everyone's surprise, Michael Howard immediately announced his intention to step down from the leadership as soon as a successor had been chosen.

He still had to choose a new shadow Cabinet and I was invited by him to become shadow Work and Pensions Secretary. He explained that he wanted a 'big hitter' against David Blunkett, the Secretary of State. Although Work and Pensions were not my strongest subjects, I was happy to return to the front bench and reconnect with the parliamentary party, many of whom had only entered the House since I had left in 1997.

Michael Howard's decision to stand down led to immediate interest as to who would throw their hats into the ring to try to succeed him. It was not the timing I would have chosen, but I decided to offer my services.

I could have been coy and non-committal and waited until I had been able to gauge my potential support in the parliamentary party. That would, normally, have been sensible but I was well aware that my candidature was a long shot.

I was fifty-nine, I had been out of Parliament for eight years and was not known personally by many of the newer MPs. I was identified with the Thatcher and Major years and, as a centrist in the party, had no band of devoted followers. Along with Ken Clarke, I was the most experienced of the Tory MPs, but the party would not be choosing a Prime Minister. They would be choosing a Leader of the Opposition with a hard slog ahead of him for at least four years.

Over the weeks that followed I had a vigorous campaign. Crispin Blunt was in charge, with Toby Vintcent volunteering to handle the logistics and administration. I had good meetings including a splendid public meeting in Westminster which over 1,100 people attended. The press gave me good coverage with both profiles and reportage of speeches.

I presented myself as the One Nation candidate and had a better claim to that title than some others who claimed it, including, ludicrously, Gordon Brown.

But in reality the campaign never took off, not least because it became clear from the start that I had only a handful of MPs backing me. David Davis and Liam Fox were attracting the right of the party, Ken Clarke continued to have a solid phalanx of pro-European devotees and as much of a claim to One Nation credentials as I had. David Cameron did not declare until some weeks later but was an obvious candidate for those who wanted a younger, new-generation Tory to be in charge.

In an interview in September 2005, with Alice Thomson and Rachel Sylvester of the *Telegraph*, I was described as 'sanguine' about the leadership contest. 'I am more relaxed than some other candidates,' I said. 'I have been Foreign Secretary. I am not an unfulfilled person.' It was how I felt.

By the time of the Tory conference in October, I knew that I did not have a serious prospect of winning. Only half a dozen MPs had pledged their support and without parliamentary backing, one would not be on the ballot for the party members as a whole. I could have stepped down over the summer but I decided that there was nothing to lose by accepting the invitation that all the candidates had received to address the whole conference in Blackpool on 3 October.

I spoke for twenty minutes before a packed hall. I did not have a text, nor did I use the autocue. I began by saying, 'I know that we have a mountain to climb and some of us an even higher mountain.' I pointed out that politics was no longer ideological. 'People don't think of themselves as right wing or left wing. They look to politicians not for ideology but for solutions.'

This was good pragmatic stuff.

My speech was well received, with repeated applause and a standing ovation. It was described as 'a thrilling old-fashioned speaking performance' but also as 'not enough to hide too much old-fashioned thinking'. The conference could not have been friendlier but it was clear they were looking to a new generation to provide a new leader. Within days I announced that I no longer considered myself a candidate.

I do not regret having thrown my hat in the ring, even if it was never picked up. I felt I had much to offer and I needed to know whether my candidacy would be as unsuccessful as I myself suspected. A political life can consist of windows of opportunity. I was not short of them between 1974 and 1997. They got me to the highest rungs of British politics. I cannot complain. But, in effect, my luck ran out in 1997.

When David Cameron became leader, he had my full support. I knew that he wanted William Hague in his team and that William wished to be shadow Foreign Secretary. That left me with the question of whether I would wish to serve in the shadow Cabinet if another portfolio was offered to me by David Cameron.

My decision that I did not was not caused by any pique that I was not to be shadow Foreign Secretary. My expertise and my main interests had always been in foreign and security policy. I preferred to speak out on these subjects from the back benches, on TV and in the press, rather than shadow, from the front bench, another domestic department.

I, of course, realised that if I decided not to serve in the shadow Cabinet I could not expect to be invited to serve in a future Cabinet if David Cameron became Prime Minister. My ministerial life would be truly over. That did not cause me any concern. Having been a minister for eighteen consecutive years should be quite enough for anyone. I have never regretted that decision.

For the ten years until 2015, that I was back in the House of Commons, I was fortunate in having the opportunity to make significant contributions to both foreign and security policy.

The most important was the five years, from 2010 until 2015, that I spent as chairman of the Intelligence and Security Committee (ISC), with oversight over MI5, MI6 and GCHQ. I shall deal with those years in the next chapter of this book.

After 2005, I also renewed a serious interest in nuclear weapons and how they should be dealt with in the post-Cold War age.

As Defence Secretary, I had had day-to-day responsibility for Britain's nuclear deterrent, though any decision as to its use would, of course, have been exclusively for the Prime Minister.

When I had become Foreign Secretary, I was informed that, in the event of an actual or threatened nuclear attack on the United Kingdom, I would be third in line to take any decision on the use of our nuclear deterrent if the Prime Minister and the Deputy Prime Minister, Michael Heseltine, had not survived. Given the end of the Cold War, that scenario was improbable, but the knowledge as to where the buck would stop was daunting and sobering to say the least.

I have always supported the need for Britain to retain its nuclear weapons but have recognised that their number and strength should be no more than the minimum required for effective deterrence. To that end, I was instrumental, as Defence Secretary, in getting rid of British tactical nuclear weapons and free-fall nuclear bombs.

In 2007, Henry Kissinger, George Shultz, Bill Perry and Sam Nunn published an article in the Wall Street Journal. Kissinger and Shultz were former Secretaries of State, Perry a Defence Secretary with whom I had worked closely, and Nunn a distinguished senator with a long record of achievement on security issues. I knew and respected all of them.

The article, entitled 'A World Free of Nuclear Weapons', made a powerful impact. Four senior American statesman, including Henry Kissinger, a noted Cold War warrior, called for a world without nuclear weapons. They had not become converts to unilateral disarmament by either the United States or anyone else. They wanted to give a major boost to multilateral negotiations to reduce nuclear weapons and the threat they represent, leading over years to their potential abolition.

I was impressed by their initiative and co-ordinated a similar article in *The Times* signed by me, Douglas Hurd, David Owen and George Robertson, former Secretary-General of NATO.

I was approached by Global Zero, an American campaigning organisation committed to multilateral disarmament, and have become one of their leading European spokesmen. I also serve as a member of the board of the Nuclear Threat Initiative, co-chaired by Senator Sam Nunn, which has done impressive work researching and promoting initiatives that would remove avoidable risks associated with nuclear weapons and fissile material.

The deterioration of the West's relations with Putin's Russia has put nuclear weapons disarmament proposals into cold storage for the time being. Indeed, Putin's rhetoric and nuclear doctrine has heightened tension because of its apparent acceptance that tactical nuclear weapons could be important in fighting an otherwise conventional war.

In 2013 and 2014, I co-chaired, along with Des Browne, a former Defence Secretary, and Menzies Campbell, the former Liberal Democrat leader, the Trident Commission, an independent cross-party inquiry into the UK's nuclear weapons policy. The Commission reached the unanimous conclusion that Trident modernisation needed to go ahead, but we combined this with strong support for the renewal of multilateral disarmament negotiations, led by the United States and Russia, in which Britain would need to play a significant part and be prepared to accept the need for change.

I remain of the view that this is one of the most important issues facing our planet, especially given the consequences that would arise if nuclear fissile material was to fall into the hands of terrorist organisations.

In 2010, I was asked by William Hague, the new Foreign Secretary, whether I would be willing to be the British representative on the Commonwealth Eminent Persons Group, which had been mandated by the heads of government to examine the future of the Commonwealth and make recommendations as to how it could be improved.

We met over the following year, under the chairmanship of Abdullah Badawi, a former Malaysian Prime Minister, and reported to the heads of government at their conference in Perth, Australia, which I attended.

Our report, entitled 'A Commonwealth of the People', had dozens of recommendations, the great majority of which were accepted. Sadly, our most important proposal, that the Commonwealth should have a Human Rights Commissioner, was a bridge too far for some of the Commonwealth governments whose record on human rights was questionable to say the least.

Our recommendation was kicked into the long grass, but it will keep reappearing and will, I am convinced, one day be accepted.

Being thought suitable for 'Eminent Persons Panels' is a sign of one's advancing years. It can also become repetitive. In 2014, I was invited to join the Organization for Security and Co-operation in Europe (OSCE)'s Eminent Persons Panel on relations between the West and Russia following Russia's annexation of Crimea and destabilisation of parts of eastern Ukraine.

During the first five years of David Cameron's government, I spoke in Parliament mainly on foreign policy issues and supported the government in the debate that, despite my intervention, led to a defeat on its proposed intervention in Syria.

I was less helpful to the government when I was one of the major rebels who helped torpedo Nick Clegg's proposed reform of the House of Lords. There is a good case for reform of the Lords, but in my view an elected House of Lords would be a mistake. It is far better that it remains a chamber which has independence and experience not found in the Commons, though as an unelected House it must leave the last word on all proposals to the House of Commons.

The end of the 2010–15 parliament turned out for me to be a truly miserable experience, though there was, in due course, a satisfactory conclusion. Jack Straw and I were the subjects of a sting by the Channel 4 *Dispatches* programme, aided and abetted by the *Daily Telegraph*.

Towards the end of 2014, I had received an email purporting to be from a Hong Kong company asking me if I would consider joining an advisory board they were intending to set up in London. The purpose of the advisory board would be to help them understand 'the various political, regulatory and legislative frameworks in the UK and across the EU'.

This sounded pretty innocuous. Such advisory boards are very common in the UK and across Europe. At present, I chair the European advisory board of LEK, a major British consultancy partnership that assists British companies and parts of the public sector.

I was asked in the email whether I would be willing to meet with their representatives in London for an informal conversation. There appeared to be no reason not to. I made clear that 'I would need to be satisfied that there would be no conflict of interest with my current responsibilities'.

In Britain, for many years, many MPs who are not ministers have had outside business interests. These interests, including the sums earned, must be entered in the Register of Members' Interests. Some people disapprove of MPs having outside business interests and believe that they should all be full-time MPs. Most opinion surveys, however, indicate that a majority of the public find such interests acceptable as they can make MPs more independent and better informed as to what is happening in the real world outside the Palace of Westminster.

I had two meetings with the 'company' representatives which were very straightforward. A high proportion of the discussion at both meetings was about their proposed advisory board and about my views on differential political risk in Russia and Eastern Europe, as well as the European Union and how it works.

The only specifically British issue they showed any interest in was HS3. This is a possible high-speed rail link between Liverpool and Hull via Manchester and Leeds. Unlike HS2, it is not a current project but an idea for the future. I pointed this out to them but they said that they would like to be better informed about it.

I made it clear that if I was to be on their advisory board I would not be able to help them obtain any information that was not already available to the general public. Channel 4, in their TV programme, acknowledged that I had said, 'You cannot give privileged information to one private citizen or company that is not available to others.'

During the meetings, they were interested in what remuneration I would expect if I helped them on their advisory board. I replied that it would depend on how much time it took, whether travel would be involved and how complex the issues would be. They asked me to be more specific and I referred them, as an example, to the Register of Members' Interests, where around £5,000 is given as a payment I had received on one occasion from a company for a speech.

At one stage, they asked me how they might assure themselves that particular countries, especially in Eastern Europe, would welcome investment by their company. I responded that as their proposed advisory board was to be based in London, one way would be to contact the ambassadors of these countries, who, I imagined, would be very happy to see them. They asked whether I could help them meet those foreign ambassadors in London and I said I could as I knew many of them.

Our discussions finished without any conclusions either by them or by me. They said they would be in touch. The next I heard was an email on 10 February 2015 from Channel 4's *Dispatches*, revealing that the 'company' was bogus and that the conversations had been secretly recorded by TV cameras. At first I was not too concerned as I was satisfied there had been no impropriety in anything I had said. That, however, was not their view.

They said that they intended to allege on their programme that I was willing to act as an MP 'for hire'; that I was willing to facilitate access to any foreign ambassador in the UK; that I could write to a minister without disclosing on whose behalf I was writing; and that my fee would be £5,000 to £8,000 per day. They also thought it reprehensible that I had said that nobody paid me a salary despite my receiving one as an MP.

These allegations were presented by *Dispatches* and the *Daily Telegraph* as 'cash for access'. The details of the charge sheet against Jack Straw were different but the conclusions essentially the same.

I had, indeed, said that I could help them meet foreign ambassadors. There was nothing remotely improper in my saying it or if I had done it. People are introduced to each other all the time, both in business and in other walks of life. At no time had I suggested that I would expect to be paid for such help.

It was correct that I had said that I did not receive a salary. The full transcript of the conversations I had shows very clearly that these remarks were made when we were discussing my business interests where I do not receive a salary but either a non-executive director's fees or remuneration based on the time required and complexity of the help provided. I could have been more careful with the words that I used but there was nothing improper in my remarks.

Likewise, I had said I could write to a minister without mentioning the company's name but, as the transcript again makes clear, it was not in dispute that this would have been only to find out what information about HS3 was already in the public domain.

Nor was the remuneration we discussed 'cash for access'. Anyone who serves on an advisory board receives a fee, whatever their background, for the advice they give and their experience that they share.

This was not how my comments were presented on the *Dispatches* TV programme or in the *Daily Telegraph*. It was a classic hatchet job. There was advance billing of scandal unearthed, 'undercover reporters', 'secret cameras' and 'politicians for hire'.

There was extensive 'cut and paste' journalism on the TV programme, used not only to sensationalise but, deliberately or through incompetence, to mislead the viewer.

Throughout the programme there were questions posed by the narrator which were combined with quotations from me presented to the viewer, incorrectly, as if my remarks were, during the actual meeting, given in response to the same question.

There were five serious examples of such shoddy journalism. In one case, the narrator says, 'We discussed with Sir Malcolm what he thought he could bring to a role on the board.' I am then shown remarking that I know many foreign ambassadors in London.

The actual full transcript, when Channel 4 eventually handed it over, shows that I never mentioned foreign ambassadors in answer to that question but referred to my experience of the European Union and knowledge of Eastern Europe. The same tactic was used elsewhere.

For example, one section of the full transcript, when the discussion turns to the information held by government departments, reads as follows:

> Ch4 reporter: 'So they won't tell us, of course, but will they tell you?'
>
> MR: 'They won't tell me either. Certainly not. Certainly not.'
>
> Ch4 reporter: 'Over a drink?'
>
> MR: 'I'd hope not because as a citizen I'd be very worried about that. No, no, no … they have to be very careful. You cannot give privileged information to one private citizen or to a company that is not available to others.'

An objective TV programme would have broadcast this full exchange, which was, clearly, the reporter trying to tempt me to say something improper. Instead of saying something improper, I had showed my strength of feeling against seeking privileged information.

That did not suit their purpose, so they only used, in the TV programme, the last sentence, as if I was only describing what would not be proper and not showing my own opposition to any impropriety.

The *Dispatches* programme makers were clever. They had obviously consulted their lawyers to be sure that they did not say anything defamatory or in breach of the Broadcasting Code. All was innuendo and inference. There was no accusation that I had broken any law.

There was even an admission that I might not have acted in breach of any requirements of the parliamentary code of conduct.

We are a society that rightly believes in free speech. Certain kinds of journalists know that you can trash not just politicians but any public figure by a combination of unsubstantiated headlines, accusations from unnamed people which appear in quotation marks, innuendo and the like, thereby leaving a smell that something fishy must be going on.

Jack Straw was treated in the same way I was. The combination of the sensationalist TV programme and accusing headlines in the *Telegraph* were very damaging in their immediate impact on our reputations. The charges being made obviously needed to be independently investigated.

I knew there had been no impropriety but, at that stage, I could not prove it. That required access to the full transcript of the conversations I had had with the Channel 4 undercover reporters. Despite my requests, Channel 4 would not provide it. In the event, when the parliamentary inquiry began, it took the Standards Commissioner six weeks to get Channel 4 to hand it over. Once they had done, I was as certain as I could be that I would be exonerated and so it turned out.

But that was months later. On 23 February, when the manure hit the fan, Jack and I were facing a media storm. I was robust in insisting there had been no impropriety. I acknowledged that, as can happen to all of us in informal conversations, I may not have been as careful as I could have been in the precise words I used with those with whom I was talking.

I was asked to see the Chief Whip, Michael Gove. He was in sombre mood and suggested that the Conservative whip would have to be suspended from me until the parliamentary inquiry had reported. That would normally not have been too serious, but as we were only three months away from a general election and there was no way the inquiry could report before the summer, a suspension would have the effect of preventing me from being an official Conservative candidate at the election.

I protested, also, that a suspension would imply I was guilty until proven innocent, which was unfair to say the least. He did not disagree with this but explained that they had a problem, as Jack Straw, who was retiring from Parliament at the general election, had already been suspended by the Labour Party. It would not look good if the Conservatives appeared to be less stern.

At my request, he agreed to report my concerns to David Cameron. I asked to see the Prime Minister before any decision was reached. In the event, the suspension was announced without a meeting.

It was a serious example of pre-election jitters. It did not necessarily follow that the whip should have been suspended when an MP's conduct was under investigation. For example, Maria Miller not only retained the whip but remained in the Cabinet until she was found to have transgressed on expenses more than a year after the accusations were made. My suspension was a tactical decision not because of any personal animosity against me but because the party leadership wanted closure on what could otherwise have been made into an election issue. I understood that, but I was very sore at their insensitivity to the consequences for me of that decision.

There were two immediate issues that needed to be addressed because of the suspension of the whip. The first was as regards my chairmanship of the Intelligence and Security Committee. My appointment by the Prime Minister in 2005 had been for five years. My tenure was due to end only ten weeks later at the general election. The business of the committee was complete apart from the publication of our final report on security and privacy.

Accordingly, I agreed to step down from the chairmanship in order not to distract attention from the substance of our final report. I remained a member of the ISC. My colleagues decided it was unnecessary to appoint a successor to me as chairman, as the committee's work was concluded for that parliament.

A more difficult decision was my position as the candidate for Kensington at the forthcoming general election. I had pondered hard and long, and discussed with Edith some months earlier, whether I should stand for another term. I was sixty-eight and would be seventy-three at the end of the next parliament. My main interests in foreign and security policy could be pursued just as easily from outside Parliament.

However, I enjoyed being the MP for Kensington, had excellent relations with my association, and, of course, being the Member for a central London constituency meant that I was not subject to weekly travel back and forth between London and the country. I had decided to stand once more.

When the sting broke, Kensington Conservatives gave me the fullest possible support. My chairman, Matthew Carrington, said he treated the allegations with the contempt they deserved.

However, I decided to stand down as the candidate for the forthcoming general election. I did so for two reasons. First, I wanted to end the media frenzy, which was causing considerable strain for my wife and family as well as for me. My decision had exactly the right effect. Within two days the story was dead and did not reappear until the Standards Committee inquiry was complete.

My second reason was that Kensington Conservatives had been very loyal to me and had given me unstinting support over ten years. Many were personal friends. There would be serious doubt as to whether I could, in fact, be their candidate while the whip was suspended. I did not think it fair to subject them to that uncertainty and to the likelihood that our political opponents would seek to exploit the issue during an election campaign.

I decided to announce right away that I would not be a candidate. I informed Matthew Carrington and then put out a press statement. Later that week, when I addressed Kensington Conservatives at their AGM at the Town Hall, I received a standing ovation from those present and the most generous of thanks for my service as their Member.

One of the sadder consequences of my decision was informing my staff, Christine Shaylor, John Sweeney and my research assistant,

Christian Davies, that I would be leaving the Commons. They had been a great team and I was lucky to have had them.

In the days that followed I received a large number of marvellous letters of support from friends, colleagues and people I did not know. They sought to assure me that my integrity and reputation had not been tarnished by the allegations. Many were angry with the behaviour of *Dispatches* and the *Daily Telegraph*. The *Telegraph* had become more like a tabloid than a serious newspaper in its love of huge front-page headlines and its indifference to any sense of fairness.

My favourite letter was from a former editor of the *Sunday Telegraph*, whom I did not know well. He began by saying, 'I am ashamed at what the *Telegraph* has done to you.' He ended his letter saying, 'Please forgive this handwriting. My hand is shaking with rage.' After I had been cleared by the inquiry, I received an email from a former editor of the *Daily Telegraph*. It was one word: 'Hooray.'

Parliamentary inquiries always take months. In my case the delay was increased by the reluctance of Channel 4 to hand over the full transcript. The Standards Commissioner, Kathryn Hudson, in due course produced her report for the Standards Committee of Parliament. They published it together with their own conclusions on 17 September. The report covered both me and Jack Straw.

The Standards Commissioner concluded that 'they have conducted themselves throughout my inquiry with dignity and honesty'.

The Commissioner then said: 'At no point was either Member explicitly asked to lobby and at no point did they offer to do so.' She added that 'although several allegations were made about each of them, arising from interviews recorded by undercover reporters, neither was in breach of the Code of Conduct or the Rules of the House'. The Commissioner then wrote: 'Both men suffered adverse publicity and were presumed guilty of the Code of Conduct before any authoritative examination of the facts had taken place…'

Her report continued:

If in their coverage of this story the reporters of Channel 4 Dispatches and the Daily Telegraph had accurately reported what was said by the two Members in their interviews, and measured their words against the rules of the House, it would have been possible to avoid the damage that has been done to the lives of the two individuals and those around them…

The Standards Committee of Parliament themselves added: 'By selection and omission the coverage distorted the truth and misled the public as to what had actually taken place.'

The news reporting on TV and the radio, on the day of publication, gave blanket coverage to these conclusions and our exoneration. I could not have been happier or more relieved. The Prime Minister kindly issued a statement welcoming the outcome and saying that my family and I could now put this distressing period behind us.

The *Daily Telegraph*, embarrassed at being hung out to dry, stopped attacking me and Jack and conducted, for several days, a disreputable smear campaign against the Standards Commissioner, questioning her ability and integrity and trying to devalue her report. As both she and the Standards Committee have been very willing to find against MPs when the facts justified it, the *Telegraph*'s smears fell on very stony ground.

The only small comfort that *Dispatches* had was that Ofcom, the broadcasting regulator, concluded that they had not breached the requirements of the Broadcasting Code with their programme.

Ofcom's conclusion did not surprise me. *Dispatches*, we assumed, had checked with their lawyers when making the programme. TV producers have the same rights of free speech as do politicians and can make whatever allegations they like as long as they do not breach the laws of defamation or the narrow requirements of the Broadcasting Code.

I am not against investigative journalism. It can often serve the public interest. The use of undercover reporters and secret cameras can also be justified in certain circumstances.

What Jack Straw and I experienced, however, can best be described as a fishing expedition. Without any reason to believe that we had acted, or would act, improperly, *Dispatches* and the *Telegraph* initiated these phony, secretly recorded conversations in the hope that we would say something that they could turn into a news story.

There never was anything of substance in their 'revelations'. They began by alleging that we were abusing our position as MPs for financial gain. Thereafter, they abandoned that claim and substituted it with a complaint that we were prepared to use the experience and contacts we had obtained as ministers to help their fictitious company.

It was a pretty silly claim. I had not been a minister since 1997, eighteen years earlier. There is nothing remotely improper, once one has retired from a particular job, in being willing to make available one's experience to others. That happens in all walks of life. Even newspaper editors have been known to do it.

These months had been the worst of my public life. I have been criticised, as have all ministers, for policies I have promoted or decisions I have taken that were unpopular or controversial. That is the stuff of politics.

But on this occasion my integrity and reputation had been attacked in an unpleasant and unjustified way. I do not conceal that the allegations caused me, and my family, considerable distress. I did not become depressed, though I was, throughout, very angry.

But all that is now behind me. The allegations were dismissed as groundless by the Standards Commissioner and, unanimously, by the Parliamentary Standards Committee. What was distressing has now become what a colleague described to me as 'a tiresome episode' in my life.

I am not in the House of Commons, but my public life is as busy as ever and my private life is more relaxed than it has been for many years. All's well that ends well.

CHAPTER 25

GUARDING THE GUARDIANS

WHEN DAVID CAMERON formed his first government in 2010, I had no expectation of being a member of it. I had burned my boats when I informed him that I would not wish to be considered for the shadow Cabinet in 2005.

I did hope, however, that the opportunity would arise to do some kind of serious job that would stretch me and use my experience and skills, such as they were.

For a brief moment I had had to consider an unexpected possibility that had arisen in the previous parliament. When it was clear that Michael Martin was going to retire early as Speaker, I was approached by the Chief Whip, who asked whether I would consider being a candidate and indicated that David Cameron would be likely to give his support.

I had never had aspirations in that direction and was uncertain whether the Speaker's office, though very grand, would stimulate me enough once the novelty had worn off.

I said that I would think about it but made it clear there was no possibility of me allowing my name to go forward unless it would have the support of a substantial number of Labour and Liberal Democrat MPs. There were too many examples of candidates favoured by the party leadership being rejected by backbenchers from all parties precisely because they were the leadership's candidate.

The Chief Whip's proposal did not have any traction with the Labour government, which was a great relief to me.

I was also sounded out, at that time, about the possibility of chairing the Intelligence and Security Committee in the next parliament. At first I said I would be more interested in the Foreign Affairs Committee, but, on reflection, decided that the ISC statutory oversight of our intelligence agencies was a much more substantial job than chairing a select committee, however prestigious.

Shortly after the general election, the new Prime Minister, David Cameron, asked me to see him and invited me to take on the ISC chairmanship. I accepted.

The ISC had been created in the 1990s when I was Defence Secretary. I was one of the group of ministers who was involved in the preparatory discussions, but, unlike the Foreign Secretary and the Home Secretary, had, at that time, no direct ministerial responsibility for the agencies.

I had had occasional contact with MI6 when I had been a junior Foreign Office Minister, and as Secretary of State for Scotland I had had the statutory responsibility for authorising MI5 warrants north of the border, which in England and Wales fell to the Home Secretary. As Foreign Secretary, I had MI6 and GCHQ under my remit.

Although I supported the work of the intelligence agencies and admired many of their achievements, I recognised the importance in any democratic society of them being subject to serious and substantial parliamentary oversight.

Intelligence agencies in any free society should not be treated with unqualified enthusiasm.

Firstly, they are secretive, and must remain so as regards a very high proportion of their capabilities and activities. This, inevitably, makes it much more difficult for Parliament to hold them to account than with any other part of government or of the public sector.

Furthermore, to fulfil their statutory responsibilities and serve the public interest they must be given lawful authority to carry out deeds which, if carried out by any other citizen, would constitute criminal offences. They have legal authority to hack computers, intercept phones or break into people's homes to plant bugs. In any democracy, that should make all of us uncomfortable.

For the public to accept such powers there needs to be proper oversight of the agencies. But it is unavoidable that that oversight can only be exercised by people permitted to have access to the secret information that the agencies gather. Apart from senior ministers and a small handful of public servants, that access is limited to the quasi-judicial Commissioners and to the Intelligence and Security Committee of Parliament, which I now chaired.

If the public are to be supportive of the work of the intelligence agencies, they must have trust not only in them but also in the independence and integrity of those who carry out the oversight task.

Some of the secrecy which used to surround the agencies has gone. Today, the intelligence chiefs are questioned in front of the TV cameras; their names are known, as are their places of work, in Vauxhall, Thames House and Cheltenham, to a degree that would have been inconceivable even thirty years ago. But although there has been much greater openness, there needs, also, to be continuing examination as to whether transparency can be further enhanced and secrecy modified without harm to their operational effectiveness.

During these years of increasing openness, the priorities of the agencies and the technical capabilities available, not only to them but also to those who would do us harm, have changed out of all recognition. The advent of the internet age and its implications for the world of intelligence is perhaps the profoundest change of all.

For many years, the primary purpose of our secret services was to find out the secrets of hostile governments and their leaders; to protect the secrets of our own government; and to guard against internal subversion. Espionage and counter-espionage were the classic priorities.

Activity of this kind is as old as the hills. Parliament first established an account to properly fund the collection of secret intelligence in 1689. In 1807, when Napoleon and Tsar Alexander I were sat on Napoleon's barge at Tilsit negotiating a joint invasion of British India, a Russian aristocrat recruited by the British secret service and stationed in the water underneath the barge listened in on their conversation and reported it to London.

In the twentieth century, intelligence capabilities and those of our adversaries were greatly enhanced by developments in signals intelligence technology. In 1917, British intelligence famously intercepted a telegram communicated via undersea cables from the German Foreign Minister, Arthur Zimmermann, to Mexico – enjoining the Mexicans to join the Central Powers in exchange, after German victory, for the recovery of their lost territory in Texas, New Mexico and Arizona. The Mexicans, very wisely, were not impressed.

During the Cold War, despite continuing developments in technology, spying was still largely conducted at a state-to-state level. The IRA campaign in Northern Ireland and on the British mainland was the one significant exception.

After the Soviet Union collapsed, the spies were brought in from the cold. The resources and manpower of the agencies was substantially scaled down.

Then, the tragic events of 11 September 2001 in New York and the London bombings in 2005 changed everything. They brought home the realisation that as well as hostile governments, international terrorist organisations now posed a very serious threat to the safety of the public. Furthermore, as we found in 2005, many of these terrorists had not come from abroad but were British citizens so alienated from our society and values that they were prepared not only to blow themselves up but to take with them as many of their fellow citizens as they could.

Over the last decade or so, Western intelligence agencies have therefore had to make international counterterrorism, rather than espionage or counter-espionage, their major concern.

At the heart of the development of the international terror networks that most threaten our safety is the rise and spread of the internet. Global terrorists communicate globally, and in practice this means communicating online, using email, social messaging, peer-to-peer sharing sites, chat rooms, webcams, online gaming platforms, mobile applications and a whole host of other media. It allows extremists to disseminate propaganda, attract and radicalise sympathisers, and ultimately to organise and prepare acts of terror, without ever having to meet face-to-face.

Just as many millions of Britons use the internet to stay in touch with people in the UK and abroad, so many young Britons, already radicalised or at risk of radicalisation, are in regular contact with people in remote, distant, hostile or ungoverned territories.

One consequence has been the jihadi volunteers who have gone to Syria. Even if only a very small proportion of those who have gone return to Britain to cause harm, the training in terror techniques that they have received and the likelihood of their being further radicalised and brutalised by their experiences poses a very severe threat to the security of the British people.

In decades past, such dangerous plotting would be countered by traditional means: conducting surveillance on people or properties, installing bugs to eavesdrop on conversations, or talking to your informants or agents.

These approaches are still relevant but do not deal, entirely, with the new evolving picture. We have to come to terms with a world in which potential terrorists today may have no leaders, where they communicate using sophisticated encryption technology, and are just as much in contact, through the internet, with sympathisers in Yemen or Pakistan as they are with those in the UK.

Most people recognise that if actual or potential terrorists are to be apprehended, there is likely to be a considerably greater degree of intrusion into the privacy of the public by the security services than was required when our enemies were restricted to foreign governments.

Because of this, some people have become increasingly anxious that our intelligence agencies are using the extensive technological capabilities now available through the internet to impose general surveillance of the public. This, it is alleged, has not been declared or approved by Parliament and may be illegal.

It is, of course, not surprising that the intelligence agencies may possess capabilities about which the public have not been fully aware. This should not be controversial in itself – any intelligence agency would be rendered obsolete were all of its capabilities to become common knowledge.

For a few of the critics, their concern is influenced by their presumption that the intelligence agencies have some sinister intent and are indifferent to the loss of privacy that their activities entail. Most, however, who express concern are more reasonable. They acknowledge that the agencies seek to operate within the law but question whether any system of monitoring that is not targeted exclusively at known or suspected terrorists is either justifiable or necessary.

These anxieties were brought to a head in the debate surrounding the leaking of stolen intelligence documents by Edward Snowden. Snowden downloaded 1.2 million US top secret documents, including 58,000 relating to GCHQ.

It is worth reminding ourselves that Britain's intelligence agencies did not have any Act of Parliament to control their activities until as late as the 1990s. They were, of course, answerable to ministers but only in an ill-defined and private manner. It was only as the Cold War came to an end that the agencies were placed on a statutory footing for the first time. The 1989 Security Service Act (for MI5) and the 1994 Intelligence Services Act (for MI6 and GCHQ) enshrined their responsibilities and protections in law.

None of the agencies are free to use their powers indiscriminately. They are permitted to exercise their functions only in pursuit of the specific objectives set out for them in statute, which are, first, the interests of national security; second, the prevention or detection of serious crime; and, third, the economic wellbeing of the United Kingdom where state security is involved. If an employee of any agency uses any of his or her powers for any other reason, he or she is committing a crime and is liable to be prosecuted.

In addition to the legislation providing the agencies with detailed statutory controls, they must also comply with the 1998 Human Rights Act, which imposes a set of human rights obligations expressed in general terms. This includes an individual right to privacy which may only be interfered with to protect the safety of society as a whole.

To meet the requirement for oversight of the intelligence agencies, the 1994 Act also established the Intelligence Commissioners and the Intelligence and Security Committee to provide accountability that would ensure that the agencies complied with their obligations.

When I became chairman of the ISC, I was already of the view that the committee needed radical reform and a substantial enhancement of its powers. I had to discuss with my colleagues on the committee whether this was necessary, but most of them were of a similar mind.

The composition of the committee was impressive. They were all, or became, Privy Councillors. They included Robin Butler in the House of Lords, a former Cabinet Secretary who had carried out, at the government's request, a major investigation of the use of intelligence in regard to the Iraq War.

Hazel Blears was the senior Labour figure. I had not known her well but I found her to be extremely able, committed to the role of the agencies in helping to ensure our national security. She was also first class at cross-examining the heads of the agencies when they came to give evidence. Menzies Campbell, former Leader of the Lib Dems, Michael Ancram, now Lord Lothian, and Julian Lewis, now chair of the Defence Select Committee, were amongst the other members.

Our clerk, Emma-Louise Avery, had served the committee for a long number of years. She was a master of detail, highly conscientious and the source of all wisdom on the committee's past achievements and problems.

The committee's first decision was to agree that the beginning of the new parliament was the opportunity to have a major review of our powers to ensure that they became sufficient to deal with our responsibilities. I also persuaded my colleagues that it was time we became a committee of Parliament rather than just of parliamentarians. We all agreed that because of our statutory responsibilities and our access to top secret information, we could not just be another select committee, but we needed to be seen to be acting within the framework of Parliament and not outside it.

Our review confirmed the inadequacies in the powers that the committee had exercised since its inception in the 1990s. Two issues stood out above all others as grounds for deep concern regarding the committee's ability to reassure Parliament and the public that they could be confident with the conclusions of the ISC's reports on the agencies.

Firstly, under existing legislation, when conducting an investigation into agency activity, the committee could only 'request' the necessary documents and primary evidence from the agencies. We had no legal right to insist on it being provided, and we could not be confident that any information provided was complete. I do not suggest that, in the past, the agencies purposely obfuscated or tried to hinder our investigations. But an ISC investigation did not impose upon them the same statutory demands to provide all the relevant material as would be required, for example, for a court case. The agencies had acknowledged that, in the past, they did not always identify documents for the ISC with the same vigour as they would if required to do so by a court order.

This vulnerability was exposed during a court case in relation to allegations of rendition and treatment of detainees. The ISC had published a report into the allegations but when the case went to trial before a judge, further documentation emerged to which the ISC had not been given access. This had done serious damage to confidence in the ISC's ability to conduct their investigations with the necessary rigour.

Secondly, while the ISC, since its formation in 1995, was formally responsible for scrutinising the agencies' policy, resources and administration, it had been given no comparable responsibility for scrutinising agency operations.

Operations are, of course, the most sensitive and important part of the agencies' activities and are what give rise, from time to time, to most public concern, as we saw with the Snowden allegations in regard to GCHQ.

In practice, the ISC was able to oversee many aspects of agency operations, but these were restricted to investigating a specific event at the request of the Prime Minister, such as the London bombings of 2005, or allegations, such as rendition, that had surfaced in the media. The ISC did not have the statutory right either to know about the operational capabilities of the agencies in any systematic way, or to investigate operations at its own discretion.

We therefore decided to make recommendations for fundamental reforms to the government. Before we did so, I met with each of the intelligence agency chiefs, Jonathan Evans of MI5, Sir John Sawers of MI6 and Iain Lobban of GCHQ, and won their support, though their enthusiasm was not uniform.

To their credit, they recognised that they and their staff benefited if the public and Parliament could have confidence in their integrity and professionalism. Their necessary secrecy prevented them from proving their own case and, while the Prime Minister and his colleagues would champion them, the government was their employer and was assumed to be unenthusiastic about seeing the agencies criticised. The ISC was independent and, although the civil liberties organisations viewed us as too pro-intelligence, we could, and did, put the boot in when the evidence justified it.

My discussions with ministers on our proposed reforms were mainly with the Foreign Secretary, William Hague, and the Home Secretary, Theresa May, though I also kept the Prime Minister fully informed. I also had regular meetings with Kim Darroch, who became the national security advisor in 2012. It was with him that much of the detail was thrashed out.

They were all supportive, although, as with the agencies, their main anxiety was that our statutory responsibility for overseeing agency operations would be retrospective and not impede operations going on at the time.

There was particular nervousness that we would expect to have the right exercised by the most senior senators and congressmen in the United States to be informed of major intelligence operations before they happened. It had been reported that they had been informed of the operation to kill or capture Osama bin Laden shortly before it happened.

At a meeting of the ISC with the Prime Minister in the Cabinet Room, I made it clear that even if the government had wanted to give us such a power we would not have accepted it. There is no benefit, and a lot of risk, in having been briefed in advance of a secret operation unless you can influence whether it goes ahead. Otherwise, you have responsibility without power, which is even worse than power without responsibility.

Having got the government's agreement to our proposed reforms, we were delighted that, far from having to wait for a slot in the legislative timetable, which could have delayed us for a year or so, the reforms were to be included in the Justice and Security Bill, which had top priority in the government's legislative programme.

The government had its own motives for being so cooperative. The Bill was to establish, for the first time, the power of the courts in civil cases to hear all or part of the evidence in camera if national security would otherwise be damaged. They knew this would be severely criticised by civil libertarian MPs and organisations.

They wanted to demonstrate that they had no sinister intent. Including our increased powers in the same Bill was politically astute.

The reforms to the ISC in the Justice and Security Act constituted a radical transformation of the committee's powers. The ISC, as a result, had statutory responsibility for the retrospective oversight of all MI6, MI5 and GCHQ operations for the first time. The committee now had the statutory right to ascertain, in detail, the agencies' capabilities in a systematic, as opposed to an ad hoc, manner. The agencies now report to the ISC on a quarterly basis with detailed information on their operational activities in the preceding period. GCHQ and the other agencies are now providing the ISC with information on the full spectrum of their capabilities.

The ISC now also has statutory authority, under the Act, to *require* as opposed to *request* all the information, including the raw intelligence, it requires in order to conduct its investigations.

The most radical change, not in the Act but which I persuaded the agency chiefs to concede, is that the ISC's own staff now have the right, and are using it, to go into the agencies' offices, access the files and, together with agency staff, decide the files that will be given to the ISC, as opposed to having agency staff doing it on our behalf. This is the first time external investigators from the ISC have been able to enjoy direct access to such sensitive material.

There have been further important reforms. The ISC is now also part of Parliament. It now reports directly to Parliament, and Parliament, not the Prime Minister, now has the last word on the committee's membership. The committee chairman is no longer appointed by the Prime Minister but is elected by the committee from its own members and can be from a government or opposition party.

Last but not least, the committee's budget has been doubled, to around £1.3 million a year. The number of its staff has risen commensurately. This was a significant increase in resources at a time of severe financial constraint.

The enactment of our new powers in April 2013 could not have been more timely. In June, Edward Snowden leaked details of US and UK highly classified intelligence gathering programmes.

Having access to these leaks, *The Guardian* ran a story suggesting that GCHQ had tried to avoid its legal obligations to get a warrant from the Secretary of State by obtaining information about communications in the United Kingdom through access to PRISM, a United States intelligence programme. If this had been true, GCHQ would have been breaking the law and would have seriously violated the rights of British citizens.

By using our new powers, the ISC was able to require complete access to all the relevant information held by GCHQ, including raw intelligence material. This included lists of UK individuals subject to monitoring, and a list of the warrants and internal authorisations that were in place for the individuals being targeted.

Far from GCHQ having broken the law by working with the Americans, we were able to establish that a warrant for interception, signed by a British minister, was already in place covering the individuals concerned.

We had carried out this inquiry very swiftly but with high professional competence thanks to our staff. It was crucial to determine whether *The Guardian* were justified in their allegations. They were not. We had the hard evidence that proved it.

The new powers were also of enormous value in the inquiry the ISC carried out after the murder of Lee Rigby in May 2013 by two terrorists who had deliberately run their vehicle into him just outside Woolwich barracks.

The two murderers, Adebowale and Adebolajo, had been subject to MI5 coverage for some years. It was essential to determine whether the murder could have been prevented if MI5 had used their powers more effectively.

Andrew Parker, the new Director General of MI5, promised his full cooperation and said that he had appointed a team within MI5 to ensure that we received all the necessary documents. He promised that the cooperation would be of the same level that they would provide if they had received an order from a court of law.

This he delivered. It was unprecedented and it enabled the ISC to carry out the most substantial and most thorough investigation in its history. In our public report, we made many criticisms of MI5 for failures in some of their processes. We also criticised MI6 for their lack of proper attention when one of the murderers had been arrested in Kenya some years earlier as a suspected terrorist.

Both men had been under investigation a number of times in the years preceding the murder, but we were satisfied that none of their actions during those periods should have indicated to MI5 their intention or planning to commit a terrorist outrage.

The only such evidence that did point in that direction became known after the murder. We saw the transcript of an online message sent by one of the murderers, Adebowale, to an acquaintance overseas. In it, Adebowale said that he wanted to kill a British soldier, and there was some discussion about how it might be done.

Our intelligence agencies do not get sufficient cooperation from internet service providers located outside the United Kingdom, especially those based in the United States. We concluded that, because of this, neither MI5 nor GCHQ could be held responsible for not having been aware of that message, sent some time before the murder.

Other inquiries and reports published by the ISC in the recent past have demonstrated the real value of parliamentary oversight.

In 2013, we published a report on foreign involvement in the critical national infrastructure and, in particular, BT's use of Huawei, a Chinese company, to provide some of the essential equipment which was being used to modernise the UK's telecommunications infrastructure.

Huawei is a state-owned company and China has a very bad reputation for cyber espionage against various countries. It was, in our view, a serious matter that a Chinese company was being used unless one could be satisfied that this would not lead to any threat to national security.

To our astonishment, we discovered that in 2005, civil servants gave the go-ahead to BT to sign contracts with Huawei without ministers being consulted. The government accepted our criticisms in this respect and agreed that ministers must always take the final decision on important issues of this kind.

We found no evidence that Huawei were abusing their position but we also made some recommendations which were accepted to strengthen the monitoring cell that had been established to provide comfort in this respect.

Our final major report was on privacy and security, which we were able to publish at the very end of the parliament. It made many recommendations, including the need for a new Act to replace the myriad of incomprehensible statutes that currently govern the work of the intelligence agencies.

We were also able to examine whether bulk interception of communications produced sufficient benefit to national security and the battle against terrorism in Britain to justify the intrusion on privacy that some civil liberty advocates believed to be unacceptable.

We concluded that the benefits were substantial and the intrusion on privacy minimal as authorisation from the Secretary of State was always required if bulk interception led to the agencies wishing to examine the detailed contents of the communications of anyone in the UK. Until that stage, the computers had been active but no human eye had perused any of these communications.

Historic was our decision to have the first ever public session of the ISC with the heads of MI5, MI6 and GCHQ giving evidence to the committee before the television cameras.

There was extraordinary media interest and the session went smoothly. We were complimented on this radical innovation, which would have been inconceivable a few years earlier.

However, there was also predictable criticism and some scorn that we had given the intelligence chiefs 'an easy ride'.

We knew this would happen. If you take evidence from intelligence agencies in public you can have a serious, mature and valuable exchange on intelligence issues and how they are combatting terrorism and espionage. What you cannot do is ask questions or make allegations that could only be answered by reference to secret and classified material.

Our critics knew that perfectly well but it did mean that the theatre of the occasion was not as exciting as they would have wished.

The ISC has a very close relationship with the US Senate and House intelligence committees and each year we spent several days visiting the CIA, the National Security Agency and other centres of the massive American intelligence community.

My first visit to the CIA had been several years earlier when, together with Madeleine Albright, I met Leon Panetta, the director of the CIA, at his office at Langley.

After the meeting, I acquired a coffee mug emblazoned with the CIA's insignia. To my amusement, I discovered that it was 'Made in China'. I asked my American colleague if that meant Taiwan or the People's Republic and, to my consternation, he said that he did not know. I did not find that very reassuring.

During my tenure as chairman of the ISC, the James Bond movie *Skyfall* came out. In the film, the head of MI6 is played by Judi Dench, but the real strongman, who eventually succeeds her, is Mallory, played by Ralph Fiennes and described in the film as the chairman of the Intelligence and Security Committee.

I pretended that I was a little miffed that they had not asked me to play myself in *Skyfall*, but as Mallory gets shot at one stage, that was probably just as well. In any event, I had some fun when the ISC next took evidence from Sir John Sawers, the actual chief of MI6, in assuring him that I was not after his job. His response was something between a smile and a grimace.

The distinction between intelligence agencies in democracies and those in authoritarian systems is crucially important.

Intelligence agencies exist in every state, both democratic and authoritarian, throughout the world. While they share certain things in common, we must never lose sight of the differences.

Intelligence agencies within authoritarian systems may wish to protect the public from terrorism and some types of serious crime. But their primary objective is the preservation of the regime they serve.

Unfortunately, the insidious use of language such as 'mass surveillance' and 'Orwellian' by many of Edward Snowden's supporters to describe the actions of Western agencies blurs, unforgivably, the distinction between a system that uses the state to protect the people, and one that uses the state to protect itself against the people. It is ironic that Snowden, in the name of privacy and the rule of law, chose China and Russia from which to launch his attack on the United States.

Some people in Britain have pointed to the different reactions of the press and the public to the Snowden revelations in the United States and Germany as evidence of some kind of uniquely British complacency. But this is to ignore the considerable political and historic differences within the free world.

For example, some cite President Obama's response to the NSA allegations as an example for the UK to follow. But Obama's most substantial promise has been to do away with the NSA's own central database of American citizens' telephone communications and to require the US agencies to access the information they need from the phone companies themselves. That is, as it happens, based heavily on the UK model, so there is no example here for the UK to follow.

People also cite Germany as an example of how we should respond. But, for many Germans, references to interception by German intelligence agencies remind them, inevitably, of their Nazi and Stasi experience. For the British, the comparable historic memory is

Bletchley Park, which shortened the war and ensured the preservation of our liberty. That should not make us complacent but it is a valid distinction.

We live in a world in which there are occasional paradoxes. When a terrorist atrocity occurs, the majority of the public tends to ask why the agencies knew so little about those who were responsible. When, however, the surveillance activities of the agencies are revealed, a smaller but vocal minority tends to ask why they need to know so much. We need to do a better job of recognising the competing demands we place upon the agencies, and do more to establish a consensus as to how these demands can be reconciled.

Our agencies are not, and do not wish to be, 'all-seeing', nor 'all-hearing'. Their capabilities have been designed to pursue their lawful, narrowly defined objectives.

True public servants operate with noble motivations and lawful authority, subject to rigorous oversight. These are the values that distinguish public servants from a public threat. That is how those who work for our intelligence agencies see themselves. That is how most of the public see them. That has been my own experience seeing them at work over a number of years. It is in all our interests that that should retain their justified reputation in the internet age.

Serving as chairman of the Intelligence and Security Committee for five years was one of the heights of my public life. It was extremely satisfying to preside over its transformation from a rather weak committee with inadequate powers into one of the most powerful intelligence oversight committees in the world.

I had great colleagues and a superb staff. I often reflected during those five years that I was getting far more job satisfaction in this work than if I had been Secretary of State in a domestic department dealing with issues which, despite their national importance, would not have been as relevant to my own interests and experience.

CHAPTER 26

FINAL THOUGHTS

I N THE INTRODUCTION to these memoirs I wrote that my ministerial life was dominated by the two existential challenges with which the United Kingdom has grappled and not yet resolved over the past half-century. They are, of course, our external relationship with the European Union and the internal issue of Scotland's future in a united kingdom.

Over the past two years, both these issues have come to a head.

In autumn 2014, there was the referendum in Scotland on independence which the Nationalists lost by 55–45 per cent, a significant though not dramatic margin.

I spoke at over a dozen public meetings during that campaign, mainly in the Highlands, the north-east and the Borders.

The meetings were very well attended and the turnout on the day was extraordinary at over 85 per cent. My most enjoyable exchange was at a public meeting in Helensburgh when a questioner introduced himself as the president of the Scottish Jacobite Society before putting his pro-independence question. With some glee, I reminded him that, as a Jacobite, he should be aware that Bonnie Prince Charlie wanted to be King of the United Kingdom not just King of Scotland. Ruefully, and to the cheers of the audience, he acknowledged that that was a fair comment.

During the European referendum the SNP warned that if the UK voted to leave the EU but there was a majority in Scotland for remaining, that could lead to a further independence referendum.

It was good rhetoric but Nicola Sturgeon and her colleagues are on shaky ground if they maintain that Euroscepticism is purely an English phenomenon. At the referendum just under 40 per cent of Scots voted to leave the European Union.

As soon as the Eurozone crisis erupted, the SNP dropped their long-held policy that an independent Scotland would join the euro. Instead, they declared their love for the pound, which became 'our pound', to try to reassure Scottish voters.

If Britain's vote to leave the EU leads to a further referendum in Scotland, it is by no means likely that any more would vote for independence than last time. Scottish voters would be contemplating not only the massive hole in Scottish revenues following the collapse of the oil price but whether, unlike at the referendum in 2014, they would wish to live with a real border at Berwick with Scotland inside the EU and the rest of Great Britain outside it.

Such a real border has not existed since 1707; perhaps not since the Union of the Crowns in 1603. No longer would Dr Johnson be able to remark that 'the noblest prospect for the Scotsman is the high road to England'.

There is a further crucial change in the Scottish political situation since the referendum in 2014. Since the Scottish Parliament election in May 2016, the Tories are now the main opposition to the SNP, with Labour languishing in third place. The large increase in the Conservative vote, which has given them over thirty seats in the Scottish Parliament, suggests that there is now a more explicit desire to demonstrate their Unionism amongst the 55 per cent of the electorate who voted for Scotland to remain in the United Kingdom.

On 23 June 2016, the people of the United Kingdom voted by 52 per cent to 48 per cent to leave the European Union. I was deeply saddened by that vote and had campaigned against it. Although a 'moderate Eurosceptic', I am convinced that we will lose more than we will gain from 'escaping' from the 'shackles' of Brussels but I will not reopen the campaign in these pages.

The EU referendum campaign had major implications for the future of the government and for the unity of the Conservative Party. Emotions had been high; hard and harsh words had been used. Ministers openly attacked their fellow ministers and cast aspersions on their integrity and honesty as well as their judgement.

Many have suggested that it will be impossible to reunite the Conservative Party and the government for a considerable period of time. While not wishing to understate the challenge, I believe they are wrong.

One of the virtues of a referendum, which is decisive and not merely consultative, is that it is the people, the electorate, who have decided. Whatever the decision, the issue has been resolved, at least for a generation. The decision has been to leave, and that will happen and be irreversible. Both sides of the campaign have been Eurosceptic, to some degree, opposed to Britain joining the euro or to significant further integration.

It should also be remembered that the Conservative Party, unlike Labour, has never been an ideological party. That is why it is the world's oldest political party and has survived and prospered for centuries. It is interested in power and will not find it difficult to reunite to try to ensure that the government will receive a further mandate at the next general election. That election is not due for almost four years. The Labour Party remains unelectable and the Liberal Democrats invisible, which puts the Tories' current difficulties into proper perspective.

In any event, most Tories will approve of Winston Churchill's advice that, in politics, you should never commit suicide as you might live to regret it.

We are to have a new Prime Minister by October 2016. History is unlikely to judge David Cameron as having been a successful Prime Minister after the disaster of the European referendum. However, he led the Conservative Party back to power after thirteen years in the wilderness. As the first Prime Minister since the Second World War to have to manage a coalition government, he did so with skill and finesse. He not only kept the Lib Dems on side for five years but managed to use the coalition as a convincing reason for not being able to adopt some right-wing Tory proposals that he didn't want anyway.

All politicians, and especially party leaders, need luck and he has had more than most. He not only presided over a majority Conservative government that he did not expect. He also faced a Labour Party that may be in terminal decline, devastated in Scotland, lacking credibility as an alternative government in England and destined to a further decade in opposition at the very least. At the same time, the Liberal Democrats have disappeared as a serious political force and are unlikely to return for a generation.

I cannot claim to know David Cameron very well. He entered the House of Commons during my eight-year absence. When I did meet him, and sat with him in the shadow Cabinet during 2005, there was no instant rapport.

In one sense, we should have been close, as we have much in common. We are both genuine One Nation Tories with a distaste for ideology, comfortable with pragmatic politics and possessing a proper respect for our national traditions and institutions.

But I suspect David saw me as a throwback to the Thatcher/Major years, unlikely to be able to contribute much to his strategy of rebranding the Tories as a modern, born-again potential government.

My decision to return to the back benches would have confirmed that judgement.

However, during the five years that I chaired the Intelligence and Security Committee, we worked well together. He believed from the very start in the need for the ISC to be reformed and given real power. He, together with William Hague, Ken Clarke and Theresa May, could not have been more helpful in signalling to the intelligence agencies that they had to cooperate with the ISC and help ensure that our reforms had parliamentary and public support.

In 2010, immediately after the general election, I was one of several senior figures in the party invited to come and see him. He indicated his intention to try to form a coalition with the Lib Dems and asked me whether I would support him. I said I would, though I doubted that he would succeed.

When he did succeed, I spoke up in the crucial meeting of the 1922 Committee of Tory backbenchers in support of the proposed coalition. During the next five years I intervened in the Commons on several issues where my views and the Prime Minister's coincided.

Two of the most important were the need to impose proper sanctions on the Russians for their aggression in Ukraine and the ill-fated debate when I supported his proposal to use air power in Syria but he was defeated in the vote. I did not support the government on the proposed reform of the House of Lords, but as the Bill that I voted against had been a sop to Nick Clegg, I doubt if the Prime Minister lost any sleep when it had to be dropped.

David was good enough to write to me to thank me for my support on a number of occasions and sent an especially nice missive after my tribute to Margaret Thatcher in the Commons. Our relationship was businesslike, friendly and correct but, in truth, has never got beyond that.

From what one hears, I don't think my experience has been very different from others of his colleagues outside his inner circle. That is the kind of person he is. I do, however, pay tribute to the ease with which he appeared able to carry the burdens of office. He had a punishing schedule, was subject to unrelenting criticism, had a divided party and did not enjoy the rapture that Margaret Thatcher received from the party faithful.

But he had a serenity, a competence and a calm fortitude that was combined with acute political skills and a self-confidence in his ability to govern. I hope he will forgive me for saying that he was a good advertisement for the benefits of an Etonian education.

I have more time than some others in the Conservative Party do for George Osborne. He has been a courageous and successful Chancellor and shown his ability to deal with the awesome challenges that the British economy has faced. There are those who don't want him to succeed David Cameron as Prime Minister. No one doubts that he could do the job.

I first met him when we were in opposition and we were active in the campaign against any proposal that might come from the Blair government to commit Britain to joining the euro. More recently, when I gave a lecture on my views on Europe at the London School of Economics, I sent him a copy. He replied saying that he had read it not once, but twice, as the views expressed in it were identical to his own. The cynics might assume that he was trying to flatter me for his own purposes. Perhaps he was. I am as susceptible to flattery as anyone.

The most important political achievement of Cameron and Osborne is the fact that they have worked so closely together over six years. There has not been a single indication of any serious rift on economic or political issues. When we recall the ghastly relationship of Tony Blair and Gordon Brown, that has been no mean achievement.

Historically, Osborne's greatest initiative, so far, may turn out to be his decentralisation of power and resources to England's cities and regions, especially in the north. He more than anyone has ensured that devolution, in one form or another, is applying to England as well as to Scotland, Wales and Northern Ireland. This is turning the United Kingdom into a quasi-federal union and may be the key to denying the SNP their dream of a separate Scottish state.

Like most people, I share the view that Boris Johnson adds to the sum of human happiness and cheers us up on dull Monday mornings. Whether he is a Winston Churchill in waiting may be another matter.

He is not a Donald Trump. He is ferociously intelligent, extremely well read and entirely civilised. If there is a serious question mark about him, it would be as regards his judgement.

Many people would not, at present, be comfortable with Boris as Chancellor of the Exchequer, or Foreign Secretary, or with his finger on the button of our Trident nuclear missiles. If he aspires to greater national leadership, he must demonstrate that he has the potential to be a statesman, not just a politician.

He has been a good Mayor of London but the Mayor does not, in reality, govern London. Most of London's governance, apart from transport, is done by the boroughs. The Prime Minister's job is incomparably more difficult, demanding and detailed. Boris has to show that he is a man for all seasons.

His role as the de facto leader of the successful Leave campaign in the European referendum has, of course, boosted his prospects of getting to the top of the greasy pole. However, at the time of writing he has just announced that he will not be a candidate for Prime Minister. He has made the right decision.

Campaigning with him is fun. When he first stood for Mayor of London, William Hague and I were asked to support him as he did a walkabout down the Kings Road in Chelsea to Sloane Square. We need not have bothered.

It should have taken a quarter of an hour. In fact, it took four times as long, as the taxi drivers honked, the crowds gathered and people surged round him to shake his hand.

I saw one young woman who had got his autograph and was looking seraphic. 'Are you going to vote for Mr Johnson?' I asked.

'No,' she replied.

I asked, 'Why not?'

'I'm voting for Boris,' she replied. I thought it unnecessary to enlighten her.

On another morning I was campaigning for him with a few colleagues in Kensington. Boris was not with us. An elderly lady, seeing our rosettes, asked me which candidate we were supporting. I told her it was Boris Johnson. 'That's all right,' she said. 'I'm his mother.'

After the election, Boris wrote to thank me for my help, in particular for persuading his mother to vote for him, as she did not always vote Conservative.

Since the general election in 2015 I have not been in the House of Commons. My public life has, however, continued uninterrupted.

I have served on an Eminent Persons Panel established by the OSCE to report on the West's damaged relations with Russia.

I am glad that the panel did not need to visit Moscow, as President Putin has banned me from Russia for the time being. I am one of several dozen prominent European politicians targeted because we were in the forefront demanding a hard response of financial and banking sanctions to Russia's illegal annexation of Crimea and deliberate destabilisation of eastern Ukraine.

If there had to be a list of people banned by Putin, I am proud to be one of them. Karel Schwarzenberg, a grand aristocrat who was recently Czech Foreign Minister, has also been banned. When he was informed, he said that his first act had been to find out who else had been. 'I am pleased', he said, 'to find I am a member of a very decent club.'

I remain, however, an ardent advocate of close dialogue between the West and Russia. While it will take years to resolve our differences, the sooner we start the better.

I am also continuing my commitment to multilateral nuclear disarmament. I serve on the board of the Nuclear Threat Initiative, chaired by Senator Sam Nunn in Washington, as well as in the European Leadership Network, which brings together former ministers, military chiefs and diplomats from throughout Europe in the cause of reducing tension in Europe.

For several years I have participated in the Aspen Ministerial

Forum, a group of former Foreign Ministers who, under Madeleine Albright's chairmanship, meet regularly.

Over the past twelve months I have been invited to speak and participate in the Munich Security Forum a new, much smaller, off-shoot of the Munich Security Conference which has become Europe's premier annual gathering on defence and security policy.

Towards the end of 2015 I was appointed a Visiting Professor at King's College London's Department of War Studies as well as becoming a Senior Associate Fellow at the Royal United Services Institute, the world's oldest think tank, founded by the Duke of Wellington in 1831.

Because I no longer have parliamentary responsibilities I am in control of my own diary. Each week I have several speaking engagements, which can be at think tanks, defence establishments, the Oxford Union or other universities, corporate dinners, schools or political events. In addition, I am often asked to write articles for journals or newspapers. Most lectures or speeches that I give are on foreign affairs, defence, intelligence or security.

Last year I was invited to give a lecture to the SAS in Hereford. Afterwards they presented me with a very good bottle of malt whisky, engraved with the SAS insignia. It is an excellent talking point when I am offering a guest a drink.

Living in central London, I can walk to most places I need to be. London can be very intimate and local despite its massive size. It is also one of the best-endowed cities for large, green, open spaces.

My most enjoyable stroll is across the bridge over the lake in the middle of St James's Park, having inspected the pelicans on my way. Then I go across Pall Mall and up St James's. St James's Street must be unique not just for its clubs but for the extraordinary number of shops that can be found there, and nowhere else, over its short length.

I can restock our brandy or malt whisky from Berry Bros, buy a hat for me or Edith at Lock's, avoid Lobb's (their shoes are way beyond my price range), purchase a pullover from William Evans, some cigars from James J. Fox (where Churchill bought his cigars) and some Grether's pastilles from the chemist, D. R. Harris.

Then I can look into White's to read the newspapers and Hugo's latest article in *The Spectator* while having a cold beef sandwich and a tankard of ginger beer.

Very occasionally, I dine at Pratt's, which is a subterranean club just off St James's Street, with just one large oval table where there will always be company and good conversation.

One evening I invited Hugo, who does not go in for clubs, to join me as he had not been to Pratt's before. As we left, I asked him whether he had enjoyed himself. He said he had but he wanted to add two points. The first was that he had been, by far, the youngest person there. When I asked him what was the second point, he said, 'You, Dad, were the second youngest.'

When I do not have engagements I can work from home and have considerably more time to be with Edith. For me, life may be very satisfactory but for Edith, her MS makes it very challenging. She copes with extraordinary courage and determination with the invaluable help of her carer, Tsonka Petrova, who has now been with us for over five years.

We both get great pleasure from our family. Hugo, in 2007, married Francisca Kellett, a fellow journalist, whom he met when they were both at Cambridge. She is now travel editor of *Tatler*. Her parents, Mike and Uschi Kellett, have become close friends of ours. Hugo and Fran have given us two delightful granddaughters, Roma, named after Edith's mother, who is seven, and Ruby, who is four.

Caroline is now a director at PricewaterhouseCoopers. She married Andrew Lennard, whom she met when he was an Army captain. Andy left the Army, got his MBA at the London Business School and now works for Shell.

To our astonishment, we discovered that not only had Edith been born in the same year and in the same nursing home in Colne in Lancashire as Andy's mother, Ann. It also turned out that before and during the war Ann's family had lived very close to where Edith's mother was living with her cousins and the two families had known each other. Ann, too, has become a good friend and we have visited her in Wetherby.

Caroline and Andy married five years ago and have a three-year-old son, George. They were kind enough to present us with a second grandson, Charlie, who was born on my 70th birthday in the summer of 2016. Edith and I have become typical, besotted grandparents.

Enoch Powell famously remarked that all political lives end in failure. He was wrong. There certainly is disappointment and sadness when those who have been fortunate in achieving their goals realise that the glory days are behind them.

But a sense of failure only exists when you were unable to realise your early hopes and aspirations. No one can seriously suggest that Margaret Thatcher's career was a failure, however disappointed and frustrated she must have been when she left Downing Street, never to return. Enoch Powell was a different matter. His career was cut short before he ever had the opportunity to deliver his full capability. David Cameron had a remarkably successful career which did end in dramatic and unexpected failure on the European issue.

In my public life I have been fortunate but have also had three major setbacks. The first was the outcome of the 1987 general election, which reduced the Tories to a rump in Scotland while we remained triumphant in the United Kingdom as a whole. That was an intense personal challenge because of my responsibilities, at that time, as Secretary of State for Scotland.

The second was my failure to win back my parliamentary seat in Edinburgh at the 2001 general election, which kept me out of the House of Commons for eight years. The third, of a different kind, was the Channel 4 sting in 2015, which threatened, for several months, to do serious damage to my reputation, until the allegations were rejected as groundless by the Parliamentary Commissioner for Standards.

Although each of these was miserable at the time, even they had a positive dimension to them. We all need to know how, and whether, we can deal with bad times as well as good. It must be very nice to have a charmed life but if you do not have to face adversity and disappointment as well, you never know whether you would have coped with it. In each case I was able to, though I do not pretend that I enjoyed the experience.

I mentioned Margaret Thatcher's career as one of indisputable success. I do not put myself in her league. Margaret Thatcher was a Titan. But I began my political life in the 1970s hoping that, one day, I might be able to play a significant part in Britain's public life and make some contribution in helping resolve some of the political problems of the wider world.

For eighteen uninterrupted years I was able to do that as a minister of the Crown, including eleven years in the Cabinet. More recently, as a parliamentarian and as chairman of the Intelligence and Security Committee, I continued that work. Now I contribute by speaking, by writing and by participating with colleagues, in Britain and abroad, who have similar interests. That, for me, is not failure but fulfilment and I am very lucky to have it.

I do realise that I may be being just a little too pragmatic in reaching such a conclusion. It is hard, after all, to change the habits of a lifetime.

Acknowledgements

THESE MEMOIRS ARE very much my own work. Every word was typed out by me on my laptop over the past year. Gone were the halcyon days when I had a ministerial office with private secretaries, diary secretaries and typists at my beck and call. To my surprise, I don't miss them, though they were superb at the time.

But I still have thanks and acknowledgements that I need to make. I had always intended to write my memoirs but assumed they would be something for the distant future. Last year I concluded that the distant future had arrived.

Part of the reason was an enjoyable lunch with Jonathan Aitken during which he not only suggested that such a book was overdue but offered to introduce me to Jonathan Lloyd, literary agent at Curtis Brown. Not long after, I received an email from Iain Dale of Biteback Publishing saying that they would love to publish such a book if I was so inclined. I am in Jonathan Aitken's debt for his encouragement. Jonathan Lloyd has also been a marvellous literary agent and I have benefited from his advice and practical support.

Writing the book has turned out to be easier than I feared and much more enjoyable than I expected. I have not kept a regular diary over the years. My overland expedition to India, when I was a student, was the one exception. But I often wrote accounts, soon after the event, of occasions that seemed of special significance, such as Margaret Thatcher's first meeting with Mikhail Gorbachev, and my own, sometimes delicate and difficult, meetings and disagreements with Mrs Thatcher. I also had box files of ministerial documents (unclassified!), press reports, letters, photographs and other memorabilia.

The book has been written as the story of my public life and not as a potted history of those years. That has not only kept the length down but, thankfully, removed the need for me to spend days and weeks in various government departments reading files and reports that I last saw decades ago. Some of the issues that I raise in the introduction I have borrowed from a lecture I gave at Mansfield College in Oxford. Likewise, the chapter on my work with the intelligence agencies has benefited from a lecture I gave at Wadham College. My light-hearted, but accurate, remarks on the relationship between ministers and civil servants I first used in an essay I wrote in the 1980s when I was a junior minister at the Scottish Office.

I am indebted to Iain Dale, Olivia Beattie, Victoria Gilder, and other staff at Biteback for their very impressive scrutiny of my manuscript, correction of its grammar and punctuation, helpful suggestions for its improvement, and encouragement to the wider world of booksellers, literary festivals and newspapers to take an interest in its publication.

While I was writing the manuscript, it was read in draft by Edith, Caroline and Hugo, who made many valuable suggestions. My family were also helpful in reminding me of some of the inconveniences and downsides of having a husband and father who was a government minister for eighteen years, some of which I had appeared either to be unaware of or to have forgotten.

I reserve the right to produce a second volume of memoirs if the years ahead were to justify it. But I would advise the reader not to get too excited at the prospect.

INDEX